RB

MEAGHER, TIMOTHY
THE COLUMBIA
IRISH AMERICAN HIS
2005.   OCT 2 5 20
35253001469893 REDB

DISCARDE

D0200909

LAKE COUNTY LIBRARY
1425 N. High St.
Lakeport, CA 95453

MO

THE COLUMBIA GUIDE TO

Irish American History

The Columbia Guides to American History and Cultures

THE COLUMBIA GUIDES TO AMERICAN HISTORY AND CULTURES

Michael Kort, *The Columbia Guide to the Cold War*

Catherine Clinton and Christine Lunardini, *The Columbia Guide to American Women in the Nineteenth Century*

David Farber and Beth Bailey, editors, *The Columbia Guide to America in the 1960s*

David L. Anderson, *The Columbia Guide to the Vietnam War*

THE COLUMBIA GUIDE TO

Irish American History

Timothy Meagher

COLUMBIA UNIVERSITY PRESS

NEW YORK

Columbia University Press
Publishers Since 1893
New York   Chichester, West Sussex
Copyright © 2005 Columbia University Press
All rights reserved
Library of Congress Cataloging-in-Publication Data

Meagher, Timothy J.
  The Columbia guide to Irish American history / Timothy Meagher.
    p. cm. — (Columbia guides to American history and cultures)
  Includes bibliographical references and index.
  ISBN 0–231–12070–2 (acid-free paper)
    1. Irish Americans — History   I. Title.   II. Series.
E184.I6M43   2005
973'.049162—dc22   2005043233

Columbia University Press books are printed on permanent
and durable acid-free paper.
Printed in the United States of America
c 10 9 8 7 6 5 4 3 2 1

To my brothers and sisters, Sean, Dermot, Andrew, Patrick and Mary,
and my aunts and uncles, Kitty, Dee, Louise and Charlie
and Peg and Myles

CONTENTS

PREFACE

This book provides a general introduction to the experience of the Irish in America for readers coming to the study of Irish Americans for the first time, as well as resources to help more experienced students in the field explore it in more depth.

Part 1 contains an introduction and a six-chapter chronological overview of the history of the Irish in America. The introduction suggests the importance of the Irish in American life and history, introduces some of the complex controversies that have emerged in interpreting their history, and offers a conceptual framework for understanding their evolution as an American ethnic group. The six chronological chapters chart the critical phases and turning points in the evolution from the first Irishman to arrive in the sixteenth century to the present day. Each of the six chapters discusses the number of Irish immigrants in that period; their regional, class, and religious backgrounds in Ireland; their reasons for leaving; and their economic adjustments and settlement patterns in America. Later chapters provide similar information on numbers, economic status, and residential patterns for American-born Irish generations as they emerged to dominate the Irish American community. Each of the chronological chapters also addresses debates among historians over critical issues, trends, and events in that period.

The first chronological chapter discusses Irish migration to America in the colonial era, the seventeenth and eighteenth centuries—the so-called "Scotch-Irish" migration—and assesses their roles in the American Revolution and analyzes the debate over whether these early Ulster Presbyterian migrants should be properly considered Irish.

The second chapter covers the period from the end of the American Revolution in 1783 to the beginning of the Great Irish Famine in the late 1840s. It traces the shift in Irish immigration patterns from northern Irish Protestants to southern Catholics, the influence of United Irish exiles on Irish America, the brief emergence of a nonsectarian republican Irish American identity, and the demise of that identity amid the rise of Irish and American sectarianism, changing politics, and the shifting backgrounds of Irish migrants to America.

The third chapter focuses on the great flood of Irish immigrants that began with the Great Irish Famine in the late 1840s and continued more or less through the early 1870s. It considers the famine's importance as a watershed in Irish and Irish American history and evaluates disputes among historians of Ireland over the U.K. government's responsibility for prolonging or relieving the effects of the famine, and historians of Irish America over the nature of the famine and its role in the Irish immigrant experience in the United States.

The fourth chapter explores a second wave of Irish immigration during the turn-of-the-century period from the late 1870s to the 1920s, concentrating mainly on the emergence of the American-born children of the Great Famine immigrants and their effect on Irish American identity and community.

The fifth chapter discusses the decline of Irish immigration to America, measures the increasing prominence and power of Irish Americans in politics and culture, and analyzes their role in the growing American Catholic community they helped build and lead, from Alfred E. Smith's defeat in the race for president in 1928 to John F. Kennedy's triumph in his race for the same office in 1960.

The sixth and final chronological chapter details the revival of immigration from Ireland, the continued economic and social successes of new American-born generations, the breakup of consensus on a strictly Catholic Irish American identity, and the emergence of multiple definitions of Irish American identity—"optional ethnicity"—in the period from Kennedy's presidency to the present.

Part 2 looks at the Irish American experience thematically rather than chronologically and addresses important topics or themes in the study of Irish American history.

The first chapter focuses on gender roles and family life among Irish Americans and explores such questions as why so many more Irish women emigrated to America than women of other groups, and why so many of those same female Irish immigrants took jobs as domestic servants.

The second thematic chapter discusses why Irish Americans have been so prominent in American politics and assesses how effectively they have used that political power for themselves and other Americans.

The third thematic chapter addresses Irish American nationalism—that is, Irish American participation in efforts to create an independent Ireland, and more recently, the struggles between Nationalists and Unionists in Northern Ireland. The chapter investigates who supported nationalism in the Irish community, why they did so, and what effect Irish American nationalism had on Irish American integration into an American mainstream.

The fourth and final thematic chapter analyzes recent debates over Irish American relations with their nonwhite American neighbors, particularly African Americans. This is the so-called "whiteness" controversy. The chapter explores what those relations have been like and discusses various theories that attempt to explain them.

Part 3 is an encyclopedia of people and organizations, including politicians, labor leaders, church figures, military men, prominent nationalists, novelists, playwrights, fraternal societies, nationalist associations, and orders of religious women, which all played important roles in Irish American life. It also includes definitions and brief histories of significant rituals (the celebration of St. Patrick's Day), economic practices (indentured servitude), cultural customs (Gaelic sports) and movements (Irish Studies), and even routes of travel for the Irish in America (the Great Wagon Road), which will help readers better understand the experience of the Irish in America.

Part 4 is a chronology of events and benchmarks in Irish as well as Irish American history that are important to understanding the background, causes, and dimensions of Irish immigration to America and the evolution of Irish Americans as an American ethnic group.

Part 5 is a guide to the best recent books and articles for understanding Irish America. Each entry is annotated to give a sense of the book or article's strengths and its particular usefulness to the study of Irish America. The guide is arranged by topic. The first three sections list books and articles that offer a broad perspective on the Irish American experience. The list includes first, relevant books on Ireland; second, reference books and broad studies of Irish American history as well as multicentury overviews of Irish American politics, religion, nationalism, and local communities; and third, books and articles on the Irish in other "diaspora" countries, such as Australia, Britain, and Canada, which provide useful comparisons to aspects of the Irish experience in the United States. The next six sections of this guide to books and articles are arranged chronologically and match the periods set out in the narrative overview: The seventeenth- and eighteenth-century colonial migration; the Irish in the new American Republic from the American Revolution to the Great Famine; the famine era; the emergence of a new generation in the turn-of-the-century era, from the late 1870s to the 1920s; Irish America's rise to power from Smith's defeat in 1928 to Kennedy's election in 1960; and contemporary Irish America from the 1960s to the present.

THE COLUMBIA GUIDE TO

Irish American History

PART I

A History of Irish Americans from the
Seventeenth to the Twenty-first Century

The Irish as Immigrants and Ethnics

The first Irishman came to America in 1584 as part of Sir Walter Raleigh's ill-fated expedition to the Outer Banks of North Carolina. The last Irish man or woman has not yet arrived and may never come, because few things have been as constant in the histories of Ireland and America as Irish immigration to the United States. There may never be a last Irish immigrant as long as Ireland and the United States exist.

Between the early seventeenth century and the end of the twentieth century, about seven million Irish men and women came to North America, the vast bulk of them settling in the United States or what would become the United States. Most would come in the nineteenth and early twentieth centuries—from the 1820s to the 1920s alone, about five million Irish entered the United States—but Irish men and women were still pouring into America in the 1980s, when some estimates suggest that as many one hundred thousand illegal Irish settled in the United States. In 2000, the U.S. Census reported that over thirty-five million Americans claimed some Irish or Scotch-Irish ancestry, more than any other ethnic group except German Americans. Billy the Kid, Timothy Leary, Spencer Tracy, Mary Harris "Mother" Jones, John C. Calhoun, Peggy Noonan, Philip Sheridan, Cardinal Spellman, Charles Carroll of Carrolton, Sam Houston, Margaret Bourke White, John McGraw, and many if not most of the firefighters who died in New York City on September 11, 2001, have traced some or all of their ancestry to immigrants from Ireland. There have probably been tens or even hundreds of thousands of Americans bearing the old Irish name of Sullivan or O'Sullivan, including the "Fighting" Sullivans, five brothers from Iowa who went down with their ship in a battle off the Solomon islands in World War II; John L. Sullivan, heavyweight boxing champion of the world in the 1880s; Louis Sullivan, the early-twentieth-century architect; Maureen O' Sullivan, film star of the 1930s who, among other roles, played Jane opposite Johnny Weissmuller's Tarzan; Harry Stack Sullivan, the noted psychiatrist; John Sullivan, the Revolutionary War general; Ed Sullivan, newspaper columnist and host of the television variety show that introduced Elvis Presley and the Beatles to America; and Kathleen Sullivan, the famed constitutional law scholar and dean of the Stanford Law School. Andrew Jackson, Richard Nixon, Ronald Reagan, Woodrow Wilson, James Buchanan, and John F. Kennedy are among the presidents of the United States who had ancestors who emigrated from Ireland.

It is hard to conceive of an America without Irish Americans.

And yet it is also hard to tell their story. The late Dennis Clark wrote ten books and scores of articles about the Irish in America, mostly about the Irish in his beloved Philadelphia. Dennis Clark knew as much about the Irish in America as anyone, but after all that work, he confessed that it was hard to pin Irish Americans down: "Almost anything you can say about Irish Americans," Clark once said, "is both true and false."[1]

Irish American history abounds in paradoxes, as Clark's statement suggests. Routinely, for example, Irish and Irish Catholic are treated as synonymous in the American media, but the majority of Americans calling themselves Irish in recent surveys are either Protestant or had ancestors that were. Routinely, the Irish are treated as one of the great nineteenth- and twentieth-century peoples immigrating to northern American cities, but again, most of today's self-identified Irish in America came here in the eighteenth century, most of them settled on the rural frontier, and most of them did so in the South. It is the mountainside and valley villages in places like Houston County, Tennessee (county seat, Erin), some historians claim, and not the narrow streets and triple-decker tenements in neighborhoods like South Boston, that make up the Irish American heartland. And when the nation tore itself apart in the Civil War in the 1860s, it was not the men of the legendary Irish brigade in the Union's Army of the Potomac who embodied Irishness, so these same historians assert, but the ranks and ranks of men in butternut and gray from Tennessee hills or Mississippi plains.

The paradoxes do not disappear even if we focus only on the heavily Catholic nineteenth- and twentieth-century Irish migrants. Easy generalizations continue to unravel. What does one say about Irish American Catholic men, who had a fearsome reputation as brawlers but were more likely than the men of almost any other ethnic group—even native-stock Yankees—to show up regularly for church? Or what do we say about Irish American women, who were fiercely independent, upwardly mobile, ambitious, committed to education and self-improvement, battlers for the interests of working women, and fighters for the cause of the homeland, but strangely passive or even hostile to the cause of their own right to vote or other rights for women? Or Irish voters, often liberal in their support of government intervention in the economy but often conservative in backing restrictions on free speech or sexual expression? Or Irish American men and women, who made themselves symbols of American patriotism but have been among the most enduringly loyal, brashly vocal, and extravagantly generous supporters of the many nationalist causes of their Irish homeland? Or Irish men and women who were among the fiercest enemies of people of color in America, but in the racist hothouse of nineteenth-century America were the whites most likely to marry Asians or Blacks in most cities where they settled in large enough numbers? Thus, just a year before the Irish-born Denis Kearney barnstormed across America in a campaign to exclude the Chinese from the United States, at the end of every speech booming in his thick Cork brogue "the Chinese must go," an Irish immigrant woman turned indignantly on a startled reporter who dared question why she and her friends had married Chinese immigrants: "Because we liked 'em, of course; why shouldn't we?"[2]

Irish Americans, therefore, have been hard to categorize and hard to pin down. Little wonder, then, that historians attempting to make sense of the history of Irish Americans have rarely agreed.

In recent years, for example, a long overdue renewal of interest in Irish migrations during the colonial era and the American republic's early years has sparked a lively debate over that migration's long-term effect on American history. Some historians—Grady McWhiney and Forrest McDonald being the most vocal and persistent—believe that those migrations created a "Celtic" South, in some ways more akin in its customs and values to ancient or medieval Ireland than to its neighboring Anglo-Saxon American North. Others dispute such a claim as so much "Celtic mist over the South," a possibly "pernicious" "patent elixir" of a historical theory.[3]

Debates over the great, largely Catholic migration of the nineteenth and twentieth centuries and its meaning have been going on longer and have been just as heated. For some, the story of Irish Catholic Americans since the Great Famine seems a tragedy. They see an Irish Catholic America born in the horrors of the famine catastrophe in the nineteenth century, long frustrated by slow upward economic progress, wracked by the pathologies of broken families and repressed sexuality, mired in benighted and corrupt politics, bewitched by nationalist pipe dreams for the old country, and throbbing with vicious racism. The assassinations of both John and Robert Kennedy seem to be appropriate caps to a history both painful and disillusioning. Slices of this perception of post-famine Irish American history as tragedy appear in the works of scholars as diverse as Oscar Handlin, Stephan Thernstrom, Steven Erie, Daniel Patrick Moynihan, Thomas N. Brown, Thomas Sowell, David Roediger, Noel Ignatiev, and Kerby Miller. Kerby Miller, who has written the fullest, richest account of Irish immigration to America, paints a harsh picture of the Irish American experience. "In spite of the diminutive size of their homeland the Irish played an important role in the commercial and industrial revolutions that transformed the North Atlantic world," he acknowledged, "however, that role was ambiguous, turbulent, even tragic, for the Irish made no easy accommodation to the changing conditions that buffeted them both at home and in North America."[4] Andrew Greeley, James Walsh, Tyler Anbinder, D. W. Brogan, David Gleeson, Jay Dolan, Dennis Clark himself, and Lawrence McCaffrey see an experience troubled with hardships, but more hopeful— even a triumph of sorts more than a tragedy. McCaffrey says, "The fact that twentieth-century descendants of nineteenth-century tenant farmers and agricultural laborers have become university professors; elementary and secondary school teachers; distinguished novelists, playwrights, and poets; important figures on stage and screen; physicians; political leaders and corporation executives classifies the Irish American Catholic experience as a tremendous success story." Indeed, McCaffrey argues, "the Irish Catholic journey from ghetto to suburbs, from despised aliens to valued members of the community has been arduous, but in historical time, relatively brief ... less than three generations after the famine washed hundreds of thousands of unwanted human refuse onto the American shore, Irish Catholics controlled the Catholic Church, most of the major cities, and a large portion of the organized labor movement in the United States."[5]

In the end, it is perhaps impossible to sort out this long and complex history and stamp a single meaning, triumph or tragedy, on it. It is better simply to recognize that an ethnic group like the Irish in America is a historical phenomenon. Irish Americans are neither inherently flawed nor gifted; neither destined for triumph nor for tragedy. They have no immutable Irish essence, and their history had no inevitable outcome in America. On the contrary, any ethnic group like Irish Americans is dynamic—it changes—and its history is contingent, not preordained.

This was not always how scholars have viewed ethnic groups. For a long time, the study of ethnic groups in America was locked into what Rudolf Vecoli, a historian of Italian Americans, called an "assimilationist model." According to this model, immigrants came to the United States and then they or their children or their children's children became Americans, their foreignness draining out until at some point they became indistinguishable from "mainstream" Americans. Irish Americans' Irishness, their "green" if you will, would be slowly diluted from bright Kelly to tepid variations of lime until they had no color at all that distinguished them from other (white) Americans. According to this model, this process is linear and unidimensional. It is linear in that it assumes only one outcome, ultimate assimilation, and a more or less steady and inevitable movement to that end. It is unidimensional in that it assumes that what defines an ethnic group in America is its distinctive culture and that as the group sheds its culture and absorbs its new American culture, it assimilates. Such a model also assumes that the progress of assimilation can be measured almost mathematically by the number of Irish customs and values given up, on the one hand, and the American ones taken up, on the other.

In the 1960s and 1970s, the African American civil rights revolution challenged not only the accuracy of the assimilationist model's interpretation of ethnic group adjustment but the value of assimilation itself. In an age that prized authenticity and reviled conformity, the struggles of blacks, Latinos, and others to retain their culture and sense of self in the face of pressures from white society seemed heroic. The renewal of ethnic pride reopened the discussion of ethnic group history but did not significantly advance its conceptualization. Social scientists, historians, and ethnic and racial activists sympathetic to the new values of diversity merely denied the assimilation model, rather than offering an alternative to it. They argued that instead of assimilating, members of groups simply and stubbornly retained their culture, but this conception of ethnic group adjustment was still linear and unidimensional, and still assumed an opposition between two static cultures: Irish (or African, Asian, Latino, Italian, etc.) and American. The dichotomy also permitted only two outcomes: stubborn retention of the old inherited culture or its abandonment and absorption of American culture.

Neither the assumption of inevitable assimilation nor cultural resistance, however, is a very useful way to look at Irish American history. Clearly, people changed, and in profound ways. This is partly a product of the passing of generations. The sharpest divide, perhaps, was between immigrants and their American-born children, the second generation. Their relationship is often depicted in stark terms: the children's unequivocal rejection of their parents' world, the second generation's deliberate "forgetting" of their immigrant parents' pasts. Their relationship was much more complex than that, but there indeed have been profound differences between immigrants and their children. There is some evidence that Irish people have been particularly attached to the concretes of their native landscapes—the rocks and hedges, streams and fields—but all immigrants, Irish or not, as Vladimir Nahirny and Joshua Fishman pointed out long ago, understand the old country in a concrete way—thick with the details of the everyday—that their descendants never can. The second generation obviously can never share their parents' experiences and culture in this way, even if they wished to do so. For them, the new land of America was natural. For most second-generation Irish Americans, in the nineteenth and twentieth centuries in particular, city streets, tenements, factories or mine shafts, corner saloons, and vaudeville houses—not fields, streams, and whitewashed cottages—were home. The second-generation Irish were born in America. America was home—they knew no other.

Yet change cannot be explained just by the passage of generations and the accumulating distance of a succession of American-born generations from Ireland. American culture changes constantly. Such a point is obvious but worth repeating, for often we treat the history of immigrants and ethnics in America as a passage from one unchanging essence to another, from some kind of Irishness to some kind of Americanness. There were undoubtedly powerful continuities in both Irish and American culture, but both were also dynamic. American identity and culture were changing and moving targets for immigrants and their descendants.

It is also important to remember that Irish Americans did not just passively adopt the American culture of their day; they helped make it. Second-generation Irish, for example, played a critical role in forging the new American urban popular culture of the late nineteenth century, the culture of professional sports and vaudeville. Children of Irish immigrants, like the baseball player and manager John McGraw or the singer Maggie Cline—not Yankee bluebloods from Boston's Back Bay or Anglo-Saxon Protestant farmers from the Kansas plains—made this new but very American popular culture.

Ireland's culture was dynamic too. Ireland after the Great Famine, for example, was still predominantly rural, but the spread of an exceptional school system and the virtual eradication of illiteracy made it very different from pre-famine Ireland. Differences in background and experiences have, if anything, been even more profound among the many waves of Irish immigrants who came to America in the twentieth century. Many who came to the United States in the 1920s and 1950s, for example, became staunch advocates of Irish republicanism in Northern Ireland after the new "Troubles" erupted there in the 1960s, but the majority of Irish who arrived in America in the 1980s have been indifferent to the Ulster question.

Harder to understand, however, is the way in which *Irish American* culture changed. Traditionally, we have thought that what makes Irish Americans distinct—what puts the "Irish" in Irish American—is what they inherited from Ireland and preserved against the powerful tides of American culture. Yet if we think about cultures as being dynamic and changing, it is possible to conceive of Irish Americans inventing new customs or recasting old values and customs in new forms. The best example, perhaps, is the **St. Patrick's Day parade**. St. Patrick's Day parades drew on some antecedents in Ireland: Fair Day customs, O'Connellite political processions, and Dublin Castle military drills. On the whole, however, the Irish in America, Australia, and Canada invented the St. Patrick's Day parades and would eventually export them back home to Ireland. Similarly, much of the music that came to stand for Irishness in the Irish American community through most of the twentieth century was written in the United States—not in Ireland: "When Irish Eyes Are Smiling," "Galway Bay," or "Who Threw the Overalls in Mrs. Murphy's Chowder" were New York Tin Pan Alley or vaudeville tunes. Even so-called traditional Irish music has felt the hand of Irish American intervention, if not invention, in the twentieth century, as recordings from traditional musicians in America found their way back to Ireland to subtly influence fiddling or other instrumental styles in the homeland.

Plotting the changes in Irish American culture, therefore, is a messy business, more complicated than simply mechanically adding up American traits gained or Irish traits lost on some measuring stick of assimilation. Yet perhaps, when thinking about the Irish in America, or any American ethnic group for that matter, it is important to think of more than just culture. Indeed, some scholars of ethnicity believe that the role of an ethnic group's distinctive culture as the source of its cohesion or the importance of cultural differences as the cause of ethnic conflicts have been overemphasized. Frederick Barth argued this point in a pathbreaking essay in 1969: "It is the ethnic boundary that defines the group, not the cultural stuff that it encloses," he contended.[6] Barth pointed out that cultural differences between an ethnic group and its rivals may be trivial and minor, but the group's members will still often emphasize the minor differences to mark their distinctive group identity. Indeed, one of the principal reasons to invent new cultural customs, like St. Patrick's Day parades, may be to self-consciously "invent traditions" that accent differences between a group and its neighbors and thus strengthen or, as anthropologists say, maintain boundaries. Jerry Seinfeld, the American comedian and an unlikely source of wisdom on American ethnic life, may, nonetheless, have suggested an appropriate analogy to the workings of boundaries and culture in ethnic loyalties and identities, when he lampooned sports fans' enthusiasm for their favorite teams. Seinfeld pointed out that most fans cheer for their team, the

Red Sox, the Giants, the Bears, or the Celtics, regardless of who the players are or even the athletes' style of play (as long as they win). In Seinfeld's words, fans root for the uniforms—"the laundry"—not the players in them. In Barth's terms, ethnic group members rally first to a sense of "us," defined by *boundaries*, not to the cultural "stuff" that "we" practice.

Among the other important characteristics of an ethnic group beyond a distinct *culture* and clear boundaries are ethnic group members' sense of identity, or *peoplehood*, their sense of sharing a destiny, the same past and future triumphs and failures. Concretely filling out boundaries and embodying a sense of peoplehood are the *networks* of clubs, organizations, and institutions that group members create. If identifications are intense and boundaries embattled, an ethnic group or community might construct a virtual parallel society of organizations for its members, sheltering them within the group from cradle to grave.

People in any society, but particularly in America, with its traditions of free association, may hold to many identities at the same time, of course. People in America have a myriad number of potential identities or loyalties: man or woman; son or daughter; child or parent; gay or straight; poor, working, middle class, or rich; New Englander, Southerner, Midwesterner; Catholic, Methodist, Jew; or Democrat or Republican.

Irish Americans could be all these things and Irish American too. In studying ethnic groups like Irish Americans, historians want to know when ethnic identities are important: when a sense of ethnic *peoplehood* becomes emotional and stirring and ethnic *boundaries* so sharply drawn that they seem charged. They also want to know when such identities are not important, or better put, when group members rally to other definitions of themselves—for example, as workers, or as Catholics, or as New Yorkers.

It is in the competition among ethnic groups that ethnic identities often catch fire. Political competition among ethnic groups is the most visible form of this, as fights for elected office, patronage, or legislation can enrich ethnic group members or simply recognize their group's importance. Almost all ethnic groups, the Irish included, have tried to make their history and their heroes an integral part of school curricula, for example. Groups do not compete only in politics; they compete in the economy as well. Irish immigrants or their descendants fought over jobs on the canals with German Americans, with African Americans over jobs on the docks, with Welsh and Cornish men over jobs in the mines, Italians over jobs in construction, Poles over jobs in steel mills, and native-stock Anglo-Saxon Protestants for jobs nearly everywhere. Yet the significant battles were not always at the bottom of the economic hierarchy. Upwardly mobile Irish Americans encountered prejudice at the top, as well, and the sting of discrimination often fired ethnic feelings even among the most acculturated and successful of Irish Americans. The ethnic outsider embittered enough by harsh treatment at the best schools to become a fiery nationalist is almost as common a story as the more conventional tale of the poor minority boy or girl who wins acceptance from admiring elites through hard work and college achievement. Fights over neighborhood turf or even football, basketball, or baseball games between colleges and high schools have also been sites of ethnic competition. Wherever the group has an *interest* at stake in a match producing winners or losers—even a symbolic one merely of group pride or reputation—such competition heightens ethnic identification and reinforces boundaries.

In one of the most important arenas for such ethnic competition, the battles were not over tangible rewards like jobs, contracts, or political offices, but over *images*. In the making of popular culture—plays, songs, cheap fiction, and cartoons, and later radio, television, and movies—ethnic group members and their enemies fought over public images or stereotypes of their people. Such images or stereotypes were powerful weapons in wider ethnic wars, for by belittling an ethnic enemy and suggesting the members' inherent unfitness to participate in governing or to hold responsible jobs, a dominant ethnic group could justify its prejudices and discrimination. Conversely, members of the persecuted ethnic or racial group sought to rehabilitate its image to discredit efforts to exclude them from power and wealth.

Yet the construction of ethnic or racial images in popular culture was never as simple as that. The images that dominant groups create of ethnic or racial minorities often reflect their own illicit desires, projected on a despised Other—a psychological exercise to displace their own guilt—in self-conscious, calculated efforts to justify their prejudices. Members of the dominant group, for example, accuse minority peoples of doing what they want to do but cannot, and then they condemn the minorities for it. On the other side, ethnic minorities often find stereotypes too deeply rooted to be simply wished away and replaced by their own benign images. Frequently, ethnic minority members have found themselves trapped into merely turning those bad old images upside down, making their vices into virtues. As William Williams has pointed out, Irish American songwriters and playwrights, for example, converted images of Irish American drunkenness into Irish American conviviality or hospitality, and the alleged Irish American lack of individual initiative to laudable loyalty to friends and family.

In a curious way, therefore, Irish Americans or any ethnic group members' relations with other groups and their understanding of those other groups as friends or enemies in competition for political or other rewards affected how they thought about themselves. Native-stock American white Anglo-Saxon Protestants of long lineage, called Yankees in New England, were probably the most important group Irish Americans had to deal with in most cities and towns. And yet, wherever they lived, Irish Americans rarely confronted only one group. American city and town populations were made and remade as fresh waves of immigrants arrived. The arrival of new groups inevitably altered the balance of ethnic group power and reshaped Irish American conceptions of their own interests and, as we shall see, affected even their own conceptions of identity and boundaries. But there are other kinds of changes that affected their relations with other groups. The economy's rise and fall, for example, often seriously affected how groups related to each other. When times were good and jobs plentiful, competition eased and ethnic tensions declined, but when times were bad, such as during the depressions of 1893 and 1929, competition for jobs and business was fierce and ethnic conflicts escalated. Irish Americans also had interests abroad—at home in Ireland or, for Irish Catholics, at the Vatican in Rome— and changes in politics in those places, for example, the rise of movements in Ireland for independence or shifts in policy made by the Pope in Rome, could have profound effects on how the Irish in America understood themselves.

Irish American ethnic identity and culture, and even the boundaries of that identity—the meaning of being Irish American—thus changed over time, as the following chronological chapters will illustrate. In the early nineteenth century, as chapter 2 describes, many Irishmen in America worked to forge an Irish American identity and boundaries of that identity that would encompass Protestant and Catholic Irish alike. Republican revolutions in America and France and the spread of revolutionary republican fever in Ireland had convinced many Irish and Irish Americans alike that they could finally overcome the bitter sectarianism that had so long troubled Ireland and now divided its immigrants in America. Alliances between Irish Catholics and Irish Protestants in the Society of United Irishmen in Ireland and in the Democratic Republican party in America gave substance to this hope and tied the two Irish religious groups together in a shared interest. Chapter 4 offers another example of how Irish American identities, culture, and boundaries would change again, at the turn of the century, when Irish American Catholics would seek to create a new group in America, the American Catholics, that would include all American Catholic ethnics.

Irish American ethnic identity, culture, and boundaries changed, therefore, for many reasons. They changed because the immigrants gave way to American-born generations, family links to Ireland and the root of family experiences there inevitably faded into distant memory, and the attitudes, customs, perspectives, and values—in short, the culture—of the American-born inevitably differed from the immigrants. Yet Irish American identity and culture changed also, because America, American culture, and what it meant to be an American changed, and thus profound differences emerged even among succeeding American-born generations of Irish. New generations of Irish Americans participated in and played crucial roles in this making and re-making of American culture. At the same time, they invented an *Irish American* culture, new customs and leisure pastimes, and recast old Irish norms and rituals into new Irish American ones. So as American as they were, they made something Irish American for themselves as well. They did so in part because being Irish or Irish American remained meaningful to them. Yet the salience or meaning of that identity would also change over time. The sense of identity, peoplehood, and boundaries—who was in and who was out—would change because the people who were their neighbors would change and sometimes the rules governing their relations with those people would change as well. That sense of identity also changed because events that demanded their response erupted in the old country or in the new. And so the Irish, like any other ethnic group, could change without assimilating, without merging into some undifferentiated American mainstream and disappearing forever as a vital and self-conscious group of people. Older, simpler dichotomies suggesting that Irish Americans (or any ethnic group for that matter) could only either assimilate or remain fundamentally the same as their ancestors are ultimately too simple.

If the American environments of Irish immigrants and their ancestors changed over time, they also differed across the country, as each region—even each city—posed its own kind of challenges and offered its own kind of opportunities to the Irish who settled there.

One of the most important variables in those environments was the local or regional economy, the kind of work local industries required, and more importantly, the opportunities the local economy offered. Industry flourished in New England in the early nineteenth century, but by the late nineteenth century the economy there was already beginning to mature, and chances for success constricted. Farther west, cities like Detroit, Chicago, or best of all, San Francisco, were just beginning to grow, and economic opportunities abounded. This was not just a difference between East and West, however. In the Philadelphia or even New York of the nineteenth and early twentieth centuries, dynamic economies seemed to generate a broader range of jobs than the New England cities.

And yet the dynamism of local economies is only one of the variables contributing to differences in Irish experiences across American space. As important has been the variation in the social mix of the cities where they settled. In New England, it was not just the slowing of a native economy that slowed Irish social progress and nourished their intense sense of alienation but also the presence and power of a Yankee population, entrenched for over two hundred years, blocking Irish mobility and exacerbating Irish Americans' sense of grievance. Relations between this powerful Yankee establishment and the huge new Irish population were more fluid than some historians have suggested, but they did often degenerate into a kind of unyielding mutual hostility of fortified boundaries and little or no social interaction. Yet the United States was still a new country, and white Anglo Protestants did not reach vast stretches of the country until well into the nineteenth century. In such places, some Midwestern but mostly western cities—large ones like San Francisco and small ones like Butte, Montana—Irish immigrants and their children arrived at the same time or even before white Anglo Protestants. The Irish, then, were part of the "founding peoples" of such cities or regions, and that status gave them advantages in the economy and freedom in the society that their fellow Irish in New England would never know.

As noted earlier, however, Irish relations with other immigrant or racial groups were also important to their adjustments, and because the mix of groups, their cultural backgrounds, numbers, and power varied from city to city, this meant that Irish experiences would vary as well. In the South, where boundaries between blacks and whites, or in the west, between whites and Asians, heightened white solidarity, Irish acceptance by the white Protestant mainstream proved easier than farther east where black or Asian populations were small or where antiabolition sentiment ran strong and racial boundaries were not quite so charged.

Rules that might facilitate strong, centralized political machines in some cities or personal and factional politics in another, for example, or even city topography, peninsulas, rivers, and islands that helped reinforce the isolation of ethnic neighborhoods or broad open spaces that made them harder to defend, could also shape Irish local experiences.

Yet it may not have been where the Irish landed in America alone that accounted for these variations in Irish American experiences in America. Who the Irish were who landed there, particularly where they came from in Ireland, may have helped shape those local cultures too. Ireland is a small country, and southern Ireland has been overwhelmingly agricultural for much of its history. Catholics have also predominated in the island's population since the Reformation. Nevertheless, there have been important differences among regions and localities in religion, types of farming, degrees of literacy, and marital behavior. Irish experiences thus might also vary across America because of which Irish went to which different cities or even how and when they got there. That is, the mix of Irishmen going to one city might have differed in their religious affiliations and the regions or classes they came from in Ireland when compared to the Irish going to another community. It might also be important whether the newcomers emigrated freely or as servants, or whether they arrived early or late in a city's history.

So in assessing variations in Irish adjustments across America, it is important to know who went where. Historians talk of immigrant chains, links of a family or friends who follow one another out to specific settlements. The ones who came first helped those who came later, paying for the steamship and railroad tickets to bring the family members or friends to America, and once there finding the newcomers housing, jobs, or simply some solace and support. Scholars of Italian, Norwegian, Dutch, and many other immigrant groups have made substantial progress tracing such chains and identifying the specific local or regional roots of American immigrant settlements. Because of their work, we know the prominence of immigrants from Avellini or towns in Sicily in Italy in Boston's Italian North End or from Fortun or Hjoringfjord parishes in Norway in the Wisconsin counties of Crawford, Vernon, and Buffalo. We know less, however, about the regional origins of Irish settlers in America, in part because sources identifying the home villages of Irish immigrants are not as good as the sources for Italians or Norwegians. We do have some scattered evidence, however, of chains from Ireland leading to communities in America: emigrants from the Dingle peninsula in County Kerry clustered in the Hungry Hill neighborhood in Springfield, Massachusetts, for example, and immigrants from the island of Aranmore off the Donegal coast settled in Beaver Island, Michigan. We also know that substantial numbers of immigrants from Kenmare in Kerry settled in the Five Points district of New York's Lower East Side, and many miners from the Bere peninsula in Cork made their way to the copper mines of Butte.

Irish immigrants did not just go to cities and towns in the United States, however, but to communities in almost all parts of the world. The phrase "Irish diaspora" has gained a certain cachet of late, as Ireland's leaders trumpet their little island's worldwide connections in a quest to accent the cosmopolitanism of a new global Ireland. For some, the phrase has a political connotation: a suggestion of forced exile, like the ancient Jews scattered over all of the Mediterranean by Roman conquest. Yet, in its most narrow sense, the phrase need not be hollow or partisan, but simply a very useful term that makes a critical if simple point: the Irish migrated to many different places throughout the world.

It is crucial for students of the Irish in America to keep in mind that Irish migration to the United States has been only part, albeit the largest part, of the flow of migrants out of Ireland. This book is about the Irish in America and it will focus on their experience, but this story will be placed in the context of the broader story of the diaspora. Not to do so would be to distort the history of Irish migration to America and to eliminate or obscure critical dimensions of contingency and change from that story. For Irish immigrants who went to the United States did not have to go there, and knowing that they had other possible destinations sheds some light on their decisions to choose America. Furthermore, as historians of the Irish in Britain, Canada, and Australia have been quick to point out, studying Irish immigrants and their descendants in those countries provides a broader range of Irish experiences as points of comparison, and such comparisons help sort out the essentials of Irish culture and tradition, thus undermining facile conclusions about what was inevitable or typical in the history of the Irish in America. Historians of Irish Americans have sometimes explained the apparently puzzling proclivity of rural, Irish peasant immigrants to concentrate in American cities, for example, as if it were the inevitable result of Irish culture and experience, the strength of their communalism, or the intensity of their disappointment with farming after the Great Famine. Such historians, however, have been unaware or have ignored the fact that most Irish migrants to Australia settled not in cities but in rural areas, communalism or disillusionment with farming notwithstanding. The comparison between the Irish in America and those in Australia thus forces us to probe more deeply and examine more carefully Irish experiences in both places.

In paying attention to Irish experiences in other nations and other continents, historians of Irish immigration look at the same variables that they look at in probing the differences between regions or cities in the United States. They look at the nature of the economies and economic opportunities, the mixes and proportions of other ethnic groups, the laws or rules governing political and economic competition, and the specific backgrounds of the Irish who settled in those places.

There is a final consideration in studying the history of an immigrant people and their descendants. Sometimes ethnic groups disappear. The descendants of immigrants no longer think that their ancestors' origins are important and no longer even think to call themselves British, Scottish, German, or perhaps even Irish American. Does the story end there?

Irish men and women had been coming to North America and what would become the United States long before the Great Famine of the 1840s. Indeed, hundreds of thousands came to America over the course of the eighteenth century. Most would settle in Pennsylvania or along the Southern Piedmont and frontier.

Interestingly, however, they have left little trace of an Irish identity there. Historians still dispute whether those immigrants even thought of themselves as Irish, though they certainly came from Ireland. By the 1840s, when the famine Irish arrived, the Irishness of these eighteenth-century Irish immigrants seemed already forgotten by many of their descendants. And yet it would be a mistake — indeed, a distortion of the story of the Irish in America — not to include them here. The history of these earlier immigrants from Ireland is as much a part of Irish American history as the well-remembered famine exodus of the nineteenth century. How and why such an Irish group consciousness died or, indeed, may never have existed at all, is as interesting as why an Irish identity took hold and endured so long among later immigrants and their descendants.

And yet the story of this earlier Irish migration underlines the question of what happens when a group becomes "extinct" — when the descendants of group members cease to think of themselves as part of the ethnic group. Has their story ended? Or can we and should we try to calculate the legacies they have left? In recent years, several historians have argued that these eighteenth-century immigrants from Ireland had a powerful and enduring influence on American culture, especially in the South, that could be traced to their Irish or more broadly Celtic origins. This is, as previously pointed out, a very controversial assertion. Yet the point they raise is important, for it is likely to become increasingly relevant for the later, largely Catholic migration as for this earlier, largely Protestant one. As ethnic consciousness weakens among the descendants of nineteenth- and twentieth-century Irish immigrants, it is appropriate to consider what their legacy has been, perhaps in their own heartlands such as New England or other states of the Northeast and Midwest.

NOTES

1. Ronald H. Bayor and Timothy Meagher, eds., *The New York Irish* (Baltimore: Johns Hopkins University Press, 1996), 533.

2. Tyler Anbinder, *Five Points: The Nineteenth Century New York City Neighborhood That Invented Tap Dance, Stole Elections, and Became the World's Most Notorious Slum* (New York: The Free Press, 2001), 420.

3. Rowland Berthoff, "Celtic Mist Over the South," *Journal of Southern History* 52, no. 4 (1986): 523, 536.

4. Kerby Miller, *Emigrants and Exiles: Ireland and the Irish Exodus to North America* (New York: Oxford University Press, 1985), 3.

5. Lawrence McCaffrey, *The Irish Catholic Disapora in America* (Washington: Catholic University Press, 1997), 9–10.

6. Frederick Barth, "Ethnic Groups and Boundaries," in *Theories of Ethnicity: A Classical Reader*, ed. Werner Sollors (New York: New York University Press, 1996), 300.

CHAPTER ONE

Irish Immigration to Colonial America

In 1980, the U.S. Census Bureau asked a large sample of Americans to identify their ethnic ancestry and *We the People: An Atlas of American Diversity* plotted their responses by county across the country in large, bright, detailed maps. One of the maps depicted the geography of Irish ethnic identifiers. The *We the People Atlas* used green, naturally enough, to show areas of Irish concentration: dark Kelly green for counties with heavy proportions; lighter shades giving way to a soft lime for counties where the proportion of Irish identifiers was smaller. Massachusetts's Suffolk County (Boston) and neighboring Norfolk County (Dedham, Quincy, and other cities and towns) were painted dark green, and those dark greens spread along the eastern New England coast, gathering in splotches on the sites of large and small cities and their suburbs across the Northeast and Mid-Atlantic region: places like Albany, Scranton, and Philadelphia. And yet, most striking was the great swath of green running from Virginia's Shenandoah Valley along the Carolina and Georgia Piedmont, then west all the way to Missouri and Texas. An accompanying table listed the five counties in the nation with the highest proportion of Irish identifiers. As might be expected, it included the Massachusetts counties of Suffolk and Norfolk, but other more surprising counties as well: Lafayette County, Florida; Smith County, Mississippi; and Houston County, Tennessee (county seat, Erin).

The people calling themselves Irish in Tennessee, Mississippi, or these other southern states were not the descendants of the nineteenth-century refugees from the Great Famine of the 1840s. The ancestors of these southerners and millions of others scattered from Pennsylvania through the Midwest and far West had left Ireland much earlier, in the seventeenth and eighteenth centuries. Of all the forty million or more Americans claiming some Irish ancestry in recent censuses, these people have probably constituted a majority, but their chapter in Irish American history has received far less attention from historians then the story of the later famine immigrants. Some observers, most notably the historian Donald Akenson, sniff Catholic biases among Irish American historians in this indifference to these earlier, largely Protestant migrants. Akenson and others suspect that recent Irish American historians have almost deliberately tried to erase an unwanted people and their inconvenient history from its deserved place in the story of the Irish in America.

Such charges border on the hysterical, but beneath them lies the first and fundamental problem of the history of these early Irish migrants: were they or, at least, were most of them Irish at all? The problem lies in the migrants' complex origins. In the seventeenth century, thousands of Scottish Presbyterians migrated from the Lowlands of their own country to Ireland's northeastern corner, the province of Ulster. Movement between Scotland and Ulster was not new. Eastern Scotland and western Ulster are scarcely miles apart at some points—some men and women who migrated to Ulster from Scotland in the early seventeenth century continued to row home to church in Scotland every Sunday. From far back into the ancient history of the two places, people had moved back and forth between Scotland and Ireland. For example, in the fourteenth century, Robert Bruce's brother Edward had crossed into Ireland with his army, dreaming of tying Ireland to Scotland in a great pan-Celtic kingdom. Yet in the seventeenth century, the migration from Scotland to Ireland took on a new and fundamentally different character. British conquerors fresh from bloody wars with Irish chieftains rooted in Ulster were intent on pacifying that province once and for all. They harried some of the old chieftains out of the country and pushed others off ancestral lands. The English then encouraged migrants from Scotland and England to settle on those lands to secure control of a part of Ireland that once had been a nursery of conspiracy and rebellion. By 1625, perhaps 14,000 to 15,000 Scots had migrated to Ireland, mainly into Antrim and Down, and by 1641, 20,000 to 30,000 more arrived, many of whom then moved further west into the confiscated lands of the old Irish Catholic aristocracy. The Scottish migration to Ulster slowed in the middle of the seventeenth century and then accelerated again in the 1690s. Between 1689 and 1715, anywhere from 40,000 to 70,000 Scots moved to Ulster. Some of these people and many of their descendants would make up the bulk of the migrants who moved to America in the colonial era. Perhaps as many as two-thirds of the eighteenth-century migrants would be either Scots who had settled in Ulster or the descendants of such Scottish settlers living in the northern Irish province.

If these people, then, were Scots who settled in Ireland or those Scots' children or even their grandchildren, were they Irish or Scottish or something in between? Many historians have called them not Irish but Scotch-Irish. The meanings and use of the term have varied significantly over time. Historian Kerby Miller claims that in its earliest incarnations in Ireland it was used to describe old Scottish-Irish clans like the MacDonnells, who claimed land and boasted members on both sides of the narrow strait separating Scotland and Ulster as well as the islands that lay between them. The term fell out of use in Ireland and Scotland altogether by the seventeenth and eighteenth centuries. In North America it reappeared, defining those immigrants who were descendants of the Scottish Presbyterians who had settled in Ireland. Yet historians do not agree how common the term had become in colonial America. Some say it was at least known in the Chesapeake Bay and Delaware River regions by the eighteenth century. Kerby Miller also suggests that conservative Irish Presbyterians began using the term in the late eighteenth and early nineteenth centuries as a political tactic. These Federalist ministers wanted the Protestant Irish to abandon Thomas Jefferson's Democratic-Republican party, which had welcomed Irish papists into its ranks. These ministers played upon the differences between the Irish Catholics and their own people by calling their own "Scotch-Irish" and pleaded with them to abandon association with the papist Irish rabble in the Democratic-Republican party. The term Scotch-Irish, however, did not really come into its own until the nineteenth century, at which point the descendants of the eighteenth-century immigrants from Ireland began to insist on calling themselves and their ancestors Scotch-Irish. As Protestants boasting ancestors who had fought in the American Revolution, they wished to dissociate themselves from the poor Catholic Irish newcomers, whom they despised as the "serfs of Rome and Tammany Hall."[1]

Were these Scotch-Irish really Irish then? Should they be included in a history of the Irish in America or is theirs a separate history? Or do they even belong to some other story, such as Scottish immigration to America? One could solve such a problem easily by suggesting simply that any immigrant leaving Ireland for America is an Irish immigrant and is thus part of the story, but some might dispute that. A historian of these colonial-era immigrants writing in the 1940s quoted an old maxim to argue that the Scotch-Irish were different: "If a man is born in a stable, does that make him a horse?"[2] There were Germans from the Palatinate who settled in Limerick in 1709 for a few years and then moved on to the English colonies in North America—are they part of Irish American history as well? Historians' treatments of other American immigrant groups suggest no easy answers: immigration historians rarely combine the histories of Jewish and Catholic immigrants from Poland, for example, but they almost always treat Catholic, Protestant, and freethinking Germans as a single people. The simple fact of living in Ireland and at some point leaving it, then, might not be enough to qualify an immigrant or his or her descendants as part of Irish American history.

Yet it is important as well not to insist on too strict a definition of Irishness and even more important not to assume that our own definitions of it should rule considerations of inclusion or exclusion. As noted earlier, ethnic and national loyalties are not givens. They change and evolve over time. When the nineteenth-century descendants of eighteenth-century immigrants from Ireland insisted on being called Scotch-Irish and not Irish, they were reacting to changes in their own time that had come to equate being Irish with being Catholic. Yet that was not necessarily how Irish was defined in the eighteenth century. Indeed, over the course of the eighteenth century a number of Protestants in Ireland, including Ulster Presbyterians in the north, forged their own version of Irish loyalties, first during the Volunteer movement of the 1770s and 1780s and later through the Society of United Irishmen in the 1790s. In short, many Protestants in Ireland in the eighteenth century called themselves Irish and identified with an Irish nation. In part, they did so because they felt free to do so. They did not worry about being mistaken for Catholics; Ireland's Catholics had been crushed after nearly one hundred years of war in the seventeenth century, and by the middle or late eighteenth century seemed finally broken. Freed from fear of Catholic rebellion, such Protestant patriots felt confident enough to assert claims for *their* Ireland against the meddling English. Fears of Catholics and disdain for them would not disappear in eighteenth-century Ireland. Even in that regard, however, as they grew frustrated with British domination of their Ireland, some Protestants began to cautiously consider some form of Catholic inclusion in the Irish political nation. All of this would change in the nineteenth century, as Irish nationalism became almost exclusively Catholic and most Protestants became stalwart supporters of a union with Britain; but in the eighteenth century, Irish national identities were more fluid, and the emergence of an enduring Protestant Irish nationalism seemed not only possible but probable.

What of these Presbyterian descendants of the Scots who left Ireland for the British colonies in America? What were they called and what did they call themselves? The historian Maldwyn Jones contends, "Most of those who had occasion to refer to Ulster immigrants continued to use the designation Irish, while the newcomers themselves, though occasionally irritated at being mistaken for Irish Catholics, generally accepted the name throughout the eighteenth century, and, indeed, well into the nineteenth century."³ They should, therefore, clearly be part of the history of the Irish in America.

Yet if such people should be considered Irish, their distinctiveness within Irish society should not be overlooked. The Presbyterian Scots and their descendants in Ulster formed a distinct people, conscious of their differences from Catholics and even other Protestants. Presbyterians were dissenters in Ireland. The heart of their separate subcommunity was their Presbyterian religion. Organized in 1642, with church elders enforcing a strict moral discipline, Presbyterianism created an almost all-encompassing world for Ulster's Scottish descendants. It was not just the internal cohesion of being Presbyterian that bound them, however, since their religion also marked them as political outsiders. In England, Ireland, Scotland, and many of the American colonies in those days, there was an established church. In England and Ireland, the established church was a variant of Anglicanism in terms of belief and organization. Like the Anglican Church in England it received state support, and like that church its members alone enjoyed full political privileges. Presbyterians could practice their religion openly in Ireland, but because they were not members of the established Church of Ireland they suffered political discrimination. The Test Act of 1704 excluded them from certain political and military offices and some of their religious rituals, even weddings, had no official sanction for many years. Economic independence underlined and reinforced the autonomy of this Presbyterian religious and political community. Presbyterians were more likely to be merchants, clerks, or skilled artisans than either Catholics or members of the established Church of Ireland. Most Presbyterian families were tenant farmers, but even many of these farm households supplemented their income by spinning or weaving for Ulster's successful linen manufacturers. On the average, Presbyterians in Ulster were richer and better housed than not only the Catholic Irish but even most of the other Protestants in Ireland. Forming a cohesive and distinctive religious community, the boundaries of its sense of identity sharpened and strengthened by gnawing political grievances and its independence sustained by economic success, Ulster's Presbyterians maintained their own culture, distinguished from other Irish peoples in ways as diverse as the bonnets Presbyterian women wore or the peculiar dialect of English that Presbyterian men, women, and children spoke.

The Presbyterians of Scottish descent were a small minority of the Irish population, consisting of only 400,000 to 600,000 of the island's approximately four million people in the late eighteenth century. They nonetheless made up the bulk of the immigrants to America in the colonial period. In 1636, a group of Ulster Presbyterians set off on the ship *Eagle Wing*, but storms drove the ship back. The migrants gave up the hope for America and instead moved to Scotland. After the 1680s, ships from Ulster carrying hundreds of migrants began arriving in the Chesapeake region. In the eighteenth century, however, this Irish Presbyterian trickle to America became a flood. In all, anywhere from 70,000 to 150,000 Irish Presbyterians came to America in the eighteenth century.

Historians once explained this torrent of Irish Presbyterian migration as the heroic trek of a godly people seeking religious freedom. Such sentiments complimented not only these Ulster Presbyterians but also the United States and its presumed special place in world history as a haven for the oppressed. Most of today's historians are more skeptical of that story. For example, David Doyle argues that the Presbyterians did not suffer grievously as dissenters in Ireland. He points out that starting in 1672 (suspended later but then reinstated under William II in the 1690s), the government subsidized Presbyterian ministers through the *regium donium*. Nevertheless, if the religious discrimination Presbyterians suffered did not cause them much pain, it did rankle. Under the Test Act, they were still second-class citizens, and this angered them. The government also compelled them to pay tithes to support an established Church of Ireland that they did not attend. For some Presbyterians, it was not just specific penalties but the broader principle of the right or wisdom of any state to establish a church that nourished a growing sense of their religious grievance in the eighteenth century. Some Presbyterians among the expanding class of successful merchants in Belfast began arguing for religious freedom and liberty of conscience as a basic right. More conservative Presbyterians, particularly rural evangelicals, did not dispute the right of the state to establish a church, but they believed that it should be their church that was established, not the oppressive, corrupt, and spiritually flaccid Church of Ireland. This suspicion of the established church radically distinguished Ireland's Presbyterians from the Presbyterians in their Scottish homeland. The ties between the two were close—Irish Presbyterian clerics often trained in Scotland—but the Presbyterian Church was established in Scotland, and so Scottish Presbyterians enjoyed the full political rights and privileges of the establishment. If their second-class religious status did not cause Ulster Presbyterians to suffer seriously, it did, nonetheless, nurture their disaffection. It may not have driven them out of Ireland, but it did help loosen the ties that kept them there.

Most historians seem to agree that what did seem to drive them from the island was an assortment of economic pressures and misfortunes that made the lure of America too attractive to ignore. One of the chief causes was the meteoric rise in rents that Irish landlords imposed on their tenants. The rise in rents in the Stewart estates in the heavily Presbyterian County Antrim in Ulster seemed typical, growing from two shillings, eleven pence per acre in 1720 to thirteen shillings, six pence per acre in the 1770s, a nearly six-fold increase. In part, a revival of the Irish economy encouraged such rising rents, but the rents seemed to grow far more quickly than the profits that tenants could manage from sales of their crops. Population pressure might have helped squeeze them higher. In 1672, Ireland, bloodied by years of war, numbered only 1.7 million people. Over the course of the peaceful eighteenth century, and especially after hard agricultural times in the early part of the century, Ireland's population grew substantially, nearly doubling between the 1740s and 1790s. Ulster in particular grew quickly as thousands of Scottish Presbyterians poured into the province in the 1690s and early 1700s. With more potential tenants seeking land, landlords took full advantage to squeeze what profits they could from their estates. Some tried to shorten leases or encourage bidding wars to take full advantage of the competition for their precious resource.

The timing of the first great wave of Ulster Presbyterian migration seems to be a direct result of those bidding wars. In the 1690s, just after the Williamite War, the landlords had invited the huge flood of thousands of immigrants from Scotland with offers of long leases and favorable rents. With memories of Catholic rebellions then still fresh, the landlords had been eager to establish a Protestant bulwark against further Catholic rebellions. Those leases came due in the 1710s and by that time Protestant landlords no longer worried about Irish Catholic rebellion. Little wonder that the first significant flow of Ulster Presbyterian migration began in the 1710s, when those favorable leases ended and the bidding wars began.

Yet rack-renting was not the only hardship these Irish Presbyterians faced in the eighteenth century. With rising rents affording them little margin for survival, bad weather and poor harvests spelled disaster for farmers all over Ireland. Drought afflicted Ireland in the late 1720s, for example, prompting the second great wave of Irish emigration to America in that decade, and beginning in December of 1739 and through all of the next year, Irish farmers suffered seriously from the misfortunes of weather, again prompting another wave of emigration.

To compensate for the rack-renting and, in part, to explore new economic opportunities, a vast number of Ulster Presbyterians became involved in the manufacture and sale of linen. The making of linen in Ulster began in about the 1660s, but only began to take off at the end of the seventeenth century. Between 1704 and 1740, the number of yards of linen sold to England rose from

700,000 to 6.4 million. As early as 1720, linen made up half of all of Ireland's trade with England. Concentrated in Ulster, more specifically in and around the booming city of Belfast, the linen industry included more than simply a few merchant manufacturers and city artisans. Thousands in the surrounding countryside participated, most of them farmers or farmers' wives spinning or weaving in their spare time to supplement the returns from their crops and livestock and then, as time passed, farming in their spare time to supplement the profits of their spinning and weaving. In good times, the linen trade could help them survive, even prosper; but if the trade expanded through the eighteenth century, it did not grow steadily. Reverses and downturns, occurred throughout eighteenth century and especially in the early 1770s, when foreign demand for linen fell by over half, causing thousands to flee to America.

Ulster Presbyterians of Scottish descent made up the bulk of the emigrants originating in Ireland who came to America in the colonial era, but they were not the only Irish to settle in the New World then. Thousands of people migrated to America from Ireland who were neither descendants of Scots nor practicing Presbyterians. Many were, in fact, of English descent. Men and women from England and Wales had settled in Ireland throughout its known history, but there were noticeably heavy migrations from parts of England in the seventeenth century. Scots were not the only Protestants recruited for the plantations in Ulster, for example. By 1622, there were 13,000 English settlers in the plantation lands in central Ulster, and another few thousand in Counties Antrim and Down in east Ulster. Established Church Protestants were also scattered throughout southern Ireland, where landlords recruited artisans and tenants from England to serve as the secure cores of their estates and towns. By 1642, 22,000 English settlers had moved into parts of Munster. These English migrants combined with the Old Irish Celts who had converted from Catholicism to the Church of Ireland to create the established church population in Ireland.

On the surface, there seemed little reason for these Church of Ireland Irish to make their way to America. After all, they dominated the Irish ruling class— all the landlords and government officials and many of the major merchants of note were Episcopalians. Even the humbler mass of Episcopalian tenants and artisans enjoyed the privileges that membership in the established Church of Ireland afforded—privileges that neither their Presbyterian nor Catholic neighbors enjoyed.

Yet there were good reasons for members of the Church of Ireland of almost every status to move to America. Gentry offspring went to America to serve as the extensions of the British Empire's ruling class, as governors, government officials, and soldiers. William Cosby would become New York's governor, for example, Joseph Murray its attorney general, and Anthony Duane and Oliver Templeton became wealthy merchants in the city. Yet there were also Church of Ireland immigrants of more modest Irish backgrounds and American accomplishments. Indeed, one historian estimates that most of these Irish immigrants to the United States were probably poorer than most Presbyterian immigrants. The poorer Anglican Irish found their own reasons for traveling west to America. Like their Presbyterian neighbors, Church of Ireland small farmers suffered from rack-renting and bad harvests. Here again, the lure of America was its opportunities for plentiful land or work, or at least its opportunity for a new life. In the end, fewer Church of Ireland Protestants went to North America than Catholics in the seventeenth century or Presbyterians in the eighteenth century. Still, they constituted maybe about one-tenth of the emigrants in the latter century and many of the most notable Irish of the entire colonial era.

The Presbyterian and Anglican migrations to America were open, visible, and numerous enough to draw widespread attention and leave abundant traces for future historians. Indeed, by the late nineteenth century most historians seemed to believe that all Irish immigrants to America in the eighteenth century were Protestant. The majority of the Irish who came to America in the colonial era were Protestants, all historians agree, but there were a substantial number who had been Catholics in Ireland, though they may not have remained so in America. Kerby Miller points to nineteenth-century local histories from South Carolina to South Dakota extolling the honorable Scotch-Irish lineage of men named O'Brien, O'Callaghan, or O'Sullivan. These are not Scottish names, as Miller notes, but proud ancient Irish Celtic ones, and in the seventeenth and eighteenth centuries many of the men and women who bore those names probably left Ireland for America as Catholics.

No one knows for sure how many Catholics left Ireland for America because their migration was so makeshift and haphazard, and once in America there was no way for them to create viable communities or even maintain their religious and ethnic identities. Most were probably people already uprooted from traditional Catholic peasant rural communities, having migrated into Irish towns or cities as individuals and shipping out from there to America, often as indentured servants. Others were prisoners tried for petty crimes or in some rare occasions for rebellion against the British Crown. These people were "transported" to America in lieu of imprisonment in jail or even execution. As anonymous drifters or former captives severed from their communities, they could establish no personal chains or networks leading back to Ireland.

However, not all were the flotsam and jetsam of a Catholic society battered by defeat in the seventeenth century and sinking into poverty and impotence in the eighteenth. **Charles Carroll** of Litterluna, County Offaly, for example, left Ireland in 1688 just before the disaster of the Williamite Wars, and prospered as a Catholic planter and lawyer in Maryland. Yet the Carrolls were the exceptions to the rule, for except in Pennsylvania and to some extent Carroll's Maryland, Catholics could not practice their faith openly in America and could not maintain their religious identity without the strongest of self-conscious struggles. Thus even the offspring of prominent Catholics in Ireland like immigrant to New Hampshire Owen Sullivan found it necessary to convert to Anglicanism to have a chance to prosper in the colonies. Irish Catholic historians in the early twentieth century like Michael O'Brien, angered by the broad claims of the descendants of Irish Protestants, would pick up on the scattered evidence of Catholic conversions and make broad claims of their own. They would claim that Catholics were a far larger proportion of the eighteenth-century Irish migrants to America than anyone had previously imagined—perhaps even a majority, albeit a hidden one, of all Irish immigrants to America in that period. This is clearly an exaggeration. Catholics may indeed have been a majority of the Irish coming here in the small migration of the seventeenth century, but they probably numbered no more than one-third, and probably closer to one-fifth, of all Irish immigrants in the far larger Irish migration of the eighteenth century. That is still a substantial number, but hardly a majority.

Even if this is more than most historians were once willing to concede, what is puzzling is why it was not greater. Why were Catholics a minority of Irish immigrants to America in the seventeenth and eighteenth centuries, when they were a majority, indeed, two-thirds, of Ireland's population at that time? Moreover, they, far more than Protestants, even the Presbyterians, had reasons to seek a better life somewhere, anywhere, other than Ireland.

To understand why, we have to retrace our steps back into Irish history. Ireland had been fought over by invading forces for well nigh a millennium by the sixteenth and seventeenth centuries, but it was the religious wars of those centuries that sealed the fate of its Catholic people. The Normans—Norsemen who settled in France—had come to Ireland in the twelfth and thirteenth centuries by way of England and Wales and overran the native Gaels, but the Gaels revived, aided by the neglect of a beleaguered England, and the mingling of Normans and Irish advanced to a degree alarming to the English court by the fifteenth century. The revival of English power in Ireland in the sixteenth and seventeenth centuries, taking place in a Europe awash in conflicts between Catholics and Protestants, would not be so easily reversed. Catholics, largely descendants of the old Irish Gaels but including many Norman (sometimes called "Old English") families—some Burkes, Fitzgeralds, De Courcys, and others—fought almost continuous battles with Protestant enemies throughout the seventeenth century.

In 1691 the Catholic cause went down for the last time when King William's armies crushed the forces of James II in Ireland and forced James's Catholic and other supporters to sue for peace. It was a final and disastrous defeat for Ireland's Catholics. Catholic land ownership had already fallen from 59 percent in 1641 to only 22 percent in 1688, but fell to 14 percent by 1703 and later even further to 5 percent at its low point in the 1770s. Some Catholic gentry hung on, pretending to conform to Protestantism while practicing their old faith surreptitiously. Others became a kind of "underground gentry," serving as the middlemen between the peasants and the new Protestant landowners. A Catholic merchant class would also begin to develop in the mid-eighteenth century, exploiting familial and other links with trading partners in European continental ports. Yet the mass of Catholics would sink into an impoverished peasantry. Penal laws enacted in 1695, 1697, and 1704 stripped all Catholics, rich and poor, of political rights, outlawed priests, stifled Catholic schooling, and severely weakened Catholic property rights. Enforcement of the laws against priests and schools would slip from haphazard to indifferent over the course of the eighteenth century, but the legislation remained on the books, and the continued exclusion of Catholics from the political nation marked them off clearly as an inferior and beaten people.

Despite suffering economic distress and political and religious discrimination, only a tiny proportion of Catholics left Ireland. Deprived of resources or redress, Catholics were the most vulnerable of all of Ireland's peoples to the misfortunes of nature. The bad weather that drowned, scorched, or froze the harvests of Irish Presbyterians and other Protestants hurt their poorer Catholic neighbors even more. In 1740 and 1741, for example, unusually cold weather destroyed crops all over Ireland (including the potatoes that were already becoming an important source of food in some parts of Ireland). Between 200,000 and 400,000 died that winter in what has been called "The Year of the Great Slaughter." Ulster Presbyterians and Episcopalians died in this catastrophe, but the overwhelming majority of victims were undoubtedly Catholic peasants. A century later, a similar disaster would send their descendants flying to America by the hundreds of thousands, but after this eighteenth-century catastrophe, at most a few thousand sought relief in migration to America. Given their degradation and misery, why did so many Catholics stay when their more fortunate Presbyterian fellow Irish left?

Perhaps a contrast with their Presbyterian fellow Irish might provide some insight into the reasons for Catholic reluctance. Kerby Miller argues that the difference in the migration rates between the two peoples is the product of deeply rooted differences in cultural values. Miller states: "In broadest terms, much evidence indicates that, in contrast to the Protestants they encountered in Ireland and North America, the Catholic Irish were more communal than individualist, more dependent than independent, more fatalistic than optimistic, more prone to accept conditions passively than to take initiative for change, and more sensitive to the weight of tradition than to innovative possibilities for the future."[4]

Miller's powerful argument has provoked strong criticism, ranging from the bitter and unrelenting assaults of Irish and Canadian Irish historian Donald Akenson to the subtler contentions of David Doyle. Akenson denies any but "small differences" in culture between Protestant and Catholics in Ireland; Doyle points to the deep communalism of Ulster Presbyterians, and thus, doubts Miller's characterization of them as the archetypes of modern individualism.

Whether or not the principal reason why Irish Protestants left and Catholics did not was rooted in deep cultural differences, it is useful to point to other important if perhaps obvious reasons for the divergences between Catholics and Protestants in their willingness to set off for America. One difference was that many Irish Presbyterians and Episcopalians had already once recently moved from their original homelands, while Catholics had not. Most Presbyterians, for example, had either themselves just moved from Scotland or were second- or third-generation descendants of such migrants. Perhaps as many as 70,000 migrants had settled in Ulster at the turn of the eighteenth century, only a few years before the great migration to North America commenced. On the other hand, almost all Catholics had deep roots in Ireland. The Catholic descendants of the Norman conquerors of Ireland, families like the Burkes or Fitzgeralds, could not trace their Irish roots back as far as their Celtic Catholic coreligionists like the Meaghers or McDermotts, but even these Norman descendants had been in Ireland for nearly five hundred years by the seventeenth century, and Ireland had clearly become their home. There had been some Catholic migration to the European continent, such as the flight of refugee gentry or the men that the gentry and others recruited for the armies of France, Spain, and Austria, but most Catholics remained in place in Ireland.

Irish Presbyterians differed from Catholics in other ways. With the development of the linen trade and the burgeoning of Ulster cities like Belfast, Protestants were drawn more quickly and deeply into the broader markets of the British Isles and the empire than the bulk of the Irish Catholic peasantry. Only slowly over the eighteenth and early years of the nineteenth centuries would Irish Catholic peasants be sucked into those broader markets. Integration into such markets had a whole host of consequences: it meant greater vulnerability to economic forces like the collapse of the linen markets, provided more exposure to information about England or North America, and offered greater access to transportation to the New World, thus probably encouraging more confident expectations of finding a better life in America among linen-trade participants. As important, though Ulster Presbyterians descended from Lowland Scots had their own dialects, they spoke English. A majority of Catholic Irish would remain speakers of Irish until further integration into broader markets would force them to learn English, the language of trade, in the late eighteenth or nineteenth centuries.

Finally, Presbyterians and Anglicans were welcome in almost all American colonies, but Catholics, open, practicing, and defiant ones in particular, were excluded, except in Pennsylvania. In fact, except in Pennsylvania and Maryland, they could be subject to trial, imprisonment, and even execution for practicing their faith. Only in Pennsylvania were Catholics allowed to celebrate mass openly. In Maryland, Catholics could celebrate mass, but only privately, and their political rights were restricted. The other colonies outlawed Catholicism and some colonies, like Massachusetts, hunted priests and practicing Catholics. In 1732, a rumor ran through Boston that Irish Catholics had attended mass on March 17, and the colony's government mobilized quickly to hunt down the priest who had allegedly presided at the service. This discrimination not only discouraged Catholics from emigrating to America, it forced those who did to change their identities, abandoning their relations with their Catholic kin and friends in Ireland. They could not, therefore, establish or maintain the networks to help bring more Irish Catholics to America and create viable albeit probably underground and hidden Catholic communities there.

For all these reasons, therefore, Irish Presbyterians were far more likely to migrate to America than Irish Catholics. For a huge proportion of the Presbyterians, migration to America seemed a reasonable alternative to the deteriorating conditions at home, and so they chose it. On the other hand, only the odd Catholic, probably one torn out of his or her rooted community and already on the road, made the trip to America.

The Irish traveled to America in the colonial era not just because they wished to, but because they could. Trade between Ireland and North America supplied the transportation links that prospective immigrants needed to carry out their plans. Through much of the seventeenth century, such trade was episodic and limited, hampered by war, the small size of the American market, and the restrictions the British Empire imposed on both Irish and American trade. Later in the seventeenth century, Irish merchants developed strong connections with the Caribbean, supplying beef and other provisions to plantations there and in the process making some tentative contacts with the North American colonies. By the 1730s, trade between Ireland and America flourished. Ireland drew on American flax seed to make its linens while America took emigrants and finished linen cloth in return. From the 1730s to the 1750s, New York and Baltimore sent an average of ten ships a year to Irish ports; Philadelphia sent from fifteen to thirty to Ireland. By the 1770s, Irish trade with America was booming: for example, twenty-six ships from Ireland made for Philadelphia in 1770 alone, while forty-nine left the Quaker City for Irish ports in the same year. By that time, Irish-born merchants prominent in Philadelphia like Thomas Griffiths and William Allen or, in Baltimore, William Patterson, emerged to facilitate trade with merchant friends or even relatives in Ireland.

This trade not only offered prospective Irish immigrants ships to travel on but schemes for defraying the costs of the tickets as well. By the time trade was booming in the 1770s, the price of traveling to America from Ireland had been cut in half. That, undoubtedly, was one reason why the volume of emigration rose through the latter half of the eighteenth century. Still throughout most of the eighteenth and certainly all of the seventeenth centuries, the price of the trip far exceeded the ability of many to pay. There were also added costs, such as the costs of lodging and food in port while waiting for the ship to sail (ships did not sail on a fixed schedule in those days). Those who could not afford the trip or these extra costs did have one recourse: for the price of the voyage, they could sell the promise of their labor to the ship's owner for a specified set of years, that is, engage in **indentured servitude**, and the ship's captain could then sell that contract in America to farmers, merchants, or artisans looking for cheap labor. Recent estimates suggest that at least 60 percent of the Irish immigrants to America in the seventeenth century and 36 percent in the eighteenth century indentured themselves to make the trip. That included a substantial proportion of Ulster Presbyterians, and probably a majority of Catholic Irish immigrants. Indeed, the trade was brisk even in some southern ports like Dublin, where two dockside inns, The Philadelphia and the

New York Arms, David Doyle reports, "served as clearing houses and ship-ping agencies for such would be servants."[5] Some Irish had their way paid to America by the government—though few or none had intended to go there or sought such "largess." About 6 percent of the Irish going to America in the sev-enteenth century and 15 percent or more of the eighteenth-century migrants were convicts, "transported" by Ireland's courts or government authorities as an alternative to prison terms or even execution. Some of them were political prisoners, opponents of Cromwell in the seventeenth century or members of secret societies in the eighteenth, but many were people transported merely for vagrancy or petty theft. In 1761, for example, Bridget Daly of Dublin was sent to America for stealing shoe buckles; eight years later, the courts trans-ported a Kilkenny man for pilfering a couple of shillings.

However Irish immigrants traveled to America, free or unfree, the trip was a long and trying one, and accommodations rugged. Living conditions on board ship were cramped, berths seldom more than five feet tall, and there were no portholes to provide passengers below the main deck with any air or light. Sailing ships were slow by modern standards and totally dependent on the wind and weather. R. J. Dickson studied emigrant ship voyages between Ulster and North America in the years between 1771 and 1774 and found that they spent an average of seven weeks and four days sailing across the Atlantic. Yet the shortest was merely twenty-seven days, while the longest some seven-teen weeks. Captains never fed their passengers on a princely scale, but few starved, and the food, largely potatoes and bread, was not much different than what the emigrants might have eaten at home. All should have been tolerable as long as the ships made good headway, but if storms or calm seas slowed them, food supplies ran low. The *Seaflower*, crossing from Belfast to Philadel-phia in 1741, experienced such troubles, and passengers resorted to eating their dead comrades before they finally made landfall.

It was a difficult and often harrowing journey, but hundreds of thousands made it. The problem is that we do not know how many thousands. It is a measure of how thin the sources and evidence are for the study of the Irish in colonial America that historians cannot agree on exactly how many im-migrants made their way from Ireland to America in the seventeenth and eighteenth centuries. Estimates vary widely. Generally, as David Doyle has pointed out, Irish historians tend to estimate more conservatively than Ameri-cans, though it is not entirely clear why this should be true. Conservative estimates of the seventeenth-century migration hover at only about 5,000 or 6,000 people, while more liberal estimates run up to double that, or more. There are big differences too in the estimates of eighteenth-century migration, from some estimates of about 100,000 immigrants to others of as many as 200,000 to 250,000. The problem here is that there simply are no sets of consistent sources to provide a more certain count. There are, for example, no complete runs of customs house records from the ports on either side of the Atlantic, and even when such records exist they do not always provide information on the numbers or identities of ship passengers, especially British subjects traveling through the empire. Historians must thus extrapolate from those records that do exist—say, from some custom house port records for Philadelphia for a limited set of years, for example, or from an Irish parliamentary inquiry into trade from Belfast and Derry in Ireland to America in the early 1770s. There are other sources but these too have drawbacks. R. J. Dickson, for example, bases many of his conclusions on the study of newspapers and their notices of ships debarking from Ireland for America. Yet Thomas Truxes suggests that Dickson and others underestimated the migration by looking only at advertisements for emigrant ships, when, in fact, almost all ships sailing to North America from Ireland and particularly from Ulster carried immigrants. Nevertheless, even by conservative estimates, Irish migration in the colonial era was probably substantial, constituting 23 percent of all white immigrants to America from 1607 to 1699, and over 35 percent of all European immigrants to America from 1700 to the beginning of the American Revolution.

Estimating the number of Irish immigrants is important, not only in itself, but because it is critical to determining how many Irish lived in colonial North America and, thus, how large their proportion of America's population was. Before American independence in 1776, there were no censuses taken in all thirteen colonies in the same year. The first national census of the new American republic was taken in 1790. This census was a simple head count, however; it records no other information such as place of birth or ethnic origin. Historians have the lists of names from the 1790 census manuscript sheets. In 1927, the American Council of Learned Societies, prompted by congressional efforts to legislate immigration quotas based on the ethnic composition of the United States, undertook a study of those names to estimate the ethnic ancestry of all the people in the nation at its birth. In that project, the ACLS committee estimated that there were about 300,000 immigrants from Ireland or their descendants in the new United States by 1790. Since then, historians have revisited the census and disputed the ACLS's old figures. David Doyle, for example, suggests that the numbers were closer to 450,000 being of Irish background, and about two-thirds of those being Ulster Presbyterians. It is not easy, therefore, to determine exactly how many Irish came to the American colonies before 1776 and their descendants' proportion of the population at the birth of the new nation.

If we do not know exactly how many Irish came in the colonial era, we also have only a dim notion of when they came. This is especially true of the tiny Irish migration to America in the seventeenth century. The first Irish settlements in the Americas in the seventeenth century were in an unlikely colony in the Amazon region of South America and in British colonial outposts in the Caribbean. The Amazon experiment would collapse, but Irish migration to the Caribbean would continue throughout the seventeenth century. In the 1650s and 1660s, the tide of Irish immigrants—Cromwell's prisoners or simply refugees fleeing the war-torn island—flowed particularly heavily into Nevis, Montserrat, and Barbados. Throughout the century, a small proportion of the Irish who landed in the Caribbean reemigrated north to North American mainland colonies, particularly Maryland and Virginia and later the Carolinas. Presumably this reemigration picked up momentum with the flood of Irish refugees to the Caribbean during and after the Cromwellian wars. Throughout the century, however, ships also carried migrants directly from Ireland to North America. Indeed, as early as the 1620s ships left Kinsale in southern Cork for the Chesapeake region. The periodization of this migration—how many came when—is hard to chart for the reasons mentioned earlier.

The ebb and flow of eighteenth-century Irish migration is much more clear. The first great burst of migration from Ulster, for example, appears to have come in 1717 and 1718, as the cheap twenty-one-year leases negotiated in the late 1690s came due and rents began to rise. Emigration rates from Ireland rose again in the late 1720s and early 1740s, but the high point came later. In the period after the Seven Years War (called the French and Indian War in America) and particularly in the last few years before the Revolution, that stream of Irish immigrants to America became a torrent. R. J. Dickson, who is very conservative in his estimates of the overall number of Irish immigrants fleeing to America, nonetheless suggests that as many as 40,000 may have come in the four short years before the beginning of the Revolution in 1775.

By 1790, there were Irish immigrants or their descendants in every state of the new American republic, but as noted at the beginning of this chapter, there was a strong Southern and Mid-Atlantic cast to Irish settlement in the colonial era, a cast that would distinguish it clearly from the Irish migration in the nineteenth and twentieth centuries. Though the Puritans of New England brought a few Irish servants with them in the 1630s—John Winthrop brought an Irish shepherd boy, for example, to tend his herds on Shawmut's (later Boston's) hills—there was little room in those self-consciously conceived and homogenous early New England colonies for many foreigners like the Irish. Irish indentured servants or convicts, however, probably fed the insatiable demand for bound labor in the Chesapeake region or later in the Carolinas in the seventeenth century, either in direct migration to North America or in reemigration from the Caribbean colonies.

Oddly enough however, when the Ulster Presbyterian migration began in earnest in the eighteenth century, it first flowed to New England. The Presbyterians who went to Boston appear to have expected the Congregationalists of Massachusetts to welcome them for their shared religious zeal and distrust of the Anglican church. There is some evidence that the Massachusetts descendants of the Puritans were enthusiastic about these early Irish Presbyterian exiles—at first. Yet shortly after the Irish arrived, the Massachusetts Congregationalists assailed the foreign Irish invaders for their laziness and obstinate insistence on their own religious practices, and harried them out of the colony. A few Ulster Presbyterians remained in less developed areas near the Bay Colony's northern and western borders, but many went farther north, where town names like Derry (in New Hampshire) and Bangor (now in Maine) reflected their presence. In any event, it is unlikely that the Irish immigration to New England would have continued, as the region's rapidly expanding population and limited and rocky land discouraged migrants seeking to establish their own farms. As important, New England's ports played little role in the flowering of trade between Ireland and America in the eighteenth century. By the 1720s and 1730s, the rising importance of Pennsylvania's flax for Ulster's linen manufacture centered that trade in the Mid-Atlantic ports. While many Anglican Irish went to New York, most Irish immigrants, of all backgrounds—Presbyterian, Church of Ireland, and Catholic—landed at the Delaware River ports of Philadelphia and Newcastle, Delaware. R. J. Dickson found that of emigrant ships headed to America and advertising in *The Belfast Newsletter* between 1750 and 1775, over half went to Philadelphia and fewer than 20 percent to the runner-up port of New York. Philadelphia itself soon developed a large Irish population, from merchants like George Fullerton and Andrew Caldwell to a large corps of artisans. At the end of the colonial period in particular, a substantial proportion of indentured servants found masters and thus homes in Philadelphia.

Still the vast majority of Irish immigrants moved out of the Delaware ports, first west into Pennsylvania's Susquehanna Valley, up into northeastern Pennsylvania and western New Jersey, and down into northern Maryland. After

1730, they moved south and west into Maryland's Cumberland Valley and along the **Great Wagon Road** into Virginia's Shenandoah Valley. David Doyle notes that in the 1750s they were "filling up the backcountry of North Carolina and spilling onto the rolling and forested Piedmont."[6] By the 1760s, they had already taken up much of the South Carolina and Georgia backcountry and began breaching the Appalachian mountain wall into western Pennsylvania to what is the Pittsburgh region today, and through western Virginia into what would become Tennessee and Kentucky.

In part, this migration to the southern and western frontiers was the natural recourse for a poor people seeking land. Few Irish immigrants arrived in America with much money and thus they were forced to the edges of settlement, where land was cheapest. Indeed, some of the earliest Ulster Presbyterian migrants were squatters occupying disputed territories along the Maryland-Pennsylvania border. Yet land owners with big grants of land to sell off or lease and colonial governors or imperial officials eager to bolster white populations outnumbered by black slaves or Indians also encouraged the Irish movement to the western and southern frontiers.

Irish adjustment to this life on the edges of America has been the source of sharp controversies among historians. The conflicting interpretations suggest a paradox. On the one hand, Irish immigrants and their children seemed to lose consciousness of being a distinct people very soon after arriving in the United States. Those that were Catholic were so detached from their own culture, so unschooled in their faith in an eighteenth century Ireland with few Catholic clergy and churches, and so severely proscribed in America, that they quickly merged into a Protestant America. Church of Ireland Irish, on the other hand, melted more easily, but for the opposite reason. If it was a new landscape with new customs, it was still the same empire, where they were part of the established church, and in many cases, a privileged people. They merged into the general white population without difficulty or delay.

Irish Presbyterians faced a different set of problems. Outside New England they faced no proscriptions and little hostility. Yet they did confront an active religious "marketplace" and fearsome competition for their adherents from dynamic dissenting denominations like the Baptists and Methodists. Ulster Presbyterians had a long tradition of revivalism stretching back to the Sixmilewater Revival of 1625. In the religious tumult of the Great Awakening, which was building in the 1730s and exploded in the 1740s, Presbyterianism in America splintered, but the more serious result of the Awakening and continuing religious competition was the Presbyterian laity's abandonment of their old faith for rival evangelical sects. In southwestern North Carolina, for example,

Irish Presbyterians accounted for about 40 percent of the local population in 1790. Yet within a decade one Presbyterian minister complained, "Our members are dropping off and our societies annually melting away."[6] By the early 1840s, there were only six Presbyterian churches in the area, but thirty-seven Baptist and thirty-two Methodist ones.

The different circumstances confronting the three different Irish religious groups in America—prohibition for the Catholics, privilege for the Church of Ireland members, and competition for the Presbyterians—eviscerated the distinctive institutional loyalties of each in its own way. Yet there may have been other reasons why these immigrants and their children seemed to melt into American society so much more easily in the eighteenth century than Irish newcomers would in the nineteenth. Irish immigrants in the eighteenth century, were, as David Doyle smartly notes, rural people settling in a largely rural America, so the nature of adjustment was not so disruptive as it was going to be for so many Irish Catholic peasants in the next century. In particular, Doyle points to the absence of the kind of fundamental discontinuity in the experiences between the first and second generations among the Irish in eighteenth-century rural America, a discontinuity that would be so characteristic of relations between Irish peasant immigrants and their American, city-bred children in the nineteenth century.

What this may have meant, as Doyle argues, is not so much that the Irish, particularly the Ulster Presbyterians, took on American culture, or as some would have it, assimilated. What may have happened is that they maintained their culture while losing consciousness of a separate ethnic loyalty: they continued to act much as they had done before in Ireland even when they lost any sense that this made them a distinctive people. For the Ulster Presbyterians who made up such a large proportion of the Irish migrants to America, not only the New World's rural nature but the sympathy of many Americans for Protestant evangelical people of British Isle origins created an environment that helped this to happen: "the readiness of many Americans ... to accept the Scotch-Irish largely as they were, meant that they could disengage from past loyalties without necessarily disengaging from their culture."[7]

Indeed, several historians have argued boldly in the last twenty years that Irish, Irish Presbyterian, or as some would have it Celtic or border country (the border country being the Scottish Lowlands, northern England, and northern Ireland) culture not only survived in colonial America but flourished in the eighteenth century and thereafter even into our own time. Historians like Grady McWhiney and Forrest McDonald, who emphasize the Celtic background of Southerners, and David Hackett Fischer, who stress their borderland experience in Britain and Ireland, have tracked the enduring power of the Scotch-Irish inheritance in aspects of Southern American culture as diverse as speech and accent, a proclivity to violence, music, farming practices, and settlement patterns. Their arguments are hotly disputed. In a lengthy catalogue of criticisms of McWhiney and McDonald's so-called Celtic thesis, Kevin Kenny points out that these historians use an extraordinarily loose definition of who is or has been Celtic. They also suggest, he contends, an essentialist concept of culture that asserts Celtic culture has scarcely changed since Roman times to the antebellum American South. Other historians have argued that rather than reflecting the persistent influence of Irish culture, most of the contentions made about peculiar Southern farming practices or high levels of violent crime reveal the powerful influence of the American South's unique geographical and social environment rather than the stubborn persistence of Celtic culture.

Few points in the history of the eighteenth-century Irish Americans have provoked more heat than the question of what role the Irish played in the American Revolution and why. Older histories dating to the nineteenth century contended that the Irish, particularly Irish Presbyterians or the Scotch-Irish, were almost uniformly enthusiastic supporters of the American cause. They frequently quoted British Army officers like Captain Joshua Pell, who cried: "The rebels are chiefly composed of Irish redemptioners and convicts, the most audacious rascals existing."[8] The argument made sense logically, if, as such historians presumed, the majority of Irish immigrants who were Presbyterians came to America for religious reasons, nourishing a grudge against a British-backed established Anglican church that discriminated against their denomination and denied them full civil rights. It is true that many Irish, particularly Irish Presbyterians, were prominent on the American, or "patriot" side in the war. They included children of Ulster Presbyterians like **James McHenry**, **Thomas McKean**, Joseph Reed, and James Smith; many Church of Ireland Irishman like **General Richard Montgomery**, and the progeny of Catholic converts like General John Sullivan of New Hampshire. Indeed, they even included some of the few openly Catholic Irish, such as Commodore John Barry, a naval hero and sometimes called the "Father of the American Navy."

And yet the reality of Irish participation in the American Revolution is much more complicated than Captain Pell contended, and it reveals in a powerful way how cultural inheritance and environment interacted in shaping Irish life in early America. In most of the middle colonies, Irish Presbyterians did in fact passionately support the patriot cause. Though some Irish sided with the British, most did not. Indeed, in Pennsylvania and to a lesser extent in New Jersey and Delaware, they were at the forefront of the American Revolution. In Pennsylvania in 1776, they led the movement to establish one of the new nation's most radical state governments. Further south, however, the Irish role was not so clearly delineated. In the Carolinas, for example, Irish Presbyterians and other residents of the colonies in the backcountry came to the patriot cause only slowly and reluctantly, and substantial numbers supported the empire. The difference lay not in the kinds of Irishmen in each colony. The majority of Irish in both the southern and middle colonies were Presbyterians. They were the same people from the same places with the same memories of discrimination and prejudice.

The difference between Irish in Pennsylvania and the Irish who went further south lay in their experiences in colonial politics before the Revolution. The difference lay in the radically different political contexts of friends and enemies that they had to negotiate at the very end of the colonial era. In Pennsylvania, Irish Presbyterians had emerged in the 1760s and 1770s as vehement opponents of the ruling Quakers. Among other reasons, the Irish felt the Quakers had abandoned them to the raids of Indians on the frontier. In 1764, Irish Presbyterians had risen up and brutally attacked some friendly Indians, and then marched on Philadelphia in the famous **Paxton Boys** uprising, to protest the ruling Quaker party's indifference to their plight. Over time, Pennsylvania's Ulster Presbyterians became more and more involved in the party opposing the Quaker rulers of the colony. That opposition party became a path to enthusiastic Irish participation in the Revolution in Pennsylvania, when many of their enemies in the ruling party sided with England. Similarly, in New Jersey and Delaware, Anglican rulers of the colonies opposed by Irish Presbyterians before the war became Tories, opposed by Irish Presbyterian patriots during the Revolution. In the Carolinas, the prewar political alignments were different. There, eastern elites controlled legislatures and were so slow to establish courts and extend representation to the frontier that those heavily Irish Presbyterian western parts of the southern colonies rebelled before the Revolution. In North Carolina, these rebels or **Regulators** were beaten at the battle of Alamance in 1771. Yet when the Revolution broke out in the Carolinas, members of the eastern elites led it. Irish Presbyterians in the backcountry, still nursing the wounds of their earlier rebellion, were slow to come around and back their longtime enemies, and thus were far less enthusiastic revolutionaries than their Irish Presbyterian colleagues further north.

During the Revolution, the first Irish phase of Irish settlement in America came to an end. Irish migration, a small stream in the seventeenth century, became a steady river in the eighteenth and then a flood in the last few years before the Revolution. Though thousands of the immigrants had been Catholics when they left Ireland, they were a minority of all Irish emigrants. This was largely a Protestant migration, and even more specifically, largely a migration of Irish Presbyterians of Scottish descent. In America, these immigrants, even the Irish Presbyterians, seemed to easily give up identification with Ireland — but whether they as easily gave up their culture and their ways of doing things inherited from Ireland is hotly disputed. Most though by no means all would settle in rural areas, many in the backcountry or frontier regions. Some landed in southern New England, but few stayed there, dispersing to the northern frontier colonies of New Hampshire and the northern portion of Massachusetts that would later become the state of Maine. Most entered America through the Delaware ports, particularly Philadelphia, and moved out from the city to northern and western Pennsylvania and south to Virginia, the Carolinas and Georgia. In 1776, then, to be Irish in America meant to be Protestant, likely of Presbyterian background if not current affiliation; to have passing or no interest in Ireland's fate as a separate nation; to be a farmer or farm laborer; and to live in Pennsylvania, or even more often, the South. It probably also meant that if you had once thought of yourself as Irish or your parents had, you would not continue to do so for very long. All this would change drastically in the next century.

NOTES

1. Maldwyn Jones, "The Scotch-Irish in British America," in *Strangers Within the Realm: Cultural Margins of the First British Empire*, eds. Bernard Bailyn and Philip D. Morgan (Chapel Hill: University of North Carolina Press, 1991), 285.

2. Wayland Dunaway, quoted in Kevin Kenny, *The American Irish: A History* (Harlow, UK: Longman, 2000), 43.

2. Jones, "The Scotch-Irish," 284.

3. Kerby Miller, *Emigrants and Exiles*, 107.

4. David N. Doyle, *Ireland, Irishmen, and Revolutionary America: 1760–1820* (Dublin: Mercier Press, 1981), 64.

5. Ibid., 56.

6. Tyler H. Blethen and Curtis W. Wood, *Ulster and North America: Transatlantic Perspectives on the Scotch-Irish* (Tuscaloosa: University of Alabama Press, 1997), 219.

7. Doyle, *Ireland, Irishmen, and Revolutionary America*, 148.

8. Ibid., 110.

CHAPTER TWO

Irish America from the Revolution to the Famine

The American Revolution would stop the flow of immigrants from Ireland, but only temporarily. Migration would begin again after the Revolution and over the next half century or so it would be much like what it had been in the colonial era. Most of the migrants would come from Ulster, Ireland's northern province, and most would be Protestant, and again most of them Presbyterians. They would also come for some of the same reasons: rents becoming too high and the occasional hard times in the linen and other trades.

And yet there would be some important differences between this migration and the earlier one, and between the Irish America these immigrants and their descendants would make and the one the colonial Irish had created. None of these migrants would be convicts and almost none would indenture themselves to travel. Though not initially, by the early nineteenth century most would settle not in the southern states but in the North, and more and more of them would flock to cities.

Moreover, some would come not because a fitful or sluggish economy forced them out but because in an age of revolution they had become revolutionaries, and when their dreams for a new Ireland were crushed, they would seek exile in America, the nursery of republicanism and revolution. There, these men and others could boast of their Irish loyalties and scheme for Ireland's redemption. Yet the Ireland that they were loyal to would not be a Catholic, nationalist Ireland, nor would the Irish America they sought to create in the United States be the Catholic nationalist Irish America of the late nineteenth century. These men's vision was of a new beginning for their old country: the birth of a nonsectarian, republican Ireland, backed by Irish Americans of all sects, Catholics and Protestants united by similar, republican sympathies. Not everyone agreed with them, and Irish Catholics and Protestants continued to fight bitter battles in America throughout the early nineteenth century. Still, it was a heady, hopeful time of revolutionary possibility and favorable circumstances, and at the turn of the nineteenth century their vision seemed as likely to come true as not. Indeed, such circumstances hinted not only at a potential healing of sectarian divisions between Irish Protestants and Irish Catholics in America but the possible peaceful acceptance of all Irishmen, Protestants and Catholics alike, by the Yankee Protestants of the New World.

Neither of these possibilities would come to pass. After the end of the Napoleonic Wars in 1815, and even more so as change coursed through Ireland in the 1830s, Irish immigration to America would change radically. More and more immigrants came to America, more came from outside Ulster, more were unskilled or poor, and more were Catholic. This new immigration, combined with changes in the culture and politics of Ireland and America, would disrupt this tentative Irish Catholic and Irish Protestant rapprochement. Embattled Irish Catholics would retreat into their own world, separated from Protestant America. The outlines of an Irish Catholic America recognizable to us today could be seen by then, even before the Great Famine. Yet those changes should not obscure the possibility that Irish America might have followed a very different path in this very fluid and decisive era in its history.

Throughout the American Revolution, migration from Ireland to America was at a standstill, but at the war's end, it began to flow again in full flood, almost as if the eight-year hiatus had never happened. Indeed, Irishmen were so eager for the new republic that they began shipping out the month before the peace treaty went into effect in 1783. By the end of that year, an estimated 5,000 had left Ireland for America, and in the next year, some suggest that as many as 10,000 left. By the end of the 1780s, the British consul in Philadelphia claimed that as many as 25,000 Irishmen had entered the city since the end of the war. Emigration continued to run strong through the 1790s, and perhaps as many as 60,000 departed Ireland for America in that decade.

British officials had already become alarmed at this tide, however. Before the American Revolution, some Irish government officials and landlords had feared that the vast migration from their island would mean not only a loss of sufficient tenants to compete for rents but also a decline in the Protestant population that could leave Ireland more vulnerable to a Catholic rebellion. Still, that colonial migration had been within the empire—Ireland's loss was the British North American colonies' gain. After the American Revolution, however, migration from Ireland drained labor and resources out of the empire to strengthen Britain's new, upstart, American rival. British officials worried in particular that skilled artisans and mechanics, for example, might carry industrial secrets to the new republic. In the early nineteenth century, they tried to choke off Irish migration altogether or at least redirect it for the Empire's benefit. Beginning in 1803, the British parliament passed legislation severely restricting the number of passengers that ships could carry to the United States. Ostensibly a humanitarian gesture meant to improve travel conditions, the act, nonetheless, drastically reduced Irish emigration to the United States by doubling or tripling the price of tickets to America—just as British foreign minister Viscount Robert Castlreagh told John Quincy Adams it was meant to do. In the next few years, the annual number of immigrants to the United States fell to 1,000. War conditions helped keep the numbers low or reduce them further. French raiders preyed on British ships carrying immigrants, but they were less dangerous than British warships prowling the American or Irish coasts, boarding ships and dragging off or impressing passengers into the Royal Navy. In 1811 and 1812 alone, the British Navy intercepted thirteen vessels off the American coast and made off with 200 passengers.

Yet even with this interference in the early part of the nineteenth century, between 1783 and 1815, at least 100,000 emigrants—probably more—came to America from Ireland. That is a sizable number, and the probability that it would have been even larger if the British government had not intervened presents something of a puzzle. As Kerby Miller notes: "At first glance this emigration seems surprising for it took place during a period of relative prosperity in Ireland."[1] Indeed, Irish people would look back on the era, especially the period 1789 to 1815, as an economic golden age. The linen industry's collapse had provoked a mass exodus from Ulster in the 1770s, but by the next decade Ireland's linen industry was booming again and even expanding into north Connaught and Leinster. Irish agriculture also prospered from the 1780s through the early nineteenth century. The British government, feeding armies at war with Napoleon on the continent and the navies on the seas, bought up as much grain and cattle as the Irish could produce, and as the hazards of shipping in wartime reduced or eliminated American or other trading competitors, the prices of these Irish goods soared. So why would anyone want to leave?

The economic good times were not without their troubles. The linen industry prospered, but erratically: a recession in 1801 and 1802 was especially bad. Other Irish industries such as silk and woolens declined in the face of British competition, and local small brewers failed in the face of the increasing concentration of breweries in the bigger cities. And for all of agriculture's prosperity, many Irish farmers faced difficult times. Those with long leases that came due in this period often saw their rents raised four- or five-fold at renewal, and those with short leases or no leases at all faced continuous squeezing by their landlords. Ireland's population rose enormously in this era, from about four million in 1781 to seven million in 1821, so there was no lack of suitors for each tenancy. Moreover, taxes skyrocketed to help pay the costs of the wars against Napoleon. As James Steele in Ireland wrote his brother in 1806: "Dear Brother ... you are happy that your country is not at war."[2]

Yet perhaps as important to Irish migration as the Irish economy's temporary downturns or continuing inequities was the new prosperity's success in pulling more and more people into a market economy, making them both more vulnerable to economic booms and busts but also more attuned to opportunities and more knowledgeable and confident about seizing those opportunities. Long before the American Revolution, migration had become a fact of life in Ulster, a recognized possibility among many possibilities for survival or even success. Now, during the Napoleonic Wars, market integration spread into all corners of the northern province and into parts of neighboring Leinster and Connaught, opening up the possibility of migration for more and more people.

Historians have not studied the backgrounds of these immigrants as intently as the colonial émigrés, but most scholars who have believe that the Irish migration from the end of the American Revolution until 1815, like the colonial migration, was largely the flight of Presbyterians and other Protestants from Ulster. Kerby Miller estimates that two-thirds of the immigrants during that period were from Ulster, mostly Presbyterians of Scottish ancestry, and the other third a mix of Catholics and Protestants, largely Anglicans, from the south. Maldwyn Jones points to the departure points of the immigrants as evidence of the immigrants' backgrounds. At the end of the eighteenth century, most left from Belfast, Derry, and other Ulster ports, just as they had before the Revolution. In 1783, for example, of the 5,000 who left, as many as 1,500 departed from Belfast. Furthermore, Jones contends that even quick random surveys of the passenger lists reveal ranks of Ramseys, Richeys, McKees, Crawfords, and others with Scottish Presbyterian names, suggesting the migration was "overwhelmingly Scotch-Irish."[3]

If there were important continuities between the colonial migration and the flight to the new republic, there were also significant changes. None of the new immigrants were convicts, for example. Britain and Ireland attempted to surreptitiously dump a few thousand convicts in America just after the American Revolution, but American officials sniffed them out and stopped the transportation of criminals to the new nation. In 1788, England and Ireland would begin to send the convicts elsewhere, to the newly discovered continent of Australia.

More important, perhaps, is that very few of the Irish leaving for America after the Revolution traveled as indentured servants. This was a dramatic change, given that at least one-third, and probably more, of the pre-Revolutionary migrants indentured themselves to pay for the trip. Historians suggest several reasons for this. Some argue that merchants and captains found enough immigrants willing to pay their way to fill their ships. Many shippers disliked taking servants because they might die on board or steal away upon landing and they took up the shippers' time and energy in bargaining contracts. It also seems that conditions in America changed too. Merchants and artisan masters had come to appreciate the flexibility of free labor, which could be hired and fired as markets fluctuated, as opposed to the fixed costs of servants, who had already been paid for and had to be fed and housed in both good times and bad. In Philadelphia, for example, only 1 percent of the city's workforces were slaves or indentured servants by 1800. There were, moreover, the changes in ideology wrought by the American Revolution as well. Gradations of the status of freedom were hard to maintain in a republic. Men and women were either free citizens or slaves. As David Roediger points out, white workers began to reject terms like master and servant, which seemed like survivals from the colonial era of monarchs and aristocrats, and opted for the more informal terminology of "boss" and "hired hand." Even the courts became reluctant to enforce servant contracts. And so indentured servitude faded away for the Irish by about the 1790s.

Through the 1780s and 1790s, Irish immigrants continued to pour through the Delaware River ports of Philadelphia and Newcastle, and through Baltimore in the Chesapeake region. In the 1790s, 10,000 Irish immigrants landed in Philadelphia, Newcastle, and Wilmington. Many of these migrants, no doubt, remained in the area; others (it is not clear how many) traveled farther south as the earlier Irish had. Irish settlement in the South had pushed out from the Carolina backcountry into the new states of Kentucky and Tennessee. As early as 1790, fully one-third of Kentucky's people were Irish, the vast majority Ulster Presbyterians or their descendants.

Yet the pattern of Irish settlement began to change in the early nineteenth century. In part this was the intended result of British officials. While making passage on ships to the United States expensive, they encouraged Irish migration to British North America (Canada) by cheapening the passage. Irish migration to the Maritime Provinces, Newfoundland in particular, had actually begun in the middle of the eighteenth century. British ships provisioning fishermen off Canada's coast had picked up both the fishermen's foodstuffs and temporary workers in Waterford, in the southeastern corner of Ireland,

and carried both to Newfoundland. Some of the temporary workers stayed in Newfoundland and settled there, but Edward McCarron has found that some began filtering south into northern New England, particularly Maine, by the early 1800s. The oldest Catholic church in Maine was built in 1808 at North Whitefield. The Waterford immigrants, however, were something of an anomaly in the Irish migration to Canada in the early nineteenth century. Ulster would send more migrants to Canada than any other province, and many would land at Quebec as well as ports in the Maritimes. Before 1815, the Irish migration to Canada was small, but it represented an important new area of Irish settlement in the New World and, as we shall see, it would eventually grow far larger.

A more important, permanent change in destination occurred with the flow of Irish immigration to the United States. Trade between Ireland and America had always centered on Philadelphia, but now the bulk of the trade shifted north to New York City. This too was just beginning in the early nineteenth century, but there were already critical signs foreshadowing the future. Between 1803 and 1805, 58 percent of the ships leaving Irish ports, for example, headed for New York, while only 23 percent went to Philadelphia. This was a major reversal of the pre-Revolutionary trend.

While most immigrants left Ireland for the time-honored reason of fleeing pinched opportunities in the old country and looking forward to the economic bounties of the "new" one, there was a special group of immigrants who left Ireland in the 1790s and early 1800s and had a powerful effect on Irish America and, indeed, the wider American Republic. These were the men and women who were members of the United Irishmen, participants in the 1798 rebellion, or sympathizers of either or both. During the American Revolution, a movement emerged in Ireland to force reform of the Irish parliament and strengthen its independence from British government meddling. That movement died about the time of the American peace, but when revolution erupted in France, a new group of political activists began to form and plot to reform Ireland's politics (eventually committing themselves to the creation of an independent Irish Republic). By 1791, such men had founded the Society of United Irishmen, which embodied those hopes. Though most of the leaders of the Society, including Wolfe Tone and Thomas Russell, were Protestants, and the bulk of the rank and file were Presbyterian artisans and small farmers, they recognized that the success of their effort depended on some support from the Catholic masses, and they began to negotiate with a Catholic secret society in the north called the "Defenders." The United Irishmen also began overtures with Revolutionary France. Britain and its conservative Irish allies, fearing this intrigue on its Irish flank while confronting France, cracked down on the United Irishmen. As government surveillance and repression tightened after 1795, a wave of United Irishmen fled Ireland for America. Some sought a permanent home; others simply a safe haven to continue plotting. In the spring and summer of 1798, harried and frustrated, the United Irishmen rose in a series of hastily organized and poorly coordinated rebellions that the government suppressed. Even the late landing of a small force of French soldiers in northern Mayo could not save the rebellion. In the aftermath, several Irish leaders or sympathizers fled to America. Others like Thomas Addis Emmett, William Sampson, and James MacNeven were arrested and later exiled, eventually making their way to the United States. Some were still coming as late as 1805 or 1806.

It is impossible to tell how many United Irishmen came to America, but whatever their numbers, their influence was enormous. As David Wilson has suggested, they "effectively took over Irish America and remodeled it according to their own revolutionary, democratic, republican image."[4] They helped create or led clubs or benevolent societies in New York, Philadelphia, and Baltimore. They created their own Society of United Irishmen in the United States, which would boast of more than 1,500 members in Philadelphia alone. Yet it was as the voice of the Irish people in America and as creators of a vision for those people that they had the most influence. They emerged as editors of no fewer than seventeen papers throughout the United States. They wrote plays, stories, and histories of Ireland and America, and became political leaders and pamphleteers.

The vision that they proclaimed was of a new kind of Ireland and thus of new kinds of Irishmen and Irish Americans. They believed that the world had entered a new age—a millennial age. Wilson argues that most of them believed in "Lockean notions of the malleability of human nature; if people were products of environment and education then it would be possible to reconstruct then as model republican citizens."[5] Among other things, this meant an Ireland that was neither Catholic nor Protestant but remade as a nonsectarian republic. Many of the United Irishmen were Protestants, some deeply devout, evangelical Presbyterians, who feared priest-ridden and corrupt Catholics. Yet the long relative quiescence of Catholics in Ireland through the eighteenth century, the fall of the church in France, and the success of religious liberty in America convinced most—at least for a moment in the 1790s—that the Irish peasantry could be led out of their religious darkness and into republican enlightenment. Thus the Society of the United Irishmen (of America) could proclaim its dedication to promoting "the warmest affection among all religious denominations of men." This was not mere rhetoric. The Society and several other Irish organizations in the period recruited both Catholics and Protestants into their ranks and elevated men of both religions to high office. Protestant lawyers like William Sampson and Thomas Addis Emmett, exiled to America after the 1798 rebellion, fought hard and long here through the courts in the United States to break down the remaining barriers blocking Catholic participation in American civil life.

It was not just the United Irishmen's vision but also party politics that helped sustain this fragile Irish Catholic–Irish Protestant alliance. Some Ulster Presbyterians or their descendants in America backed the Federalist party after the American Revolution. County Antrim–born **James McHenry**, for example, became Washington's secretary of war in the 1790s. Most Scotch-Irish Protestants, however, had come out of the Revolution sympathetic to the Republicans led by Thomas Jefferson and others. Second-generation Irish **Thomas McKean**, for example, was a powerful force for Jefferson's Democratic-Republicans as governor of Pennsylvania from 1799 to 1808. Many Irish Catholics, remaining true to the Church's Old World conservatism and appalled by the French Revolution's attacks on the Church, gravitated initially to the Federalists. Through the 1790s, however, controversies over the **Whiskey Rebellion** of 1794, the Federalist's capitulation to an aggressive Britain in John Jay's treaty ratified in 1795 or over the Immigration and Naturalization Acts passed in 1798 to limit the political power of Irish immigrants, combined with the increasing influence of United Irish exiles, helped bring a broad range of Irish rank and file of all sects into Jefferson's party. Presbyterians and Catholics alike, then, became stalwart Democratic-Republicans.

Rooted in the self-interest of politics and nourished by the continuous power of the revolutionary age's ideals, a definition of Ireland, Irishness, and Irish America that was nonsectarian and republican seemed not only possible but likely in the first two decades of the nineteenth century. Moreover, this was not a definition of Irish Americans that set them apart from most other Americans. They could wear this Irishness easily as earnest republicans and mingle freely in the broader society.

Images of Ireland and Irishmen reflected and perhaps encouraged this sentiment. The "Stage Irishman," the character of a blundering, ignorant, comic peasant quickly became a staple of the American theater. Before 1828, no less that twenty-two plays featuring such Irish characters appeared on American stages and variations of the character showed up often in magazine and newspaper stories and popular literature. Yet before the Great Famine, historian Dale Knobel has argued, Americans believed Paddy ignorant but not stupid—not condemned to degradation by any inherent defects, but capable of redemption in the wholesome and free environment of the new American republic. Perhaps strengthening such sentiments was a romanticization of Ireland itself in American popular song. As William Williams has pointed out, Ireland became a popular image of a lost, premodern, rural idyll even to white Anglo-Saxon Protestant middle-class Americans in the antebellum era. Tom Moore's songs in particular, such as the "Meeting of the Waters," "Let Erin Remember," and "Tho' The Last Glimpse of Erin" invoked a misty, romantic Ireland of dead heroes, moody rural landscapes, and lost loves. Such songs became broadly popular as sheet music to be played and sung by families around the piano—presumably by the mostly Protestant, middle- or upper-class American families wealthy enough to purchase the instrument.

Cooperation, rough alliances, and even friendships between Protestant and Catholic Irish were not unique to America in this period. They had, of course, taken place in Ireland before the rebellion of 1798. In Australia, exiles from that rebellion, many of them Protestants, played roles similar to those played by the United Irishmen in America in the early 1800s, mentoring later Catholic and Protestant arrivals, helping them establish themselves on farms or ranches of their own, and setting a tone of tolerance and civility in the new colonies. Through the middle of the nineteenth century in Britain's new penal colony, sectarian boundaries were often overcome or blurred. In Canada, even Protestant Irish with a bright Orange tint to their politics (members or sympathizers of the Orange lodges that were strongly opposed to an independent Ireland and to Irish Catholic assertions of their rights) forged unlikely alliances with their erstwhile "Green" Irish Catholic enemies in the 1810s and 1820s. Within the context of Canadian politics, at least for a few years anyway, the Orange Irish Protestants and the Green Irish Catholics found more in common with each other than either group found with the Canadian Tories or even Canadian republican radicals.

If this cooperation across religious lines seemed like a broad trend at the turn of the nineteenth century, it was still new to the Anglo-American world. Interreligious alliances were fragile and visions of a republican Ireland and Irish America still just hopes at best. Throughout the period, sectarian clashes still erupted frequently. In New York, Protestant workers mocked Irish Catholics by carrying "paddy effigies" and fought with them in 1799. Irish Catholics and Protestants in New York battled again in 1824 and 1825. More disturbing had been the degeneration of the United Irishmen's 1798 rebellion in Ireland into brutal and vicious sectarian violence, despite all the high ideals of the Irish republicans. From the beginning then, it was never clear whether the

United Irish definitions of Ireland and Irish America would take hold among the Irish in America.

Still, they might have blossomed had not circumstances emerged in both Ireland and America to destroy them. In Ireland, it was the death of republican nationalism among its Protestant supporters. The Orange order, founded in Ireland in 1795 and encouraged as a means to counter the United Irish radicals and rally Protestants to the Crown, began to spread in the early nineteenth century. In part, this growth of the Orange order reflected a revival of Protestant suspicions of Catholics in the wake of the 1798 rebellion's sectarian violence. Yet there were also long-term trends at work. After the Act of Union tied Britain and Ireland together into a United Kingdom in 1801, Belfast and Ulster continued to evolve into a prosperous industrial center while southern Ireland's economy floundered and even regressed. Ulster Protestants of all denominations began to see their interests in trade and industry as being the same as Britain's, and saw the interests of both as very different than those of southern, rural, Catholic Ireland. At about the same time, a religious revival, a mighty wave of evangelical fervor, swept through Ulster's Presbyterian communities, encouraging the abandonment of old radical notions rooted in enlightenment rationalism and reinvigorating not only Protestants' religiosity but also their suspicion of Catholics. Ironically, by focusing belief and practice more narrowly on individual salvation rather than old communal responsibilities, the revival also helped wash away a sense of a distinct community among Ulster's Presbyterians. As Sean Connolly argues, the cultural and social distinctiveness of the Presbyterians, as well as vestiges of their interest in Irish nationalism, slowly faded into a pan-Protestant Irish unionism.

While Protestants in Ulster and throughout Ireland defined a new loyalty to the union, Catholics took over the nationalist crusade. The two processes were linked and mutually reinforcing. Catholic nationalism emerged largely out of the efforts of Daniel O'Connell to win full civil rights for Catholics. William Pitt, the British prime minister, had initially intended to include a provision for Catholic emancipation in the Act of Union that united Britain and Ireland under one parliament. Pitt believed that a grateful Catholic middle class could be tied to the new United Kingdom, preventing Catholic discontent from ever fueling Irish nationalist rebellion again. There were good reasons to believe such a strategy might work, but King George III refused to sanction the incorporation of Catholics into public life through a Catholic emancipation act. Catholics would eventually be admitted to the political nation—at least those of sufficient property to qualify, for the United Kingdom imposed property qualifications for voting and office holding throughout the nineteenth and early twentieth centuries—but only after nearly thirty years of frustration and only after Catholics had angrily wrung those rights from a reluctant parliament through Daniel O'Connell's emancipation movement. The result of this movement was precisely what Pitt had hoped to avoid: the linkage between Catholic grievances and Irish nationalism. More important, it meant a definition of Irish nationalism as now exclusively Catholic. From now on, most Irishmen who sought an independent Ireland understood that they fought for an Ireland where the Catholic majority would rule. In the process, O'Connell explicitly repudiated the broadminded, nonsectarian republicanism of the United Irishmen that he himself had flirted with in the 1790s.

Not just in Ireland but in America too, important trends were afoot to set Catholics and Protestant Irish apart and isolate the Catholic Irish as an embattled minority. America had its own evangelical revival, the "Second Great Awakening," and while its effects were complicated and its results diverse, the new revival in the United States, like the one in Ireland, helped resuscitate religious identities and revive Protestant suspicion of Catholics. At the same time, the bloated Democratic-Republican ruling party exploded in the 1820s, initially into factions and eventually splitting into two new parties, the Democrats and the Whigs. The new parties reflected and reinforced religious antagonism, as the Whigs became a vehicle for evangelicals seeking state-backed moral reform and the Democrats became home to most opponents of these "reforms." In the northern United States, Irish Protestants and Irish Catholics who had once found common cause in Jefferson's Democratic-Republicans now split and went their separate ways. As Kerby Miller has suggested, from the 1820s through the 1850s "nearly all Irish American Protestants and Catholics in the northern United States were mobilized in opposing political camps … the former [Irish Protestants] in the Whig cum Know-Nothing cum Republican parties, the latter [Irish Catholics] in the Democratic coalition."[6]

Yet it was not just these changes in social and political contexts but also changes in the nature of Irish emigration that began to transform America and revolutionize the Irish American identity. In 1815, with the end of both the Napoleonic Wars and the War of 1812, the small river of Irish emigration burst its banks in a flood. After years of an annual flow of but a few thousand per year, a full 20,000 left for America in 1815 and 1816 alone. Economic depression in America in 1819 dampened the enthusiasm of some, but even in the early 1820s Irish migration was running to at least 5,000 to 10,000 people per year. After 1828, the numbers fell under 10,000 only once, in the depression year of 1838, and as early as 1831 and 1832, the numbers were so high—more than 50,000 a year—that it had truly become a mass migration. In all, as many as

800,000 to one million men and women left Ireland for North America from 1815 to 1845, the thirty years before the Great Irish Famine.

In part, this mass migration reflected the ease of movement that the new peace permitted. Ships no longer worried about privateers or navy press gangs. British passenger legislation still kept ticket prices to the United States high, but those same acts and government-aided trade made passage to Canada relatively cheap. A half million Irish thus went to Canadian ports between 1815 and 1845. Not all of these people stayed in Canada. One estimate suggests that only about one-third remained in the British colony between 1816 and 1842. Most went to Canada simply because it was cheaper to ship there first and then make for the United States than to travel directly to New York or Philadelphia. In 1818, one observer estimated that it cost only half as much to go through the port of St. John in New Brunswick and then to the United States than to travel to an American port directly.

By the late 1830s the tide had begun to turn, and more migrants began to go directly to the United States. This change stemmed in part from repeals of British passenger legislation, but also from the emergence of Liverpool to New York as the critical trading axis of British-American trade. Liverpool, on England's western coast, had emerged in the early nineteenth century as the great hub of Britain's vast Atlantic trade and in particular its commerce with North America. Liverpool's shipping tonnage increased fifteen times from 1750 to 1800, another six times by 1825, and four times again by 1850. In the process the city soaked up the emigrant traffic, which, in the eighteenth and early nineteenth centuries, had passed directly from several Irish ports to North America. Immigrants from Ireland thus began to take the new cheap steam packets to Liverpool and then ship out from there to New York on vessels that had carried cotton, timber, or other goods to England. As early as 1834, 80 percent of Irish emigrants left for the United States from Liverpool. In America, New York did not dominate quite so much as the receiving point, but by the 1830s, over 280,000 British and Irish immigrants to America traveled through New York.

In the end, however, it was not because the journey to America became easier that so many Irish emigrated. That hundreds of thousands took a complicated and circuitous route through Canada to get to the United States testified that it was not only—or even mostly—improvements in transportation that lured them out. Irish men and women were on the move in all directions in this era. Thousands migrated to Britain. At first, many went there temporarily to help out with harvests or to take laboring jobs or even to beg, to pick up a few pounds to tide over their families before returning home to Ireland or shipping out to the United States. Yet others went to stay. By 1841, there were over 400,000 Irish-born living in England and Scotland.

They left Ireland for Britain, the United States, and Canada (and even a few hardy souls for Australia) not because it was easy but because they felt they had to leave. Ireland's economic "golden age" ended with the end of the Napoleonic wars. The seemingly limitless demand for Irish agricultural products shriveled and prices began to fall. How much they fell or how quickly is disputed by historians, but the "golden age" was clearly over and the agricultural economy was stagnant. Landlords, feeling squeezed themselves and impatient with their middlemen and hordes of tenants, sought to clear their lands in hopes of reaping profits by turning from the labor-intensive and price-stagnant growing of grains to the promising, largely labor-free cattle trade. Between 1839 and 1843 alone, one source suggests, Irish landlords may have evicted as many as 150,000 families from their tenant farms. Meanwhile, opportunities for women and men to earn money by weaving or spinning textiles at home began to decline in the face of English or even Belfast factory production. These hard times would have been difficult in any circumstances, but, as noted before, the population had nearly doubled during the Napoleonic Wars, and though population growth would slow after the war, competition for land grew fiercer than ever before, just as the profit return on crops for tenants declined. It is not clear that rents rose much—only 30 to 40 percent, Irish economic historian Cormac O'Grada estimates—but that may have been because of the peasants' stubborn resistance. From the 1810s through the 1830s, Ireland was awash in secret societies pledged to violence: Whiteboys, Rockites, and Ribbonmen, among others. In the latter decade, a struggle over tithes convulsed a large swathe of eastern Munster and southern Leinster. It was, a historian has suggested, as if the country was engaged in a secret, "night war."

In the new conditions, richer Irish tenants and the strong and middling farmers tried to adjust by keeping their holdings intact and passing them on to a single heir, not dividing them up among all their children as some had done previously and some poorer farmers still did. That, of course, meant that the younger children had to find other means to support themselves, either in Ireland or outside it. These excess young, single males would dominate the new migration, though it would include some families as well, all intent on leaving Ireland before its spiraling economic descent brought them down.

While conditions worsened throughout Ireland, the volume of the migration suggested it was not just the return of hard times but that an increasing number of people in Ireland were unwilling to simply hunker down and bear the hardships as their parents or grandparents had done. It was not just changes in material conditions but also changes in attitudes and in the perceptions of the world and the opportunities it might offer.

Through the late eighteenth and early nineteenth centuries, roads and canals had begun to tie all parts of the island together and connect more and more of its people to broader markets. That increased their familiarity with a broader world, but it also made them more vulnerable to market changes far beyond their local community. Indeed, as economic integration moved from roughly the north and east to the south and west, the secret society wars moved with it, as the demands and dislocations of the new economy provoked resistance as it spread. Yet migration became another alternative. It was people connected to the broader world who would be most likely to leave, while others still hidden away in remote areas and still rooted in traditional cultures would be less likely. In a small but a telling statistic, Ruth Anne Harris found that in mapping the home villages in Cork of immigrants listed in the Boston's Irish newspaper **The Pilot's** Missing Friends column in the 1830s and 1840s, most of the immigrants' home towns were located on or near a major road.

What this spread of the marketplace eventually meant was a revolution in Irish migration to America. It was as we have seen a revolution in numbers as Irish migration became a mass phenomenon. But because it became a mass phenomenon, the kind of people who emigrated changed too. They were, for example, from a different class. In general, Irish migrants during this entire pre–Great Famine era were wealthier and better skilled than those who would come during the famine or even through much of the post-famine era. Yet over the course of the pre-famine period, the pool of potential migrants deepened, reaching down to poorer farmers and workers over time. Kerby Miller reports that as early as 1836, nearly 60 percent of the Irish arriving at New York were laborers or servants. Just ten years before, the proportion had been only 28 percent.[7]

As the migration process pulled from lower in Ireland's class structure, it also began draw more widely regionally and religiously. Ulster would continue to send most of the migrants to North America through the 1830s, and most of the Irish migrants to cross the ocean over that period would be Protestants. Indeed, perhaps twice as many Ulster Protestants left Ireland for America between 1783 and 1845 as left in the colonial era. Yet there were important changes afoot. First, in the early nineteenth century, large numbers of Ulster Catholics were drawn into the flight for the first time. These Catholic Ulster men and women thus figured prominently in the early histories of Irish Catholic communities across America. In a recent study, Edward O'Day has found that 40 percent of all Irish immigrants naturalized in New England from 1784 to 1825 were from Ulster. Ulster Catholics, Brian Mitchell also reports, dominated the early Irish American community in Lowell, Massachusetts, and Oscar Handlin found that Ulster Irish, presumably largely Catholic, made up over one-third of the Boston area's backers of Daniel O'Connell's Repeal Association in the early 1840s. These Catholics came from all parts of the province—even the heavily Protestant areas around Belfast—but their numbers were especially large from the Catholic-dominated counties in the province's southwest, such as Monaghan and Cavan.

Gradually through the 1820s and 1830s, migration fever began to spread south into northern Leinster and northern Connaught counties like Longford, Meath, Sligo, and Roscommon. At the same time, migrants began pouring out of specific parts of Munster, the southwestern province, particularly County Cork. Many of the first Irish settlers in Worcester, Massachusetts, for example, came from the southern coasts of Leinster and Munster. Since roughly the further south one went in Ireland the more Catholics predominated, as the migration pool expanded into the southern counties of Ulster and into other provinces, the proportion of Catholics among the migrants to America increased. By the 1830s, for the first time, Catholics became the majority of America's Irish immigrants.

These post-1815 Irish migrants all but shunned the American South, the heartland of the Ulster migration of the eighteenth century, instead pouring into the cities, mining patches, and mill villages in the North. This "spread," as David Doyle has argued, was "in almost exact proportion to the incidence of expanding economic opportunities"; their preference "for the Northeastern and Midwestern," he states, "reflects the development of transportation, trade, commercial temperate farming and manufacturing there."[8] Some of the thousands who shipped out to Canada would stay there. As Donald Akenson has found, Catholics as well as Protestants would find land in upper Canada, what is today called Ontario, and carve out respectable livings there in the 1830s. Yet Canada's economy was still too raw and small to absorb large numbers of migrants. Catholic immigrants also seemed to find Canada less hospitable. An increasing proportion of those who did stay in Canada were Ulster Protestants even as the sources of migration in Ireland turned to Ireland's heavily Catholic southern provinces. It was in the United States, especially the northern cities, where populations began to rise far faster than the American population as a whole in the 1830s, that the Irish—particularly, Irish Catholics—would seek homes.

These new immigrants transformed the meaning of being Irish in America for good. The new Irish American was Catholic. Irish Protestants began melting away into the broader Protestant mainstream or, in fewer cases, vehemently distinguished themselves from the Catholic Irish, defining themselves as Scotch-Irish. The new Irish America was also embattled and militant; Irish Catholics would see themselves not just as different from Protestants but in competition with and fighting against all Protestants, Irish or otherwise.

This did not happen all at once. Through much of the 1830s, Protestants and Catholic workers allied together in Workingmen's parties in some cities. In other communities in the 1830s, particularly in smaller northern cities, Irish Catholics managed to work out amicable relations with at least some factions of local Protestant elites and live in relative peace with their Protestant neighbors. In the South, too, Irish Catholics seemed to achieve some sort of accommodation with white Protestant majorities

Yet very few Irishmen were moving to the South in this era, and conditions were changing rapidly in small northern cities like Worcester and Lowell, moving toward a new conception of Irish America that was taking hold already in bigger cities in the north. In those large cities, anti-Catholic nativism had become a critical factor in local politics. In New York, for example, anti-Catholic nativists took over the mayoralty in 1844, and bloody riots pitting Catholics against Protestants erupted in Philadelphia in the same year. These new Irish Catholic immigrants were perhaps themselves conditioned to be suspicious of their new Protestant neighbors. David Doyle points out that many of the new Irish Catholic immigrants came from the Ulster borderlands, southern Ulster or northern Leinster and Connaught, where Protestant and Catholic populations were roughly equal and sectarian conflict as intense as anywhere in Ireland. Yet whether or not the Catholic Irish flooding the United States brought especially bitter experiences with sectarian violence with them might not have mattered. For in the United States of the early nineteenth century, religion was shaking out as—next to race—the critical cutting point in politics, society, and culture, and it seemed almost inevitable that these Irish immigrants would begin to identify themselves and define their community in embattled religious terms.

Thus from the masses of these Catholic communities a new kind of sectarian leadership rose to power. As David Doyle has pointed out, these leaders founded their own newspapers, the *Pilot* in Boston, the *Catholic Herald* in Philadelphia, and the *Catholic Telegraph* in Cincinnati, which spoke self-consciously to and for this Catholic community and made no pretence, as the old United Irish–edited sheets had done, to represent a broader "community-wide" interest. They also founded and led new organizations like the Hibernian Universal Benevolent Society which were more exclusively Catholic.

Support for O'Connell's Catholic Emancipation movement came from both Catholics and Protestants, but seemed to draw more heavily from Catholics in the 1820s and 1830s. The Repeal Association in the 1840s also drew largely middle- or even working-class Catholics in its initial phases. Irish Americans also took over the Catholic church in this era. As David Doyle has noted, in 1819 there was only one Irish bishop in America (in Philadelphia), but by the Great Famine, Irish bishops led dioceses in New York, Boston, Chicago, and Cincinnati, as well as other important sees. As they rose to power, Irish bishops and priests often displaced the French or other continental clergy still smarting enough from revolutions in Europe to be wary of the new American republic, and some of the Irish-born bishops like John England of South Carolina articulated a remarkably liberal and sympathetically republican Catholicism. Yet many of the new generation of Irish American bishops, the rough-hewn, bullying "Dagger" **John Hughes** of New York or the steely intellectual Francis Kenrick of Philadelphia, for example, were less interested in accommodating the church to America than in jealously defending its interests and guiding it by the Vatican's light. Similarly in politics, a new rough and ready leadership emerged, with a machine politics style of governance. **Michael "Mike" Walsh**, a Protestant born of a '98 rebel in Youghal in Cork, who became a leader of the "shirtless" Democrats in New York City was one example, but there were others. Inevitably, these new political leaders clashed with and displaced the United Irish exiles who found some of the ideas of the new men dangerous and their style of politics crude. In the election that perhaps best symbolized this change, in 1834, the Irish American voters of New York City's Sixth Ward roundly rejected the United Irish exile and longtime New York Irish leader William Sampson. Sampson had switched to the Whigs over what he had considered Jackson's reckless destruction of the national bank, but new Irish immigrants would brook no criticism of their Democratic party.

And so in these years between the American Revolution and the Great Famine, the whole nature of Irish America had begun to change. What had been since the earliest years of the eighteenth century a migration largely of Protestants, specifically Presbyterians, became one largely of Catholics. What had been a steady and measured migration had begun to take on the look of a mass flight, and what had been a community where Irishness could be defined in nonsectarian terms and asserted confidently in an accepting environment as harmonious with the best traditions of the republic had now become a community defined as exclusively Catholic, embattled, and suspicious.

NOTES

1. Kerby Miller, *Emigrants and Exiles: Ireland and the Irish Exodus to North America* (New York: Oxford University Press, 1985), 171.

2. Ibid., 177.

3. Maldwyn A. Jones, "Ulster Emigration, 183–1815," in *Essays in Scotch-Irish History*, ed. E. R. R. Green (London: Routledge, Keegan and Paul, 1969), 60.

4. David Wilson, *United Irishmen, United States: Immigrant Radicals in the Early Republic* (Ithaca: Cornell University Press, 1998), 3.

5. Ibid., 97.

6. Miller, *Emigrants and Exiles*, 143.

7. Ibid., 198.

8. David Doyle, "The Irish in North America, 1776–1845," in *A New History of Ireland*, vol. 5, *Ireland Under the Union*, ed. W. E. Vaughn (Oxford: Clarendon Press, 1989), 689.

CHAPTER THREE

The Famine Years

It sits astride the path of Irish and Irish American history like some colossus—some kind of gigantic, nightmarish tangle of horrors and deaths, tragic political judgments, painful uprooting and migration, and difficult settlement in a new and very different world. It is, for many people, the only landmark that they recognize in that road from an Irish past to an Irish American present. If most people have heard of anything about Irish or Irish American history they have heard about the Great Famine. Indeed, it may figure more prominently in the American popular imagination of Irish American history now than ever before, understood in recent years by many in America as both a kind of Irish analogue to the Jewish Holocaust or the African American middle passage, and as a kind of Irish American "origin myth"—a story of "how it all began." It might then seem that we should know this era of Irish and Irish American history better than any other. Its story should be more clear and distinct than any other in Irish American history, and it should be easy to reach a consensus on what happened, why, and what it means.

That is not the case. First, perhaps surprisingly, historical study of the Great Famine is relatively recent. For many reasons, not least the pain and perhaps the shame of the event—a reminder to a still-poor Ireland of its poverty and dependency—Irish historians seemed to shy from it for scores of years. In the early 1940s, the Irish government pledged money to encourage Irish historians to undertake a study of the famine, but that history did not appear until 1956 as *The Great Famine: Studies in Irish History*. It stood with a few other books—the most notable being *The Great Hunger*, a popular history by Cecil Woodham Smith—almost to the present. Yet in 1995, with the coming of the one hundred and fiftieth anniversary of the famine, all that changed. The newly confident Irish, riding an economic boom and reveling in a cultural renaissance, were no longer afraid that the famine image might reinforce perceptions of their contemporary shortcomings. Indeed, many Irish historians and social activists, eager to cast Ireland as a broker between the developed or First World and the underdeveloped or Third World, saw in the famine a key event legitimizing Ireland's place as a First World people with a Third World past. Other revisionist historians were eager to cast off what they thought was a narrow and nationalist interpretation of Irish history unfit for the new, cosmopolitan Ireland in its exaggerations of English perfidy and Irish virtue. Interpretations of the famine thus became a touchstone in Ireland's process of remaking itself in the 1990s and produced a sudden abundance of excellent and often pointed and contentious scholarship on the subject. Debates among these scholars revolve around several questions: why did the Great Famine happen? Was it inevitable? Was the United Kingdom's British-dominated government responsible—morally culpable—in any way for this disaster? Was Ireland's largely Protestant establishment also culpable? And, perhaps strange to ask for a catastrophe of this magnitude, ultimately how important was the famine in the course of Irish history? Was it a watershed or turning point?

The study of the Great Famine's place in Irish American history has taken a somewhat different course. The famine's effect in pushing a flood of Irish immigrants to the New World has always figured prominently in Irish American scholarship. Most studies of the Irish in America have begun with the famine or have made it central to their story. Indeed, most historical studies of Irish American communities focus on this era in the middle of the nineteenth century, slighting both earlier and later periods. This reflects both American ethnic historians' preoccupation generally with immigrants as opposed to later generations of ethnics as well the sense, pervasive among scholars and the general public, that the famine era was *the* era of Irish immigration. The famine has also generated heat in Irish American historiography. Many historians of famine Irish experiences in America depict a horror, a mass of impoverished, ignorant, bewildered Irish peasants washed up like so much ocean flotsam in American ports where they suffered all the hardships that a new, raw, industrial, urban America could visit upon them. Other historians suggest that this depiction is too harsh. They argue that it does not take into account the regional diversity of Irish experiences in America—for example, that the Irish had more success in Western cities than in the East. Others have argued that even where famine immigrants seemed to suffer most, in Boston or New York, there was evidence not only of hardy resilience but active and successful agency among these famine Irish.

In 1845, a fungus, *Phytopthora Infestans*, descended on Ireland and much of western Europe. Probably originating in South America's Andes mountains, it made its way to North America, wiping out much of the potato crop on the East Coast of the United States in 1843 and 1844 before appearing in Belgium in June 1845 and in Ireland in September of that year. Later, some Irish peasants would claim that they saw it settle on their fields like a cloud. The fungus had a peculiarly devastating effect on potatoes, rotting them into a black putrefied pulp while they lay in the ground or even as they were stored in pits. The blight turned potatoes to black mush all over western Europe, but nowhere did the fungus wreak as much havoc as in Ireland, for nowhere else were the people more dependent on potatoes than in Ireland.

The fungus struck late in the season in 1845 and thus crop losses were minimal, but the destruction was near total the next year. Farmers planted fewer potatoes for the 1847 harvest and thus the harvest was far below normal. Yet tantalizingly, the fungus was less destructive that season, and buoyed by the hope that they had weathered its worst effects, Irish peasants sowed a full crop of potatoes for the 1848 harvest. But the blight returned in full force and turned nearly all the new potatoes black in the fall of 1848. Not until 1851 did the horrific effects of the blight recede into insignificance in many places. Ireland would not suffer from the blight on this scale ever again, but a scientific cure for the *Phytopthora Infestans* would not be found until 1882.

Without the potato or some food substitute available in sufficient quantity to replace it, the Irish simply died. Historians dispute how many died but the best of the experts, like Cormac O'Grada, estimate that about one million did. Some died of outright starvation, perhaps as many as 9 percent in Mayo, but most died of the diseases that easily infected and ravaged the malnourished, like dysentery or diarrhea. Whatever the cause, they died everywhere: in their mud cabin hovels, on the roads, in the fields, even in the squares of towns where they had fled looking for relief. In Kenmare in Kerry, the local priest, Archdeacon O'Sullivan wrote, they were "dying by the dozens in the streets."[1] Even nearly a hundred years after the famine, old men and women told the Irish Folklore Commission that there were mounds in fields or the ruins of cabins scattered around the country where no one would walk because they believed famine dead lay there.

Yet there were patterns and trends in this mortality. People did not die in the same numbers everywhere. Mortality was worse in the west, in the province of Connacht and western counties of the province of Munster. There people were most dependent on the potato and often lived close together in communal settlements called *clachans*. When diseases appeared in these densely packed communities they spread like wildfire. In southern Wexford in the province of Leinster in the southeastern corner of Ireland and in north Down in the province of Ulster in Ireland's northeastern corner, people suffered little from the famine, but in Mayo in Connacht or Clare in western Munster, they died by the thousands. Residents of Munster and Connacht were twice as likely to die as the people of Leinster and Ulster. Mortality rates were lower in villages along the coast than inland, perhaps because of the greater availability of fish and seafood there or because of easier access to grain shipments in port cities and towns.

The variations were not just geographic. As might be expected, the poor, agricultural laborers who worked for wages, or cottiers, who sold their labor for a patch of land to grow their own potatoes, were more likely to die than any others (although doctors and medical students, relentlessly exposed to fevers and infections, died in disproportionate numbers as well). Men were more likely to die than women, though historians are not sure why. Perhaps it was because women had hardier constitutions because they store more body fat, or, as historian David Fitzpatrick speculates, that their skills of nurture, cooking, and even consolation earned them access to a little more food in the midst of scarcity.

Even as the famine unfolded in all its horror, the debate began on why it occurred. Many British observers focused on Irish population growth and overdependence on the potato, and ultimately blamed the Irish peasantry's fecklessness and irresponsibility for both. Irish nationalists, on the other hand, pointed to the effects of an oppressive and inefficient land system in the long term, and greedy or profligate (or both) landlords and the niggardly callousness of the United Kingdom's government in the short term.

To some extent, those two positions still structure the debate over the causes of the famine horror today. The growth of Ireland's population in the late eighteenth and early nineteenth centuries was so rapid that it seemed natural to observers then and some since to see the famine as the inevitable if painful winnowing of a population that had become too bloated for its land to sustain it. Much of western Europe's population began to grow in the eighteenth century, but Ireland's population grew especially fast. From 1750 to 1845, for example, while the population of France grew at a rate of 0.4 percent a year and that of England's increased at about 1 percent a year, Ireland's population grew by 1.3 percent annually.

As far back as Thomas Malthus in 1796, observers of Irish population growth ascribed its high rate to reckless early marriages and subsequent unchecked fertility. The Irish, so this version went, were self-indulgent and incapable of self-control, and thus married early and had children without care or concern for how they might feed them. K. H. Connell, in his influential study *The*

Population of Ireland, 1750–1845, argued that early Irish marriage was the ultimate root of Ireland's population explosion, but that the story was more complicated than that. Connell suggested that the Irish had begun to marry earlier
and earlier in the second half of the eighteenth century. They did so because
the economy was so good, and particularly the demand for labor-intensive
tillage products like grains and cereals was so high, that even young couples
would have no trouble finding the means to support themselves. Yet in some
other societies the possibility of economic success might well cause men and
women to postpone marriage and childbearing while they took advantage of
new opportunities. The cruel irony of the Irish situation, Connell suggested,
was that the economy might provide enough for young couples to survive,
but the oppressive rigidities of Ireland's land system would not allow them to
improve their position. There was then no reason to postpone marriage. In
recent years historians have become skeptical of Connell's argument. Many
have pointed out that Irish population growth slowed at least after 1821, and
there is substantial evidence that by that time Irish marriage ages were little
different than the European norm. Irish tenant farmers were neither reckless
nor desperate at that point. Timothy Guinnane believes that Connell places
too much trust in Parliament's massive inquiry into Irish poverty in 1836, which
produced a parade of witnesses lining up to decry early marriage among the
Irish peasantry as the source of the island's overpopulation and poverty. When
pressed, Guinnane notes, few of these witnesses could cite any real evidence
of early marriage among the Irish at the time. What prompted those "experts"
to blame early marriage? Guinnane argues that these witnesses, largely gentry,
officials, merchants, or other members of the Irish Protestant Ascendancy,
were so blinded by their stereotypes of the Irish peasantry that they simply assumed that the Irish indulgence in reckless and improvident early marriages
had led to the island's poverty. As Guinnane points out, similar prejudiced
explanations have been used throughout history by representatives of richer
established nations or classes to explain away the plights of poorer ones.

Yet if the Irish marriage age was not especially low and population growth
not very high at the time of the famine, it is still not clear why the Irish population grew so rapidly in the crucial years of the late eighteenth century. Historian Cormac O'Grada believes that early marriage among the Irish may,
indeed, have been the cause of population growth. However, unlike Connell,
he believes that the Irish marriage age did not start to fall in the late eighteenth
century; it had already been low and merely stayed that way. O'Grada points
out that populations in Ireland and almost everywhere in the world before
the modern era did not remain static, but ebbed and flowed, growing rapidly

in good times until they outran their resources and the number of people grew too large for the land available to support them. Ireland had previously suffered a grievous famine in the 1740s. In the second half of the eighteenth century, however, there were no catastrophes in Ireland to check population growth or scare couples into delaying marriage and children. Indeed, the booming economy seemed capable of absorbing all the new children Irish parents might want to have, and so they married young and produced many children. The pendulum of Irish population swung back naturally from the famine of 1740, encountered no friction or felt no drag, and kept rising.

Timothy Guinnane is not convinced that Irish marriage age is the key variable at any point. He suggests instead that the Irish married about the same time as most other Europeans, but Irish women simply had many more children than women from any of these other countries. The reasons for this are not clear, he states. It may have been because of the Irish diet's dependence on the potato. Its cheap nutrition made more women healthy enough to bear more children. Or perhaps because the potato required wives to work harder to cultivate it, mothers stopped breast feeding more quickly, making them more likely to become pregnant (breast feeding has a mild contraceptive effect). Or it may simply have been because the Irish depended deeply on children in old age or in sickness or were, as many observers noted at the time, "unusual in the degree to which they enjoyed children."[2]

Whatever the reasons, Irish population grew rapidly through the eighteenth and nineteenth centuries but was already beginning to slow down at least a couple of decades before the Great Famine. Even without the famine, rising levels of migration might have not only slowed the population's growth but, perhaps, even checked or reversed it. The Irish, then, were not necessarily reckless when it came to having children, and Irish population growth was not a runaway train out of control. Without the failure of the potato, the famine need not have happened.

Yet if population growth did not make the catastrophe inevitable, did the near total dependence of the Irish on one crop make it so? In retrospect, such dependence seems foolhardy. No other people in Europe relied on the potato for a food source by the nineteenth century as much as the Irish. As Cormac O'Grada suggests, the Irish were "Europe's 'potato people' *par excellence*" in Europe, or, indeed, the world, by the middle of the nineteenth century.[3] Irish people consumed an average of five pounds a day; Irish adult men ate an average of an astounding ten to twelve pounds a day. By contrast, the French ate an average of only six ounces of potatoes daily, the Dutch only twenty-eight ounces a day, and though potato consumption was higher in Flanders or in

Germany than in France or Holland, nowhere in Europe did people match the Irish consumption of potatoes. First appearing in Ireland in the late sixteenth century, the potato was already a critical food source for many of the poorer Irish by the late seventeenth and early eighteenth centuries. By the end of the eighteenth century, it had become the central source of nutrition (supplemented in most cases by a little buttermilk) for a majority of the Irish. In the early nineteenth century, the spread of a new inferior breed of potato, the "lumper," poor in nutrition and subject to frequent failures, made that dependence increasingly precarious. Chronic food shortages in summers when the old year's stocks of potatoes had given out and the new crop had yet to be harvested also led to recurring hunger crises for the poor.

And yet on the whole, Cormac O'Grada suggests, the potato served the Irish very well. O'Grada cites data from military records revealing that Irish soldiers appear to have been taller and even heavier than their English counterparts in the pre-famine era. All in all, he notes, "their physical stature and relative longevity suggest that the pre-famine Irish poor were healthier than their lack of material wealth would predict"; they were, he argues, "relatively well fed."[4] The potato made this possible because of its nutritional value and its abundant yield (up to six or seven tons per acre). Irish men, on average, consumed over 3,000 calories per day, hundreds more per day than either English men in the late eighteenth century or French men in the early nineteenth century, and nearly double the average number of calories consumed by the people of Bangladesh today. Indeed, one observer found that adult male laborers working in Clare in 1839 consumed nearly 5,000 calories a day when they ate their average daily fare of thirteen pounds of potatoes. Moreover, the potato rarely failed, Cormac O'Grada states, and thus "only a very tiny fraction of the Irish people starved in an average year."[5] From today's vantage point, the Irish reliance on the potato in the early nineteenth century might seem to have been tempting fate, but in their own time, such reliance seemed not only necessary for such a poor people, but reasonable and indeed a practical response to the constraints their economy imposed on them. If O'Grada is right, the Irish could not have foreseen the blight that destroyed their crop so thoroughly and killed or scattered so many of them. If the Irish were already curbing their population and could not anticipate the failure of their staple food, then it seems less likely now than it once did that the Irish themselves could have forestalled such a catastrophe.

Yet what remains controversial is whether the government of the United Kingdom, its political and social leadership, and local leadership in Ireland could have softened the effects of the blight when it struck. As James Donnelly reports, almost since the time of the Great Famine itself Irishmen and Irish Americans have charged the British government with genocide—a deliberate effort to eliminate the Irish Catholic peasantry. Some have likened British policy to the Nazi extermination of the Jews in the Holocaust. Yet the effort to equate Ireland's fate in the 1840s with that of European Jews in the 1930s and 1940s may obscure more than it explains. O'Grada, not at all sympathetic to the United Kingdom's governmental policies during the famine, nevertheless claims: "Any worthwhile definition of genocide includes murderous intent and it must be said that not even the most bigoted and racist commentators of the day sought the extermination of the Irish."[6]

That being said, O'Grada, Donnelly, and several other historians who have analyzed famine relief policy and practice in Ireland have judged such policy and practice misguided, mean-spirited, and inspired and constricted by both an inflexible ideological dogmatism and by prejudicial stereotypes of the Irish peasant. They argue that the Irish need not have suffered as terribly as they did, that the United Kingdom's leaders and local Irish leaders did not do as much as they could to prevent that suffering, and that the failure was the result not only of poor policy choices but also moral failures. The charge of genocide may be a red herring, but a test of culpability does not begin and end with that charge. The culpability of United Kingdom's officials and their policy in Ireland need not be judged only against the horrors that the Nazis visited upon the Jews—it can and must be judged in its own context.

The longest and most bitterly contested claim against Ireland's rulers focuses on the paradox that Ireland exported food while its people starved. This claim is rooted in the peculiar economic necessity forced on the Irish peasant to grow wheat or other grains to pay the rent to the landlord while growing potatoes for his own family's food; or to labor in the raising of livestock for a larger farmer while being allowed the use of a small plot to grow potatoes as payment. The blight that turned the potatoes to black mush did not affect the other crops or livestock. Production of these other foods did suffer as well in these years for various reasons: poor peasants ate the pigs that they raised for cash crops without replacing them, for example, and sheep owners sold off herds hurriedly lest too many of their animals disappear to became last feasts for the desperately starving. In 1847 and 1850, poor weather also cut into harvests, particularly wheat. Exports of cereals and flour fell from 514,000 tons in 1845 to 147,000 in 1847 before bouncing back to 293,000 tons in 1848. Sheep exports also fell from 324,000 head in 1847 to 152,000 head in 1851. Nevertheless, Ireland was still exporting food even in the worst days of the famine. Moreover, in 1847, more acres were devoted to the cultivation of grains

(3.3 million) than to potatoes, and even more land was devoted to cattle and sheep raising.

For many observers then and now, this irony was too cruel and inexplicable to seem anything less than a calculating or even criminal indifference to Irish life by the United Kingdom's and Ireland's own ruling classes. John Mitchel, a Young Ireland revolutionary who remained a fierce nationalist after moving to America, is perhaps most responsible for making the case against Irish rulers over the exportation of food. In his famous *Jail Journal*, first published in 1854, he recounted: "When the Irish nation then being nine millions, produced by their own industry on their own land and growing food enough to feed 18 millions, one cannot well say that Providence sent them famine."[7] Mitchel's argument was not the first time the charge had been lodged. During the famine itself, Young Irelanders like Gavan Duffy sought a policy to stop exports and "hold the harvest" to feed the dying.

Most historians question whether a check on food exports would have helped the Irish much. James Donnelly, who has been very critical of the United Kingdom government's policy during the famine, argues that much more of the grain grown in Ireland was consumed there during the famine than before it—as the fall in grain exports suggest. As Donnelly argues, the loss of the potatoes could not be made up by Irish grain: "The food gap created by the loss of the potato in the late 1840s was so enormous that it could not have been filled even if all the grains exported in those years had been retained in the country."[8] Furthermore, he points out, the inflow of food from abroad exceeded the outflow from Ireland after 1846 by almost three to one, and these imports were more useful in making up the estimated 50 percent of total food calories lost with the destruction of the potato than holding the grain exports would ever have been. Even adding in the calories of meat and dairy exports from livestock would have done little to offset such a loss, Donnelly argues. He concludes that the Irish did not starve in the midst of abundance but rather that the potato's failure was too fundamental for the rest of Irish agriculture to compensate.

Most historians today probably accept that judgment, but Christine Kenealy raises an exception. She contends that though shutting down exports throughout the famine by itself might not have saved the Irish, there was a critical period when it would have been very helpful: the winter of 1846 and 1847. Little grain was coming into the island then, but exports continued. On a single day in December of 1846, six ships left Ireland carrying hundreds of pigs and sheep and tons of oatmeal to Liverpool, even as Ireland slipped further into disaster. At that point, food exports exceeded food imports, as the persistence

of the blight and the scale of the catastrophe it had worked was only beginning to become apparent. Kenealy's point notwithstanding, even the sharpest
critics of the United Kingdom's leadership among today's historians would
suggest that limiting exports would have saved at best only small numbers of
Irish from death and may have even hurt the larger population by forestalling
the importation of cheaper food.

However, many recent historians raise serious questions about that leadership's response to the famine. Cormac O'Grada and others have criticized, for
example, the government's initial reliance on a program of public works as opposed to outright provisions of food through publicly administered soup kitchens. Modern experts in the economies of famines such as Anya Sen endorse
public works schemes as famine relief because pay for work gives the afflicted
money and thus some power to acquire food, even when—as often happens
today—corrupt bureaucracies or warring raiders might try to siphon it off. The
presumption is that enough food exists somewhere and can be made readily
available to the starving, and more specifically, in a modern world it can be
moved quickly to meet demand, so all that is necessary is to create the demand
among the famine victims. It is not a lack of food, this argument goes, but a
failure to distribute it that causes famines. Yet in Ireland in the 1840s, O'Grada
suggests that the potato's failure was so sudden and so widespread and distribution systems so slow to respond that the money paid to the blight's victims
did not attract enough food. Moreover, forcing Irish peasants already suffering
from hunger out into winter climates to undertake construction work for the
few pence that work relief offered probably made them only more vulnerable
to disease and death. As the potato had provided the peasant Irish with cheap
and plentiful nutrition, turf from local bogs had provided them with cheap
and plentiful fuel for heating their homes. So impoverished that they could
afford nothing better than broken—if any—shoes and mere rags for clothing,
they were not well equipped to face the cold winter climate. In normal times,
the Irish did not have to venture far from their well-heated if often squalid hovels during Ireland's cold and raw winters, because there was little work to do
in their fields in the winter. Yet they were forced to do so by the government's
relief policy in the winter of 1846 and 1847, an exceptionally cold winter by
Irish standards. As O'Grada concludes: "Forcing masses of half-starving and
poorly clothed people to build roads and break stones in all weathers often for
less than a substantial wage, was no way to minimize mortality."[9] O'Grada also
suggests that some of the conditions that make contemporary experts like Sen
recommend work relief did not exist in Ireland. Most notably, unlike many
modern famine-stricken countries, Ireland was not at war, and thus the distri-

bution of food could proceed with relative ease and little fear of interdiction or wholesale theft. Moreover, as O'Grada suggests, the bureaucracy responsible for the Irish famine was certainly more honest and probably more sophisticated than many of its Third World counterparts today.

If the public works policy was neither a necessary nor useful solution to Ireland's famine, was there an alternative? Historians like O'Grada and Donnelly suggest that there was: the direct provision of food by the government through soup kitchens. The government did, in fact, turn to such a policy in the summer of 1847, doling out 2.6 million rations a day, feeding about one-third of the island's population by early July. There were several problems with this policy: the "soup" was so thoroughly watered in some cases that it was of little value, the peasants complained of the humiliation of taking a public handout from sometimes unfeeling administrators, and eligibility requirements sometimes rewarded the unemployed with more food than the employed who could pay for it. Yet for all those problems, James Donnelly has argued that "the [soup kitchen] scheme was by far the most effective of all the methods adapted by the government to deal with starvation and disease between late 1846 and 1851."[10] Deaths from starvation and incidences of disease like dysentery and typhus fell substantially during the soup kitchen era.

Yet the United Kingdom's government had instituted the direct provision of food to the famine-stricken only as a temporary measure to tide Ireland over until the harvest of 1847. The government's long-term strategy was nothing more than to throw the problem of the blight and the famine it caused back on to the people of Ireland themselves and let them resolve it. The instrument of this strategy was an adjustment to Ireland's Poor Law. The original Poor Law had been instituted in 1838 and had established workhouses for the poor in 130 poor-law unions across Ireland (this was later increased to 163 unions). The workhouses were already crowded in the early years of the famine, but the government's public works schemes and soup kitchens had relieved some of the pressure on them. After the cessation of government-sponsored work relief and outdoor soup kitchens, the impoverished and starving would have no other recourse but to go to the poorhouses. Aggravating the government's abandonment was the petering out of private relief. The Quakers, who had labored bravely and tirelessly during the early years of the famine, gave up much of their work in disgust and frustration after the government adopted its new policy of falling back on the Poor Law. Exasperated Society of Friends officials pointed out that they could hardly fill the gap after the government pulled out.

More important, perhaps, was that the United Kingdom's government had decided that Ireland should support Ireland's famine victims. Local taxpayers (or "rate" payers, in the terms of the day) would have to support the work-houses on their own without subsidies from the national government. This meant that Ireland's landlords would have to meet the brunt of the expenses for poor relief, for they would have to pay all the rates for small tenants and half the rates for larger ones. For many landlords already unable to collect rents from starving tenants, the additional burden of rising rates could be crushing. Substantial numbers had entered the famine years already heavily in debt from mismanagement of their estates or their profligate lifestyles.

Their temptation was to clear the land altogether: to evict their tenants and push them to emigrate before they became an excessive burden. The "Gregory Clause" in the new Poor Law of 1847 (named after Sir William Gregory, hus-band of the famous literary figure Lady Gregory and a notorious gambler who squandered his inheritance on horse races by the early 1850s) helped them to do this, for it made only tenants with but one quarter-acre of land or less eligible for workhouse relief. Tenants with more land than that had to give it up if they needed the food only the workhouse could provide. Thus, in 1847 evictions began to soar in Ireland as the government abandoned relief for the island's poor and landlords scrambled to shed the rising burdens of their re-sponsibility. Historians have disagreed about how many evictions actually took place in Ireland, however. Mary Daly, for example, argues that only about 19,000 families were evicted from 1846 to 1848. Timothy O'Neill, on the other hand, contends that landlords might have evicted as many as 98,000 families in those early years of the famine. James Donnelly estimates about 50,000 families, comprising about 250,000 people, between 1849 to 1854. Whatever the number, Ireland was left to fend for itself and the poorest and most vulner-able in Ireland suffered for it.

Why? Why did Britain ultimately abandon Ireland? And why then in turn did Britain appear to encourage Irish landlords to abandon their tenants? The answer to the first question appears to lie in attitudes that mixed simple, raw prejudice against the Irish with laissez-faire economic orthodoxy and a kind of providential faith that God had sent the famine to transform poor, backward Ireland. This caused British leaders of the United Kingdom and their voters to give into a kind of "compassion fatigue" only two years into the famine—about three to four years before the catastrophe ended. The Irish were slothful, the peasants feckless, and the landlords wastrels, and it began to appear that only by being forced to face the cold hard realities of famine by themselves could they be trained in the proper self-reliance—or so the British seemed to think. As O'Grada suggests: "From 1847 on most of the English print media con-veyed an impression of the Irish poor as devious, violent, and ungrateful, and relief as a bottomless hole."[11] As Prime Minister Lord John Russell summed up the prevailing English mood in 1849: "We have granted, lent, subscribed, worked, visited, clothed the Irish; millions of pounds worth of money, years of debate etc.—the only return is calumny and rebellion. Let us not grant, clothe etc. etc. any more and see what they will do."[12]

The "they" became the Irish aristocracy, who were charged after 1847 with responsibility for the famine. There were landlords who managed to survive the famine and succor their tenants at the same time: The Earl of Kingston in Cork or the Grattans and Fitzwilliams families in Wicklow. Yet many of them—if, by no means, all—abandoned the poor. As many historians have pointed out, it was impossible to expect many landlords to manage the burdens of disappearing rents and rising taxes. If thousands of peasants were evicted, then scores or hundreds of landlords also lost their estates. In 1849, Parliament passed the Encumbered Estates Act, creating a special court to sort out the tangle of debts and conditions that tied up many heavily mortgaged Irish estates and help spread their sales. Some of the largest landowners in Ireland, Lord Mountcashel in Cork, for example, were brought to this court and forced to sell off their lands to meet their debts. Yet for most such landlords, as Cormac O'Grada suggests, the famine's "true role was that of a catalyst: getting rid of landlords who were doomed in any case."[13] Most of the estates sold in the early 1850s had debts far in excess of their rents, so much so that the bulk of their debts had clearly come before the famine and thus were the result of "conspicuous consumption and poor estate management rather than bad luck or investment plans thwarted by the famine."[14] If many landlords lost their lands in the famine then, most of them lost them not because of that calamity but because of years of their own imprudent spending or neglect of their holdings.

Abandoned by their government and in many cases by their landlords, over two million Irish sought survival by escaping Ireland and its miseries altogether. "To contemporary observers," Kerby Miller notes, the famine emigration seemed "a lemming-like march to the sea by Irish men and women of all classes and from all parts of the island."[15] Observers at the time could be forgiven if they could see no patterns in those huge crowds choking roads and ports or could detect no distinct streams or rivers feeding the flood. Historians, however, believe that they can see such patterns—though they disagree about what patterns they see. There are no reliable emigration statistics from before 1851 suggesting which provinces or counties emigrants came from. The only means of determining the immigrants' origins is to estimate from the fall in population from the 1841 to 1851 censuses, but, of course, such determinations would have to take into account an estimate of the number of deaths and births as well. Cormac O'Grada's estimates suggest that about 580,000 of the emigrants left from Munster and Connaught and about 460,000 from Ulster and Leinster. Better statistics from the 1851 to 1855 period reveal that nearly 300,000 left from Munster—nearly 60,000 from Tipperary and 90,000 from Cork alone—and about 170,000 each from Ulster and Leinster, and about 100,000 from Connaught. Miller and some other historians see continuity from the pre-famine era to the famine era, noting the continued heavy migration rates from South Ulster, particularly counties like Cavan and Fermanagh as well as the Leinster midlands. Even the rising Connaught migration by O'Grada's estimate may reflect simply a spreading and deepening of "migration fever" that had already penetrated northern Connaught from south Ulster before the famine. Miller points out importantly that the areas with the highest death rates did not necessarily have the highest emigration rates; indeed, the reverse was often the case. County Clare, for example, had the highest death rate on the island, but relatively low migration rates.

David Fitzpatrick sees the regional patterning of the famine migration very differently. He argues that the catastrophe of the famine "generated an immediate and lasting transformation in the regional pattern of outward migration."[16] The "epicenter" of migration, he argues, clearly shifted west and south to Connaught and especially Munster during the famine. Bits and pieces of evidence—depositors in the Emigrant Savings Bank in New York City, naturalization records for New England, parish records in Cambridge and Newburyport, Massachusetts and the Lower East Side of New York, a census taker's notation in a Milwaukee ward, and organizational records in Worcester, Massachusetts—suggest such a shift from Leinster and Ulster to Connaught or Munster too. Yet there is evidence here—subtle, localized patterns that subvert broad generalizations. Historians like Donald Jordan argue that in poor western countries like Mayo, it was the people from the rich central plains that left for America, not the poor peasants from the rocky, mountainous, peripheral parishes. Moreover, if there is a general relation or even an inverse correlation between county death rates and county emigration rates, some counties with high death rates like Mayo and Sligo did send large numbers of migrants. Interestingly, when the analysis is refined to look at smaller local units, it appears that high death rates in some of the towns or parishes in rich counties in the east spurred increased migration from those places.

Is there any way to make some sense of this seeming crazy quilt of patterns? In a broad sense, it seems safe to say that if the famine migration began running in some of the same channels as the pre-famine movement, the sheer volume of the flood of famine refugees clearly broadened as well as deepened the flow. The spread of the famine disaster or even simply the fear of its creeping doom scoured out the richer counties of the east and north that had long sent immigrants to America, pulling people now with less means or ambition than before but who were now convinced there was no alternative to flight. In the poorer counties of the west and south that had not sent as many emigrants in the pre-famine era, the famine migration seemed to come from the richer areas. Peasants there often elected to migrate because they had been evicted from valuable lands. Poorer peasants in the rocky upland areas, however, struggled to hang on in their mountain fastnesses or died; they did not have the networks, knowledge, confidence in migration, or money to leave. Thus in the rugged, stony regions of County Clare or Mayo, where suffering and death was intense, few escaped to the New World. In sum, the famine accelerated a trend that had been going on for some time: the widening of the sources of emigration, expanding them further west and south to pull in more and more parts of the island.

Similarly, while the overwhelming proportion of migrants were rural peasants, the flood did include others. There were large numbers of artisans already suffering from English industrial competition, now also deprived of even the remnants of local markets. An estimated 2,000 skilled tailors settled in New York City in the mid-nineteenth century, for example.

And so they fled from Ireland, two million of them, the small or middling farmers, a few fortunate cottiers or laborers, and artisans fleeing not only the famine but the demise of their industries. In the late 1840s, during the worst years of the famine, the proportion of Irish migrating as part of a family rose over pre-famine levels. By the late 1850s, however, most migrants again were likely single people traveling alone. More Irish left their island between 1845 and 1855 than had left in the previous two-and-a-half centuries. Nearly a whole generation disappeared from Ireland, dead or emigrated. Only one-third of those born in Ireland in 1831—only one in four of those born in the province of Munster—would die in their homeland.

The vast majority would make their way first to Britain. Thousands, usually the poorest of them, would stay there and settle, or make a home in some English or Scottish city. In 1851, there were 727,000 Irish in England, just a few hundred thousand less than the 924,000 the United States counted in 1850. By 1861, the number in Britain had risen to 805,000. By mid-century, one-fifth of the people in Liverpool, Glasgow, and Dundee had been born in Ireland. The flood of famine refugees thus capped a steadier migration into British cities since the 1820s and created an increasingly noticeable Irish population among the British urban proletariat.

Even most of the Irish bound for North America, however, first went through Britain, more specifically Liverpool. By the mid-1840s, over 90 percent of the Irish going to Canada or the United States went through Liverpool and over one million Irish passed through the city between 1847 and 1853. As Robert Scally notes, few Irish emigrants have left records of their impressions of the great English port but it is hard to believe that they could not have been anything but awestruck: "For all but a few it was their first sight of the inner core of the civilization that had ruled them for centuries ... peasants who had never seen seagoing ships of sail or steam now saw hundreds in motion at once. They had just left a world in which a few cabins of piled stones and turf were the center of life and now saw giant geometrical walls of thousands of multistoried buildings lining the shore and crowds more numerous at a single glance than all the strangers they had seen in a lifetime."[17] It was not just huge and awe inspiring, however, but for ignorant, impoverished immigrants awaiting passage, the brief stay in Liverpool was often a nightmare of squalor and fear, as they packed into dilapidated boarding houses and tried to ward off the con men who preyed upon the unwary. Settling in the crowded Irish wards of the North End of Liverpool and weakened by the famine, they were also still easy marks for the typhus epidemic that struck the city in 1847 and the scourge of cholera that came two years later.

The vast majority who came with the means and the intention of leaving for North America did so. It was not an easy trip. Though most immigrants probably traveled from Ireland to Liverpool by steam ferry, the trip across the Atlantic was still by sail. Trips were, on average, somewhat shorter than they had been in the eighteenth century, but still often lasted six weeks. Calms with no breezes or storms with too much wind and rough seas could stretch that out much longer. Poor provisions, cramped quarters, and delayed trips took tolls on the passengers. The cheap ships to Canada packed with panic-stricken peasants in the first few years of the famine suffered extraordinary death rates. In 1847 alone, "Black '47," at least 20,000 Irish died en route to Canadian ports. Many more died in the quarantine station at Grosse Isle, in the St. Lawrence River outside of Quebec City. Death rates were far lower on ships carrying Irish to American ports. Though in a few years death rates on America bound ships may have reached as high as 9 percent in some famine years, over the long run, Irish immigrants on such ships seemed to fare no worse than Germans coming to the United States. Still, outbreaks of epidemics like cholera could wreak havoc among Irish emigrant passengers as late as

1853. The disasters of Black '47 on the Canadian routes had a significant effect on redirecting the emigrant traffic. Until then, enticed by cheaper ticket prices, almost as many Irish shipped out to Canadian ports as to ones further south in the United States. Yet horrified by the death tolls on ship or in the quarantine camps and the flood of impoverished and disease-ridden immigrants into their small cities, Canadian officials began imposing heavy taxes on immigrant ships and the Irish flow into Canada began to fall precipitously after 1847.

Long before they stopped coming to Canadian ports, however, the vast majority of Irish had set their sights on the United States as their ultimate destination. Canada by the 1840s could no longer absorb them: easily accessible lands were already taken, and Canadian industries and thus cities had not yet begun to grow fast enough to employ the masses of Irish workers arriving on their doorstep. Many Irish took advantage of the cheap passage to Canada in 1846 or 1847 and simply shipped out again for the United States soon after they landed at Canadian ports. Of the over 9,000 Irish who debarked in St. John, New Brunswick in 1846, over half moved on immediately to the United States. At least 25 percent of those arriving in Quebec in 1847 also went on to the United States immediately. The Irish who went to Canada came south down the East Coast by ship or overland through New England or New York by railroad, river and canal boats, wagons, carriages, or simply on foot. As Cecil Huston and William Smyth argue, the famine marked the end of substantial Irish migration into Canada.

It was the United States that became the magnet for Irish immigration during the famine and its aftermath. As late as 1851, about as many Irish-born lived in Canada and Britain together as in the United States. Yet thereafter, the number of Irish-born in the United States would rise dramatically, while Irish immigrant populations in Canada and Britain would stop growing. The famine migration helped establish a base in America that continued to renew itself over time thorough remittances. Already, by 1853 and 1854, Irish immigrants had sent twenty-one million dollars back to their families, often to pay for tickets to get relatives out of a stricken Ireland. In the 1850s, Australia would emerge as an important destination for Irish immigrants, as government assistance encouraged movement there, particularly from the counties of Tipperary, Limerick, Kilkenny, Cork, and Clare. The small river to Australia would never match the torrent traveling to the United States, however, approximating only about one-eighth of the Irish who headed for America in the 1850s.

Irish immigrants who came directly to the United States as likely as not went through New York City. There were some shipping lines that linked

Irish ports directly to other American ports, such as an important Derry to Philadelphia line, but most Irish immigrants—indeed, most immigrants of all nationalities—came through New York. Between 1847 and 1851, 1.8 million immigrants, including 848,000 Irish, landed in the port of New York. Just as the increasing systemization and rationalization of Atlantic trade had elevated Liverpool to the United Kingdom's hub, so were the same processes making New York City the center of American trade.

Not all of the immigrants stayed in New York City, of course, but enough of them did to make it the largest Irish community in America by far. In the period between 1847 and 1851, about one of every eight Irish immigrants in the United States lived there—add the Irish who lived in the then separate city of Brooklyn, and it was closer to one in six. By 1855, there were 175,750 Irish immigrants in New York City—nearly double the number from 1845—and they made up nearly a quarter of the entire city's population.

For modern Americans, even modern New Yorkers, it is hard to imagine what the city looked like then—much less what life was like for its immigrant Irish. Before builders could use iron or steel framing to permit buildings to rise several stories, city populations grew by packing more people into low-rise buildings tucked into every nook and corner of the landscape. Most settlement in New York City was still below Fourteenth Street and the tip of Manhattan teemed with people more densely crowded than in Calcutta. This "walking city" was not only extraordinarily dense, it was also a jumble of land uses, with few distinct neighborhoods devoted solely to one economic function or one class of residents. Rich and poor residences and businesses, retail stores, warehouses, factories, and small artisan shops often sat side by side in city blocks carved up into warrens of alleys and lanes more reminiscent of contemporary Beijing or Taipei than today's New York or Boston.

From our own time, the settlement of tens of thousands of poor, bewildered Irish immigrants, many still suffering from hunger and illness, in this great, complex, and busy metropolis seems like chaos. The Irish lived almost everywhere in the city. They made up over one-fifth of the populations of sixteen of the city's wards and over one-third in nine of them. Thousands of Irish squatted in the open lands along the northern border of the city's development, lands that would become Central Park. There with their pigs and dogs, living in huts or even caves, they carved out an ironic and pitiful recreation of Irish rural life. Most, however, lived in the Lower East Side, not far from where they had landed. In the chaotic mélange of the old walking city, the Irish did not make many wards or even one ward entirely their own. There was no Irish ghetto here. They did make up a majority in the Sixth and Fourth

Wards but a bare majority in both. Yet even in the "Five Points" neighborhood in the "Bloody Ould Sixth" Ward, the Irish often shared their streets with members of other ethnic groups. Neither the Lower East Side nor any of these other downtown neighborhoods would ever approximate the faux-rural Ireland like the villages in what would become Central Park. The Lower East Side neighborhoods were dense with tenements and businesses. There were twenty-nine groceries and nineteen "porter" houses or taverns on Mott Street alone, a short street in the heart of the Irish Sixth Ward. Looking back from today, the overcrowding, squalor, and degradation seems suffocating. Fifty-five Irish families, for example, were packed into a narrow seven-story tenement on James Street. The worst buildings were Sweeney's Shambles and the Old Brewery. The brewery, converted to a residence in 1837, was a notorious home to criminals, prostitutes, and several hundred Irish immigrants. On Elizabeth Street, a three-story tenement was surrounded by pigsties and horse stalls. Graham Hodges describes: "A slimal filth made the ground impassable so boards covered the yard. The partly decayed boards when pushed up yielded a thick, greenish fluid through the crevices."[18] Disease, understandably, was rampant. The first cases in the city's cholera epidemic in 1849 were an Irish immigrant named Gilligan and his family. The five of them lived in a rear basement room on Orange Street with no furniture—not even a door.

It was not just cramped, squalid, and diseased, but to people who had spent much of their lives in stable if impoverished communities among longtime family and friends, it must have seemed anarchic. Contrary to myths of old ethnic neighborhoods, populations in these early Irish settlements in New York City were constantly turning over. People might find fellowship there but they did not remain in any one residence for very long. Jay Dolan has found that nearly two-fifths of the parents who baptized their children in the Lower East Side Parish of the Transfiguration in 1850 had left the city by 1859. Even when they lived in the city, they did not stay in the same apartments: four-fifths moved at least once while living in the city; two-fifths moved at least twice. The confusion of uprooting and restless movement and the squalor and overcrowding bred violence as well as disease. Gang fights, like the Dead Rabbits brawl in 1857, or mob actions, like the Astor Place riots of 1849, were the most visible evidence of the rough and harsh world of the Five Points and the other poor Irish neighborhoods.

Fleeing a familiar if hopeless world for survival, and now landed in a harsh and complex one as different from their own rural villages as they could have imagined, some Irish simply broke down. From 1849 to 1859, they made up about 60 percent of the inmates admitted to the New York Lunatic Asylum.

Most of the patients were women, and many of them were immigrants who had been in the city less than a year. Yet for most of them and even most who managed to slog through their new hardships without emotional trauma, there really was little chance for escape. They endured the squalor and hardship because they had to: they were poor. Poverty trapped them in this world, and many if not most of the famine Irish immigrants in New York would not escape it.

Few Irish came to America with any serviceable skills. Archbishop John Hughes of New York, himself an immigrant from Tyrone but crusty and hardly sentimental, lamented them: "the poorest and most wretched population that can be found in the world—the scattered debris of the Irish nation." Joseph Ferrie has found that of those entering New York City between 1840 and 1850, for example, only about 6 percent were skilled artisans compared to about 23 percent of the British immigrants and over 28 percent of the Germans. Upward mobility was also slow for the Irish, seemingly painfully slow. In 1855, nearly half of the employed Irish-born men and women (46 percent) in New York City were either laborers or domestic servants. So many at the bottom of the economic hierarchy had so little margin for error that any number of setbacks—an accident to a father or working children, a short spell of bad economic times, illnesses, or new infants—could push them to seek charity. In 1852, half those treated by the Association for the Improvement of the Poor in New York were Irish and as late as 1858 the Irish still made up 60 percent of the inmates in the New York Alms House.

They need not have stayed in New York, of course. From Ferrie's sample it appears that a larger proportion of Irish arriving in New York City between 1840 and 1850 were still there by decade's end than British or German immigrants. Yet that was still only 18 percent of all Irish immigrants who landed there. Only 13 percent of the 1840s Irish immigrants who landed in New York City still lived there by 1860.

By the late 1840s, it had become easier to travel throughout the country than ever before. Railroad and canal companies and even a few New England factory owners had stationed recruiters in New York by then, and by 1847 the Commissioners of Immigration had established a labor exchange. Transportation inland had also become faster and cheaper by the late 1840s and early 1850s, as railroads supplanted the old canals. Thus, while the trip to Pittsburgh by train and canal took six days in 1845, by 1855 it took only two days. The most popular route to the Midwest had also become faster. That trip went up the Hudson River to Albany by boat, then via the Erie Canal or by railroad to Buffalo, and then by steamer to Chicago or other cities on the Great Lakes. The canal took eight days; the railroad thirty hours.

Such trips inland, especially as far west as St. Louis or Chicago, could be costly to immigrants of few means, however. Tickets to Midwestern cities cost about the same as the price of the passage that had carried immigrants over the ocean. Irish immigrants, as compared to British or German ones, were far less likely to move very far from New York. Joseph Ferrie contends that nearly 70 percent of the Irish who landed in New York in the 1840s settled within 250 miles of the city. By contrast, 60 percent of the Germans arriving in New York in that decade moved to cities or towns *over* 250 miles away, nearly 40 percent moving at least 500 miles from New York. In 1850, nearly 80 percent of the Irish-born in Ferrie's sample who had arrived in America in the 1840s had settled in the New England or the Mid-Atlantic states. Of Ferrie's sample of immigrants, nearly 19 percent of the Germans settled in Ohio but only 3.2 percent of the Irish did; by contrast 24 percent of the Irish landing in New York worked their way further east to the New England states but only 2.5 percent of the Germans did.

The Irish making their way to New England encountered conditions that were much like New York City—or worse. Boston was ill-equipped to receive the thousands of Irish who landed at its port, made their way south from New Brunswick and Quebec, or moved north from New York. The local economy's growth was modest, the city's area was still largely confined to its original tiny peninsula, and it had little housing suited for a flood of impoverished refugees. Conditions for the Irish in Boston, then, were probably worse than in New York. Nearly half the men could find jobs only as laborers. Irish families found housing wherever they could: basements, converted middle- or upper-middle-class homes, or newly built ramshackle tenements in neighborhoods from Boston's North End to the South Cove. Broad Street, today part of the city's financial district, was then a mixed business and residential area and a "perfect hive of human beings."[19] Several Irish families lived at the notorious Half Moon Place, where twelve constantly overflowing privies stood in the yard. Irish in the surrounding ramshackle tenements found coal and wood so expensive that they spent as much time in bed as they possibly could during the harsh New England winters. Meanwhile, cholera spread like wildfire in neighborhoods like Broad Street or the North End. During the famine era, the city's death rate zoomed up until it was higher than the rancid slums of England's industrial cities, and it was twice as high still in Irish areas like Broad Street than in the rest of the city. In one year, 1850, no less than one in seventeen of all the Irish men, women, and children residing in the Broad Street neighborhood died.

Such dismal conditions were not just true of New England's biggest city. In the new mill town of Lowell, north of Boston on the Merrimack River, more than half the male heads of Irish households in the principal Irish neighborhood "the Acre" were laborers. In 1850, tuberculosis and ship fever plagued the Irish community there and when cholera struck Lowell in 1849, three-quarters of those who died were Irish immigrants. Families staggered under such hardships. Husbands died or deserted and wives were left raising children with few resources. In 1850, women headed 23 percent of the Irish households in Lowell. And like Irish immigrants in other cities, Lowell's Irish suffered from violence: Irishmen often preyed on other Irish in crimes ranging from petty assaults to gang battles and riots that pitted Corkonians against Connaught-men. To the west of Boston in Worcester, the Irish-born population jumped from 600 to 3,000 from 1840 to 1850. There too the story seemed largely a tale of hardship. Hundreds made their way to Worcester from their famine ships only to die of ship fever, dysentery, or other diseases almost immediately in the central Massachusetts city. Like Lowell, bad blood between southern or eastern Irish and westerners erupted into gang fights and worse, including a major riot on Palm Sunday in 1847 that ripped the community apart.

Further west through upstate New York, Irish hard times continued. In Troy, the Irish had a far higher proportion of single-headed households than any other group as late as 1880. By 1860, Buffalo, at the end of the Erie Canal and the principal shipment point for goods going further west, had almost 10,000 Irish-born men and women. Three-quarters of the Irish household heads who lived in the city in 1855 had come there since 1846; over half had come since 1850. In Buffalo, as in much of New England, nearly half the Irish men were day laborers and almost 90 percent of the single working Irish women toiled as domestics. In Buffalo, too, the Irish seemed trapped in the worst housing, along the canal or the "Beach" on the lakeshore. Some lived with their pigs in nothing better than shacks. Irish men and women in Buffalo, like in New York and so many other cities, also made up a majority of the poorhouse population and a substantial proportion of the men and women in jail.

In sum, the experience of Irish famine immigrants in the United States was usually neither easy nor happy, and, indeed, was often quite harsh and painful. Joseph Ferrie's study of the immigrants arriving through the port of New York in the 1840s is the closest we have to a national study of Irish immigrant economic mobility and Ferrie's conclusions are sobering. Comparing Irish economic achievements to that of the Germans or British immigrants arriving in

New York in the same decade, he found that the "Irish clearly had the worst out-comes; the highest percentages moving down and the lowest moving up." Even worse, for the Irish, "the percentages moving down [from white-collar or skilled workers to unskilled] exceeded the percentage moving up [from unskilled to white-collar or skilled worker]."[20] The Irish also fared worse in accumulating wealth than their fellow German or British immigrants in Ferrie's sample.

Such difficulties were not common only among the Irish in the United States. The Irish in Britain may have suffered even more than the Irish in New England and New York because the Irish immigrants who settled in Britain were probably poorer than those who made it to the United States. Though some of the Irish in Britain continued to meet the other island's need for farm labor, which had long attracted Irish immigrants there, most settled in English or Scottish cities. There they started and generally remained at the bottom of the economic hierarchy. Sir James Tenent claimed in 1860: "The Irish immi-grant competes only for the coarsest ... and generally the most repulsive con-ditions of labor."[21] The Irish in British cities also suffered from drunkenness, crime, and disease just as the Irish in northeastern cities in the United States.

In the best of political conditions, the lives of America's famine Irish would have been difficult, but the late 1840s, 1850s, and 1860s were not the best years for them to arrive in the United States. Nativist—that is anti-Catholic and anti-immigrant—movements had already emerged before the famine migra-tion, electing a mayor in New York, for example, and prompting brutal, bloody riots in Philadelphia. Yet the nativist surge would reach its high point in the 1850s with the rise of the Order of the Star Spangled Banner and the Know-Nothings and their political party. Founded in 1850, the Know-Nothings rose like a rocket in 1853 and 1854. By the latter year they had a million members. By 1854, they either had control of the legislature or had won governorships or both in Massachusetts, Maine, and Pennsylvania, and were powerful in Indiana. By 1856, they were still strong enough to nominate Millard Fillmore for president and carry eight electoral votes, but by then they had all but spent their force and would soon disappear.

As Tyler Anbinder has suggested, it was frustration over the slavery issue more than fear of immigrants or even antagonism over religion that seemed to lift the Know-Nothings to prominence in the North. The spectacular rise of the party came in 1854, when many northerners began to suspect that the existing parties were cravenly capitulating to the "slavocracy" and failed to address the national crisis. The nativist party declined in the North and then disappeared when the new Republican party emerged by 1856 to absorb its antislavery voters.

Nevertheless, if the new Know-Nothing voters worried first about the power of slavery, they were also obsessed with the threat of immigrants, particularly Catholic immigrants. The two fears, fear of slavery and fear of Catholic immigrants, were in fact related. In many northern states, Catholics, particularly Irish Catholics, had become mainstays of the Democratic party—the northern allies of the southern slave owners. The flood of famine refugees only heightened those fears by vastly increasing the number of potential Democratic voters. Moreover, Irish Catholics were among the most strident of the antiabolitionist Democrats.

Yet there was also a deeper association between the political power of slaveholders and Irish Catholics in the Know-Nothings' and Republicans' minds. As Eric Foner has suggested, many antislavery men in the North hated slavery as much or more for corrupting the South and potentially the entire country as for mistreating African Americans. They saw it as a root of the South's backward civilization and the ruin of Southern whites: it sapped their initiative, hindered education, bred laziness and petty sensitivities to honor and violence, and dragged people down into reactionary decadence. The South, they believed, looked backward—not forward, as the North did, to industry and the economic development that free labor would produce. Kevin Kenny suggests that this image of the South was easy to transfer to Irish Catholics, a people with seemingly no interest in education or self-improvement and fatally corrupted by a reactionary Catholicism, which was itself rooted in aristocracy and monarchy and an enemy of liberal progress. Irish Catholics, then, were not merely temporary allies of Southerners but products of similarly flawed cultures. In the early nineteenth century, American observers assumed Irish immigrants would grow out of their backwardness after sustained exposure to the bracing free market and civil liberties of the United States, but by the late 1840s and early 1850s, Anglo-Saxon Protestant Americans were no longer so confident. This "racializing" of Irish Americans became prominent in literature, magazines, and histories, but was most powerfully conveyed in cruder graphic forms in cartoons or on the stage. As L. Perry Curtis has pointed out, newspaper and magazine cartoonists on both sides of the Atlantic, prompted by rising fears of the Irish and motivated by vague influences of a distorted Darwinism, began to draw Irishmen as inhuman apes and monkeys. In the United States, Thomas Nast of the *New York Times*, the best-known cartoonist of his day, consistently offered the simian, bestial, and violent "Paddy" as the typical Irish American. Dale Knobel argues that more and more such observers despaired of Irish self-improvement, suggesting that Irish fecklessness, conservatism, and irresponsibility were genetic traits bred in the bone and thus immune to the American environment's beneficial effects. Knobel dates such changing attitudes to the great Philadelphia riot of 1844, but clearly the arrival of so many famine immigrants packing overcrowded slums and filling jails, almshouses, and lunatic asylums contributed to the new despair over and aversion to the Irish.

Nativists had other reasons to fear Irish immigrants. Skilled blue-collar workers made up a substantial proportion of the members of the Order of the Star Spangled Banner. Though Anbinder notes that their proportions among Know-Nothing members were no greater than among native populations at large, these workers had special reasons for fearing immigrants, particularly Irish immigrants. Joseph Ferrie, for example, points out that new evidence on wages, prices, and economic mobility reveals that native-born workers in the northeastern United States may have suffered from a "hidden depression" between 1843 and 1857. His own research suggests that the advent of the Irish even more than other immigrant groups may have had an adverse effect on native-stock workers in big cities, as the Irish provided the cheap labor to accelerate the "deskilling" of old crafts such as shoemaking.

Whatever the causes of nativism in the 1850s, it could not but help the alienation that the famine Irish felt. Impoverished and suffering, they were also unwanted.

Within a few years after the demise of the Know-Nothings, the nation plunged into civil war. Despite being diehard Democrats and staunch opponents of abolition, initially Irish Americans rallied to the war. About 140,000 Irish-born and an unknown number of second-generation Irish fought in the war. The twelve most heavily Irish regiments in the Union's Army of the Potomac suffered nearly 50 percent killed, wounded, or dead of disease over the course of the war. The heroism of some of the Irish regiments has been justly praised. The Irish Brigade, the best-known Irish unit, made valiant charges at Antietam, Fredericksburg, and Gettysburg. But as the casualties piled up, Irish American enthusiasm for the war waned. When Abraham Lincoln announced that he would issue the Emancipation Proclamation, many Irish American newspapers were outraged. The war's aims had changed from preserving the Union, they cried, to the abolition of slavery, and they wanted no part of the latter. Irish American disaffection peaked when implementation of a military draft sparked **riots** in Boston, northeastern Pennsylvania, and especially New York. Many Irish immigrants would continue to fight valiantly until the end of the war, but many others in the Irish community had soured on the union's cause. Irishmen also fought for the South, though in much lower numbers.

Even with the close of the war the trauma did not let up for famine-era immigrants. Those who managed to survive into the 1870s suffered, as the country as a whole did, from the effects of the Panic of 1873, which lingered on until the late 1870s.

It is easy, therefore, to see the experience of the famine Irish immigrants as an unrelieved travail, but that would oversimplify the complexity of their history. Though the Irish concentrated on the East Coast, in New England or the Mid-Atlantic states, by 1860 nearly one-third of them lived in the Midwest or West. There social and economic opportunities were usually better for them: economies were just beginning to grow, entrenched elites were nonexistent, and societies were fluid. Wages for skilled workers were usually higher in the West, and in parts of the Midwest, like Minnesota, land came cheap in the 1850s and appreciated quickly in value. In short, the West offered famine Irish immigrants a much better chance for a better life.

No place seemed better for the Irish than San Francisco. There the Irish arrived just as every other European American did. In 1848, San Francisco was but a hamlet of 1,000 people and 200 buildings, but as early as 1852, there were 4,000 Irish immigrants living there. The population of the "instant city" was exploding. Many of those early Irish came to San Francisco by way of Australia, moving from the gold fields in Victoria to the "gold mountain" of California. With no whites preceding them or resisting their upward climb, and the local economy enjoying skyrocketing growth, the Irish flourished. By 1860, 15 percent had already found white-collar work. By that decade too, Irishmen were already breaking into the local elite, a process that would not happen in New England cities until the middle of the twentieth century. James Donahue was owner of the San Francisco Ironworks, one of the largest manufacturers in the city, and Donald Murphy owned the biggest dry goods store west of Chicago. Even the San Francisco Irish in blue-collar jobs fared far better than their East Coast counterparts, enjoying wage rates double or nearly triple that of eastern urban wages, and they still could find good housing and reasonable food prices. Upwardly mobile, prosperous, and easily accepted, the San Francisco Irish spread across the city. The Irish-born made up at least 10 percent of the population in ten of the city's wards in 1880 but no more than 27 percent in any one of them. If the famine refugees in Boston's North End and Broad Street or in New York City's Five Points seemed to merely exchange Irish rural horrors for American urban ones, Irish immigrants in San Francisco found one of the most hospitable places on earth for their people.

And yet Irish men and women did not have to go that far to find a respite from the famine or sample their new country's potential. There were opportunities east of San Francisco too, in cities like Detroit, Milwaukee, Natchez, or Memphis. Detroit, for example, was a prosperous little community enjoying steady growth when the famine struck Ireland. Famine Irish refugees to the city clustered initially in the poorer jobs and in their own streets and neighbor-hoods on the city's West Side around Most Holy Trinity Parish. These famine immigrants, Jo Ellen Vinyard notes, were twice as likely to be laborers in 1850 as earlier Irish-born settlers in the city. Steady rather than sudden popula-tion increases, however, helped promote a diversified economy able to absorb workers who came with a range of abilities, and upward mobility was within reach of the hard-working or savvy immigrant. The proportion of Irish labor-ers was about one-third in Detroit, far lower than in Boston, and young im-migrants found jobs as painters, plumbers, and in iron foundries and stove factories. Wages were also higher in Michigan than almost anywhere in New England, Mid-Atlantic, and even Midwestern states except Illinois. Land as well as housing were easily accessible as well in Detroit, and after some ini-tial clustering, Irish immigrants spread throughout the city's west side and spilled over into the east side as well. By the early 1880s, about half of the city's Irish and German immigrants owned their own homes. Detroit's advantages seemed to attract special kinds of immigrants: long-time married couples, not single people — immigrants who were willing to set down roots in this stable, prosperous community. Almost half of the Irish and Germans living there in 1850 were still in Detroit in 1870 and two-thirds of the Irish residents in 1870 were Detroiters thirty years later. Such figures contrasted sharply with the con-stant turnover of Irish populations in New York City.

Even on the East Coast there was considerable variation in Irish immigrant experiences. As in Boston or New York, the Irish made up a majority or more of the paupers taken in by Philadelphia's Almhouse and House of Industry. The Irish in Philadelphia also suffered terribly from the ravages of the era's cholera epidemics. Yet on the whole, the experience of the famine Irish in Philadelphia was far better than that of the Boston or even the New York Irish. Not hemmed in by water as on Boston's narrow peninsula or on the island of Manhattan, Philadelphia could expand easily. Moreover, legal legacies of the Penn proprietorship reduced the value as well as the costs of much of the city's lands. One result of these circumstances was the creation of neighborhoods in Philadelphia that were far less dense than those in Boston and New York and thus less unhealthy. Mortality rates in Philadelphia Irish neighborhoods, for example, ran to one-third of Boston's heavily Irish wards and nearly one-half of New York's in the 1850s. A second result was that even Irish immigrants of modest means could purchase their own dwellings. In the working-class neighborhoods of Moymensing and Schuylkill, for example, one-quarter to one-half the property owners were Irish by 1860. Combining these living conditions with a dynamic manufacturing economy that opened up many opportunities, in 1860 Philadelphia could offer even its nearly 95,000 Irish immigrants a reasonably comfortable new home and hope for the future.

Even in New York and the New England cities, amid the confusion of the famine and the squalor of Irish neighborhoods there were some signs of hope and stability. Not all the immigrants settling in those cities were unskilled and hapless peasants. New York, as noted earlier, attracted substantial numbers of Irish tailors, who found work in the city's burgeoning ready clotheswear industry. Most toiled in the bottom ranks of the city's clothing manufacture industry, but some became successful manufacturers or merchants themselves. Even for the unskilled, New York was rich with opportunities, offering some of the highest wages for laborers in the nation. In other northeastern cities like Troy, New York, and Worcester and Lowell, Massachusetts, Irish immigrants had also already begun to break out of the ranks of day labor and into better jobs as ironworkers, boot and shoe makers, or textile operatives by the 1860s and 1870s.

Yet more than the few short steps up the economic ladder, it was the ties of family and friends that sustained immigrants and nourished their hopes in trying times. Historians are just beginning to trace how Irish immigrant chains extended across the Atlantic from Ireland to America, but there is substantial evidence to show they existed. A disproportionately large number of the Irish living in the notorious Five Points Slum in the 1850s, as Tyler Anbinder and Cormac O'Grada point out, hailed from Kerry and Sligo, and it appears the they not only lived near one another for mutual support but chose wedding partners from among their old country neighbors and friends. Over four-fifths of the Kerrymen lived in but two of the Five Points' twenty city blocks, for example, and people from the same counties dominated in single tenement houses or small clusters of buildings. They also often married within the old country's networks. Cormac O'Grada found that two-thirds of the Sligo or Kerry people marrying at Transfiguration Parish in Five Points chose partners from the same county. For many the choices were more narrow than that: ten of fifteen grooms from the parish of Tuoist in Kerry married women from Tuoist and three more from parishes bordering on Tuoist. Such networks of friends, Anbinder argues, helped Irish immigrants even in this, the most notoriously degraded neighborhood of America, put aside surprisingly large amount of savings. Even amid the filth, hardship, and violence of the Five

Points, America's worst slum, it seems clear that such chains or networks were at work, facilitating both the migration and the adjustment afterward.

There are hints of such networks in other cities as well. In Buffalo, one-quarter of Irish immigrant households had kin in the city, compared to only one-eighth of the Germans, and in cities like Buffalo and Lowell in Massachusetts, communal networks sustained Irish workers on strike or helped move immigrants out of day labor or domestic service and into mill work. County loyalties were a mixed blessing—gangs rooted in county allegiances ravaged the Irish communities in Worcester and Lowell—but such loyalties revealed that the immigrants were not mere individuals, pounded by the famine's havoc into "debris" as Archbishop Hughes put it, impotent to affect their fate and merely drifting as circumstances carried them.

It was not just the networks that carried them from the old country that sustained the famine Irish in a new land and gave some stability to their new communities. It was, as well, the networks and institutions they created or remade for themselves in America. One such source of community were the saloons, groceries, and small shops that emerged in Irish neighborhoods. The businesses themselves served important functions in building a new community. Saloons and taverns could be raucous dives, easing already demoralized Irish immigrants down paths to alcoholism. Yet saloons should not be dismissed that easily. Saloons were also clubhouses and gathering places, informal, most often, but sometimes formal meeting places for ethnic organizations and unions. Groceries offered credit to immigrant families newly caught in the topsy-turvy cycles of booms and busts. Owners of both kinds of shops also served as a kind of petty neighborhood elite, potential help for immigrants in intervention with the government, and mobilizers of community protest.

Such men filled the lower ranks of the Democratic party and were the immigrant's link into a new kind of political organization that was transforming American urban politics: the political machine. A few Irish immigrants or American-born Irish had already fought their way into the leadership of the Democratic party in New York City by the 1860s, for example, but the vast bulk of the Irish were still largely "foot soldiers" in Tammany or other Democratic organizations by that decade. Nevertheless, politicians reaching down into the ranks of the new immigrants for votes offered in turn some access to power and reward, potential help and cushioning in hard times, and protection against enemies. The emergence of this leadership from the masses had begun before the famine, as such new rough men replaced the old remaining elites of the United Irishmen. Paul Gilje has found, for example, that even before the famine, saloonkeepers or the grocers on New York's Lower East

Side often provided bail for neighbors who fell afoul of the law. This leadership cut two ways. Grocers and saloonkeepers earned their livings off the poor and they rarely mobilized their people behind the kinds of broad, fundamental economic reforms that might have helped immigrants the most. Still the lineaments of some stability and lines of connection and loyalty had begun to emerge and grow.

Irish American Catholics flocked to the Democrats because that party offered an alternative to the Whigs or Republicans, who seemed to insist on imposing some kind of Protestant cultural conformity on cities, states, or the nation at large by outlawing Sunday recreation, advancing public schools imbued with Protestantism, or, most importantly, prohibiting drink. Yet to say most of the famine Irish hewed to the Democratic Party for such reasons is to simplify a politics that was much more complicated and personal. Democratic Party organizations in Irish immigrant neighborhoods were rarely cohesive and paid scant attention to issues. Rather, they were congeries of factions and fiefdoms, allying, squabbling, compromising, and even openly brawling with one another in struggles for the rewards of patronage and contracts.

The Catholic Church was probably a more important focus of community coherence and identity than the Democratic Party. It would exist in some form in every town and neighborhood, its rules would govern every aspect of the lives of its people, and its organizations, sodalities, temperance societies, institutions, churches, schools, hospitals, and orphanages would supply much of the infrastructure for the new Irish American community. By its constant attention to who was in or out or of good standing, it would also be the most effective police of this community's boundaries. In the end, the new Irish America that emerged in the mid-nineteenth century would be an Irish *Catholic* America more than anything else, and all of the Irish Catholic immigrants' other loyalties and allegiances would be influenced by their Catholic identity.

That is not to say that the church had as yet achieved this pervasiveness and power in Irish America during the famine years. It was, in fact, a ramshackle organization in the 1840s in most cities, plagued by massive numbers of impoverished lay men and women who left Ireland with little knowledge of their faith, and consisting of a motley band of often undisciplined clergy. As Jay Dolan has pointed out, it seems likely that no more than 40 percent of Irish Catholic immigrants attended church regularly in New York City in the 1840s and 1850s. In some cities like Boston and Worcester, new Irish immigrants fought openly with priests in the 1840s. Getting proper priests was also a constant problem, as America sometimes attracted renegade or malcontented clerics. With few priests and tens of thousands of new laity to accommodate, dioceses were hard pressed. As late as 1865, the average population of a parish in New York City was about 11,000, and there and in other cities like Chicago, parishes of 20,000 or even 30,000 were not unknown.

Nevertheless, slowly the church managed to get control. Diocesan synods helped tighten regulations and impose some discipline on the clergy. Priests and people also came together in the face of the increasing anti-Catholic militancy, and bishops also began to build on a huge scale to accommodate the new huge members. **Archbishop John Hughes** built twenty-two new churches in Manhattan alone from 1839 to 1864. In the Boston Diocese of the four northern New England states, there were forty-eight churches in 1846, but by 1866 there were 109 churches in Massachusetts alone. It was not just a change of bricks and mortar but changes in lay attitudes, knowledge, and devotion that transformed the church in the famine era. The "Devotional Revolution" or Catholic Revival sweeping Europe and Ireland in the middle of the century also caught fire in America, transforming Irish immigrant faith from a chaotic blend of scattered doctrine, magic, and encrusted traditions born in rural peasant life to a disciplined institutionalized religious life of regular mass attendance, frequent devotions, and respect for the clergy. Only slowly would the church establish its primacy, but it had survived a difficult period of crisis and had laid a foundation for future development by the end of the famine era.

The final pole of identity to become established in the famine Irish era would be a new version of Irish American nationalism. The United Irish exiles had already planted Irish nationalism in America, and, just before the famine, Daniel O'Connell's Repeal movement had flourished briefly. Even the Young Ireland with its grand talk and tiny "cabbage patch" rebellion in 1848 had its backers in the United States. It would be the Fenian movement, founded just before the Civil War and growing to extraordinary popularity by the late 1860s, however, that would make Irish nationalism truly a mass movement in America. The **Fenians** were bunglers at revolution. Riddled with spies and plagued by grandiloquent but ineffectual leaders and bitter factionalism, the Fenians tried to snatch Campobello Island from Canada, invaded Canada unsuccessfully twice, and failed when they tried to run guns and men into Ireland to incite a revolution there. Still, they were extraordinarily successful in mobilizing public opinion. Capitalizing on lingering bitterness—maybe even survivors' guilt—from the famine, the Fenians' frenetic activities of picnics, meetings, and parades, and blizzards of pamphlets, speeches, and songs won backing throughout Irish America. The breadth and passion of their support

suggest how they made Irish nationalism a third pole of the new Irish identity in America and how nationalist organizations would become but another
critical piece of the infrastructures of Irish American communities. Anchored
by the growing strength of the Catholic Church, the Democratic Party, and
nationalists like the Fenians, the Irish American community slowly developed
cohesiveness and coherence after the famine disaster.

Yet it was not just forces inside the community but forces outside it that
reinforced that cohesiveness. The most important of those forces was probably
the Know-Nothings. The embodiment of anti-immigrant anti-Catholic prejudice, the rising power of the Know-Nothings in the mid-1850s helped unite
Irish Catholics around the church and the Democratic Party and sharpened
the emotion of nationalism. In cities like Lowell and Worcester, it helped end
internal conflicts among county gangs and rally Irish immigrants around new
aggressive lay and Catholic church clerical leadership.

The Know-Nothings would fade away by the end of the 1850s. Though
the Irish in the North had become increasingly ambivalent about the Civil
War, especially as the Union's goals shifted to the abolition of slavery, most
of their neighbors remembered Irish valor at Antietam, Fredericksburg, and
Gettysburg, not the **Draft Riots of 1863**. Irish American Union army veterans
like General St. Clair Mulholland cultivated such good feeling by trumpeting
Irish heroism in speeches and histories after the war. Irish Americans fought
back against nativism not only on the Civil War's battlefield but in urban
theaters. Irish immigrants and their children had became become a sizable
proportion of America's songwriters, singers, comics, actors, and playwrights,
and these men and women worked hard to rehabilitate the Irish image. None,
perhaps, worked harder than the immigrant **Dion Boucicault**, who did not so
much eradicate the "Stage Irishman" Paddy in the 1860s and 1870s as begin in
a series of his extraordinarily popular plays to transform him from buffoon or
even sympathetic simpleton to a sly and brave if still comic hero.

Nevertheless, Irish Americans were clearly now a distinct people. The
Catholic Church, the Democratic Party, and fierce Irish nationalism defined
them as different. The boundaries were sharply drawn. The Protestant Irish
America of the eighteenth century was now long gone, and even the United
Irish vision of the early nineteenth century—Protestants and Catholics united
in behalf of a republican Ireland and Irish America—seemed distant by the
1860s and 1870s. The **Orange Riots**—the bloodiest riots yet—pitting against
each other "Orange" Protestant Irish and "Green" Catholic Irish in New York
on the anniversary the Battle of the Boyne in 1870 and 1871 made clear that
there could never again be an Irish America including Protestants and Catho-

lics. In the latter riot, over sixty people died on the city's West Side. By the late nineteenth century, most descendants of the Ulster Presbyterians of the eighteenth century and even many new Protestant Irish immigrants turned their backs on all associations with Ireland and melted into the American Protestant mainstream. A smaller number, proud of their Ulster Presbyterian colonial roots but disdainful of the new Catholic Irish, insisted on a Scotch-Irish identity. Some of the latter founded the **Scotch-Irish Society of the United States of America** in 1889 to keep this identity alive.

Yet was it the famine migration that made this Catholic Irish America? For all its horrors and for all the numbers of immigrants who fled to America, did the famine create an Irish America that had not or would not have come into existence without it? Was the Irish America forming in the late 1840s and 1850s and maturing in the 1860s a significantly different Irish America than the one in the early 1840s before the potatoes blackened and the people starved? This is hard to answer. David Doyle suggests that "on the eve of the Famine the themes and structures of Irish America were all in place."[22] Migration had already become a mass movement by then, and Catholics had already begun to dominate that migration. Tensions had also emerged in many places between Catholics and Protestants and the dream of a nonsectarian Irish American community had begun to fade long before the potato blight's fearsome devastation.

Nevertheless, it seems hard to conceive of the famine migration as anything but crucial in the shaping of Irish America. Migration fever had been creeping slowly down from Ulster, jumping parts of Connaught and infecting Munster for a generation or more by the time of the famine, but, as we have noted, the famine accelerated that trend from a creep to a gallop, shifting the whole center of the migration farther south and west. It was not just where the Irish immigrants came from in Ireland, however, but where they went to overseas that marked the famine as a watershed event. Before the famine, Irish immigration to England and Canada rivaled the exodus to America, but as noted earlier, Canada virtually dropped out shortly after the famine and the movement to Britain would also slow significantly by the 1860s. Though the flight to Australia began in this era, it was never more than a small stream compared to the American flood.

Yet it was not its origins or its destinations that made the famine migration so distinctive or decisive. It was the numbers. It was the torrent of Irish that seemed to make a difference. As Doyle so rightly points out, New York and Philadelphia already had large Irish communities by the late 1830s and early 1840s, and the tensions building between religious groups in those cities had already heightened and divided Catholics and Protestants. Indeed, Philadelphia exploded in interreligious warfare in the riot of 1844, a little over a year before the blight settled on Irish fields. Yet in smaller cities like Worcester, Lowell, and Buffalo, these tensions were just emerging before the famine and there was some sense that it was not too late to ease them. Even in Philadelphia, Dale Light suggests that middle-class Catholics were horrified at the violence of the 1844 riot, blamed their poorer coreligionists for it, and hurried to accommodate their Protestant neighbors. After the famine, in small cities and large, Irish communities were simply too big to permit a retreat to the ambiguous possibilities of these earlier years. Without the famine, the ethnic balances of power would have been altered, not only because there would be fewer Irish, but perhaps also because there might have been more Germans, Chinese, or others who would be sucked in by America's voracious appetite for labor to meet the needs that the smaller numbers of Irish could not.

Yet it may not have been their effect at the time but rather the legacy of memories that the famine Irish left that might have had the greatest influence on the future of Irish America. As Andy Bielenberg, Donald Akenson, and David Fitzpatrick note, the memory of the famine never seemed to linger much in other parts of the diaspora like Britain or Australia. It was in the United States that John Mitchel's and Jeremiah O'Donovan Rossa's bitter fulminations accusing Britain of extermination seemed to take hold, and there more than any other site of Irish migration it fueled the angry bitterness of physical force nationalism. The famine migration grew into a memory of oppression that the Irish in America would neither forget nor let their enemies forget. It also created a people too huge and too distinct to hide their potential power or for others to ignore.

NOTES

1. Tyler Anbinder, *Five Points: The Nineteenth Century New York City Neighborhood That Invented Tap Dance, Stole Elections, and Became the World's Most Notorious Slum* (New York: The Free Press, 2001), 62.

2. Timothy Guinnane, *The Vanishing Irish: Households, Migration, and the Rural Economy in Ireland, 1850–1914* (Princeton, N.J.: Princeton University Press, 1992), 85.

3. Cormac O'Grada, *Black 47 and Beyond: The Great Irish Famine in History, Economy, and Memory* (Princeton, N.J.: Princeton University Press, 1999) 17.

4. Ibid., 25.

5. Cormac O'Grada, *Ireland: A New Economic History, 1780–1939* (Oxford: Clarendon Press, 1994), 86.

6. Ibid., 10.

7. James Donnelly, *The Great Irish Potato Famine* (Phoenix Mill, England: Sutton Publishing, 2001), 218.

8. James Donnelly, "The Construction of the Memory of the Famine in Ireland and the Irish Diaspora, 1850–1900," *Eire/Ireland* 31, no. 1–2 (Spring 1996): 32.

9. O'Grada, *Black 47*, 66.

10. Donnelly, *Great Irish Potato Famine*, 90–91.

11. O'Grada, *Black 47*, 83.

12. Christine Kinealy, "Potatoes, Providence, and Philanthropy: The Role of Private Charity During the Irish Famine," in *The Meaning of the Famine*, ed. Patrick O'Sullivan (London: Leicester University Press, 1997), 166.

13. O'Grada, *Black 47*, 133.

14. Ibid., 130.

15. Kerby Miller, *Emigrants and Exiles: Ireland and the Irish Exodus to North America* (New York: Oxford University Press, 1985), 293.

16. David Fitzpatrick, "Emigration, 1801–1870," in *A New History of Ireland*, vol. 5, *Ireland Under the Union*, ed. W. E. Vaughn (Oxford: Clarendon Press, 1989), 571.

17. Robert James Scally, *The End of Hidden Ireland: Rebellion, Famine, and Emigration* (New York: Oxford University Press, 1995), 195.

18. Graham Hodges, "'Desirable Companions and Lovers': Irish and African Americans in the Sixth Ward, 1830–1870," in *The New York Irish*, eds. Ronald H. Bayor and Timothy Meagher (Baltimore: Johns Hopkins University Press, 1996), 113.

19. Report of the Committee on Internal Health, quoted in Oscar Handlin, *Boston's Immigrants: A Study in Acculturation* (New York: Athenaeum, 1972), 113.

20. Ferrie, *Yankeys Now: Immigrants in the Ante Bellum United States, 1840–1860* (New York: Oxford University Press, 1999), 79.

21. David Fitzpatrick, "'A Peculiar Tramping People': The Irish in Britain, 1801–1870," in *A New History of Ireland*, vol. 5, *Ireland Under the Union*, ed. W. E. Vaughn (Oxford: Clarendon Press, 1989), 641.

22. David Doyle, "The Irish in North America, 1776–1845," in *A New History of Ireland*, vol. 5, *Ireland Under the Union*, ed. W. E. Vaughn (Oxford: Clarendon Press, 1989), 723.

CHAPTER FOUR

The Turn of the Twentieth Century

If the famine was one the great watersheds in Irish American history, the half-century straddling the turn of the century was another. Immigration from Ireland had dwindled to a small river in the mid-1870s, but in the last few years of that decade and the first few of the next one, people had once again begun fleeing Ireland by the tens of thousands. This migration was different from the old one in important respects: a higher proportion of the immigrants were women, and larger numbers were from the West: the province of Connaught and the counties of Kerry or Donegal. Yet it was not the new migration that made the turn-of-the-century era such a decisive period. It was the maturing of vast numbers of a whole new generation of Irish Americans, a people born in America. There had always been children of Irish immigrants in America, second-generation Irish, because there had almost always been Irish immigrants in America. Yet it is appropriate nonetheless to talk of the emergence of the second generation at the turn of the twentieth century, for these were the children of the vast famine migration, a huge and resounding echo of the explosion of Irish immigrants on to the American landscape in the famine years. During the turn-of-the-century era, the number of foreign-born Irish would finally stop growing. The American-born Irish would exceed them first in the Irish American general population by the 1870s and 1880s, and then among Irish American adults by the 1890s and 1900s. Irish America was now dominated by people literally Irish American.

Yet what would this mean for Irish communities in America? This would be harder to determine, for the new generation's cultural perspectives were complex. Born in the United States, most were proud of their American patrimony, embraced American popular culture, and moved up and out of their parent's occupations and neighborhoods. Yet it would be a mistake to describe the lives they tried to create as rebellions against their parents or an embrace of assimilation into an American mainstream. Many were devoted Catholics who, oddly, acted even more like their cousins in Ireland than their immigrant parents when they made decisions about when to marry and bear children. Even had their culture been simply defined, they were buffeted by events and trends—depressions, wars, labor upheavals, religious tangles, and the rise and fall of nationalist movements—that shaped their adjustments, scrambling simple paths to assimilation into much more complicated adjustments. Nearly a century ago, William Shannon caught the contingencies and confusion caused by the emergence of this generation when he described the turn of the century as an age of identity crisis for the Irish community. The Irish at the turn of the century, he argued, had entered an "ambiguous, indeterminate state." They "found themselves with a foot in both worlds … the desire to join the ins conflicted with the desire to lead the outs," and as they "reached towards a new definition of themselves within an American context … they were, in effect, asking themselves, who am I?"[1]

Out of the wreckage of the famine, Ireland's agriculture began to stabilize and even recover as early as the mid-1850s. By the next decade, the country's farmers even seemed to be enjoying a modicum of prosperity. Transportation improvements integrated more and more of the country into broader markets and the export value of Irish wool, dairy, and meat products rose steadily. These trends, combined with the famine's destruction of an entire underclass of small landholders, hastened the consolidation of farms into larger units and the conversion of agriculture from tillage to pasturage, from the labor-intensive cultivation of wheat, barley, oats, and other grains or cereals to the relatively labor-free raising of cattle, dairy cows, and sheep. Landscapes once clotted with peasant hovels and *clachans*, clusters of houses, were now cleared and would remain open fields into the twentieth century. In most places the famine probably abetted changes already underway, by eliminating the peasant resistance and landlord indifference that had hindered them. Such trends and the prosperity for most survivors that followed them were not happening everywhere after the famine, however. Many parts of the west remained desperately poor, locked into a version of the small-farmer pre-famine economy, with heavy dependence on potatoes for food and tillage crops to pay the rent, until late in the nineteenth century. Change would eventually come, but much more slowly and never as completely as in the east.

By the middle and late 1870s, however, even the modest and bitterly earned prosperity of the post-famine era was in jeopardy. Prices for Irish agricultural products began to decline in that decade as Britain's economy slumped into its "Long Depression." Then at the end of the 1870s, bad weather blasted the west of Ireland, wilting the crops there. To some it seemed like 1845 all over again, and many worried about a new famine. Thousands fled. Emigration numbers rose from 14,569 in 1877 to 81,486 in 1883. Others stayed and fought, joining the Land League founded in Mayo in 1879 and battling for land system reforms that might give them a chance to survive at home. Yet, as Donald Jordan notes, when the League failed to deliver, or even to seek modest redistribution of land from big farmers to small ones, many tenants on small farms in western counties like Mayo gave up the Land League fight and joined the exodus to America.

The fluctuations in Irish migration—the decline and resurgence through the 1870s, for example—should not obscure the fact that amid these ups and downs, migration had become an established part of Irish life by the late nineteenth century. It was not the specific causes of shifting prices or bad harvests that were important, but chronic structural weaknesses in the Irish economy that spread to most parts of the island after the famine that made migration not an occasional outlet but a continuous necessity. Before the famine, farmers in the east and "strong" farmers (renting thirty acres or more) almost everywhere passed their farms on intact to a single heir to preserve their holdings' economic viability. In the consolidation of farms after the famine and the shift to pasturage, this practice of impartible inheritance became more broadly pervasive. In this system, only one son could inherit a farm and only one daughter receive a dowry so she could marry the heir of another farm. Irish sons who did not inherit or Irish daughters who did not marry the heirs to other farms had only cruel choices: they could stay home and probably never marry, becoming perpetual laborers and bachelors or old maids, or they could migrate. But if they chose to leave, they could not stay in Ireland. They had to go overseas, because southern Ireland, unlike virtually all of western Europe and the United States, continued to deindustrialize over the latter half of the nineteenth century. Only eastern Ulster in the north of Ireland prospered, but Belfast's Protestant workers jealously guarded their monopoly over the region's best manufacturing jobs there. And so southern Irish Catholics left Ireland.

Ireland's troubles thus forced its poor people to become, in Richard White's terms, "cosmopolitan peasants" playing "musical chairs" with America, for it was there they looked to emigrate.[2] Between 1876 and 1920, 84 percent of Ireland's emigrants went to the United States. Irish migration to Canada fell away to tiny numbers by the end of the nineteenth century. When the flow into Canada began to rise again in the early twentieth century, it was made up largely of Ulster Protestants. Britain's attraction proved more enduring, but Irish migration fell off even to there. Irish migration to Australia remained heavier for longer but never rivaled the American totals. Over the period from 1881 to 1920, 90,000 Irish went to Australia. By contrast, about two million Irish immigrants poured into the United States between 1871 and 1920. The number of Irish born in America would thus continue to climb long after the famine, not peaking until 1890. Such numbers belie the myth common among Irish Americans themselves today that they are not only largely but exclusively a famine people.

Why America? In large part it was because of the American economy. Though growing through a roller coaster ride of booms and busts, the American economy was, nonetheless, rapidly becoming the industrial colossus of the world. In America, the value of manufacturing rose from one billion in 1850 to nine billion in 1890 and twenty billion in 1909. The number of farms also grew from one and a half million to four and a half million over the latter half of the nineteenth century. Great Britain's economy, meanwhile, stalled after the 1870s, and its dominions, Canada and Australia, could not come close to matching the economic development in the United States.

In part it also appears that America was the destination of choice because of the large base established there by the famine migrants and their immediate predecessors. Immigrant chains and networks rooted there during the famine flood now continued to bring migrants to the United States through the end of the nineteenth century. Irish immigrants in the United States sent an estimated $260 million home to the old country; 40 percent of that sum was for prepaid tickets for relatives or friends. In Worcester, a local agent of the shipping lines sold sixty tickets on White Star Lines and sent them overseas between December 4 and December 31, 1884; forty-three of the tickets were sold to people with same last name as the prospective passenger.

The clustering of immigrants from specific counties or parts of counties in certain cities or even city neighborhoods also suggests the importance of such chains or networks. In Massachusetts, for example, Worcester and Springfield attracted large numbers of immigrants from west Kerry: Worcester from Killarney and Castlemaine (in 1901, no less than five of Worcester's twenty-one Irish-born policemen were from Killarney) and in Springfield, a host of Irish speakers from the Dingle peninsula and the Blasket Islands. In the Boston area, Galway men and women predominated among the parishioners of Our Lady Help of Christians Church in Newton on the Boston border in the 1880s, and Roscommon immigrants clustered on Mission Hill in the city itself. Immigrants from all counties settled in New York City, but there were discernible differences among immigrants from various counties in their choices between Manhattan and Brooklyn, for example. As John Ridge's data reveals, Donegal and Cavan migrants were more likely to prefer Brooklyn than Galway or Kerry men and women in the early 1880s. Such clustering was not just common on the East Coast. Migrants from the West Donegal island of Aranmore made Beaver Island in Lake Michigan their special destination over the second half of the nineteenth century, and out in the Rocky Mountains, immigrants from the Bere peninsula in Cork made up the core of the Irish population in the new city of Butte, Montana, in the 1880s.

If the destination was still America, there were changes in how Irish immigrants traveled there. In the 1850s, steamships began carrying immigrants to America. By 1863, 45 percent of the Irish came to America on steamships; by 1866, over 80 percent did. Steamships were hardly luxurious for the poorest of their passengers, but the journey was far more comfortable and safer on them than on the old sailing ships. That was because most steamships provided kitchen galleries and sleeping berths. Government regulations, combined with the concentration of the shipping trade into a few well-capitalized steamship lines like Cunard and White Star, contributed to such improvements. Perhaps most importantly to Irish immigrants, steamships made the trip faster than it had ever been. In the 1860s and 1870s, the 2,500- to 5,000-ton steamships had cut to two weeks the crossing time from the sailing ship's six or seven weeks. By the beginning of the twentieth century, the much larger 15,000- to 20,000- or even 30,000-ton ships made the crossing in nine or ten days. Better accommodations and a quicker trip did not mean higher prices, however. By 1894, Kerby Miller reports, Irish immigrants could purchase tickets to America for as little as $8.75. Moreover, after 1870 most no longer had to travel to Liverpool to pick up a ship to America. By then the steamship companies, vying for the immigrant trade, had begun to put in regularly at Irish ports, most notably Queenstown (renamed Cobh after the Irish Free State was established in 1921) in County Cork and Moville near Derry in the north of Ireland. Immigrants, especially immigrants from the west, thus found it far easier to make their way to America.

It was so easy, in fact, that a bit of folklore developed in West Kerry. It was a story about Sean Palmer from Rineen Ban who had a craving for tobacco. One night he was lured aboard a magical boat with the promise of a pipe's smoke and the boat took him to New York in an evening. While there he met his childhood sweetheart, best friend, and a brother who had already emigrated before he was whisked home as fast as he had come.

As pervasive and routine as migration had become in the latter half of the nineteenth century, the character of the flow and the people who made it up changed very significantly. By the 1880s and 1890s, as economic change finally spread through the west of Ireland, for example, the Irish migration was increasingly composed of men and women from the province of Connaught, County Donegal in western Ulster, and Counties Clare and Kerry in western Munster. The numbers from Connaught nearly doubled from 86,000 in the 1870s to 161,000 in the 1880s. Clare migrants also rose from about 19,000 to 32,000, and Kerry migrants from about 27,000 to over 50,000 in that period. Meanwhile, the number of migrants leaving the eastern province of Leinster and counties like Cork increased only incrementally. The shift was evident at the other end of the journey as well. Of the Irish immigrants arriving in the port of New York in the early summer of 1882, nearly 40 percent were from the five counties of the province of Connaught and the western counties of Kerry in Munster and Donegal in Ulster. Yet Connaught, Kerry, and Donegal together made up only about 25 percent of Ireland's total population in the previous year.

The Irish migration of the late nineteenth and early twentieth centuries not only included more people from the west, it also included more women. There had been a large number of young single women among Irish immigrants as early as the 1850s, but in the 1880s the number of single women actually drew even or began to surpass the number of men among Irish immigrants. Janet Nolan notes that "between 1885 and 1920, females outnumbered males among the 1.4 million people leaving Ireland by almost twenty thousand."[3] Nolan argues that the rising number of women immigrants followed from changes in Irish agriculture and the decline of Irish industries. Before the famine, in areas where families raised wheat and grains to pay the rent, Irish women played critical roles in household economies that needed everyone's labor to raise crops. In those years, too, women also brought in extra money by spinning or weaving, particularly in the counties of northern Connaught and southern Ulster. Yet famine evictions and post-famine market changes routed the old tillage economy in most places, replacing it with cattle and sheep raising. Meanwhile, English and north Ulster industrialization destroyed the cottage industries. The new cattle and sheep farms did not need women's labor as much as old wheat or cereal farms did, and with the virtual disappearance of cottage industries of weaving or spinning, women's roles shrunk to mere domestic duties by the late nineteenth century. For daughters as well as sons the new farm economy also limited opportunities for marriage. If only one son could inherit the farm and be sure of supporting a family, in most families only one daughter could be assured of a dowry sufficient to entice such a man. The other daughters, like the other sons, had to make do elsewhere.

There were broader, more general changes that seemed to distinguish the new immigrants from the old. The United Kingdom, for example, had established a national school system in Ireland in 1831, and in the years following the famine it spread rapidly across the country. By the end of the nineteenth century Ireland had one of the highest literacy rates in the world. In the wreckage of the famine, Catholicism had changed too. A "Devotional Revolution," emerging in parts of the country as far back as the eighteenth century, swept the nation after the famine, entirely transforming Catholic religious practice. Mass attendance and ritual observance among the laity shot up and clerical vocations grew exponentially. The Irish peasant of the late nineteenth century, Lawrence McCaffrey argues, seemed less feckless and more disciplined than ever before.

And yet the new education and religious discipline immigrants gained in Ireland did not seem to help Irish immigrants much in America. Most still began and ended their occupational careers in America at or near the bottom of the economic hierarchy. In 1900 about 23 percent of Irish immigrant males in America still found no jobs better than as day laborers. Only 1.9 percent were professionals and 2.9 percent were merchants. By contrast, only about 10 percent of the foreign-born Germans that year were laborers, 2.4 percent were professionals, and 5.2 percent were merchants. Irish immigrant women did little better. A full 54 percent of working Irish immigrant women were domestic servants in 1900, and they were overrepresented in occupations like laundresses and underrepresented in positions like clerks. There were some signs of success. Irish-born men were overrepresented in some skilled artisan positions like masons and other building trades. Moreover, as before, there was a distinct variation in success from region to region and even from city to city. New England remained the most difficult place for Irish immigrants to make any upward progress and California the easiest.

Largely working class, the new immigrant Irish, like the old ones, had limited resources to spend on housing. Yet only a small proportion of them would remain in the old Irish neighborhoods in urban downtowns like the North End in Boston or the Five Points in New York. In part this was because new immigrant groups overran Irish settlements in those old neighborhoods: the Italians in Boston's North End or the Italians, Jews, and Chinese on New York's Lower East Side. In part, this was also because transportation improvements began stretching cities out, opening up new neighborhoods. So Irish immigrants in New York moved north through the city's West Side to Hell's

Kitchen in midtown Manhattan by the turn of the century; in Boston they moved into Charlestown or South Boston; and in Chicago into Bridgeport. By the second or third decade of the twentieth century, transportation improvements and building booms in New York City, Marion Casey has pointed out, opened up new residential opportunities in the city's outer boroughs, the Bronx and Queens, even for Irish immigrants who had made little progress up New York's occupational ladder.

Irish immigrants at the turn of the century might move into mixed neighborhoods or even set up households in tenements with a German family above or a British immigrant below, but chances were still very good that their household would remain entirely Irish. As late as 1910, the odds for an Irish-born man to marry an Irish American woman was nearly four to one, and the odds that a boarder in his household would be Irish American were about three to one. Gender imbalances tilting heavily toward men in the West and less heavily toward women in the East and the more general ease of Irish relations with their white neighbors in the West complicate these figures. Women were more likely to marry outside the group in the East, and Irish-born immigrant men would marry outside the group in the West. Yet in most places where Irish immigrant women could find Irish men, or vice versa, they chose each other above all others.

Despite the steady stream of new immigrants pouring into America from Ireland over the course of the turn of the century, it was not they who would play the critical role in the casting or better the recasting of Irish America for the twentieth century. As noted earlier, there had always been second-generation Irish in Irish America. Yet the children of the great eighteenth-century Irish migrations largely dissolved into a broader American mainstream. If they carried the cultural traditions of their ancestors as some historians suggest, they helped secure them as foundational cultures for the southern and western regions where they settled. Those cultural values and practices—if these historians are correct—became American values and practices in those areas, and the children of those early American Irish immigrants lost any memory of their Irish origins. Even Andrew Jackson, rumored to have been born on a ship while en route from Ireland to America with his parents, made little of his Irish past and hardly worried whether his Irish culture and identity would have an American future.

The children of the Catholic migrations of the 1840s and 1850s would be different than the offspring of immigrants to the colonies or the early republic. They would hardly mimic their parents, but neither would they blend into an

American mainstream and disappear as the earlier second-generation Irish had. Instead, they would take over the Irish America that they had inherited from their famine immigrant parents and transform it.

Some historians have seen this second generation emerging as early as the first few years after the Civil War. In 1880, when the U.S. Census first began reporting figures on the children of immigrants, the second-generation Irish already outnumbered the first by to 3.2 million to 1.8 million. Yet certainly in the 1860s and even as late as the 1880s, the bulk of the American-born Irish were still young. In Worcester, scarcely 3,700 of the 12,000 second-generation Irish were over the age of eighteen in 1880, and they were outnumbered by immigrant adults by almost three to one. It would not be until the 1890s or even early 1900s that the children of the famine immigrants would begin to reach maturity in large enough numbers to dominate Worcester's and the country's Irish population. By 1900, the U.S. Census reported that second-generation Irish males in the nation's work force (ages fifteen and over) outnumbered immigrant Irish males by 1,009,000 to 714,000; for women, the proportion over age fourteen and in the workforce was 388,000 second-generation to 245,000 immigrants. For the first time in the history of the Irish in America, the American-born defined Irish America's identity, determined its boundaries, shaped its culture, and defended or advanced its interests. The steady influx from Ireland's seemingly inexhaustible reserves of young men and women would still be important to the evolution of Irish American history at the turn of the century, but it would be the second-generation Irish, the American-born children of the famine Irish immigrants, who would take over Irish American communities and begin to remake them according to their own values, customs, and aspirations.

This new generation was very different than their parents. In the 1890s, the term "lace curtain Irish" was invented, along with other less popular adjectives like "cut glass Irish," to describe the new phenomenon of an emerging Irish middle class. The term was a bit presumptuous or premature. Second-generation Irish males would still be underrepresented among lawyers, agents, brokers, and bankers in 1900, but they were overrepresented among such solid if less glamorous white-collar positions including bookkeepers, clerks, and salesmen. Moreover, few of the second-generation Irish were mired like their fathers had been in the bottom ranks of the American economic hierarchy as laborers. The most impressive gains the second-generation made, besides the purchase many had found in the lower ranks of the middle class, were in skilled blue-collar jobs as painters, printers, machinists, and other trades. Second-generation Irish women did as well as—maybe even better than—their brothers. Most impressive was the number of American-born Irish women who became teachers. In 1900, there were over 31,000 of them throughout the nation, consisting of about 8.1 percent of all second-generation Irish women in the work force, and that percentage exceeded the proportions of both second-generation German and British women who were teachers. By 1910, in cities as diverse as Lowell, Buffalo, and Scranton, second-generation Irish women made up over one-quarter of all public school teachers. In Worcester, they were a near majority: 49 percent of all the city's public schoolteachers.

Members of the new generation not only moved up but out—out of their parents' older city neighborhoods into new residential districts emerging in the farther reaches of cities or even across city borders into suburban towns. As noted, transportation improvements in the late nineteenth century, particularly the electrification of street car lines in the late 1880s and early 1890s, broke down the old limits of the densely packed and jumbled-up walking cities and spread city settlements all over the landscape. In New York, the trains pushed up the island of Manhattan and jumped to Bronx and Queens; in Chicago, the city swallowed up a whole swath of once sleepy farmlands on the South Side; and in Boston, trolleys rolled relentlessly farther to the southeast, tying once proudly independent towns like Dorchester and West Roxbury into the expanding city. Again, as noted earlier, such changes helped pull the Irish immigrants and second-generation Irish alike out of their old downtown neighborhoods, but while Irish immigrants moved, the second generation, it appears, moved out farther and faster than the Irish immigrants. As early as 1890, for example, the second-generation Irish outnumbered the immigrants in mid- and uptown areas of New York City, while the Irish-born continued to outnumber them in the oldest neighborhoods farther south below Fourteenth Street. In Boston, while immigrant movement seemed to stall not far from the central city in neighborhoods like South Boston and Charlestown, many members of the second generation were already riding the trolleys farther south into Dorchester or even West Roxbury. In Chicago, the Catholic Archdiocese created forty-three new English speaking (and usually Irish-dominated) parishes between 1880 and 1902. Although these churches were scattered to all points of the city, most of the second-generation Irish seemed to settle in the South Side. There, for example, the Archdiocese founded St. Bernard's in Englewood—eight miles south of the Loop—in 1887. St. Bernard's filled up quickly with upwardly mobile, apparently largely second-generation Irish and by 1895, the pastor, Rev. Bernard Murray, could boast more than 600 families in his parish.

Moving up and moving out, the new generation revealed a new openness to the world around them even in the most personal of decisions, such as whom to marry. Intermarriage rates for the second-generation Irish were consistently much higher than for the immigrants, though they too varied from city to city. A nationwide sample of the 1910 census suggests that the odds were no better than even that the second-generation Irish would find spouses from among members of their own ethnic group.

Perhaps more than anything else it was the new generation's enthusiastic participation in American popular culture that seemed to distinguish them so clearly from their famine Irish parents and suggest their openness to the possibilities of their new country. "There were sixty or seventy years" at the turn of the century, as Daniel Patrick Moynihan has said, "when the Irish were everywhere."[4] Moynihan was talking about New York, but he might as well have been speaking about the entire nation. From "King" Kelly, the flamboyant and self-destructive hero of Chicago's White Stockings and Boston's Beaneaters in the 1880s, to John McGraw, the hard-bitten, tactical genius of the original Baltimore Orioles in the 1890s and the New York Giants in the 1920s, the Irish certainly seemed prominent wherever baseball was played. They included owners, Charles Comiskey of the Chicago White Sox; owner-managers, Connie Mack of the Philadelphia Athletics; and managers such as Bill Carrigan of the Red Sox; as well as scores of players and hundreds of thousands of fans. When a novelist created a fictional "everyman" baseball fan in 1909, he called him Mickey O'Hooligan, and when a young school-teacher from Worcester came to write the poem that became baseball's lyric signature, he named the batter Casey, not Smith or Brown or Saltonstall or even Wagner or La Joie. If anything, the Irish seemed even more dominant in the newly popular sport of professional boxing. Second-generation Irish heavyweight John L. Sullivan, the "Boston Strongboy," embodied Irishness for the entire country in the 1880s: tough, loud, alternately sentimental and mean, and addicted to drink. He reigned until another second-generation Irishman, Jim Corbett, "Gentleman Jim" from San Francisco, took his title away from him. On stage, American-born Irish **Edward "Ned" Harrigan and Tony Hart** created a series of musical farces, the Mulligan Guards plays, that were enormously popular in New York, and songs from their plays were sung throughout the country. Maggie Cline, "Pat" Rooney, and ultimately George M. Cohan, all American-born, carried on this stage tradition until the birth of the movies. Whenever Americans paid to watch people play, dance, or sing, often as not they seemed to pay to see second-generation Irish men or women perform.

The Irish were everywhere on stages and playing fields at the turn of the century, but it was not just their special talents or pluck that such prominence reflected, but the depth of their passion for American popular culture. Behind every King Kelly or John McGraw there were thousands of American-born Irish playing on local teams, and there were so many Irish boxers that members of other groups took up Irish names when they entered the sport—almost as a rite of passage in order to be taken seriously. Similarly behind the vaude-ville headliners, too, there were small-time or bit professional players or young men and women putting on plays or revues like "The College Freshmen" or "The Man from Broadway" for parish benefits or Knights of Columbus or Catholic Knights' socials.

By the 1920s, indeed, even by the early 1900s, the economic progress of the second-generation Irish, their dispersal throughout the cities and towns they lived in, their propensity to marry outside the group, and their avid par-ticipation in American popular culture seemed evidence of an easy assimi-lation into American society and culture. The popular stage reflected these changes. The peasant Paddy, even Boucicault's heroic Conn, was now disap-pearing from the theater, replaced by Harrigan and Hart's denizens of New York's Lower East Side, who celebrated their American savvy in songs like "We All Fellows Bran' New." And after all, who could have been more American than Casey at the bat, or the second-generation Irish vaudevillian George M. Cohan, the Yankee Doodle Dandy born on the Fourth of July?

And yet to conclude that Irish Catholics had been neatly assumed, merged, and assimilated into American society would be hasty, glossing over what was in fact a much more complicated adaptation for them and their communi-ties. If they moved up the economic ladder, for example, the move up in most places was often tough sledding and still left them behind native-stock Yankees and the second generations of more favored English and Scottish immigrants. Moreover, opportunities at the very top of the American social and economic hierarchy may have become more restricted, not less, by the turn of the century. The new elite of America's second industrial revolution of the 1890s and early 1900s began to harden into a caste, a "Protestant Estab-lishment." This establishment justified its boundaries with a new racist social Darwinism that deemed the Irish, if not as outright inferiors like the Italians or Jews (not to mention the Chinese or African Americans), then still as suspect and as outsiders. This new white Anglo Protestant elite also defended its bor-ders jealously with a bulwark of new or transformed institutions like prepara-tory schools and men's clubs that decided who would be in and would be kept out. Irish Catholics might cross these boundaries more easily into elite circles in San Francisco, but never in Boston, rarely in New York or Philadelphia, and occasionally and, perhaps, only uneasily in Chicago.

Similarly, second-generation residential dispersal did not mean that the ties of the Irish Catholic community had frayed for them or that they had achieved easy integration into welcoming American communities. Ellen Skerret suggests that the movement of the Irish south through Chicago was less a quiet dispersal than a deliberate and conscious invasion. Protestant-Catholic conflict shaped parish creation in this movement, as Irish Catholics built new churches and forged new communities in deliberate defiance of suspicious Protestants. Skerret points out that when Fr. Murray dedicated St. Bernard's in Englewood in the 1880s, he "scheduled the cornerstone laying for the same day—at the same hour that Presbyterians were to do the same for their new church just a stone's throw away." Five thousand Catholics from parishes all over the South Side, including the Clan na Gael Guards, paraded to the church through the streets of Englewood. Skerret concludes: "However American the Irish in these outlying areas considered themselves to be, their religion and ethnic heritage continued to set them apart from native-born Protestants."[5]

Even second-generation intermarriage rates perhaps warrant a second look. Rates varied significantly not just from east to west, but according to the size and intensity of communal loyalties in local communities. Thus in Worcester, over 70 percent of the second-generation Irish married among their own in 1900. In Lowell, it was about the same for men and a little lower for women in 1880. New England's Irish have been notorious for their insularity, but in this regard they may not have been a special case. In New York City, a study of ethnic intermarriage for the years between 1908 and 1912 found that 70 percent of second-generation Irish men and 62 percent of the women married within the group. Up in Buffalo, the proportions remained similar even into 1920. Out west in the most Irish city in America, Butte, percentages in 1900 and 1910 were much like Worcester's, and a substantial proportion of second-generation Irish married fellow Irish in San Francisco in 1880. Thus even in the West the Irish American ethnic base was slow to erode, at least in places where Irish populations were large enough to provide an Irish American marriage market offering some choices. Moreover, it seems likely, as Robert McCaa has argued, that many of the second-generation Irish throughout the country marrying native-stock Americans, particularly those in cities with large Irish populations, were marrying members of the still small but growing number of third-generation Irish, not counted as Irish by the census or marriage registers.

Not just who but when the second-generation Irish married also offers reason to pause before reaching hasty judgments about assimilation. That reason
is the strikingly late age when second-generation Irish men and women married, and the equally striking large proportion who never married. Second-
generation Irish men and women married later than their parents, later than
their Irish immigrant contemporaries, later than even almost all other ethnics
and native-stock Americans, and almost as late as the Irish in Ireland. Scattered evidence suggests that second-generation Irish men married, on average,
in their early thirties; women married in their late twenties. The causes of this
second generation's late marriage are a complex mix, but among them was
the persistence and flourishing of their Catholicism: an institutional loyalty
and subculture of distinct values and customs that marked the Irish off and
separated them from an American mainstream. As we shall see, there is good
reason to believe that the American-born Irish did not simply carry on their
parent's Catholic traditions but, in fact, were far better Catholics than their
immigrant forebears, if "better" means better disciplined to its institutional
structures and more observant of its rituals and obligations.

Finally, even the second generation's avid enthusiasm for American popular culture cannot be taken as assimilation. If by that term what is meant is giving up one's own culture and taking up another, then it is not at all clear that is
what the second-generation Irish were doing at the turn of the century. American culture has not been static over the nearly four-hundred-year history of the
North American colonies and nation. Rather than absorbing another people's
American popular culture at the turn of the century, the second-generation
Irish were working along with many others, ethnics and natives alike, to forge
the new urban-based popular culture of baseball, professional boxing, summer vacations, vaudeville, and popular melodrama. John L. Sullivan, John
McGraw, Maggie Cline, and Harrigan and Hart were not learning American
popular culture—they were making it.

Indeed, Irish Americans not only helped make American popular culture,
but made American culture over in their own image. In newspapers around
the country, Americans delighted in seeing events through the eyes of "Mr.
Dooley," **Finley Peter Dunne**'s fictional bartender. On stage, Harrigan and
Hart's young men may have boasted of being "bran' new" and of their urban
American savvy, but they were different than other Americans and representative of a distinct people, Irish Americans. Indeed, as William Williams suggests, Harrigan and Hart and other Irish playwrights and songwriters in the
turn-of-the-century era, continued the trend begun by Boucicault in reversing
but not replacing the old Irish stereotypes: making drinking a sign of good fellowship, violence evidence of manly "heart," and lack of ambition a reflection

of communal loyalty. Thus, for example, Harrigan and Hart's characters sang of the "Bucket of Beer" as a rough, male sacrament of sharing and friendship. The image of Irish Americans on stage and in song was certainly American, but just as certainly, distinctly Irish American.

Changes in Irish American life at the turn of the century cannot be understood only by looking at trends in individual behavior in everyday life like earning a living, marrying, finding a home, or even choosing leisure diversions. The transformation of Irish American life during that period occurred not only at the personal level, but also at the community level, where Irish Americans struggled to hammer out new understandings of group identity. The maturing of the second generation with their own, new cultural perspectives was crucial in this process, but immigrants, too, had a voice in those community debates. More important, this struggle was not played out in a vacuum. It was shaped by the trends, events, and movements of the environment that they lived in: the economy's boom and bust, the influx of millions of new immigrants from many nations, the confusion of political alignments here in America, nationalism's rise and fall in the homeland, and even the Vatican's struggles to adjust an ancient church to a modern world.

In the 1880s, combinations of these circumstances and the gradual emergence of the new generation seemed to offer the American Irish a variety of potential courses of evolution: those choices stretched from class-conscious labor radicalism to an embrace of American culture led by a liberal Catholic church. Yet in the 1890s, most of those alternatives would close down, and by the 1910s and 1920s, the Irish American community and Irish American understandings of themselves would harden into a single mold.

The emergence of two movements in particular appeared to open a range of new possibilities for Irish Americans in the 1880s. The first was labor resistance to the late nineteenth-century changes in the American economy that produced vast corporations, widespread mechanization, and centralization of management that some have called the "second industrial revolution." This resistance was touched off by the great railroad strike of 1877, spread with waves of thousands of strikes large and small throughout the nation in the 1880s, and finally culminated with the bloody strike at Homestead in Pittsburgh in 1892 and the Pullman strike in Chicago and along the western rail lines in 1894. Much of this strike activity was spontaneous. Workers in a shop, for example, might have grown dissatisfied over hours, wages, or conditions and simply walked off the job. Yet there was an organization at the core of this resistance for at least some of the period—the Knights of Labor, the first mass-based union in American history. At its height in 1886, the Knights could count close to 700,000 members. Irish Americans were heavily involved in this upheaval. Some have estimated that they made up as many as one-third of the strikers in 1877, and an estimated half or more of the Knights at points in its history were Catholics (a majority of them very likely to be Irish Catholic). Both the Grand Master Workman, **Terence Powderly**, his deputy, John Hayes, and many of the Knights leaders, like Leonora Barry, were first- or second-generation Irish Catholics.

Not all the Knights were workers; middle-class reformers and sympathizers were numerous in its ranks. The Knights ideology was also a homegrown, motley mix of ideas largely distilled from American republican traditions. Some historians have judged the Knights naïve and backward looking, spouting mushy, anachronistic ideas about reviving a society of independent artisans and yeoman farmers that perhaps *had never been*, but, in any event, certainly *would never be* again.

Yet if the Knights eschewed class conflict and even politics in principle, the bite of their economic critique and their increasing self-confident aggressiveness by the mid-1880s made a future of class politics seem distinctly possible. As Leon Fink and others have written, in towns and cities across the country as diverse as Rochester, New Hampshire; Richmond, Virginia; New York City, Chicago, and Rutland, Vermont, Knights of Labor–backed workingmen's parties had a powerful influence on local politics by the mid-1880s.

Often, as Fink and Martin Shefter have shown, these parties or labor slates drew their strongest support from second-generation Irish skilled workers frustrated by the obstacles that industrialists and corrupt bosses had put up to their self-improvement. Fink, for example, points to strong second-generation Irish support for public services in Rutland, Vermont, such as the public library, better schools, and adult education, as a reflection of Rutland's second-generation Irish Knights' interest in self-improvement.

In Australia, Irish immigrants and their children were becoming heavily involved in a Labor party that seemed like a national version of the local Knights' slates in America. The Australian Labor party would emerge as a powerful force on that continent by the end of the nineteenth century. Many Irish immigrants and their children would also become supporters of the emerging Labor Party in Great Britain. If it could happen in those countries, could it not happen in the United States?

While growing labor conflict seemed to offer one possibility for how the Irish might define themselves in the new era, a very different opportunity opened up in another important institution in Irish American life, the Catholic Church. This was the emergence among some Catholic bishops and priests of an effort to engage American culture and society, embrace American culture's virtues despite its Protestant roots and, perhaps, even reach some kind of accommodation with contemporary Protestants, who still saw themselves as the nation's special guardians. These priests and bishops have often been called liberal Catholics. Most, like their leaders **Archbishop John Ireland** and Bishop John J. Keane, were born in Ireland and brought to America as children, or like **Cardinal James Gibbons** were born in the United States as the children of Irish immigrants. Men like Ireland and Keane waxed rhapsodic about their love for the United States. They believed that it was destined to become the world's supreme power and to spread its ideals of democracy and individualism around the world. They thought the Church—their Church— should be part of this mission, indeed, should lead it, but could not do so if its people remained sunk in their old country culture and isolated in religious or ethnic ghettoes bulwarked by a defensive array of separate schools and institutions. These liberals thus strongly backed Catholic temperance societies, for example, decrying drunkenness as a peculiar Old World curse of the Irish that needed to be extinguished in the new one. Father James Cleary of the St. Paul Archdiocese claimed the tradition of drinking was Irish and not American, and that "we are not to be ruled by the customs of other lands; the sound judgment of the American of the American public is competent to regulate its own customs in accordance with the best interests of our common country."[6] The Catholic Total Abstinence Union, dubbed a "Hibernian Crusade" by its historian Sister Joan Bland, grew steadily over the course of the late nineteenth century. John Ireland, Keane, Gibbons, and their allies also fought frequent battles with German and French Canadian Americans over the persistence of these other Catholic ethnics in the use of old-country languages. The Irish Catholic liberals sought schemes that would permit Catholics to attend public schools and still receive a religious education as well. More radical still was the second-generation Irish New York priest Edward McGlynn, who not only became the church's strongest advocate for the poor and working classes, but also endorsed a wide range of church reforms, from a vernacular English liturgy to abolition of parochial schools altogether.

In the late 1880s through the early 1890s, the liberals seemed to have the upper hand in the American Church. Their ideas were popular, particularly on the periphery of the concentration of Catholic settlement, in the West or the South, where Catholics were few and forced to mingle, or where cities were new and more fluid and open, or where Irish Catholics confronted powerful German Catholic rivals and needed to assert American loyalties as a weapon to stave off German ethnic challenges. Yet there were also advocates of liberalism in the East, in cities like Worcester, where local political alignments encouraged accommodation between Protestants and Catholics. There were also more general reasons why such a spirit of accommodation seemed so popular in the 1880s. It was, for example, then that memories of the Civil War, even nostalgia for its shared sacrifice, seemed to wax strong, reminding potentially hostile Protestants and Catholics alike of their wartime coopera-tion and common valor. More important, a new pope, Leo XIII, seeking to adjust his church to a changing world of industry and republican politics, seemed to encourage the liberals—at least at first.

Both these trends, labor assertion and Catholic liberal accommodation to American culture, seemed reflected in the revival of Irish American national-ism in the 1880s. This Irish American nationalist resurgence was prompted by the rise of a new nationalist movement in Ireland. A new leader, Charles Stewart Parnell, took over Ireland's Home Rule party in the 1870s and began to make it a more aggressive voice for returning some political autonomy to Ire-land. Meanwhile, the plunging Irish economy in the west of Ireland provoked the emergence of an organization, the **Land League**, dedicated to carry on an agitation for relief from an oppressive land system. In what became known as the "New Departure," John Devoy, head of the **Clan na Gael** in America, Michael Davitt from the Irish Republican Brotherhood, and Parnell worked to bring the disparate elements of the nationalist movement—the physical force revolutionaries, the land agitation, and the Home Rule members of Parlia-ment—together into a single force. Though these men would soon fall out again, the unification of these three elements made Irish and Irish American nationalism enormously powerful in the early 1880s. Land League clubs sprung up all over America—as many as 1,500 branches with 500,000 members. Some of these branches were recruited largely from workingmen, had close affilia-tions with Knights of Labor Assemblies, and reflected the enormous energy of labor's "Great Upheaval." Indeed, some Land League branches were nurseries for such assemblies. These radical nationalists were led by **Patrick Ford**, editor of the Irish World. On the other hand, moderate nationalists led by John Boyle O'Reilly, editor of the Boston **Pilot**; Patrick Collins, a prominent Boston poli-tician; and Father Thomas J. Conaty of Worcester advocated constitutional, parliamentary methods to achieve limited goals of Home Rule for Ireland in an imperial federation. Such nationalism, often dressed up in rhetoric reso-nant with American heroes and ideals and comparing Ireland's struggle to the American Revolution, attracted strong support from native-stock Yankees and easily complemented the aspirations and ideals of liberal Catholicism.

Looking forward from the 1880s, it would have been hard to predict the future identities and conceptions of community for Irish Americans. As vague and even self-contradictory as the Knights of Labor ideology may have been, the possibility of deepening class conflict in America seemed very real in the 1880s, and the possibility then too that the bulk of Irish Americans, still largely working-class, would define themselves principally in class terms through union agitation and labor politics seemed real enough. Indeed, was not that already happening in Australia, where a labor party was forming that would receive Irish backing? On the other hand, especially for more mobile Irish Americans, the time seemed ripe for breaking down old barriers separating them from the American Protestants and gaining some acceptance from their erstwhile antagonists. Perhaps they could even become a simply Catholic-tinged current swirling in an American mainstream. There is some evidence in recent studies of the Irish in Ontario and parts of Australia that something like this process occurred for the second-generation Irish there.

Yet in America, the alternatives of the 1880s began to close down rapidly in the 1890s. The Knights of Labor's power peaked in 1886 and then the union disintegrated, reeling from corporate suppression of strikes, heightened fears of labor radicalism after the Haymarket Tragedy, and its own internal rancor and petty personal squabbles. The American labor movement and the American left would then change drastically in the 1890s. One of the most important trends was the rise of the American Federation of Labor and its conservative business unionism. The AFL, founded as the Federation of Organized Trades in 1881 and renamed the American Federation of Labor in 1886, was already in place during the Knights of Labor's rise, but was overshadowed by the Knights until the early 1890s. The Federation and its craft unions of skilled workers had little interest in changing the capitalist industrial economy that they confronted; they sought merely to manipulate it to their best advantage by controlling labor markets and tough negotiating. The vast majority of AFL leaders had no interest in class politics and a labor party. The other important trend was the emergence of a hard-edged Marxist socialism in the principal left-wing opposition to American industrial capitalism. Older ideologies rooted, as the Knights had been, in working-class republicanism faded in turn. Confronting these changes, most Irish Americans workers opted for the AFL and its conservative unionism. Although there were occasional exceptions, individuals like the fierce labor organizer, **Mary Harris "Mother" Jones**, or communities such as Irish American workers in Haverhill, Massachusetts in the early 1900s and Butte, Montana in the 1910s, Irish Americans were conspicuously absent from the ranks in most of the Socialist Party's strongholds, like New York City. Conversely, the Irish became powers, dominating the new conservative union movement embodied in the AFL. In the first decade of the twentieth century, first- or second-generation Irishmen headed no less than fifty of the AFL's 110 unions.

While labor was transformed in the 1890s, liberal Catholicism was killed in that decade. Almost simultaneously, the Pope in Rome soured on the liberals while the revived nativism of the American Protective Association in America mocked their easy confidence in accommodation with American Protestant culture and society. In 1899, Pope Leo XIII, once the liberal's friend, condemned a vague heresy called Americanism, which many understood as a condemnation of the American Catholic liberals. Subsequent papal attacks on modernism in 1907 seemed to seal the Vatican's prohibitions of the kind of experimentation the liberals had attempted in adjusting Catholicism to modern culture. Suddenly, "liberal" became a dirty, dangerous word for American Catholics. To be a "liberal" meant to be a "toady" or social climber who hid or apologized for his faith to win Protestant acceptance.

The nationalist movement also foundered by the 1890s. By the mid-1880s, Parnell had routed the economic radicals and stifled the physical force nationalists and gained control of the movement both in Ireland and America. Yet by 1889, he too was in trouble. Named as the "other man" in a divorce trial, his powerful Home Rule Party broke into factions and remained broken through the 1890s.

The possibilities of class radicalism however vague, as found in the Knights of Labor, or accommodation, as found in the Catholic liberals, were thus dead in most parts of the country by the 1890s. Irish American ethnic identities and conceptions of their role and place in America were therefore in flux as some of the possibilities of the 1880s faded away. It is difficult to say what replaced them in the 1890s, for there are few studies of Irish American communities after 1890. In Worcester, the community retreated in on itself into a kind of ethnocentric isolation. Interest in Irish culture boomed and physical force Irish nationalism became more popular than ever. In Butte, Irish nationalists like the **Clan Na Gael** also flourished. There Irish Americans raised money for the Boers fighting Britain in South Africa. There was some evidence of an Irish ethnocentric revival generally throughout the nation as well, though it is unclear how much this new ethnocentrism dominated communities elsewhere as much as it did in Worcester or Butte. The **Ancient Order of Hibernians**, for example, grew enormously throughout country in the 1890s and early 1900s. Between 1886 and 1907, the Hibernian membership almost quadrupled. In part, the Hibernian's success reflected their new better relations with the Catholic clergy after long years of clerical suspicion. Yet it must also be read as evidence of the popularity of the Hibernians' ethnic—if religiously orthodox—militancy. As Kerby Miller has noted, after 1897 the Hibernians seemed especially and aggressively ethnocentric, promoting **Gaelic Sports in the United States**, actively encouraging study of the **Irish language in America**, pressuring local schools to teach Irish history, assailing demeaning stereotypes on the stage, and sliding toward physical force nationalism. The national AOH also endorsed the Boers in their struggles with the British in South Africa, and in 1908 concluded an alliance with the German American National Alliance to counter growing sympathy in America for England. As Matthew Jacobsen and David Doyle have pointed out, for some militant Irish American nationalists, identification with colonial struggling Ireland meant more than mere opposition to an alliance between Britain and America—it also meant, more interestingly, opposing American colonialism in the Philippines. As popular as the AOH was through the 1890s and early 1900s, however, it is impossible to say how popular their new militant ethnocentrism was in communities across the country.

If the Hibernians with their militant ethnocentrism did dominate in such cities as Worcester in the 1890s and 1900s, they did not and could not do so for long. Indeed, after the 1900s, the Ancient Order of Hibernians' membership would fall off, first slowly, then drastically in Worcester and across the country. Militant Irish ethnocentrism could not persist for several reasons, but the most obvious, perhaps, was that the era of the immigrant was passing in Irish American history, and Irish America would only be defined in the future by the American-born Irish. Members of the new American-born generations were more respectful of their immigrant parents' homeland and traditions than many scholars would have it. Yet as noted earlier, they were Americans first, fiercely proud of their native country, and the vast majority were thoroughly taken by American popular culture. Any new definition of group identity would have to take that into account.

By the early twentieth century, Irish American definitions of themselves began to harden into a fixed form that would dominate in most Irish American communities. This was a militant American Catholicism. It had several hallmarks. Its first hallmark was an uncompromising, almost jingoistic American patriotism. Irish Americans of diverse backgrounds seemed to agree that these Irish and American identities should somehow become one, or as the vaudevillian Pat Rooney sang: "Patrick's Day will become the Fourth of July." Many Irish Americans pointed to proof of their American patriotism in their increasingly virulent antiradicalism. That did not mean that most Irish Americans became conservative reactionaries. Indeed, in the limited spectrum of American politics, as John Buenker suggested long ago, they might well have qualified

as American urban liberals, an emerging political position they were helping to define. They backed state intervention in the economy, help for labor
unions, and social welfare policies, while they opposed prohibition, Sunday
closing laws, and restrictions on nonpublic schools. Yet as the old working-
class republicanism of the Knights of Labor faded away, and the American left
began to embrace a harder-edged Marxist ideology, Irish American Catholics
attacked it strongly. Indeed, led by Irish American bishops like James McFaul
of Trenton, James Quigley of Chicago, and **Cardinal William O'Connell** of
Boston, and by enlisting labor leaders like Peter Collins of the Boston Central
Union, the Catholic Church launched a vigorous campaign against socialism
in the 1910s.

Perhaps as important in this new definition of themselves, Irish Americans
were also militantly Catholic. There would be no accommodations and no
outreach, however tentative, to Protestants now. The increasing conservatism of the Vatican, the shocks of the APA in the 1890s, the resurgence of an
anti-Catholic Ku Klux Klan in the 1920s, and the hardening of an exclusive
Protestant establishment at least on the East Coast all bolstered Irish Catholic militancy. The new symbol of the Irish American–led church was not
the suave liberal Gibbons or the earnest, forceful Americanist John Ireland
but the imperious and pugnacious conservative, **Cardinal William Henry
O'Connell** of Boston, who worked hard to expand the Catholic infrastructure
in his Archdiocese. Such building of the Catholic institutional network took
place almost all over the country, however: for the period from 1890 to 1920,
the number of parochial schools in the United States rose from 3,194 to 5,852
and the number of students from 633,000 to 1.7 million. A Catholic ghetto had
finally and now irrevocably emerged, a parallel society that matched mainstream or Protestant society women's club for women's club and Boy Scout
troop for Boy Scout troop. This ghetto had been foreshadowed as far back as
Archbishop "Dagger" John Hughes, and many of the elements had long
been in place, but what made it different now was that with liberalism dead
there would be no further flirtation with the Protestant mainstream. What
also made it different were the new Catholic resources of people and money.
It was these numbers and dollars that allowed the Church to elaborate its
ghetto, to fill its holes, and more fully encapsulate its people. But it was also
these numbers and dollars that permitted O'Connell and others to define an
Irish Catholic identity that was not just militant, but triumphant. As Cardinal
O'Connell himself would say: "The Puritan has passed; the Catholic remains.
The city [Boston, O'Connell's see] where a century ago he came unwanted he
has made his own."[7]

Irish Catholic power was not just reflected in the Catholic church. Indeed, it was probably more evident—and even more threatening to Anglo-Saxon Protestants—in politics, where Irish Catholics led by their second generation finally came into their own. Throughout the last two decades of the nineteenth century, Irish Catholics had broken through to the top positions in politics in cities large and small: they had elected a mayor of Chicago in 1893, a mayor of New York in 1880, in Boston in 1884, and also in Worcester in 1901 and in Burlington, Vermont in 1903. In 1894, John Paul Bocock wrote a famous magazine article that worried about "the Irish conquest of our cities." It was not just the elections of Irish Americans to offices but the capture of real power by the Irish in such cities that began to trouble and frighten their enemies. It was at the turn of the century that Irish Catholic–led machines and bosses appeared all across the country. From **Martin Lomasney**, James Michael Curley, and John F. Fitzgerald in Boston to Frank Hague in Jersey City, to "Hinky Dink" Kenna and Johnny Powers in Chicago, and Christopher Buckley and P. H. McCarthy in San Francisco, Irish Americans emerged as the powerful leaders of ward and city machines. In New York, for example, Grace's election was hardly as important as the steady emergence of Irish Catholic power in Tammany Hall, the city's Democratic Party organization, culminating in the selection of "Honest John" Kelly as Grand Sachem in 1871 and ultimately more importantly, in Tammany's rout of its factional enemies and development as a powerful, efficient machine under second-generation Irishman **Charles Francis Murphy** in the early 1900s. In the 1900s and even more so in the 1910s, Irish American Catholics rode a wave of Democratic Party popularity to assert power in state politics as well. Rhode Island elected James Higgins governor in 1906, Illinois elected Edward Dunne in 1913, Massachusetts David I. Walsh in 1913, and New York made **Alfred Emanuel Smith** the state's second Irish Catholic governor in 1918. Irish Catholics, even in the face of gerrymandering and discrimination in apportionment, also achieved a new prominence in state legislatures. By the 1920s, Charlie Murphy would work to get his protégé Smith nominated by the Democratic Party. Though Murphy would not live to see it, Smith would, in fact, eventually become the first Catholic, Irish or otherwise, nominated for president by a major party, in 1928.

Certainly the maturation of the second generation had dramatically enhanced Irish Catholic power in America. It was not just their numbers, nor even the greater resources they could command because of their movement up the occupational ladder, nor even the fact that because they were born in America they were automatically eligible to vote. It was also a savvy about the American world and their ambitions for some recognition and achievement that helped the new generation make Irish Americans far more potent than in the famine era, when the community was dominated by the immigrant generation.

The numbers and financial resources that built the new Catholic ghetto and powered the new Irish-led machine did not come from the Irish alone. Rather, both in the church and politics, they had emerged as leaders of a co-alition of Catholic ethnics: Germans, French Canadians, Italians, Poles, Lith-uanians, and others. For Irish Catholics, their fellow Catholic ethnics would always be both a threat and an opportunity. They were a threat because they competed with Irish Americans for jobs in the lower ranks of the economy and for recognition in American urban and church politics. They were an oppor-tunity because taken together, Catholic ethnics could dominate almost any Northeastern or Midwestern city by the 1910s and 1920s. Irish Catholics under-stood that if they could weld such ethnics together into an effective coalition, as leaders of such a coalition they could rule such cities and states. The need to do so reinforced their need to assert the American and Catholic aspects of their identity—what they had in common with other Catholic ethnics—not their Irish loyalties, which set them apart from other Catholics. Most second-generation Irish, born in America and proud of it, might have been inclined to do that anyway, but practical demands for gaining power in the church, politics, or the labor movement now also made it necessary.

If the hallmarks of this new identity were fervent, militant, and uncom-promising American patriotism and panethnic Catholicism under Irish leadership, then no organization better embodied this new definition than the **Knights of Columbus**. Though founded as far back as 1882 and mod-estly successful through the 1890s, the Knights did not really begin to come into their own until the early twentieth century. Between 1899 and 1922, the Knights' membership skyrocketed from 42,000 to 782,000. No other Catholic lay society could match their popularity, which stemmed from their combina-tion of intense patriotism and devoted, aggressive Catholicism. Much of the surge in the Knights' membership, for example, followed World War I, when their hard work tending Catholic soldiers in camps in the United States—and overseas as well—and selling war bonds won them a reputation for intense patriotism. Yet the Knights were also vigilant Catholics, ever ready to defend their Church here or abroad. They were particularly active in the 1920s, com-bating the Ku Klux Klan in America and the new revolutionary government in Mexico. Finally, though Irish American–dominated, the Knights recruited members from all Catholic ethnics. Taking Christopher Columbus, the first American and first Catholic, as a common ancestor, they tried to construct a panethnic Catholic people that would become a powerful force in the twentieth century.

Yet if Irish Catholics looked out at a hostile Protestant America and talked of a vast band of Catholic ethnics united by a common religion, when they looked back at that band they rarely recognized the other Catholic ethnics as equals. Discrimination and exclusion by Irish Americans against the new ethnics would be commonplace, particularly in unions, but also in politics and the Catholic church. Irish Democratic politicians battled constantly in the turn-of-the-century era with Italian, Polish, French Canadian, and Lithuanian immigrants, who sought recognition of their power in tangible benefits like jobs and contracts and symbolic recognition in everything from nominations for important offices to appropriate commemorations of their holidays. Similarly, Irish bishops were often at war with members of the same groups over control of their churches. Polish-Irish conflict grew so hot that some Polish American Catholics broke from the Roman Catholic Church and created their own Polish National Catholic Church in 1897. If Irish Americans called themselves militant American Catholics, they believed that they were different from other Catholics who might use that name. They were different if only because they were better American Catholics—models to others of what American Catholics should be. Yet they also retained some sense of ethnic identity, nourished by an invented Irish American culture of Tin Pan Alley music, Harrigan and Hart or George M. Cohan plays, and St. Patrick's Day parades, which gave some cultural substance to this separate identity.

Yet there was more concrete and telling evidence that their Irish loyalties still tugged at them. In 1916, Ireland erupted in rebellion. The revolt was quickly put down, but nationalist sentiment still simmered in Ireland nonetheless, exploding into full-scale revolution by 1918. Irish American nationalist diehards like **John Devoy** schemed and labored to aid Germany (and thus hurt Britain) at the beginning of World War I, but many Irish Americans, especially later American-born generations, paid little attention to Ireland's cause during that war. When the rebels rose during Easter Week in 1916, they roused little interest among Irish Americans. Yet in the fall of 1918, as revolution erupted in Ireland, Irish America exploded in a frenzy of activity in behalf of the new revolutionaries in Ireland. The secretive **Clan na Gael** formed the **Friends of Irish Freedom** (FOIF) as a popular front for itself in 1916, but the FOIF did not become really popular until after the end of World War I on November 11, 1918. Over the next few weeks, the FOIF would sponsor meetings around the country, including a mass meeting in Madison Square Garden in New York City that featured Cardinals **Gibbons** of Baltimore and

O'Connell of Boston. Over time, the nationalist movement would split over a dispute between Devoy and Eamon De Valera that ended with De Valera forming his own organization, the American Association for the Recognition of the Irish Republic. After England conceded virtual Irish political autonomy in the Irish Free State in December, 1921 and Ireland broke into a civil war between the Free State and republican loyalists shortly thereafter, the nationalist movement in America deflated quickly. Still the nationalist mania, which enlisted all Irish American generations from the end of World War I until the treaty creating the Free State, testified that Irish Americans still understood themselves as a distinct group with links to the homeland.

Through the turn of the century, then, Irish Americans reached a crossroads, made their choices, and moved on. At the beginning of the era, it appeared that many possible paths seemed open to them, including participation or even leadership in a new class-conscious labor movement or some kind of reconciliation with their heretofore hostile Protestant neighbors. Those possibilities closed down with the destruction of the Knights of Labor, the revival of anti-Catholicism, and the Vatican's tightening of Catholic ideological orthodoxy. In the end, most Irish American Catholics began to define themselves as militant American Catholics. Such a conception of identity seemed to best embody the aspirations of American-born Irishmen, but also seemed to best fit the changes in social and political circumstances confronting Irish Americans at the turn of the century. It would prove to be a very durable conception of their identity, lasting well into the twentieth century.

NOTES

1. William Shannon, *The American Irish: A Political and Social Portrait* (New York: Collier Books, 1974), 132, 145.

2. Richard White, *Remembering Ahanagran: Storytelling in a Family's Past* (New York: Hill and Wang, 1998), 80.

3. Janet Nolan, *Ourselves Alone: Women's Emigration from Ireland, 1885–1920* (Lexington: University of Kentucky Press, 1989), 49.

4. Nathan Glazer and Daniel Patrick Moynihan, *Beyond the Melting Pot: The Negroes, Puerto Ricans, Jews, Italians, and Irish of New York City* (Cambridge, Mass.: MIT Press, 1963), 217.

5. Ellen Skerrett, "The Catholic Dimension," in *The Irish in Chicago*, ed. Lawrence McCaffrey (Urbana: University of Illinois Press, 1987), 40–41.

6. Timothy J. Meagher, *Inventing Irish America: Generation, Class, and Ethnic Identity in a New England City, 1880–1928* (Notre Dame, Ind.: University of Notre Dame Press, 2001), 165.

7. Robert H. Lord, John E. Sexton, and Edward T. Harrington, *The Archdiocese of Boston in the Various Stages of Its Development* (New York: Sheed and Ward, 1944), 3:511.

The Twentieth Century

Gary Wills has written of the Catholic world he grew up in, in the 1940s and 1950s: "We grew up different. There were some places we went, and others did not—into the confessional box, for instance…. We spoke a different language from the rest of men, not only the actual Latin … [but] odd bits of Latinized English…. It all spoke to us of the alien. The Church was stranded in America, out of place."[1] Wills was not Irish, but Irish Catholics had constructed this different world and they led it now. It was as much theirs—probably more theirs—than anyone else's. Many of them still understood, then, that they remained a separate people of sorts. Even as Irish Americans moved three or four generations from their immigrant pasts, they were still somehow "different." It was not that they were not Americans: its popular culture was second nature to them now—it was their culture. Bing Crosby was the nation's "crooner," Notre Dame's "Fighting Irish" the nation's college football team, and Jimmy Cagney, Spencer Tracy, and Pat O'Brien among the nation's best-loved movie stars. Irish Catholics were patriots too; some thought they were too fanatically patriotic, as they spurred on the anticommunist crusades of the 1950s. It was not, then, that the Irish American was not an American; it was just that after three generations he or she was still a different kind of American.

In the middle years of the twentieth century, Irish Americans thus changed but remained separate and distinct from an American Protestant mainstream. They continued to move up the occupational and income ladder; indeed, they made significant gains in this era. They also gained significant political power. Al Smith's defeat in 1928 notwithstanding, Irish Catholic prominence in state and national politics grew apace as the Democrats became the nation's majority party in the 1930s. Their power in shaping American culture grew as well: Irish American priests and soldiers became movie icons. It was not an untroubled rise, however. Indeed, Irish Americans, like others, suffered from the great upheavals of the early and mid-twentieth century: the great Depression, World War II, and the cold war. Out of the pain of those experiences would come the bitter excesses of Irish ghetto sensibilities: **Father Charles Coughlin**, Father Leonard Feeney, and **Senator Joseph McCarthy**. On the whole, for Irish Catholics in America, the middle years of the twentieth century were decades of progress, mobility, and new power. Yet the militantly Catholic world they had set in place by the early twentieth century would persist until mid-century. They were still different.

Ironically, the persistence of this difference owed little to the new life injected into America's Irish community by immigration. It was not that Ireland did not continue to hemorrhage young emigrants. The newly independent Irish state could not prevent emigration from the island from continuing and even increasing in the middle of the twentieth century. Through most of the twentieth century, even the now independent Ireland remained a poor, agricultural country with little industry to employ new sons and daughters as they came of age. Some would say the new state may have inadvertently fostered such migration with its flirtations with economic nationalism and its cultural oppressiveness. In 1932, for example, the Irish government touched off an economic war with Britain (then its most important trading partner) that lasted for about six years and sapped the Irish economy. Yet it was not the state's policies so much as Ireland's persistent, precarious economic position in a turbulent, dangerous world of economic depression, global war, and cold war that encouraged immigration. Ireland remained a rural country of small farms and little opportunity throughout this period. As late as 1951, Linda Dowling Almeida notes that half the population lived in rural areas and the most rural counties in Connaught and the rest of the west lost jobs continuously in the middle of the century. Yet with weak urban industries scrambling to sustain themselves in hard economic times, the Irish economy could produce few nonagricultural jobs to offset the loss. Darker still, even as much of the rest of Europe pulled itself out of the wreckage of World War II, Ireland, which remained neutral during the war, did not improve, falling further behind its European neighbors. Between 1949 and 1956, Ireland's income rose only one-fifth as fast as the rest of western Europe's, and unemployment in southern Ireland reached record levels.

The same painful dilemma that had become nearly universal for Irish young people throughout the island by the end of the nineteenth century persisted and even sharpened through the first six decades of the twentieth century. They could remain in Ireland and, if unlucky, confront likely unemployment or a marginal, hopeless existence as an unmarried worker on a brother's or a stranger's farm. Luckier men could inherit a farm, and fortunate women with a dowry could marry an heir, but they often faced a long wait and a consequent delay of marriage before they took over their farm, and then they often found it to be too small to afford them anything but a hardscrabble existence. For many, even those who might inherit, escape seemed a better option.

Emigration thus continued from Ireland throughout the period from the 1920s to the 1960s. As before, however, it ebbed and flowed as conditions changed both at home and overseas. The number of emigrants fell from the onset of the Depression in the late 1920s until there was actually a net inflow in 1932. Emigration rose again during World War II, as the needs for Irish labor rose, and it persisted after the war through the 1960s, as the Irish economy continued to flounder. Thus from relatively modest emigration totals of about 16,000 people per year in the late 1920s and 1930s, the numbers rose to nearly 25,000 by the late 1940s, and to nearly 40,000 by the 1950s. Between 1946 and 1961, 531,255 people left Ireland.

Yet if emigration continued, surprisingly fewer and fewer of these immigrants came to America. As Kevin Kenny notes, between 1876 and 1921, 84 percent of Ireland's emigrants went to the United States. By 1926 to 1936, Kenny points out, the proportion was down to 54 percent and it continued to plunge thereafter, dropping to about 16 percent by 1946 to 1961.

Some have suggested that America's new immigration restriction laws of 1921 and 1924 forced Irish migrants to seek other destinations. While the quota for Irish immigrants was relatively generous, especially compared to the severe and perniciously racist limits placed on southern and eastern Europeans and the exclusion altogether of Asians, the laws did set a ceiling on Irish newcomers and introduced rules that complicated when and how Irish immigrants could enter the United States. The new laws may have discouraged some prospective migrants to the United States, but they hardly explain such a momentous change in Irish migration. By the 1930s, the Irish were not even reaching their quota of migrants to America.

A more important reason for the fall in the number of emigrants to America was the increasing attractiveness of nearby Britain over the distant United States (and distant Canada and, indeed, even farther Australia as well, for Irish migration to those overseas dominions declined too) in troubled economic times. As early as 1930, three Irish migrated to Britain for every one going to the United States. Thus while the number of Irish-born in the United States plunged from little over one million in 1920 to less than 700,000 in 1940 and

338,000 in 1960, the number of Irish-born in Britain rose from an early twentieth century low of 505,000 in 1930 to 716,000 in 1951 and 950,000 in 1961.

What drew the Irish to Britain over the United States and other overseas economies? Perhaps surprisingly it was the British economy, which if receding in world importance, offered the Irish better or perhaps safer chances to escape their own island's economic trap. Britain's economy, for example, rallied more quickly and successfully from the depths of the global depression in the early 1930s, and when World War II began, Britain was desperate for workers for its labor-starved war industries. In a trend not unlike that for black workers in the United States, the wartime crisis permitted Irish workers to penetrate a wide range of new industries and occupations in Britain and make some important advances up the British economic ladder. In the postwar era, Irish migrants in Britain not only profited from earlier gains and newly established networks, but from their ability to establish themselves easily and take advantage of government benefits.

Yet it was not just that Britain offered the Irish better prospects; by the time of the war, the British economy was hardly better than America's. The British option, however, was a safer and easier one for Irish emigrants to take. That was quite literally true during World War II, when German U-boats made crossing the North Atlantic almost impossible. Yet it was also true earlier in the 1930s. As Enda Delaney suggests, the move to Britain amid the economic turmoil of the 1930s was a safe and easy stop, cheap and easily reversed if opportunities never fulfilled their promise. Going to the United States, on the other hand, was a major effort, more expensive and time consuming to undo, as might likely be the case in hard times.

Nevertheless, if Irish migration to America declined to a trickle relative to earlier floods, becoming a small stream beside the river to nearby Britain, it never stopped. In the 1920s alone, before the shift to Britain picked up momentum, over 210,000 Irish men and women poured into the United States. Even later in the first fifteen years after World War II, almost 90,000 came here. In the early 1920s, some came as political refugees from the turmoil surrounding the establishment of the new state. Though more diehard unionists or Protestants fleeing the new Catholic-dominated Irish Free State made their way to Britain or Canada, some Republican nationalists, embittered by the outcome of Ireland's brief civil war, went to the United States. Yet even many of these former IRA men were probably motivated more by economic necessity than by political oppression, and for the vast majority of Irish who came to America, the hard realities of making a living was the principal, or even only, reason that they came.

Almost all the trends that had become dominant by the 1880s in Irish migration to America still characterized this one: an excessive proportion of the migrants were from the impoverished areas of the west; they were largely young, unmarried men and women in their teens; and the proportion of women rose and fell but was always high and sometimes—as between 1955 and 1961—a majority. Often the larger part of entire families left Ireland, following in one another's footsteps in the time-honored fashion of immigrant chains. Historian Richard White's mother Sara Walsh, for example, left her home in Ballylongford in County Kerry in 1936, reaching New York, where she met Jack Hegarty, her cousin, before moving on to the South Side of Chicago, where she settled in with her Aunt Kitty, her sister Nell, some cousins and in-laws, and her father, Jack (a sign of Ireland's economic desperation was the fact that her father left his wife and family to work in America for about twenty years to earn money to support his Kerry farm). More than ever before, such chains led Irish immigrants to America's big cities. In 1920, one-fifth of all America's Irish immigrants lived in New York City, but Linda Dowling Almeida reports that one-third of all the Irish entering the United States between 1958 and 1961 were heading to New York City and half to the other largest cities in the nation.

Irish immigrants found a more comfortable, hopeful environment in twentieth century America than any time since the famine. After all, those big cities had been "Irish" for nearly a century. Earlier Irish immigrants and the American-born Irish dominated political and religious hierarchies there and were ensconced as potential employers in positions of influence, such as in utility or transit companies. Moreover, hostility and discrimination by now had long since deflected on to "newer races": first Italians, Jews, and Poles, and later, blacks from the South, Puerto Ricans, and Mexicans.

Irish immigrants themselves seemed equipped for their new life. National schools had long since all but eliminated illiteracy in Ireland and given every young Irish man and woman a solid elementary education. Routine immigration along established chains of family and friends should also have made New York, Chicago, and Boston seem easily familiar. Boasting these advantages, some of the new immigrants did "take" to America quickly and successfully. William and Paul O'Dwyer, born in County Mayo, came to New York in the mid-1920s. William would become mayor of New York and ambassador to Mexico; Paul became a crusading civil rights lawyer and ultimately to many the conscience of New York.

Still the achievements of most Irish immigrants in the twentieth century were much more modest. In 1950, over three-quarters of the Irish immigrants in the New York Metropolitan Area were blue-collar workers; only 3 percent were professionals. Irish immigrants, as Stephan Thernstrom and others have pointed out, continued to lag behind native-stock Americans and more successful eastern European Jews in New York and Boston through the 1940s. For all they knew about the United States and for all the friends who had journeyed there before, Irish immigrants could never be fully prepared for their new life in America. Though some in power in Ireland, like Eamon de Valera, found some benefits in Ireland's rural, peasant character—an isolated island of premodern virtue in a sea of modern corruption—it did not help immigrants to America who had to make their way in the biggest and most modern cities of the most modern nation in the world. Moreover, while almost all immigrants had sound elementary educations, few had more than that. Linda Dowling Almeida notes that their average educational level in 1960 was at about the eighth grade, still respectable in many parts of the United States, but hardly likely to significantly ease upward mobility. Dowling Almeida does point out that in the 1950s more and more of the immigrants were white-collar workers. By the late 1950s, over 15 percent were professional or technical workers and another 10 to 15 percent were clerical workers. Still, the vast bulk who had come until then had fled backward, impoverished farms with only a sound but limited education to sell in America's industrial marketplace.

Low rents or mortgage costs and the need for easy access to public transportation governed these blue-collar immigrants' searches for housing. They confronted other constraints too, as black, Mexican, and Puerto Rican immigrants and their children flooded northern American cities. Still, the twentieth-century Irish had some advantages in finding residences as well. Unlike racial minorities, their movement around the metropolises they settled in was largely unimpeded. Blacks and Puerto Ricans would become more segregated over time in the twentieth century, walled up by prejudice and hostility in their New York Harlem or Chicago South Side ghettoes. Irish immigrants, on the other hand, could take advantage of improvements in public transportation that allowed them—even with their blue-collar incomes—to escape downtowns and find homes in newly developing areas. In New York City, as Marion Casey points out, transportation improvements and a building boom in the 1920s created a glut of apartments in the housing markets of the outer boroughs that were both accessible by public transportation and offered larger, cleaner homes for the same or less money as apartments in Manhattan. In 1920, 57.4 percent of Irish immigrants in New York City lived on the island of Manhattan and merely 9.2 percent in the borough of Bronx and 5.2 percent in the borough of Queens. By 1950, only one-third of the Irish-born lived in

Manhattan, 26 percent in the Bronx, and 17 percent in Queens. As Casey notes, a substantial permanent Irish settlement far from Manhattan grew out of an Irish beach resort in Rockaway Beach on the far southern side of Queens in the 1930s and 1940s. Even those who lived in Manhattan increasingly concentrated in neighborhoods at the island's very northern tip, in Washington Heights and Inwood. Similar trends were at work in Chicago, Boston, and the other major points of Irish immigrant settlement, with, perhaps, greater dispersal in Chicago and somewhat less in Boston.

If Irish immigrants now seemed freer to roam through big cities than ever, the settlement patterns of most were not random. Instead, many sought out and found housing among other immigrants and Irish Americans. In 1950, Morris Winsberg points out, about 60 percent of the Irish-born in Boston settled in city census tracts with a significantly disproportionate share of other Irish immigrants. The proportions were smaller among the Irish immigrants in New York City or Chicago, but still noticeable: 48 percent and 41 percent respectively. In Washington Heights and Inwood, Robert Snyder reports, older Irish American residents remembered "family gatherings with kitchen music on accordions or fiddle, Saturday night social visits to taverns with neatly dressed children in tow … Irish dances at places like the Innisfail or Leitrim House and Irish football matches at Gaelic Park just to the north in the Bronx."[2] Marion Casey notes that in the 1930s and 1940s, several Irish-speaking families from Donegal clustered in what became Donegal Hill in Flatbush, a part of Brooklyn.

Even in mixed ethnic neighborhoods, however, Irish immigrants found their own "communities" of friends. Sara Walsh, an immigrant from Kerry, remembered her neighborhood on the South Side of Chicago in the 1930s as Irish, though the census reveals that it was composed of broad array of Germans, Poles, and Lithuanians. But as her son, historian Richard White, has suggested, these others may have "even lived next door … but they were not the people that Sara talked to, cared about, or met in private places."[3]

This mix of dispersal and the easy acceptance that permitted it suggested how early and mid-twentieth-century Irish immigrants differed substantially from that of their nineteenth-century predecessors. They were far more likely, for example, to marry outside the group. As Kevin Kenny points out, over three-quarters of Irish immigrants in 1920 married first- or second-generation Irish, but fewer than half did in 1960. Linda Dowling Almeida found that postwar Irish immigrants to New York City seemed largely uninterested in the formal activities of the Gaelic League, a once flourishing organization committed to the preservation of the Irish language. Memberships dropped in the

AOH across the country, falling to 20,000 by 1940. Even the county societies in New York City found that they could not hold on without opening ranks to second- or third-generation Irish after immigration fell off after the 1920s.

And yet there was evidence of stubborn efforts to hold on to old-country culture or to reinvent it for American conditions. If Irish immigrants were more likely to marry outside the group, Irish immigrant women as late as 1960 continued to have more children than American natives and all other immigrants except Mexicans. In New York City, if the county societies and Gaelic League (see **Irish Language in America**) grew only slowly in this era, they were still able to foster appreciation of Irish culture through an annual Feis, or festival, of Irish music and dance. Founded in 1932, by the 1940s the New York Feis attracted over 15,000 patrons to the campuses of Iona College and Fordham University to witness competitions in Irish music and dance.

Irish immigrants could not and did not merely preserve a culture they had brought with them from Ireland. They were forced to change, trim, resituate, or even hide it even while they tried to maintain it. The Feis, as Rebecca Miller has pointed out, did not try to foster the traditional Irish arts of music and dance as the communal, folk rituals that they had been in Ireland, but to celebrate them as fine arts equal to classical music and dance. In the process, the Feis transformed those folk arts into something radically new. A more telling symbol of the complexity of Irish immigrant cultural adaptations in the mid-twentieth century was the City Center dance hall, which opened in New York City in 1956. Linda Dowling Almeida suggests City Center was far more popular for 1950s immigrants than events staged by traditional Irish organizations like the Gaelic League. At its peak in the late 1950s, Rebecca Miller states, 2,000 people packed City Center every Saturday night. At City Center, Irish immigrants found a diverse musical mix. The featured performers were Brendan Ward's twelve-piece orchestra, which played American dance tunes and Americanized Irish songs. But the ballroom also featured shorter sets of Irish jigs and reels, often played by Paddy Noonan on the piano accordion. These tunes, Rebecca Miller points out, were rooted in traditional Irish music, but were simplified for the constraints of the big ballroom and the "modern" tastes of its patrons. In short, Miller notes, "the resultant Irish dance and music offered by City Center followed a standardized and semi-traditional style, a compromise gesture toward Ireland's folk culture and the more palatable commercial culture preferred by Irish America."[4]

In the end, Irish immigrants' life in mid-twentieth century America may not have been shaped by their lack of desire to perpetuate old-country culture as much as by the power and urgency of forces trying to Americanize them and their own weak capacity to resist those forces. The pressure to conform during World War II and the cold war was enormous. As Rebecca Miller points out, even Irish musical patrons were quick to make clear that the celebration of Ireland's arts in no way diminished Irish American loyalty to America. Moreover, as radio and later television joined movies in broadcasting a powerful American commercial culture, the preservation of Irish traditional culture in its communal settings became a hard business. *Saisuns* staged in kitchens in Bronx apartments or Washington Heights taverns were lonely, scarcely audible voices in the din of American popular culture. Yet as big a problem for the immigrants was that there were just so few of them. They might cluster in the big cities and especially New York City, but even there the struggle to maintain Irish culture was difficult.

That last fact suggests perhaps the most important and striking point about Irish immigrants in Irish American life at mid-century: their irrelevance to Irish America. Irish immigrants like the O'Dwyer brothers or Archbishops Hanna of San Francisco or Curley in Baltimore still exerted influence in the Irish American community. Yet increasingly after 1930, Irish immigrants seemed a quaint oddity amid so many more American-born Irish Americans. Irish immigrants became almost an ethnic community within an ethnic community, with traces of a brogue, differing tastes in music, and tight connections with family members setting them apart from native-born Irish Americans. The immigrants were Irish Americans to be sure, but they not only did not now define what that meant, but they could not even offer a significantly challenging alternative definition to those who did define it.

If they did not define Irish America, then who did? Just as there would always be Irish immigrants, there would also always be children of immigrants. And yet the second generation's time seemed to also pass, over the course of the twentieth century. Their numbers had peaked and fell steadily to only a little over 1.4 million by 1960. It was, then, the third and fourth generations, the demographic echoes of the famine flood, who made up the bulk of the Irish American population now. Yet their predominance and influence is difficult to chart, if for no other reason than that there are no good sources to reasonably estimate their numbers. From a series of national surveys conducted in the late 1960s and early 1970s, Andrew Greeley concluded that almost three-quarters of all Irish Catholics then were of the third generation or later (put another way, he concluded that only a little over one-quarter were immigrants or the children of immigrants). This was about the same proportion as German Catholics, but contrasted sharply with Italian American Catholics, of whom only about 28 percent were of the third generation or later.

Just as the absence of national census data makes it hard to determine how many third- or fourth-generation Irish there were in mid-twentieth century America, that lack of hard data also makes it difficult to determine how economically successful they were. For much of the twentieth century, Irish Americans, men in particular, have been object lessons of economic failure in a capitalist economy for any number of prominent historians and social scientists, ranging from Thomas Sowell and Daniel Moynihan to Steven Erie and Stephan Thernstrom. The speed with which new immigrant Jews raced by the plodding, resentful Irish, especially in New York City, seemed the best evidence of this contention. Irish Americans seemed handicapped by a backward Catholic culture that made them fatalistic, communal, suspicious of ambition and individualism, obsessed with conformity and security, and fearful of risk. To find such security, they seemed to eschew anything entrepreneurial and burrow into the lower echelons of government bureaucracies or safe, stolid, public utilities like electric or telephone companies. In Boston, as William Shannon noted, there were virtually no Irish among the city's economic elite at mid-century even though they completely dominated the city's politics. The same might have been said of Worcester, forty miles away, where Yankees along with Swedish Protestant allies retained firm control of the city's homegrown local corporations. Yet even outside of New England in the dynamic economy of New York City, the Irish, Moynihan has claimed, seemed to lag far behind other groups, most notably the Jews, in starting their own businesses or managing the major companies of others. Stuck in the lower middle class, Moynihan argued, Irish Americans seemed too comfortable and respectable to produce swaggering boxers or charismatic singers and dancers to compete with newer, hungrier immigrant groups, but neither could they seem to rouse themselves to vault into the forefront of the economy. Faceless, they seemed to fade into invisibility and disappointment. They had made gains, Daniel P. Moynihan acknowledged in 1963, but "for the moment ... the relevant question is not how the Irish have succeeded, but why they have not succeeded more."[5] Such depictions suggest a despairing, torpid dullness to Irish American life in the twentieth century. And yet the evidence of this failure was often impressionistic, based on limited data, or skewed by comparison to groups like the Jews, who were not only more successful than the Irish but spectacularly more successful than almost any other ethnic or religious group in American history. Sowell and Thernstrom, for example, had suggested that Irish indifference to education had held them back, but this could not be supported by the facts. A host of sources suggest that the American-born Irish were at or above national and even eastern urban levels in educational achievement by the early twentieth century. Andrew Greeley, drawing on a series of national survey samples, argues that American-born Irish Americans only continued to move up from there. He contends that the proportion of Irish Americans going to college rose steadily from World War I to the cold war, from 24 percent to 38 percent, and that those numbers exceeded all other Protestants and Catholics except Protestants of British origin.

Yet did the American-born Irish manage to translate this education into economic success? In his massive study of mobility in Providence, Joel Perlman found that the second-generation Irish there had achieved virtual parity with city's native-stock Yankees by the 1920s in both educational and occupational achievement. Moreover, Perlman found no evidence in that study that parochial schools—alleged nurseries of all the values and attitudes such as fatalism, communalism, and otherworldliness that held Irish Americans back—retarded Irish American upward mobility. Similar studies in New York City found the second-generation Irish about as successful as the city's native-stock Yankees in 1920 and 1940 (though both lagged far behind the city's American-born Jews). It is harder to determine how the third- and fourth-generation Irish were doing economically in the early and middle years of the twentieth century, but Greeley's retrospective data based on his 1960s and 1970s samples suggests that they were actually doing quite well. Greeley suggests that the Irish had pulled about even with the native-stock Americans nationally by the late 1920s, suffered setbacks during the Great Depression, and finally began making rapid progress up the occupational ladder during and after World War II, aided by the Roosevelt and Truman administrations' many policies favoring blue-collar workers and veterans. By the time John F. Kennedy was elected in 1960, Irish occupational status exceeded national averages and was higher than every other white ethnic group except the Jews.

Because of the same lack of good sources, it is also difficult to trace American-born Irish residential patterns through the middle of the twentieth century. Across the nation, of course, the great movement was the exodus from cities to suburbs. A first wave of suburbanization crested in the 1920s and receded during the Depression, but a second, far larger wave surged in the late 1940s and 1950s, unleashed by postwar prosperity, government-built highways, and federal programs backing cheap mortgages and providing benefits to veterans. In the earlier period, the American-born Irish, like Irish immigrants, found it easy to range to at least the edges of cities, if not over their borders. In New York City, that meant movement up into the Bronx or out into Queens; in Boston, southwest through Jamaica Plain to West Roxbury or south through Dorchester; and in Chicago, farther south and west on the city's South Side. After World War II, the movement carried Irish Americans further afield. Between 1940 and 1965, the archdiocese of Chicago created seventy-two new parishes in the suburbs and twenty-eight on the city's fringes. Those new churches constituted one-quarter of all the archdiocese's parishes by 1965 and served half of all its Catholics. Few were probably self-consciously Irish and none probably had only Irish members, but many of them, probably most, were made up largely of third- and fourth-generation Irish Americans, with smaller numbers of Americans born of other ethnic groups.

Irish American upward social mobility and outward geographical mobility over the first half of the twentieth century seemed to occur almost silently or invisibly, but the growth of Irish political power in the twentieth century was open, noticeable, and impressive. In his novel *The Last Hurrah*, published in 1956, Edwin O'Connor lamented the demise of the old Irish political machines and blamed it on Franklin Roosevelt. A character in the novel argues, "All you have to remember is one name: Roosevelt ... because he destroyed the old line boss. What Roosevelt did was to take the handouts out of the local hands. A few little things like social security and unemployment insurance and the like."[6] That insight became something of an article of faith for historians and social scientists. They pointed to the dramatic downfall of the fabled, once almighty, Irish-led Tammany machine in New York as proof of its point.

And yet a better case might be made that Roosevelt and the political revolution he led that made the Democrats the nation's majority also made the political fortunes of the Irish. Roosevelt's troubled relationship with James Michael Curley in Boston did little to undermine Irish power in that city, and Irish machines survived intact under Frank Hague in Jersey City and under Dan O'Connell in Albany, New York. While Roosevelt had no love for Tammany, it was not his personal opposition or his programs so much as a surge of Italian and Jewish American power, an electrifying opponent in Fiorello La Guardia, and Irish-led Tammany's own mistakes that did them in. As importantly, the Roosevelt revolution seemed to create or strengthen Irish rule in several other cities. Chicago's politics had been hotly contested between Republicans and Democrats through the 1910s and early 1920s, until the Czech ethnic Anton Cermak finally forged a Democratic majority after the **Alfred E. Smith** campaign of 1928. That Chicago Democratic majority was still fragile when Cermak's Irish American successors **Edward Kelly** and Patrick Nash tied the Chicago Democratic machine's fortunes to Roosevelt and strengthened it with New Deal patronage and benefits. By the 1950s, under **Richard Daley**, the Chicago machine would become the symbol of machine politics in America. In Pittsburgh, as Bruce Stave has shown, the Democrats were a woeful minority before the New Deal. Irish American David Lawrence then used New Deal patronage and programs and Roosevelt's blessing to create a solid Democratic majority in the city.

Irish power in the cities thus hardly faded, but it was not their power in cities alone that was so impressive now. It was the ever-expanding Irish power on the state and federal levels that made them seem to be America's "governing class." In many states, the Irish had just begun to break into governorships in the 1910s and 1920s. By the 1930s, 1940s, and 1950s, Irish rule in statehouses had become commonplace. In Massachusetts, James Michael Curley, Charles Hurley, Maurice Tobin, and Paul Dever served as governors in the 1930s, 1940s, and 1950s; in Rhode Island, Robert Emmet Quinn, J. Howard McGrath, John McKiernan, and Dennis Roberts; in Michigan, Frank Murphy; in California, Patrick Brown; and in Pennsylvania, David Lawrence. Archaic constitutional rules or political gerrymandering that discriminated against cities and the simple inertia of entrenched traditions slowed the Democratic triumph in state assemblies and sometimes produced a decided lag between Irish and Democratic triumph in gubernatorial races and their dominance of legislatures. In Massachusetts, for example, David I. Walsh won the governorship in 1913, but not until 1948 did Democrats seize control of the state House of Representatives in the state's General Court and elect **Thomas P. "Tip" O'Neill** their speaker. In Rhode Island, the Irish-led Democratic takeover in the legislature came earlier, in 1935, but it required a "bloodless revolution" in state government to change ancient constitutional provisions that discriminated in favor of rural Republicans in that overwhelmingly urban state. Irish power was evident in Congress as well; in 1958 over thirty Irish Americans were elected to the House of Representatives. They included the majority leader and a future majority leader, both future Speakers of the House, John McCormack and **Thomas P. "Tip" O'Neill**. Michael Mansfield of Montana, a future majority leader in the Senate, was also elected that year. Chairmen of the Democratic Party in this era included James Farley under Roosevelt and J. Howard McGrath under Truman, and behind them stood the informal power of some of the party's biggest "heavyweights," like Lawrence of Pennsylvania, Daley of Illinois, or John Bailey of Connecticut.

Inevitably, such electoral muscle paid off in appointments to the highest offices. Frank Murphy in 1940 and William Brennan in 1956 were appointed to the Supreme Court. At lower levels, George Flynn estimates one in four of Franklin Roosevelt's new judges were Catholic, compared to one in twenty-five for the previous Republican administrations. There is no evidence of the ethnicity of the new Catholic appointees, but given Irish prominence within the Democratic Party and Catholic population, it seems likely that they made up the majority of these new Catholic judges. Irish Americans also became more prominent throughout the bureaucracy, including cabinet level appointments: Attorney General Thomas Walsh and Postmaster General James Farley under Roosevelt; and Attorney General J. Howard McGrath, Secretary of Labor Maurice Tobin, and Postmaster General Robert Hannegan under Truman.

Yet the new Democratic majority and the New Deal did not just bolster Irish power in politics. It sustained and expanded their power in other areas too, such as labor unions. Already well established in labor's leadership, the New Deal offered a potential threat as well as an opportunity to Irish American labor leaders. They were strongly entrenched in the old skilled unions of the AFL, but the emergence of mass industrial unions in the CIO nourished by the pro-labor environment of the 1930s threatened to outstrip the AFL. Irish Americans, however, soon became prominent in the CIO as well as the AFL. **Philip Murray**, Irish by way of Britain, became the CIO's second president, American-born Irishman James Carey its secretary, and John Brophy (also Irish by way of Britain) its national director. In 1955, after the AFL and CIO merged, the third-generation and self-consciously Irish **William George Meany** would become the new AFL-CIO's first president.

As in the labor movement, Irish Americans had already long ago established their leadership in the Catholic Church. The proportion of Irish Americans among the hierarchy remained more or less the same at mid-century as it had been at the turn of the century. The names of the bishops or archbishops in some of the nation's largest dioceses in the middle years of the twentieth century suggest the continued Irish dominance in America: O'Connell and Cushing in Boston; Farley and **Francis Spellman** in New York; Curley and Keough in Baltimore; McIntyre in Los Angeles; O'Boyle in Washington; Gallagher and Mooney in Detroit; and Glennon in St. Louis. Yet their power and influence in a broader American society was far greater by the mid-twentieth century because the strength and influence of the church was so much greater. One reason was simply numbers. The echo of the vast Catholic immigration of the turn of the century in new second-generation Catholics, and by the 1940s and 1950s, even third-generation Catholics enormously increased the Catholic population. Indeed, it meant more than a rise in numbers: it meant a significant expansion of the Catholic proportion of the American population, from 19 percent to 23 percent in the 1950s alone, and from one-third to 40 percent in the northeastern states in the same decade. The church's power grew too as Catholics moved up the occupational ladder, reaped the economic and political benefits of the new unionization, and became critical elements in the new Democratic majority. The Roosevelt administration nursed contacts and friendships with Catholic leaders as ideologically diverse as liberals such as Chicago Auxiliary Bishop Bernard Shiel and Catholic University social theorist and activist John A. Ryan, on the one hand, and the conservative New York **Cardinal Francis Spellman** on the other. Catholic power grew also because the church created and strengthened national organizations that could become the instruments of power. Such organizations as the National Catholic Welfare Conference, the National Catholic Education Association, and the National Conference of Catholic Charities, all headquartered in Washington D.C., had been founded earlier in the 1900s and 1910s, but came into their own in the middle of the twentieth century. Leaders of such organizations, such as the second-generation Irish John Burke of the Welfare Conference or the Irish-born John O'Grady of Catholic Charities, lobbied hard in Congress for the Church's positions.

Complementing this Irish power in the Church, labor, and politics was a kind of Irish cultural power. It was not a dominance of the intellectual or literary elite. There were notable Irish figures in literature and drama, of course: **F. Scott Fitzgerald**, John O'Hara, **James Farrell**, **Flannery O'Connor**, and Eugene O'Neill. Yet there were few Catholic intellectuals in general, or Irish Catholics in particular, who reached great prominence in the middle years of the twentieth century. In the mid-1950s, Monsignor John Tracy Ellis, a distinguished historian of American Catholicism, and Bishop John J. Wright, an Irish American from Boston, lamented the lack of Catholic intellectuals. This was not simply a matter of numbers and group pride to Wright or Ellis. The absence of Irish Catholic intellectuals meant that perspectives born out of Catholic thought or Irish American experiences would have little effect on American thinking in this era, a kind of weakness, that if rarely visible, could be telling. Yet, if Irish Catholics played little role in American intellectual life, they continued to have some effect on the shaping of American opinion. Historian James Fisher points in particular to popular Irish American newspaper columnists who were plainspoken but broadly influential in the 1950s. Men such as James Kilgallen, Ed Sullivan, Jack O'Brian, and Bob Considine "influenced a whole culture" in that decade, Fisher argues, with their celebration of "regular guys" and "vision of gritty urban sophistication."[7]

Perhaps as important, the Irish "came into their own" in American film in the 1930s and 1940s, gaining wide and usually complimentary play in characterizations on screen. If Irish gangsters were prominent in films, so were

Irish priests and policemen, and in World War II and the cold war, the Irish seemed to embody a special kind of patriotism, from the *Fighting Sullivans* to George M. Cohan as the *Yankee Doodle Dandy*. The representation of the Irish in the movies reflected Hollywood's appreciation of their unique position as a brokering median people, accessibly positioned somewhere between distant white Anglo Protestant elites and the still seemingly foreign newer ethnics of the Italians, Jews, and Poles. Irish Americans were Americans, but of a distinct and special kind. In part, however, the benign Irish image also reflected Hollywood's appreciation of Irish power, not just the power of Irish politicians, but the new direct power that an Irish-led Catholic Church had over the film industry. In 1927, the National Catholic Welfare Conference had led a vigorous protest against a film, *The Callahans and the Murphys*, which it felt denigrated Irish Americans and their religion. In 1934, the Catholic Church established the Legion of Decency to judge the moral content of films and mobilize the Catholic faithful to support its judgments. An Irish-dominated church, working to influence Irish Americans like Martin Quigley and Joseph Breen of the Motion Picture Production Code office, did not insist on the inclusion of favorable depictions of Irish Americans, but such power must have made movie studios receptive to the celebration of Irish American priests and patriots.

Irish Americans, by any count, seemed to be making it in America by the middle years of the twentieth century. But what did "making it" mean? It did not seem to mean assimilation, if that is cast in simple terms. The Irish were Americans; the vast majority never wavered in that allegiance (though they did question the allegiances of others). Even as late as the 1950s, however, Irish Catholics were still more outsiders than insiders. If they were outsiders, however, they were not alone. Indeed, the source of much of their power was their ability to continue to lead of the largest and most powerful group of white outsiders in the nation, white ethnic Catholics, through politics, the unions, and the church. And if they were outsiders as we have seen, they were clearly on the rise. The middle years of the twentieth century then were a paradox for the American Irish, one best summed up by James O'Toole's phrase, "militant and triumphant." The militancy, born of the tensions and insecurities of a people still on the outside battling an Anglo Protestant majority and establishment; the triumphalism prompted by their leadership of a large minority growing larger and more powerful. As in everything else in Irish American life, geography qualifies such an easy generalization. In Boston they may have been more militant and in Chicago more triumphant, and in St. Louis, San Francisco, and other cities, both Irish American militancy and triumphalism both may have been tempered by an earlier, easier acceptance. Still on the whole, if Irish Americans were a people on the rise, they were also a people still separate in most places, still playing out an older role.

Irish Americans were more successful and powerful in the twentieth century than they had ever been, but in most of America they still had not penetrated the nation's ruling economic and social elite. That elite throughout this period was Protestant, a "Protestant Establishment," in Digby Baltzell's phrase. Though Protestants had long made up the vast majority of the nation's business leaders and social "swells," it was only in the late nineteenth century that a new business corporate elite began to try to develop the institutional and associational infrastructure and community rituals that would forge them into a caste. It was then that old elite preparatory schools like Philips Andover and Exeter and newly created ones like Groton and St. Mark's Schools were meant not only for the academic preparation of the elite but the social exclusion of those unwanted—Jews, all racial minorities, and all but a few Catholics. Feeding into Ivy League universities, these prep schools and universities became a nursery of networks for elite members. The universities were more open, however. Though several Ivy League colleges set quotas on Jews, there is no existing evidence that they deliberately limited Catholic admissions in the twentieth century. They were, however, home to clubs such as Harvard's Porcellian, which preserved social exclusion in the environments of somewhat more democratic universities. Men's eating clubs, women's clubs, and country clubs in cities throughout the Northeast and Midwest were further extensions of this Protestant establishment. In Boston it included the Somerset, in New York the Knickerbocker, in Philadelphia the Union League Club, and in Pittsburgh the Duquesne Club. Topped off by community rituals like debutante balls, this network of schools, organizations, and rituals defined and defended the boundaries that separated the Protestant elite's members even from other whites, particularly white Catholics and Jews.

This exclusion was not merely social, however. Few Catholics, especially Irish Catholics, could be found in the top ranks of major corporations (and for all their economic success, even Jews were rare among executives in the core, heavy manufacturing industries before the 1960s). Even in government, certain positions in the state department or the foreign service seemed set apart for the "striped pants" men of the Protestant establishment. As noted, there were significant regional variations in the Protestant elite's hegemony. In Boston, the Protestant hegemony seemed iron-fast, but in San Francisco and possibly even St. Louis, Irish Catholics had long been welcome in elite circles.

Still there was a profound sense, perhaps strongest even among the most ambitious of Irish Catholics particularly in the Northeast, that they were outsiders, and different. It ran as a powerful theme through F. Scott Fitzgerald's fiction, but burned even hotter in John O'Hara's work. In a famous passage from his *Butterfield 8*, O'Hara wrote: "I want to tell you something about myself that will help to explain a lot of things about me. You might as well hear it from me. I am a Mick."[8] Such a sense of exclusion clearly motivated Joseph Kennedy's actions, and though his children moved more easily in an Anglo-Protestant world, they remained aware of their differences. The only sure way for an Irish Catholic to break through the walls of the elite, perhaps, was to become someone else, as James Forrestal did. Born and raised an Irish Catholic in Matteawan (now Beacon), New York, Forrestal seemed to simply jettison his Irish background, made his way to Dartmouth, Princeton, and Wall Street before becoming Secretary of the Navy and Defense under Truman.

If an Irish American sense of exclusion from the Protestant establishment remained, so did an ideological enmity with the liberal intellectual elite. Thrown together in the same Democratic Party coalition after 1932, Irish Catholics and liberal intellectuals clashed often. As John McGreevy has pointed out, liberals feared growing Catholic power and in a fascist age, also suspected that the rigid discipline of Catholic clericalism was a potential breeding ground for American fascism. There were specific issues too. One source of tension was Catholic sexual conservatism as it manifested in staunch resistance to changes in birth-control laws. In the heavily Irish city of Holyoke in western Massachusetts, this issue became a *cause celebre* after World War II. Many liberals also worried that the burgeoning Catholic school system was dividing the nation and isolating Catholic children from the beneficent effects of public education, and they resented Catholic lobbying to gain public money for Catholic schools.

Perhaps no issue was more divisive, however, than controversy over the threat of communism. It is important to remember that a broad anticommunist agreement cut across almost all religious and ethnic lines in middle of the twentieth century. Still, there were issues that seemed to pit Catholics led by Irish Catholics against at least liberal, if not all, Protestants and Jews. The battle over the Spanish Civil War in the 1930s seemed to draw those lines starkly. The religious and ethnic implications in **Joseph McCarthy**'s anticommunist crusade are more complicated. As Donald Crosby and others have pointed out, some Catholics including Irish Catholics opposed McCarthy, and there was widespread enthusiasm for his charges among non-Catholics. Still, Catholic and especially Irish Catholic support for McCarthy was especially high, particularly in cities like Boston and New York. Polling data varies: in 1952, a Roper poll showed Irish Catholic support for McCarthy exceeding opposition by 18 percent; but two years later an International Research Associates poll found that supporters among Irish Catholics outnumbered opponents by only 5 percent. In Massachusetts, the anticommunist hysteria appeared to feed off the long and bitter grievances of Irish Catholics against the Yankee elite. Back in 1937, when the Massachusetts legislature was debating the imposition of loyalty oaths for teachers to root out "Reds," Timothy Murphy, Massachusetts state representative, cried: "I plead with you members who come from the same stock as I do to ignore the whispering of that class of people who use their arts and wiles to gain an objective but who would consign you to political oblivion. [Democrats] should consult their own common sense rather than surrender to any inferiority they may feel in relation to holders of elaborate college degrees."[9] As other observers noted more generally, the McCarthy era seemed a time when graduates of Holy Cross and Fordham were arresting the alumni of Yale and Harvard.

Intergroup tensions over McCarthyism infected relations not just between Irish and other Catholics and Protestants, but between the Irish and Jews. This relationship was more recent: truly only becoming important at the turn of the century, and more localized and crucial in New York City, where the Jewish population was so large, or in Boston and some other major cities. It was also a relationship that by the 1950s was already steeped in tension and mutual suspicion. Such tensions stretched back to the turn of the century but were softened by smart Irish political bosses like "Big" Tim Sullivan and Charlie Murphy in New York and Martin Lomasney in Boston. Rapid Jewish social mobility, "turf" wars in neighborhoods like Washington Heights in New York and Dorchester in Boston, and Irish resistance to surging Jewish political strength, however, combined with the rise of anti-Semitic fascism abroad and the economic plunge into depression at home to revive the hostility and thrust it from pushing, shoving, and catcalls on urban side streets into broad open conflict and national attention.

In 1926, **Father Charles Coughlin**, a Canadian born of Irish heritage and a pastor in Royal Oak, Michigan, began speaking on Radio Station WJR in Detroit. At first his topics were devotional, but as he developed a following and the nation's economy crashed, he began addressing national political issues. Originally enamored of Roosevelt, he soon became disappointed in the New Deal, and eventually Coughlin began to see a Jewish conspiracy in the Depression and its suffering. Millions listened to him but his strongest support seemed to come from Irish and German American members of the lower middle class who had seen their hard-fought climb to respectability wiped out or threatened by the Depression. In 1936, Coughlin launched his own political party, the Union Party. Washed away in the Roosevelt electoral tidal wave that year, the party did boast some success in parts of Boston and New York City, where Coughlin's Christian Front organizations were also popular. Relations between Irish and Jews were tense in those areas, sometimes erupting in spasms of violence. Despite the 1936 loss, Coughlin remained powerful until the United States entered World War II and his venomous anti-Semitism began to seem not just vile but traitorous.

Irish relations with Jews quieted during the war and its aftermath, but underlying tensions persisted before exploding again in the 1950s. In 1947, Father Leonard Feeney of Boston began a crusade emphasizing the Catholic Church's role as the sole path to salvation, which soon took on an anti-Semitic edge. Feeney's harangues attracted thousands until his defiance of Catholic Church authorities finally undermined his popularity. McCarthyism was a source of tension between Jews and Irish in the early 1950s as well. Jews had traditionally backed the left in American politics and many prominent Jews were hounded out of the movies, the academy, or other professions for their leftist loyalties by McCarthy-inspired investigations. Mixed into the ideological conflicts were battles for power between Irish or Italian-led old-line, regular Democratic organizations and new Jewish and Anglo Protestant–led reform, or what James Q. Wilson has called "amateur" Democrats. As Wilson points out, older Irish Democratic organizations brushed off the challenge of Jewish and Anglo Protestant amateur Democrats in Chicago and Massachusetts through this period, but in New York City, the heavily Jewish reformers were much more successful. Such battles stiffened ideological struggles between Jews and Irish with battles over power and patronage.

Irish American relations with other Catholic ethnic groups also sparked and flamed in competitive rivalry. By the 1940s and 1950s, American-born generations of the new immigrants were growing to maturity, and they grew restless under Irish American leadership in politics and the Church. In 1950, New York City elected its second Italian American mayor, Vincent Impelleteri; in 1946, Rhode Island its first Italian American governor, John O. Pastore; and in 1956, Massachusetts its first Italian American governor, Foster Furcolo. All of the above were Democrats but in the rough and tumble of ethnic politics of New England, New York, New Jersey, and Pennsylvania, Italians often battled the Democratic Party for the Republicans. An Irish American politician in Massachusetts grumbled in the late 1950s that the state really had three parties: the Republican, Democratic, and "Italian" parties. Not surprisingly then, the second Italian American governors in Massachusetts and Rhode Island, John Volpe and Christopher Del Sesto, were both Republicans. Ethnic rivalries had become more muted in the Church since the early twentieth century, but through the century's middle decades there was still a clear and distinct sense of the importance of ethnic differences. In his study of Chicago Catholics from the 1910s to the 1940s, Edward Kantowicz talks about different ethnic "leagues" of priests: the Irish being members one of three "major leagues," and the Italians, one of the four "minor leagues." The priests of the "major leagues" were eligible for posts in the best parishes, and were much more likely to be promoted to positions of power such as bishop, while the Italians and other "minor league" ethnic groups such as the Poles remained stuck in marginal national parishes and minor diocesan appointments.

Such rivalries among Catholics, however, did not detract from the ongoing effort by largely Irish Catholic church leaders to forge an American Catholic people out of its constituent ethnic elements. In 1938, the American Catholic hierarchy created a Commission for American Citizenship to produce materials for parochial schoolchildren that did precisely that. Producing readers, youth magazines, and even Catholic comic books for up to three-quarters of American parochial schools in the 1940s, the Commission emphasized Catholics' common early American ancestors: Commodore John Barry of the American navy, Archbishop John Carroll, Pere Marquette, the great explorer of the Midwest, as well as common contemporary Catholic heroes from Babe Ruth to Cardinal Spellman to **Tom Dooley**, the CIA-backed doctor working in war-torn Laos.

As Irish Catholics worked hard to make American Catholics out of other Catholic ethnics in one of the three great American religious melting pots, there was evidence that it paid off. Observers in the 1950s like Will Herberg certainly believed that it was happening. Research studies conflict, but it appears that the proportion of Catholics marrying *outside* the Catholic Church may have leveled off in the twentieth century—even as ethnic intermarriage *within* Catholicism grew. The completion of the Catholic ghetto—the building of multiethnic Catholic high schools in the 1920s and 1930s, and the proliferation of Catholic youth groups like the CYO about the same time—probably helped both trends. The multiplication of multiethnic Catholic parishes in peripheral areas and then the suburbs, coupled with the decline of national parishes and national parish schools in the city, also reflected and reinforced such trends.

If the tensions with groups outside the Catholic Church continued to feed Irish Catholic militancy, the success in forging a new, growing, and powerful people encouraged their triumphalism. These were heady days, indeed, for the Irish-led Church. The Depression slowed new construction and threatened mortgages of churches and schools already built, but in the 1940s and 1950s the Church exploded in a construction binge that spread a blizzard of yellow brick buildings across America. Between 1950 and 1960, Catholic elementary school enrollment grew by 174 percent; public elementary school enrollment by only 142 percent. The proportions were about the same for high schools: 174 percent for Catholic schools; 148 percent for public schools. By 1960, the Catholic church could boast 808 hospitals, 279 orphanages, 9,897 elementary schools, and 1,567 secondary schools. The places were staffed in part by orders such as the **Sisters of Mercy** and the **Presentation Sisters**. More than 160,000 Catholic religious women made this network possible.

As if Catholics could hardly restrain themselves showing off all these numbers and thus their power, the Catholic hierarchy delighted in a new kind of ritual in the middle years of the twentieth century, the mass devotion. The first important one was a celebration of the Eucharistic Congress in 1926, when 400,000 Catholics packed Soldiers Field in Chicago for a mass, and another 800,000 somehow made their way twenty miles north to the Diocesan seminary in Mundelein, Illinois, to watch a magnificent procession make its way around the seminary's manmade lake. Over the 1930s, 1940s, and 1950s, similar huge marches or giant meetings took place in Boston, Pittsburgh, Worcester, Providence, and other Catholic-dominated cities. It was a Catholicism ascendant and a Church triumphant.

Yet it was not just a matter of numbers that fed that confidence but a philosophical perspective that seemed to offer a sense of certainty and moral clarity in a turbulent world. As old-line Protestant denominations seemed to falter in their encounter with modernity and begin hemorrhaging members, Catholics built their expanding Church on philosophical principles traced to Thomas Aquinas that appeared to inoculate them from the angst of the modern era. As William Halsey points out, neo-Thomist philosophy, a faith in clear first principles and a rational design for the universe, became the central perspective in American Catholicism after World War I and dominated it until the 1960s. In response to the despair of much of modern thought in the years after the Great War, "Thomism offered a philosophy which secured a structure of civilization whose soul is absoluteness, objectivity, wholesome common sense and reign of intelligence." As Halsey argues, "optimism and confidence were its marching orders."[9] It was, it appeared, well suited to a people like the Irish Americans, who made up the largest proportion of Catholic college students and were ascending from the working class into the middle class, challenging older, suddenly troubled and defensive elites in the process. It seemed to provide a confidence about issues of right and wrong that bolstered the steady climb of such people to respectability. Yet it also seemed to bolster them in their address of the fallen world outside. It was this attitude of moral certainty as well as personal charisma that made Bishop Fulton J. Sheen, partly of Irish ancestry, such an effective and popular television preacher in the 1950s.

Complementing this rigorous and disciplined morality in the lives of the faithful was the rich thickness of Catholic ritual and devotion. The devotional revolution that had begun in the nineteenth century continued apace into the twentieth century. In Detroit, Leslie Tentler suggests, devotional practices probably reached their peak in the 1930s. Such devotions included novenas, group rosaries, "First Fridays," and special celebrations of holy days. While many devotions flourished in Irish American churches, the newer ones established in the nineteenth or early twentieth century, such as the devotions to St. Theresa of Lisieux, "The Little Flower," Our Lady of Fatima, or St. Jude, the patron of "lost causes," were panethnic in their appeal and especially popular. By the 1950s, family rosaries in the home, sometimes said in concert with a bishop or priest on the radio, had become commonplace throughout the Northeast and Midwest. Catholic material culture, statues, paintings, or prints of the Little Flower, the Infant of Prague, the Sacred Heart of Jesus, or the Immaculate Heart of Mary decorated churches and homes through the 1940s and into the 1950s as well. The Catholic world, a world of sacred objects, special languages, and rituals, continued to set all Catholics, even third- and fourth-generation Irish Catholics, apart. As Gary Wills said, it made them "different."

In the early and middle decades of the twentieth century, Irish American Catholic parishes ranged all over the lot, from the inner city church composed of a few old families still holding on amid an influx of minorities, to the second settlement, largely blue-collar parish still flourishing in the zone of emergence, to the postwar yellow brick suburban church set amidst the ranch houses and split levels in a new suburb.

No parish, therefore, was typical, but, perhaps, looking at one parish, St. Sabena's in Chicago, can give the life of twentieth-century Irish Catholics some concreteness. St. Sabena's was established in 1916 in the Auburn-Gresham neighborhood on the far south side of Chicago. This was not an inner-city district, historian Eileen McMahon notes, but a peripheral area of Chicago, if still well within the city's borders. It was also an ethnically and religiously mixed area, consisting of about half Catholics, but with a large Swedish Protestant population. The people of St. Sabena's divided up into roughly the same economic categories as Irish Catholics nationwide. In an analysis of the occupations of parishioners in the late 1950s and early 1960s, MacMahon

found that a little less than one-tenth were high white-collar workers, professionals, managers, and the like; close to two-fifths were low white-collar clerks
and salesmen; and one-quarter were machinists, plumbers, electricians, and
other skilled blue-collar workers. It was, both parishioners and outside observers understood, an Irish American parish. In 1954, the church's members and
clergy would sponsor South Side Chicago's first **St. Patrick's Day** parade. One
hundred thousand spectators came out to see twenty-three bands, forty floats,
and thousands of marchers from the Knights of Columbus, Catholic War Veterans, and Veterans of Foreign Wars parade through the city's South Side. Yet
it was Catholicism, not Irish ethnicity, that was central to the parishioners' life.
McMahon found that "their everyday activities revolved around the church,
which kept the parish, rather than their more intangible Irishness, central in
their lives and hearts."[10] She quotes one parishioner: "At St. Sabena's it was
Catholic. Nothing ethnic really. You were definitely Catholic."[11] "Definitely
Catholic" implies a sense of embattlement in an atmosphere of religious rivalry. Another parishioner claimed: "You were brought up with the idea that
you were as good as anybody else." T. O'Rourke echoed: "They [Catholics]
were on the defensive and I think it brought them closer together. They were
raised in a kind enclave, maybe you should you call it a ghetto."[12]

That ghetto, or at least St. Sabena's little piece of it, thrived in the early and
middle years of the twentieth century. Originally housed in a storefront on the
muddy prairie, the parish soon built a grand Gothic edifice. The congregation grew by nearly 50 percent between 1930 and 1960, and as late as 1957 the
church offered no fewer than eleven Sunday masses. Meanwhile, the school
grew from 240 children in 1917 to over 1,200 twenty years later. The parish
also built a huge Catholic Youth Organization community hall that sat 1,500
people for boxing matches and basketball and could be converted to a roller-
skating rink or dance hall. Block rosaries and novenas to Our Lady of Sorrows
flourished in a rich devotional life, and a men's church organization like the
Holy Name Society boasted over a thousand members. One old parishioner
summed up: "There was no reason to stretch out to any other place, because
you had that wide territory of your own people. And naturally you feel toward
your own kind."[13]

Upwardly mobile and increasingly powerful, then, many Irish Americans
nonetheless still understood themselves as part of a people set apart—their
"own kind"—in the middle years of the twentieth century. Often they understood this people, their people, to be American Catholics, thus potentially
including other Catholics. Within that group, however, they often understood
themselves as distinct or were reminded of their distinctiveness by Catholic

rivals such as Italians and Poles. Of all American Catholic ethnic groups, they made the most unstinting commitment to this American Catholic identity. They were the leaders of the new group and the models of its culture as well as its most passionate advocates and defenders. Paula Fass has contended that in the twentieth century, ambitious and upwardly mobile Irish Americans, unlike most other Catholic ethnics, were more likely, not less, to attend parochial schools. Though Catholicism and its rituals and rules made up much of the stuff of their separate world, there was a conglomeration of markers: **St. Patrick's Day** parades, Tin Pan Alley songs like "Mother Machree" and "When Irish Eyes are Smiling," and movie images of Irish American priests played by Pat O'Brien, Spencer Tracy, and Bing Crosby, all of which helped mark Irish Catholics off from fellow Catholic ethnics.

If many or perhaps most Irish Catholics still considered themselves to be a distinctive people within the American Catholic people they were trying to create, it was as American Catholics that Irish Americans continued to define themselves most often in the twentieth century, as members of a church militant and a church triumphant. Tensions with groups outside Catholicism continued to nourish the militancy. Growing numbers of members, institutions, clubs, and associations fed the confident sense of triumphalism. Militant and triumphant, cohesive yet upwardly mobile and powerful, Irish Americans did seem to themselves and observers as a people on the move.

Yet their success masked the seamier or harsher sides of Catholic life. Working-class Irish neighborhoods like Boston's Charlestown and South Boston, for all their bravado and rich local lore, often seemed locked in despair of alcoholism and self-destructive behavior. In Charlestown, for example, locals competed in a carnival of reckless self-destruction in the 1930s, driving crazily through the giant pillars supporting the trolley car tracks above their neighborhood's streets.

Irish Catholic life in the mid-twentieth century also gave pause to some of the best of their own writers, both then and later. Novelist **James Farrell** worried not just about violence in neighborhoods like Boston's Charlestown or his own South Side, but also about the intellectual impoverishment of a lower-middle-class Catholic world that insisted on simple answers. By the 1950s, it was the mixture of suburbanization, embourgeoisement, and unyielding puritanical and dogmatic Catholicism that troubled many. For **Edwin O'Connor** in *The Edge of Sadness*, it was a kind of spiritual hollowness as the thickness, richness, and earthiness of immigrant life receded farther and farther away, to be replaced by the bland and starchy respectability of the new suburban Catholicism of the 1950s. Later novelists, like Tom McHale and **Mary Gordon**, would look back on this time and see not a confident, cohesive people, but a repressed one, trapped between the expectations of their new class status and the iron rigor of their religion.

And yet Irish Catholics were not a people at rest. There were forces at work not only among them but in the country at large that were converging on the next decade, the 1960s, when events at home and abroad would touch off a revolution transforming much of America, and changing Irish America utterly. As the 1950s closed and the old church was at its apogee in mass attendance, school enrollment, and numbers of nuns and priests, it was already changing. The old devotionalism seemed to be waning by then. As early as the 1930s, the popularity of saints' devotions had begun to slide in places like Detroit, and Timothy Kelly reports that in Pittsburgh the mass meetings and marches were beginning to decline by the 1950s. People were learning new ways to pray, Joseph Chinnici suggests.

Yet there were other changes occurring as well. Irish American power had rested on power brokering between new immigrant whites, largely Catholics, and the Protestant establishment, on acting as leaders of a large group of "outs" while dealing with the "ins." Such a position had little to do with non-whites, Asians, Latinos, and Blacks, whom Irish Americans had helped push to the margin of American society or kept out of the country altogether. Yet race was being redefined in America, changing political alignments along the way. Those changes had been gathering momentum since World War II and would lead to a dramatic reconfiguring of racial and ethnic life in America in the 1960s, a reconfiguring which would also dramatically change Irish American life.

NOTES

1. Gary Wills, *Bare Ruined Choirs: Doubt, Prophecy, and Radical Religion* (New York: Dell), 15.

2. Robert W. Snyder, "The Neighborhood Changed: The Irish of Washington Heights and Inwood Since 1945," in *The New York Irish*, eds. Ronald H. Bayor and Timothy Meagher (Baltimore: Johns Hopkins University Press, 1996), 442.

3. Richard White, *Remembering Ahanagran: Storytelling in a Family's Past* (New York: Hill and Wang, 1998), 183.

4. Rebecca Miller, "Irish Traditional and Popular Music in New York City: Identity and Social Change, 1930–1975," in *The New York Irish*, eds. Ronald H. Bayor and Timothy Meagher (Baltimore: Johns Hopkins University Press, 1996), 493.

5. Nathan Glazer and Daniel Patrick Moynihan, *Beyond the Melting Pot* (Cambridge, Mass.: The MIT Press, 1963), 256.

6. Edwin O'Connor, *The Last Hurrah* (Boston: Little Brown, 1956), 374.

7. James Fisher, "Alternative Sources of Catholic Intellectual Vitality," *U.S. Catholic Historian* 13, no. 1 (Winter 1995): 83–88.

8. John O'Hara, *Here's O'Hara: Three Novels and Twenty Short Stories by John O'Hara* (Cleveland: World Publishing Company, 1946), 147–148.

9. John Aloysius Farrell, *Tip O'Neill and the Democratic Century* (Boston: Little Brown, 2001), 81.

10. William Halsey, *The Survival of American Innocence: Catholicism in an Era of Disillusionment, 1920–1940* (Notre Dame, Ind.: University of Notre Dame Press, 1980), 149.

11. Eileen McMahon, *What Parish Are You From?: A Chicago Irish Community and Race Relations* (Lexington: University of Kentucky Press, 1995), 100.

12. Ibid., 102.

13. Ibid., 53.

14. Ibid., 114.

The 1960s to the Present

The story had come full circle, or so it seemed. In June 1963, John Fitzgerald Kennedy had come "home." He walked through the lanes of Dunganstown in County Wexford, where his great grandfather Patrick Kennedy had lived one hundred and twenty years before, and spoke from the quay in New Ross, where Patrick had boarded a boat and fled famine-stricken Ireland on a journey to America. Now Patrick's great-grandson stood on that same soil, that same dock, as the most powerful and most widely recognized man in the world, as president of the United States. Indeed, John F. Kennedy had landed in Ireland fresh from making a stirring speech in Berlin, whose translated refrain "I am a Berliner" was still reverberating around the world.

Reversing the journey of his ancestor, Kennedy had neatly and symbolically retraced the long Catholic phase of Irish American history that had begun with the famine. From the bedraggled poor stepping off their stinking sailing ships at Castle Garden in New York or East Boston and huddling in squalid slums on Fort Hill in Boston or the Five Points in New York, they had produced not just a president of the United States, but a man who was wealthy, intellectual, and self-confident, an apparent model of gentility. Kennedy himself would recall some of that long historical journey of Irish America from famine to "Camelot" in a speech to the Irish parliament, the Dail, just before he set out for Dunganstown, conjuring up images of the Irish Brigade at Antietam and Fredericksburg in retracing some of his people's past.

The Kennedy story is often told. The immigrant Patrick Kennedy's son, P. J. Kennedy, became a prominent political boss in East Boston, a power among powers in the rough-and-tumble world of Boston ward politics that included colorful John F. Fitzgerald of the city's North End. Kennedy's son Joseph P. and Fitzgerald's daughter, Rose, wed in a marriage of local Irish political "petty nobility," but, despite their fathers' prominence, Boston's Yankee establishment could not accommodate their, or particularly Joseph's or Joe's ambitions, and the family moved to New York. Piling up fortunes in a variety of ventures, some brilliant, some merely seamy, Joe Kennedy groomed his family for the political triumphs and social successes that he had not enjoyed. After the first son, Joseph or "Joe" Jr., died, John, or "Jack," became the chosen one, and began his ascent up the political ladder, first as a congressman representing the gritty urban neighborhoods of Boston, and after 1952, the entire Commonwealth of Massachusetts as U.S. senator. In the latter election in a nice symmetry, the new Irish aristocrat Jack Kennedy defeated a scion of the old Yankee aristocracy, Henry Cabot Lodge Jr. Though Irish Catholic, young, and still hardly seasoned, Kennedy was poised in 1960 to make a run for the presidency.

Kennedy's nomination for president that year was not unexpected. His aide Theodore Sorenson had made a powerful case that the Democratic Party needed to nominate a Catholic after Catholic voters had defected to the Republican Dwight Eisenhower in large numbers, in the elections of 1952 and 1956. Kennedy money, grace, intelligence, and chic made him a formidable candidate, if seemingly still callow in many respects, and the help of Irish Catholic political professionals like John Bailey of Connecticut, David Lawrence of Pittsburgh, and of course Richard J. Daley helped push Kennedy through to a razor-thin victory. For all that, most estimates suggest that Kennedy's Catholic religion still may have cost him more votes than it won, though the Catholic vote did return for him, and the Irish Catholic vote for him was even greater.

Much has been written about the Kennedy presidency, and much that soberly revises his heroic image: his timidity on civil rights, the bungling at the Bay of Pigs, the youthful arrogance and womanizing. Still the wit, the rich and stirring rhetoric, and the episodes of purpose and resolve, sanctified by his later murder, had a powerful effect on the lives of Irish American Catholics. Kennedy's election, by itself, broke the last political barrier for Irish Catholics in America, but the assassination that raised him into the pantheon of American heroes helped undermine and topple all the remaining barriers, social, economic, or otherwise. However, Kennedy's assassination would not be the only cause, and perhaps not even the most important cause, of a revolution in Irish American life that is still being felt today. It would not be a revolution wrought by new Irish immigrants, though Ireland would continue to send its youth abroad until the 1980s. It would be revolution in the lives of the American-born Irish. It was a revolution made in part because of the movement of the vast majority of Irish Americans up the economic ladder to the middle class and out of cities and into suburbs. Yet there were other important causes as well: the changing configuration of race in America, the "disestablishment" of the Protestant establishment, the Second Vatican Council, the Vietnam War, and the breakup of the old New Deal coalition in the Democratic Party. Kennedy's election and assassination, then, would not be the sole or even principal cause of this revolution, but it would be as distinct a marker of the timing of this revolution as any other. Kennedy's election and assassination would clearly signal the end of an Irish America that had been born when Kennedy's great-grandfather left Dunganstown during the famine, been transformed at the turn of the century when his grandfather came to power, been challenged by his frustrated father seeking something better in the twentieth century, and finally would die with the young president in Dallas.

John F. Kennedy's ascension to the presidency of the United States coincided with a new beginning in Ireland too. In the late 1950s, under the new Taoiseach or prime minister Sean Lemass, the Irish government took a more aggressive approach to economic development, rejecting earlier policies of protectionism in the search for broader markets. As a result of these policies and the general effects of a European boom, Ireland's long-stagnant economy began to stir. Emigration, largely to Britain but also to America, had been chronic through the 1940s and 1950s, but it slowed noticeably in the 1960s, and some emigrants began to return home to share in Ireland's prosperity. Emigration to the United States fell from about 4,000 a year in the 1960s to about 1,000 a year by the 1970s. Indeed, in the latter decade, Ireland enjoyed a net *in-migration* of over 100,000 people, most of them returned emigrants. Marriage ages also dropped in Ireland and as fertility rose, Ireland experienced a mild population boom.

Yet the economic good times did not last. In a pattern not unlike an earlier economic boom at the turn of the nineteenth century, Ireland's economic rise in the 1960s had sparked a growth in population, but like that earlier period, that growth became a population excess when the economy crashed again. It had been a recipe for mass emigration in the nineteenth century, and it became a recipe for emigration, if on a smaller scale, again at the end of the twentieth century. By the 1980s, Ireland's economy was suffering severely. Joseph Lee reports that the unemployment rate skyrocketed from 7.1 percent in 1978 to 17.1 percent by 1987. Officially, the net outward flow of Irish immigration was 216,000 between 1980 and 1990, with the average emigration rate reaching 34,000 between 1986 and 1990. Officially too, the number of legal immigrants into the United States for the same period was about 25,000. Yet there is every reason to believe that not only did more people than that leave

Ireland, but far more than these official numbers came to the United States. Some estimate anywhere from 100,000 to 200,000 uncounted immigrants made their way from Ireland to the United States alone.

The vast bulk of the latter were illegal immigrants because the dramatic change of American immigration laws in 1965 had eliminated the European preferences of the old laws and the fat quotas allowed northern European nations like Ireland. None of the architects of the 1965 law had anticipated this, but as a result of the law, the sources of emigration to America shifted quickly and decisively to Asia and Latin America. That shift had a built-in momentum, for as Asians and Latinos settled here, the law helped them bring relations in as well, through the family preference system. Since Irish immigration to America had slowed to a trickle in the 1960s and 1970s, few young Irishmen and women seeking to escape their country's economic downturn a decade later had close relatives in the United States who could sponsor them for legal, permanent settlement.

As illegal Irish immigrants began to flood the United States in the mid-1980s, the newly founded newspaper, the *Irish Voice*, representatives of Irish community organizations, and Irish American politicians began looking for means to open up more opportunities for Irish men and women to settle permanently in the United States. In 1986 alone, over 98,000 Irish arrived under temporary visas and fewer than 2,000 qualified for permanent status. In 1987, the Irish Immigration Reform Movement, with the help of Senator Edward Kennedy and under the leadership of Congressman Brian Donnelly of Massachusetts, attached a provision to the Immigration Reform and Control Act of that year providing an extra 40,000 visas for European immigrants over the next few years. In due course, the Irish would win about 16,000 (40 percent) of them. A subsequent provision for more visas sponsored by Congressman Bruce Morrison of Connecticut afforded the Irish another 16,000 visas.

Immigration rules even after the reforms permitted some of the new Irish to create rich, hopeful lives in America, but by no means all, perhaps not even a majority, of the Irish newcomers did so. According to sociologist Mary Corcoran, legal immigrants profited quite a bit from their move to America, but illegals lived in a shadowy world of limited opportunities. In her study of Irish immigrants in the 1980s, Corcoran found a number of engineering or technical school graduates who came to America legally and confidently to exploit the advantages of their skills in a vibrant economy. In 1988, Corcoran notes, nearly half of all of Ireland's engineering graduates left the country. These "eirepreneurs," as Corcoran calls them, found a useful and productive niche in American corporations and as legal immigrants could travel back and forth to Ireland at their leisure.

The lives of the much larger numbers of illegal immigrants were much harder. Some of these immigrants were the sons and daughters of middle-class families in Ireland who overstayed their holiday visas just to sample American life. They returned to Ireland when they became bored, frustrated with restricted opportunities, or simply homesick. Most, however, came simply because there were not any opportunities in Ireland or just not the right kind of opportunities. Opportunities in America for them as illegal immigrants, however, were restricted as well. As illegals, not only was their pay low but they were always in danger of being reported to the Immigration and Naturalization Service, and they could not leave the country and expect to return. Because they feared exposure, they had to work with the informal contacts of family and friends to find work or places to live. As Mary Corcoran explains: "News of jobs travels largely through word of mouth so it is incumbent on the immigrant to extend his or her network of contacts. Ethnic contacts and ties must be cultivated because of the exigencies of survival and the structure of job opportunity in the illegal immigrant market."[1] Corcoran quoted one illegal migrant from eastern Ireland who suffered in New York because he could find no one from his part of Ireland to help. Irishmen from the west did not know him or were indifferent: "I would have starved on the street before someone from the west of Ireland would come to my aid."[2] Many of the men worked in construction, most in the small firms on the informal nonunion side of the industry, where pay was low. Other men and many of the women worked at pick-up jobs in bars, restaurants, and shops. Substantial members of the women also found jobs cleaning homes or taking care of children as au pairs. It is important to note that as difficult as their lives were, they were white English speakers—and thus better off than their Latino or Haitian brown or black fellow illegals. A study in New York, for example, found that Irish illegal workers still earned as much as twice the pay that Dominican illegals did. Still, it was a hard life of limited opportunities for most Irish illegals in America.

Desperate for communal links, the illegals clustered together in cities with already large Irish communities, most of them settling in New York but also in Boston, Chicago, or San Francisco. And in those cities, they usually settled in surviving old Irish neighborhoods like Woodside in the borough of Queens in New York City or Brighton in Boston. There they mingled with older Irish Americans, often with the immigrants who had fled Ireland in the 1940s and 1950s. Indeed, the new immigrants often depended on these old Irish immigrants for jobs in construction firms, bars, and restaurants, or for other tips on how to adjust to their new world. That did not mean that those relationships were easy or even amicable, however, for the new immigrants, shackled by the constraints of their illegal status, resented their dependence on the older generation of foreign-born Irish. There were significant cultural differences as well. Many, perhaps most, of the immigrants of the 1940s and 1950s had come from an Ireland locked into a traditional rural life imbued with Eamon De Valera's vision of a Holy Ireland of simple peasant people. When Northern Ireland erupted in violence, many of these older immigrants became strong nationalists. The new immigrants of the 1980s came from an Ireland rapidly if painfully being integrated into a broad European and world culture, and they themselves had become active participants in its new youth culture of rock music, continental sports, and modern fashions. In a way, though both groups of immigrants had come from the same island, they had not come from the same place.

By the 1990s, as the spectacular revival of the Irish economy created a new demand for workers, Irish immigration to the United States and elsewhere began to fall precipitously. The steady investment of European Community funds into improving Ireland's infrastructure, government policies that held down taxes and encouraged agreements between labor and business to keep wages low, and investment from America all helped Ireland capitalize on some of its existing inherent assets: a well-educated and English-speaking but still cheap workforce and a foot in the European market as a member of the European Community. As a result, pharmaceutical and technology industries, particularly producers of software, boomed in Ireland and the country became known as the "Celtic Tiger"—a robust, quickly growing economy that was the envy of Europe. The effects of the boom were uneven. There were still pockets of poverty in the old slums of Dublin or Limerick, which had been trying to live on sick, old manufacturing industries, and the income of rural farming regions in many parts of the country grew much more slowly than the Dublin metropolis. Still, immigration to America slowed to a trickle and, by the late 1990s, thousands of Irish-born men and women were returning to enjoy the boom. Immigration to America would never end, if only because Irish executives in international companies would move where the global economy dictated, but the history of Irish immigration to America had come to a historic pass.

The revival of Irish immigration embodied in the flood of illegals in the 1980s suggested an image of continuity in Irish life in America. It was not just the continuity of immigration, but a picture of a poor, vulnerable people huddling together in big city neighborhoods that recalled images of Irish America extending back to the famine.

And yet it was a misleading image. If immigration from Ireland did continue, the immigrants were now but a tiny slice of the people who claimed Irish ancestry in America, less representative of a broader Irish American population or even an Irish Catholic one than ever before. In 1980, the United States census counted not merely immigrants and their children but in a special sampling of households, counted Americans' ethnic ancestries as well. At a time when there were officially less than 200,000 Irish-born in America, over forty million people claimed Irish ancestors in the United States. These numbers were obviously the sum total of some four hundred years of Irish immigration to America—not just the one hundred and thirty or so since the famine—and thus a majority of the forty million or more were the descendants of the largely Protestant Irish migrations of the eighteenth and early nineteenth centuries. This accounts for the vast spread of Irish identifiers in the 1980 census across the South cited in chapter 1 of this book. Looking at people who identified as principally or totally Irish, rather than as Irish among multiple ancestral backgrounds, yields a somewhat different picture. While the number claiming single and multiple ancestries was roughly the same for Irish Americans in the New England and Mid-Atlantic states, the number claiming single ancestry was half as large in the Southern states. Social surveys that were able to distinguish Catholics and Protestants drew this difference with more precision. Andrew Greeley reports that such recent surveys reveal that while nearly half of all Irish Catholics live in the New England or Mid-Atlantic states, only about 7 percent of Irish American Protestants do. Conversely, only about 14 percent, or one-seventh, of today's Irish American Catholics live in the South, but more than half of Irish American Protestants reside there.

Perhaps what is most noticeable about this recent census and social survey data and what most clearly contradicts the image of continuity suggested by the illegals' plight is the substantial occupational and economic achievement of Irish Catholics. In Greeley's surveys, there is evidence that Irish American Catholics had surpassed Irish American Protestants as early as the 1920s in the economic hierarchy, a product probably as much of geography as of any special Catholic cultural advantage. Irish Catholics had settled in the northern United States, where the economy was dynamic and grew to be the economic engine of the world. This had been no great advantage to many of the famine era or later Irish immigrants, rural people who were chewed up in the maw of this industrial monster, but the descendants of those who survived were well placed to take advantage of the region's economic dynamism. Irish Protestants had moved into the expanse of the Pennsylvania and southern frontiers. Yet the South never developed as quickly or as completely as the North, and those

Appalachian areas, in particular, remained economically backward, as they were too mountainous for easy railroad access.

The achievements of Irish Catholics now did not merely surpass Irish Protestants but carried Irish Catholics finally into the highest reaches of the American economic hierarchy. Their proportions attending and graduating from college and finding professional jobs exceeded all but the Jews and the most successful Asian Americans, the Japanese, and equaled the achievements of old-line Protestants such as Episcopalians. Irish Catholics had "made it." Moreover, they appeared to have made it everywhere. There had long been important distinctions in economic success between Irish Catholics in New England and the Irish farther west in California or Michigan or even in New York or Pennsylvania. Yet by the 1980s at least, if not earlier, those differences seemed to have disappeared. In the 1980 census, a higher proportion of Irish American men and women worked in professional or managerial jobs in Massachusetts than in either the states of New York or Illinois.

It is important not to overdraw this picture. There were qualifications. Even in this new era of Irish Catholic success there were some odd patterns. There was some evidence, for example, that even the Irish who were successful were overeducated for the income that they earned. In addition, a higher proportion claiming only Irish ancestry in the 1980 census were likely to gravitate to government positions than the population at large. Both trends pointed perhaps to the persistence of old values: prizing safe positions over entrepreneurial risk and security over wealth. Irish Americans sometimes complained in the 1970s about their own timidity—the "$50,000 lawyer" who made a safe and tidy income but somehow did not aspire to more.

There were some more serious qualifications to this rosy picture as well. The busing controversy in Boston revealed an Irish working class left behind in physically and socially rotting neighborhoods of South Boston—"Southie"—and Charlestown, where children had little more hope for a college education or a white-collar job than poor blacks in nearby Dorchester or Roxbury. When the busing crisis passed in those neighborhoods, the crisis of despair only seemed to deepen. As Michael MacDonald movingly describes in his memoir *All Souls: A Family Story from Southie* and Joe Hayes in the short stories in his collection *This Thing Called Courage*, scores of young adults in places like Southie felt locked into a no-win world of drugs and crime. South Boston was special, but, as David Reimers points out, there were Irish American neighborhoods in New York City with similar levels of poverty and despair. A mid-1970s study of three Irish neighborhoods in New York City, he notes, revealed a considerable number of Irish Americans using food stamps and collecting unemployment insurance and a substantial proportion of elderly barely eking out a living.

Still, most Irish American Catholics in the North were doing well, and their success meant that while they were still a metropolitan people there, most were no longer an urban people. Greeley reports that some 29 percent of Irish Catholics lived in the nation's largest metropolitan areas in the late twentieth century and that another 58 percent resided in the next one hundred largest cities. Yet in the New York metropolitan area, where the Irish concentration was the largest in the nation, less than one in four lived in the city in 1980; three-quarters lived in the suburbs. By contrast, Irish Protestants were less likely to be a metropolitan people. Greeley found that only 11 percent of them lived in the nation's twelve largest metropolitan areas, and 34 percent in the next one hundred largest cities. In the 1980 census, while the two heaviest concentrations of Irish identifiers in the North (most likely overwhelmingly Catholic) were in the city of Boston and the Boston suburbs of Norfolk County, the heaviest concentrations of Irish identifiers in the South (probably Protestant in religion) lived in rural Lafayette County, Florida; Smith County, Mississippi; and Houston County, Tennessee.

In the 1950s, to be Irish in America meant for most people to be a militant Catholic, an American patriot, and a Democrat. After the 1960s, it still meant that for some Irish Americans, but for others, it meant a passion for Irish music, a devotion to Irish literature, a genealogical obsession, or perhaps all of those things, or, for many people of Irish ancestry, none of them—no Irish identity at all.

Even as late as the 1950s, many Irish Catholics were wary of how they interacted with non-Catholics. They belonged to different clubs than their non-Catholic neighbors, their children often went to different schools, and they almost never married across religious boundaries. In the 1950s, Catholics, third- or fourth-generation Irish Catholics, might still believe that certain jobs were beyond their reach, certain companies or firms coolly, if tacitly, discouraging. Many Catholics thus believed that they had their own interests, distinct from the interests of non-Catholics, interests that might cut across class lines, regional boundaries, or even city-suburb divides. In short, Irish Catholics still felt that they were part of a separate group with distinct boundaries, a clear sense of peoplehood, and a calculable common interest. If the group they identified with now was more often defined as broadly Catholic than narrowly Irish Catholic, it did not diminish their sense of separation.

During the 1960s and after, that sense of separation and distinction would wash away for most Irish Catholics. The intense identification, the sharply delineated social boundaries, and the dogged pursuit of ethnic interests had been fired by ethnic and religious competition and rivalry and the prejudice and discrimination that such competition generated. Irish Catholics had been Irish Catholics before the 1960s because, in many ways, they had to be. If Irish Catholics identified as Irish Catholics after the sixties, it was because they chose to do so, and they could slip such an identification by choice as well. After the 1960s, they were Irish when or if they wanted to be and because they wanted to be.

This was a revolution of great importance, because it was the first time since Irish Catholics had begun migrating to America that they had that choice in all parts of the country. Irish Protestants had long since had such an option in America, almost from the first years of their migration (New England in the early eighteenth century was a possible exception), and Irish Catholics in some western or southern communities had seemed to have such a choice as early as the nineteenth century. Why was it now possible for Irish Catholics everywhere?

In some respects, it was the result of the long-term trends of upward economic mobility and geographical mobility, noted earlier, that had been carrying Irish Catholics up and out since the last part of the nineteenth century. Such trends had made the Irish American Catholics a powerful people who could use their power to strengthen themselves and punish their enemies.

Yet it is important not to see this process as simply a "natural" one, an inevitable outcome of the working out of a beneficent American democracy and capitalism. Beneficent both may have been to white groups like the Irish—though the too-frequent horrors of Irish life in nineteenth-century American cities demand that even that statement be qualified—it still does not explain Irish "arrival" in the 1960s. For one thing, the emergence of Irish Catholics as national political powers depended on the Democratic Party's triumph after 1932. Looking forward from 1928, that would been hard to predict. It would have seemed more likely, then, that the Irish might have been condemned to being an emerging force in a permanent minority party. Furthermore, that unforeseen Democratic Party power in turn helped accelerate Irish and other white ethnics' economic rise and suburbanization through the backing of unions, redistributive tax plans, and government subsidies of education and housing.

Moreover, rising social and economic status and growing political power—however accrued—need not automatically result in easy assimilation. Indeed, they did not for Irish Catholics earlier in the century. Early in the twentieth century, economically and geographically mobile second- or third-generation

Irish Catholics were, indeed, likely to be proud American patriots and eager advocates of American culture. Yet those same ambitious and successful second- and third-generation Irish Catholics in many parts of the country were also more likely to be fierce and unyielding in their Catholic militancy than their working-class fellows. The Knights of Columbus, after all, was built on such ambitious and successful second- and third-generation Irish Americans. This is all simply to say that while the processes of Irish American social and geographical mobility accelerated by World War II were important in the dissolution of Irish Catholic ethnicity in the 1960s, they were not its sole cause.

There were other long-term trends at work. One was the transformation of race in America, both in its conceptualization and its political and social alignments. The conceptualization of race, as Matthew Jacobson has shown, changed dramatically in the middle years of the twentieth century for white ethnic peoples. Once categorized as "races"—inferior races along a complex hierarchy at that—white ethnics like the Irish, Italians, and Poles were increasingly lumped together as "Caucasians" in the 1930s and 1940s. World War II popularized the new white egalitarianism, as Gary Gerstle has pointed out, by setting American ethnic diversity—the inevitably multiethnic platoon in the foxhole of every World War II movie—starkly against Nazi obsessions with ethnic and racial purity. By this time, the Irish, as noted already, boasted a favorable image in the movies, burnished only further in their depictions as heroes on screen during World War II and the cold war.

As Gerstle argues, this celebration of diversity usually stopped short of black inclusion, but the economic demands of the war prompted a new black migration north and west, opened industries to black workers, and energized the African American civil rights movement. That movement helped push civil rights to the head of the American political agenda and brought racial issues to the fore of American political life. As the nation focused on differences between whites and blacks, differences among whites seemed trivial. A more sinister result was that whites in northern cities like Detroit and Chicago began to overlook ethnic distinctions among themselves and band together against black movement into their neighborhoods. These trends were already at work in the 1950s but came to a head when the civil rights movement peaked in the mid-1960s, and eventually gave way to Black Power and a host of other minority movements among Asians, Native Americans, and Latinos.

The civil rights movement triggered a whole series of other movements in the 1960s as well: a revival of feminism, a struggle for gay rights, and after the nation became bogged down in the morass of Vietnam, an antiwar crusade. These movements shared a skepticism of authority and celebrated individual liberation and personal authenticity. They thus encouraged rebellion against old institutions and the trampling of longstanding boundaries in the name of individual self-fulfillment. According to these ideas, artificial distinctions such as religious differences, for example, should not be an obstacle to true love and marriage.

This assault on authority helped to undermine the social and cultural pretensions of the old Protestant elite. Economic restructuring with the rise of new technology, information, and media industries in the 1980s and 1990s also undermined the economic power of that old elite, which had been based in heavy industry corporations that dated to the nineteenth or early twentieth centuries such as steel, automobiles, and the like. The Protestant establishment thus began to crumble, as Irish Catholics as well as Jews and others moved into top positions of Fortune 500 companies and mingled with Anglo Protestants in the most exclusive clubs. This did not mean that there was no establishment anymore or even that it did not include Protestants. It was just that Anglo-Saxon origins and Protestant faith were no longer required to be a part of it. Even in Boston, where Irish American mobility had been painfully slow, Irish Catholics began to vault to the top of the economic ladder as the heads of big businesses, such as Peter Lynch at Fidelity Investments or Terry Murray at Fleet Bank. Some of the structures, therefore, that had helped lock Irish Catholics into a separate world had begun to break up, crumble, and set them free.

Yet the changes were taking place not just outside the group but inside it as well. A new pope in Rome, John XXIII, ascended to Peter's throne in 1958 and he almost immediately called for a worldwide council for the Church, the Second Vatican Council. The changes resulting from the Council for American Catholics were momentous, from the specific revisions in the Catholic liturgy—such as now saying the mass in the vernacular, English—to a drastic rethinking of the church in the modern world. One of the most important changes was the reevaluation of Catholic relations with non-Catholics—Jews and Protestants in particular. After years of militant hostility, the church now sought to explore common ground with these other religions: ecumenism became the watchword of Catholics in the early 1960s. The changes outside (the transformation of race relations, the revolt against old institutions and authority in general, and the decline of the old Protestant elite in particular) and the changes inside (the Vatican Council's ecumenism) undermined the old Catholic militancy and defensiveness.

Yet this did not mean just a change in attitudes. Because the vast edifice of Catholicism was built as a defense against the dangers outside, the decline of hostility outside and militancy within caused the Catholic Church's institutional structure to begin to crumble. It did not collapse entirely, but it would never be the same. Between 1966 and 1978, about 10,000 men left the priesthood in America, and the number of religious women dropped by about 50,000 in roughly the same period (from 180,000 to 126,000 between 1966 and 1980). In the two decades after 1964, 40 percent of Catholic elementary schools and 27 percent of Catholic secondary schools closed. Regular mass attendance, which had been as high as 71 percent in 1963, plummeted to 50 percent in 1974. This affected all Catholics of all ethnic backgrounds, of course, but the transformation of the church in the 1960s was particularly important for Irish Catholics. It had been their church after all. They had led it since the nineteenth century and they would count more priests and bishops in it than any other ethnic or racial group even through the first years of the twenty first century. Yet, if the church had been theirs, they had also been the church's. It had been the center of Irish Catholic life since the end of the Revolutionary War, or certainly since the famine, and it had probably grown more important, not less, for them through the twentieth century.

The church was not the only old anchor of Irish American Catholic life to loosen in the 1960s. Irish Americans' particularly intense kind of American nationalism, manifested in an unyielding anticommunism and antisocialism, had been a second hallmark of Irish American identity since the early twentieth century. Indeed, it was the Knights of Columbus' peculiarly effective merger of American nationalism and Catholicism that had made them the most popular organization in the Irish American community in those early decades and throughout most of the twentieth century. In 1954, long after most other fraternal societies were dead and buried, the Knights still boasted nearly a million members. Other organizations like the Catholic War Veterans had also profited from this marriage of fierce nationalism and Catholicism. Irish American church figures were also identified with it, none more than **Cardinal Francis Spellman**, the archbishop of New York and Vicar of Military Affairs. When Hollywood came to define a figure to represent this kind of jingoistic nationalism in 1970, it naturally enough made him an Irish American and called him Joe Curran, the principal character in the movie *Joe*.

As that movie detailed in horror, the country had not just plunged into a war in Vietnam in the 1960s but also into a war with itself, and it seemed like few groups were so torn apart by the struggle as Irish Americans. As might be expected, Irish Americans were among the fiercest war "hawks," long-time backers of the Catholic anticommunist leaders of Vietnam. In the late 1960s, a young Irish American Catholic doctor from St. Louis, **Thomas "Tom"**

Dooley, had been the poster boy for that struggle, and his death gave America its first "martyr" in the Vietnamese conflict. As the war escalated with no resolution in sight and the nation at home split apart, Irish American leaders like Spellman, Mayor Daley, George Meany (head of the AFL-CIO), and the filmmaker John Ford were prominent among the "hawks" who assailed war protestors for their lack of patriotism. Daley in particular became a symbol of pro-war, antiprotest stridency during the tumultuous Democratic convention of 1968.

Yet there was growing sentiment against the war, not only in the country at large, but among Irish Americans. Ironically, two Irish American senators, Eugene McCarthy of Minnesota, early on and unequivocally, and Robert Kennedy of New York, later and more cautiously, rose to challenge President Lyndon Johnson and his war policy during the Democratic primaries in 1968. In the church, the Berrigan brothers, Philip, a Josephite priest, and Daniel, a Jesuit, were prominent in radical protests against the war. Irish and other Catholic students at Catholic universities like Georgetown, Boston College, Holy Cross, Catholic University, and Notre Dame joined the more mainstream student protests, albeit perhaps more slowly than other college students and with less ideological rigor. Yet such a stalwart anticommunist as Fulton J. Sheen, now bishop of Rochester, also joined the antiwar movement by 1967. **Thomas P. "Tip" O'Neill**, then a power in the House of Representatives and later majority leader and Speaker of the House, reflected the shifting attitudes even among many old-time, "regular" Irish American Democrats. O'Neill had been a stout anticommunist himself in the Massachusetts House of Representatives in the 1950s and as late as February of 1966 upbraided a delegation from his district when they came to Washington to lobby against the war. By the summer of that same year, however, pressure from liberal intellectuals in his Cambridge, Massachusetts district and increasing doubts about the conflict among his city's blue-collar constituents pushed O'Neill to oppose the war.

It is hard to say on which side the average Irish American came down on the war. The stereotypical image embodied by the movie character *Joe* was of course the Irish American hawk. Andrew Greeley, citing data from his own National Opinion Research Center and other surveys, adamantly rejects that notion. He argues that there was considerable "dove" antiwar sentiment among Irish American Catholics as early as 1967. Whatever the balance of alignment within the group, it was at least clear that there was no longer a community consensus on the kind of intense American nationalism imbued with a strong anticommunism that had once characterized the militant American Catholicism of Irish Americans throughout most of the twentieth century.

The war, the transformation of race, the changes in the church, and the rise of a new sexual ethic all combined to confuse old political alignments, weakening yet another longtime anchor of the Irish American community: the Democratic Party. There had been defections in the 1950s, as noted earlier, by Irish and other Catholics. Those wanderers returned in the 1960 election and appeared to hold for Lyndon Johnson in 1964. One estimate suggests that Johnson won as much as 78 percent of the Irish American Catholic vote. It is not clear whether either of the two Irish American Catholics, Eugene McCarthy or Robert Kennedy, would have had a special appeal to their fellow ethnics in the 1968 election. Though both were intensely Catholic in their own ways, the more charismatic and hard-nosed Kennedy seemed to have more appeal across class lines. Still, Hubert Humphrey, the eventual Democratic nominee, held the Catholic vote and what is more, polled an even larger percentage among Irish American Catholic voters: 64 percent.

There were signs of change, however, As far back as the 1950s, Irish Catholics like William Buckley had helped launch a new kind of American conservatism. Buckley, editor of the new conservatism's voice, the *National Review*, began his first book, *God and Man at Yale*, in 1951 with his stern anticommunist credo: "I ... believe that the duel between Christianity and atheism is the most important in the world. I further believe that the struggle between individualism and collectivism is the same struggle reproduced at another level."[3] Buckley and others, like Clarence "Pat" Manion, played critical roles in helping push the Republican Party to the right in 1964 with the nomination of Barry Goldwater. At this time, the movement appeared to have little effect on the Irish American electorate, as the previous figures suggest.

Yet there were signs in the 1950s and increasing evidence in the 1960s that the Irish American commitment to the Democrats was loosening. Such signs were evident first and most notably in the state of New York. There, a combination of factors seemed at work early on to pry the Irish away from the Democrats and push them toward the Republicans. The particularly strong conservatism of New York's Irish Catholic bishops like Cardinal Spellman probably had an effect. Suburbanization into Long Island and Westchester Republican strongholds did as well. Yet the decline of Irish power in the Democratic Party, particularly in the city, was important too. After caving into the Fiorello La Guardia coalition in the 1930s, Irish Democrats in New York had rallied to get one of their own, William O'Dwyer, elected mayor in 1945. Yet thereafter, Irish power in the Democratic Party began to decline as Anglo Protestants from mainline Protestant congregations and Jewish reformers pushed them out of the Democratic leadership. Kevin Phillips would later document the shifts in New York in his blueprint for the future rule of the GOP, his book *The Emerging Republican Majority*. He pointed to heavy Catholic defections from the Democrats, partially countered by a smaller Wasp movement out of the Republican party, in his analysis of New York voting data from the 1950s and 1960s. In 1960, when an estimated 70 percent of Irish Catholics around the nation voted for Kennedy, only 60 percent of the New York Irish did. Indeed, in heavily Irish American middle-class areas of the borough of Queens in New York City, Nixon ran neck and neck with Kennedy. Daniel Patrick Moynihan liked to point out that only the votes of the largely Jewish School of Social Work prevented the Catholic Fordham University straw poll from going for Nixon in the 1960 election. In 1961, two young Irish Americans, Kieran O'Doherty and J. Daniel Mahoney, founded the Conservative Party in New York. By 1970, that party had nominated and elected Irish American James Buckley to the post of U.S. senator. By the 1980s, New York's Irish Catholics were voting for Republican presidential candidate Ronald Reagan by a healthy margin. It had been quite an odyssey, from icons of the Democratic Party as Tammany's faithful to Republican enthusiasts.

In no state did the exodus from the Democrats seem as pronounced as in New York, in part because of the special conditions there: the Irish-Jewish rivalry, the rapid Irish descent from power in the Democratic hierarchy, and the local church's exceptional conservatism. Yet the changes were not just occurring in New York. All across the country some Irish American Catholics reacted to the antiwar movement, the sexual revolution and, perhaps, most important, the transformation of racial politics, by moving into the Republican Party. Indeed, in 1984, Reagan carried the Irish Catholic vote handily not only in New York, but in several other states as well.

As Irish Americans rapidly and apparently decisively swung to the Republicans, Irish American men quickly became icons of conservatism, indeed, of reaction, in American popular culture. Most often these images were not flattering. Indeed, Irish American males often appeared on screen as agents of a corrupt, oppressive old order trying to stifle liberating change. Such depictions began with the movie *Joe* in 1970, extended through such notable films as *Serpico, Ragtime, True Confessions*, and *L.A. Confidential* and through less visible films like *January Man* and *Q & A*. This representation of Irish American men also appeared on television, occasionally in dramas like *Law and Order* and consistently in *Homicide: Life on the Street*. Irish American men's conservatism has also been the central conceit of television comedies like *The Fighting Fitzgeralds* and *It's All Relative*. In part, this depiction of Irish American men reflected the entertainment industry's attention to changing political trends as well as overt outbreaks of Irish American racism and reaction, such as the resistance to busing in Boston in the mid-1970s. It, no doubt, also became easier to depict Irish Americans as "heavies," since Irish Americans after the 1960s had neither the cohesion, organizational clout, nor really interest to protest unfavorable images of themselves. Yet ironically, this harsh image of Irish American male, sometimes racist, reactionaries of the 1970s, 1980s, and 1990s, was rooted in earlier celebrations of Irish Americans as priests, patriots, and policemen in the 1930s, 1940s, and 1950s. Irish Americans have been depicted as agents of the established order and its institutions in both instances; the difference is that in the earlier period Americans revered authority and institutions, but after the 1960s many Americans suspected both as corrupt and oppressive. Irish Americans' identification with the older values of respect for authority and institutions did not condemn them among all Americans. Indeed, such an identification with an older America combined with a longtime Irish American male image as the quintessential common man—a "regular guy"—has probably enhanced the popularity of conservative Irish political television personalities in the 1990s like Bill O'Reilly or Sean Hannitty as well as more moderate political television commentators like Tim Russert and Chris Matthews.

Whatever recent movies or television might say, however, it is important not to make too much of the Irish American swing to conservatism. White Catholics are still more likely to vote Democratic than white Protestants, and Irish Catholics are more likely to do so than Catholics as a whole. Moreover, there were important regional distinctions in the Irish Catholics vote even in the 1980s. While Irish American Catholics in the state of New York and other states swung decisively to Reagan in 1984, their fellow Irish Catholics in Massachusetts did not. Southern New England, the Irish Catholic heartland in America, remains a Democratic stronghold, indeed, it is probably the most thoroughly Democratic region in America.

Nevertheless, the political fragmentation of Irish America signaled the evaporation of a common interest holding the group together. Now religious as well as ethnic boundaries meant little in dividing Irish Catholics from other whites. Catholic outmarriage skyrocketed from the 1960s on, and Irish ethnic outmarriage was even greater than that. Reginald Byron found that that the vast majority of people born after World War II calling themselves Irish Americans in Albany, New York in the 1990s actually came from ethnically mixed ancestries.

With no interests inside or forces outside the group holding them to a common conception of their identity, Irish Americans could now choose what it meant to be Irish American themselves or choose to forsake their roots altogether. For many, perhaps, it has meant what it had meant since at least the turn of the century: fiercely devoted Catholicism, American patriotism, and social conservatism. Yet for others, there was no going back to that old identity and culture. As Charlie Fanning has pointed out, in the first flush of the sixties liberation, several Irish American writers lashed out bitterly against that old world. Thomas McHale, for example, viciously satirized middle-class Irish American life and its puffed up hypocrisies, racism, and jingoism in his novels *Farraghan's Retreat* and *Principato*. No writer was more pessimistic, perhaps, than **Mary Gordon**, who traces the bleak middle-class life of Irish Americans in New York City's outer boroughs back to tragic defects in Irish culture itself.

Yet for Irish Americans who wanted to shed the old militant Catholic identity, and even some who did not, the 1960s opened up a variety of new potential meanings for the identity Irish American. There was for example the return of nationalism, as Northern Ireland erupted after nearly a half century of Unionist Protestant rule and seething Catholic resentment. The struggle there began as a civil rights movement modeled closely on America's own, but quickly degenerated into a brutal hit-and-run guerrilla war. Irish Americans rallied to the cause from its beginnings. During the civil rights phase, support was broad in Irish America and probably tilted left, but as the struggle turned into armed conflict, active support and contributions narrowed to a small if passionate slice of Irish Americans who were ironically often conservative in their American politics but militant in their Irish nationalism. **NORAID** was the principal organization in America backing the IRA provisionals who were carrying out the guerrilla war. By the late 1970s, a number of leading Irish American politicians, nicknamed the "**Four Horsemen**," staked out a more moderate constitutional nationalist position. Despite such splits and the narrowness of concern, for the first time in decades, Irish American nationalism, the cause of uniting Ireland's thirty-two counties into a single nation, became a touchstone of Irish identity, intensely emotional and deep-seated for a few Irish Americans and at least occasionally important for many more.

For most Irish Americans, the meaning of their Irish identity had a less politically purposeful focus. If the changes in the 1960s had seemed to blur boundaries among white ethnic groups, it had, paradoxically, encouraged white ethnics' pride in their ancestries. White ethnics were prompted by the black search for equal rights to mobilize their own claims for respect and inspired by Black Power rhetoric to proclaim their own ethnic pride. The white ethnic revival emerged in the late 1960s and 1970s and spread through almost all ethnic groups. By the late 1970s, the ethnic revival's organizations and activities sputtered out but the rhetoric of white ethnic pride became a critical part of mainstream American culture. In time, Ellis Island became an icon of equal status to the Mayflower in American national culture, and "Ellis Island Whiteness" in Mathew Jacobson's phrase became the equal of "Mayflower Whiteness."

Many Irish Americans, moved like other white ethnics to assert their ethnic identities, now looked back to Ireland for the sources for their new ethnic pride. One of the results of the new emphasis on group pride was the democratization of genealogy, and by the late twentieth century Irish genealogical organizations like the Irish Ancestral Research Association of Boston, the Buffalo Irish Genealogical Society, and the Ballykilcline Society had sprung up all over America.

For many Irish, the search for their ethnic roots was more general. It involved not just a tracing of ancestors but an immersion in the culture of the old country. As noted earlier, Irish traditional culture had almost disappeared in America in the middle years of the twentieth century. Yet the cultural revolution that swept the United States in the 1960s, with its rejection of modern bureaucratic civilization's spiritual emptiness and its consequent passion for the "authentic" and the "natural," sparked a startling new interest in folk music and folk arts. Irish traditional music was at the center of this revival and enjoyed a new popularity in America unparalleled in the nation's history. Led by the Clancy Brothers and Tommy Makem in the early 1960s but really reaching full flower with the Chieftains and other groups like them in the 1970s, 1980s, and 1990s, it exploded into American popular culture. Self-consciously retrieved from Ireland's distant past and played on instruments like the bodhran, an Irish drum, fiddles, tin whistles, and uillean pipes, it was a kind of music that most Irish Americans, accustomed by the 1940s to Tin Pan Alley Irishness, had never heard before. Even in cities like Washington, which had had little Irish immigration to speak of but was filled with third-, fourth-, and later-generation Irish American transplants working the Capitol's halls of power, the effect of the traditional music revival was electric. As Terry Winch, an Irish musician and poet living in Washington, explains, today's Irish community in Washington is not "rooted in any geographical locale, it coalesces around cultural, social, and political events and interests. This floating subculture came into existence in the mid-1970s, when certain visionary and half-crazy businessmen and musicians conspired to create a music scene that was as unlikely as it was catalytic. Out of that world of bars and ballads a new Irish network evolved."[4] One- and two-day Irish music festivals and concerts, featuring numbers of Irish bands and selling everything from soda bread to Irish themed T-shirts, sprung up in places like Washington, Milwaukee, and North Easton, Massachusetts. By the 1990s, "Celtic music" had become almost omnipresent in American culture, from the blockbuster movie *Titanic* to telephone commercials and television detective shows. Irish bars, which had largely descended into quiet, smoky, working-class neighborhood taverns by the early twentieth century, now spruced up, expanded, and staged shows of Irish music. Irish dance was somewhat slower to emerge. Finally prompted by the Riverdance phenomenon, Irish dance schools mushroomed around the country. Emerging Irish music and dance groups began to affiliate with Ceoltas Ceoltari Eirann, founded in Ireland to promote Irish music and dance. By 2003, there were more than forty such branches of Ceoltas spread across North America. They included the O'Neill/Malcolm branch begun in the Washington D.C. area in 1969, the Hanafin/Cooley branch founded in Boston in 1975, and the Cooley/Keegan branch organized in San Francisco in the 1970s.

The new meaning of Irishness could be found not only in Irish music and arts but in the formal study of Irish literature and language. **Irish Studies** programs began booming in American universities in the 1970s and 1980s and have flourished since. In 1966, the American Conference of Irish Studies had 300 members; by 1997 it had 1,500 and had established regional branches in Midwest, New England, Mid-Atlantic, Western, and Southern regions. In addition to these academic programs, a number of cultural organizations both national and local have emerged to encourage broad public interest in Irish Studies. Eoin McKernain, a faculty member at St. Thomas University, created the Irish American Cultural Institute in 1962. Over the years, the Institute published a scholarly journal, *Eire/Ireland*, imported lecturers from Ireland for nationwide tours in its "Irish Perspectives" and "Irish Fortnight" programs, and provided funding for research in Irish American history. Irish American communities in New York and Chicago also established their own local arts or cultural centers to nurture interest among Irish Americans and others in a wide range of Irish traditional and contemporary arts.

A dramatic, new, and broadly supported interest in Irish culture, then, was already underway by the 1990s, when Ireland, flush with new prosperity as the Celtic Tiger, experienced a cultural revival of its own in theater, film, dance, and performing arts. The export of this culture to America on top of indigenous efforts in the United States made some recognition of their Irishness easy and, indeed, attractive to many Irish Americans. As Marilyn Halter has argued, there was not a little hucksterism in much of this new ethnic pride from airlines encouraging returns "home," to beer companies underwriting festivals, to retailers selling sweaters (woolen and usually white) as identities. Halter argues, however, that for all that, millions of Irish Americans have been working to forge an Irish identity for themselves through the passionate embrace of Irish culture and consumerism.

Still, what was important now was that it was a choice. It was not determined by social or political constraints but chosen to fill some personal need for identification. For every Irish American who made the choice to take their Irish American identity seriously there would be another, or several others perhaps, who felt that they did not need to find fulfillment in an ethnic identity. What it also meant was that there was no agreement or consensus on what it meant to be Irish in America, either.

The absence of such consensus could lead to friction and controversy. In New York, for example, the meaning of being Irish was played out every March in dramatic confrontations between gay and lesbian Irish Americans and older organizations like the **Ancient Order of Hibernians**, who ran the **St. Patrick's Day** parades in their communities. Such protests began in New York City in 1991, when Irish American gays and lesbians asked to be included in the annual St. Patrick's Day parade. The Ancient Order of Hibernians, which sponsored the parade, refused, and the protests have gone on since then. These disputes were contentions not so much over a parade, but over what it meant to be Irish in America and whether a group publicly self-identified as gay and thus in conflict with the Catholic Church's teachings on homosexuality could be included in the parade, which passed by St. Patrick's Cathedral and received the greetings of the archbishop of New York. A similar dispute arose between the South Boston Allied War Veteran's Council, the organizers of the parade in that heavily Irish Boston neighborhood, and Irish American gays and lesbians of Boston about the same time. In both cases, the courts permitted the sponsors to exclude the gay Irish American marchers, but the exclusion hardly resolved the issue. There was no way now to impose one version of Irish American identity on American people descended from Irish immigrants, for there was no authority to do so and no outside constraints forcing the compromises that solidarity in defense of Irish American interests had once demanded. There were no Irish American interests now, and therefore, there were many ways to be Irish American now as well, and they were all choices to be taken up or abandoned as personal need or desire required.

NOTES

1. Mary Corcoran, "Emigrants, *Eirepreneurs,* and Opportunists: A Social Profile of Recent Irish Immigration in New York City," in *The New York Irish,* eds. Ronald H. Bayor and Timothy Meagher (Baltimore: Johns Hopkins University Press, 1996), 471.

2. Ibid.

3. Patrick Allitt, *Catholic Intellectuals and Conservative Politics in America, 1950–1985* (Ithaca, N.Y.: Cornell University Press, 1993), 21.

4. Terence Winch, "A Bit of Ireland," *Washingtonian Magazine,* March 2000.

PART II

Issues and Themes in Irish American History

CHAPTER ONE

Irish American Gender and Family

Few dimensions of Irish American life are less studied than family life and gender roles, despite the fact that few such dimensions appear to be as rich and intriguing fields for historical investigation. Serious studies of Irish families or male and female roles in the colonial era are rare, and little work has been done on twentieth-century Irish American families. What follows here, then, is a discussion of family life and gender roles among first- and second-generation Irish American Catholics in the nineteenth and twentieth centuries, since most of the current scholarship focuses on that era. If this discussion traces this topic largely through only a narrow slice of Irish American history, it nonetheless reveals Irish American family and gender roles that clearly distinguish them from the family and gender norms and customs of native-stock Protestant Americans and other ethnics. It therefore suggests that this area of Irish American life is worthy of further investigation.

This distinctiveness of Irish American gender roles has been evident from the very act of migration from Ireland to America in the nineteenth and twentieth centuries. Irish immigrants to America at that time included a far higher proportion of single women than any other groups migrating to this country. This was largely a post-famine phenomenon. In the colonial era, the vast majority of migrants were single men or men and women as parts of families. Even in the pre-famine period, when most of the migrants were single, most were men. During the famine, the proportion of migrants fleeing as part of families increased significantly. After the famine, most migrants were once again single people. At this point, the proportion of single women among Irish migrants began to rise. By the 1870s, women began to outnumber men among Irish migrants in many years, and the proportions remained roughly even through the early twentieth century.

For no other immigrant group was the proportion of single women among the migrants so high. For ethnic groups like the Jews, families migrated, so husbands, wives, and young daughters and sons came to the United States together in a unit. Many groups—Italians, for example—were top-heavy with males, particularly initially. These men were often "birds of passage," planning ultimately to return to their homes in Europe, but when some settled down, female immigrants began to follow. Scandinavian immigrants included more single women than many other immigrant groups, but the proportion of single women was not as high among Swedes or Norwegians as it was among the Irish. Indeed, at the turn of the century when the proportion of single Irish immigrant women was reaching its peak and running to about half of all Irish immigrants, the percentage of females among *all* immigrants fell to its lowest levels ever: 38 percent in the 1880s and a mere 30 percent between 1900 and 1909.

Why were there so many Irish women among the migrants? Janet Nolan argues that women left Ireland to regain something of the status and freedom that they had enjoyed in the pre-famine era and were losing or had lost in the economic and social changes that followed the famine. More specifically, the trend from tillage to pasture and complementary trends from earlier to later marriage increasingly constricted women's economic roles and limited their social freedom. Nolan suggests that in pre-famine Ireland, women worked in fields with men and made money for the household by spinning yarn. Almost all women had a chance to marry then as well, and pre-famine society offered women in Ireland ample opportunities to socialize. So as Nolan argues: "Female emigrants between 1885 and 1920 sought to regain their pre-famine status as wives and economic partners within the family, something they could no longer do in the changed world of post-famine Irish life... . The legions of young women leaving rural Ireland in the late nineteenth and early twentieth centuries were discarding their newly subservient and marginal positions in their home communities, not their traditional expectations."[1]

Nevertheless, whatever compelled Irish women to come to America, there had to be something more fundamental and broadly based in Irish culture for such an emigration to occur, no matter what the circumstance. Almost all European peasant societies were experiencing disruptive economic and social changes in the nineteenth and twentieth centuries, but many of those societies continued to jealously guard women's "virtue" by maintaining male control of women at all times. Men and women in Mediterranean cultures would have been shocked at the freedom Irish women were allowed in migrating. Some might argue that the sexual puritanism that increasingly pervaded

Irish society seemed to inure the Irish to fears or worries about their daughters' virtue. Yet one could also read this permissiveness another way, as a kind of backhanded gender egalitarianism forced by necessity, an acknowledgement that women had the right to emigrate as much as men because they needed to leave as much or more than the men.

Whatever the underlying values that permitted the migration of women, the gendering of the very process of Irish migration was unique. This meant, by necessity, that the gendering of Irish immigrant experiences in America would be unique too, if for no other reason than that there were so many female immigrants among the Irish than among any other group. The vast majority of both Irish male and female immigrants were unmarried when they came to America. They needed to establish a home and find work when they landed. Most Irish men worked at a variety of unskilled occupations and boarded with Irish immigrant families already established in America until they themselves married. Irish immigrant women also needed jobs and places to live. The majority found a single solution to both theses needs: domestic service. Of all the immigrant women in America, again Irishwomen were far and away the most likely to become domestic servants. Hasia Diner points out that domestic work offered Irish women many advantages: high pay, secure work, and ample openings. Yet Jews, Italians, and almost all others but Scandinavians avoided such work—as did native-stock Americans. Some of these other ethnics objected to the control exerted by mistresses; others feared that it placed young women in sexually vulnerable positions. Irish women, however, needed service in a way that these other women did not, for they needed not just a job but a place to live. They might board out like their brothers, but most manufacturing wages for women were significantly lower than for men, and paying rents for apartments or, more likely, boarding fees would eat up their paychecks quickly. Moreover, manufacturing jobs were also more precarious than service and more subject to seasonal or cyclical booms and busts, making Irish women's living arrangements outside service even more insecure.

Kevin Kenny wonders whether historians like Diner and Nolan have perhaps overestimated the benefits of service for Irish women and underestimated its drawbacks. "It is surely important," Kenny contends, "not to romanticize domestic service and remember ultimately that it is based on domination and subordination."[2] He points in particular to the potential for sexual harassment of servants by male employers and the number of women who seemed to fall from their positions as domestic servants into prostitution. Kenny's argument is sobering and helpful, but it is useful to remember as well, as he acknowledges, that service was often the best of difficult choices for Irish women, who needed affordable housing as well as a job when they came to America. Moreover, Nolan and especially Diner make powerful points in their suggestions that the wages and security of service, as well as the lessons in American culture learned in that work, helped Irish immigrant women establish themselves in their own communities and nourish the independence and ambitions of their daughters—even if those lessons and resources were hard earned in subservience to masters and mistresses.

Irish immigrant men and women thus often lived apart when they arrived in America, but Irish women did not forsake their local Irish communities. They were fiercely loyal to the Catholic Church—many pastors would thank the "live-in girls" for contributions to church buildings—and participated in the social life of the community whenever they could. By the 1890s, Irish immigrant women also joined formal social organizations like the Ladies Auxiliary of the **Ancient Order of Hibernians** or the Irish National Foresters. Men too had their associations, but they also had the men's world of the saloon, where women were not welcome and where few went.

Both male and female Irish immigrants married later than most other immigrants to America through the nineteenth century, and the average age of marriage for both seemed to creep upward as time passed. This was perhaps a reflection of the spread of delayed marriage throughout Ireland itself in the late nineteenth century as the conversion to pasturage—raising cows, cattle, and sheep—erased the old tillage economy of growing wheat, barley, and oats. In the cattle, sheep, and dairying economy, open land was at a premium and thus farmers refused to break up their farms to distribute land to all their children. Parents were also reluctant to give up their farms until they grew old and feeble. With no other economic options in deindustrialized southern Ireland, heirs to farms as well as their potential wives had to wait for their fathers to give up the land before the new couple could wed. Other sons and daughters had few chances to marry at all if they stayed at home, and many remained single "boys" or "girls" living and working on relatives' or others' farms until their deaths. All this drove up the average age of marriage in Ireland for both men and women to heights unique among western nations. Hasia Diner also contends that once Irish immigrant women arrived in America they encountered new reasons for postponing marriage. Diner suggests that in America, Irish immigrant women came to fear marriage because of the real possibilities that their husbands would die, desert, or beat them. Irish immigrant women here were also reluctant to give up their independence as working women, Diner argues: almost no Irish American women worked outside the home after marriage, in contrast to women from some other groups, such as the French Canadians.

Still, many historians note how much *earlier* Irish immigrants, male and female, married in America than men and women in Ireland, even though they
tended to marry later in life than other immigrants to America. Widowhood
and domestic violence were real problems for Irish Catholic women, but in
the end only a very small proportion of Irish immigrant women actually fore-
swore marriage altogether—a smaller proportion, in fact, than native-stock
American women at the turn of the century. This may have been because of
the high proportion of Irish immigrants from the west of Ireland, where the
island's custom of late marriage was new and just being established. These
women from the province of Connaught and western Munster or western
Ulster may simply not have been accustomed to marrying late like their fellow Irish from farther east on the island. Yet it was also because marriage, or
more specifically, the eventually employable children that could come from
marriage, offered both men and women virtually their only guarantee of security or hopes of modest prosperity in their own homes. Few Irish immigrant
women, even among the servant girls, expected or hoped to work all their
lives. So they married, nine-tenths or more of them marrying fellow Irish, and
when they married had children at rates far higher than native-stock women.

If Irish immigrant women and men needed each other, there still appears
to have been some profound differences between them. As noted earlier, domestic service, for example, may have not just been a necessity for immigrant
women, but for many, some historians argue, it may have also proved a training ground. There, Irish immigrant servants had a daily lesson in American
bourgeois norms and customs: how respectable Americans acted, furnished
their homes, ate, and brought up their children. Few women could then easily
translate this knowledge into their own family lives, as they and their husbands
and children struggled for survival in some of the worst city tenements, but
some of their experience did apparently rub off on their children, particularly
their daughters. A number of historians have also suggested that immigrant
mothers may have played a critical role in the family's religious life as well.
This should not be surprising, as women seemed to have been far more likely
to be religious than men among virtually all ethnic and religious groups in
nineteenth-century America. Yet immigrant women in the famine era and
shortly after, from the 1850s to the 1870s, may have played a particularly critical role in the evolution of Catholicism in North America. As Brian Clarke
has pointed out in his study of the Irish in Toronto, Irish immigrant women
may have been the principal participants in the Catholic "Devotional Revolution" of that era and thus helped introduce the new devotional Catholicism

into their families. An argument can be made, then, that immigrant women were active agents of respectability and cultural change in Irish families.

While Irish immigrant women looked forward, Irish immigrant men may have been more likely to look back. Historians such as Diner and Kerby Miller have suggested that women were more likely to shrug off the homeland and embrace their new country, but male emigrants left Ireland with regret, had trouble accepting America, and often viewed themselves as exiles forced out of their homeland. In large part this may have been because men sacrificed the possibility of power in their families as ruler of the family's land (or at least the illusion of achieving that possibility). In America, there was no land and thus fathers had no such power. In the American family, wives who had worked as domestics may have known as much about their new home as their husbands did, and American-born sons and daughters might be bringing home as much or more money as carpenters, plumbers, clerks, or even schoolteachers as immigrant fathers still stuck in day labor. Looking homeward nostalgically, Irish men, Clarke, Colleen McDannell, and others suggest, seemed more interested in the issues of Irish nationalism than in the church. Their saloons, men's clubs, and work also oriented them to the communalism and rough masculinity of working-class male culture rather than to the ideals of bourgeois respectability.

As the immigrant father's power diminished, the immigrant mother's power increased—all the more so when Irish immigrant fathers were absent, which they often were. Irish men, working in heavy labor, the worst jobs that the economy offered, were unusually susceptible to industrial accidents and illnesses. Many also often wandered the country, looking for construction work on railways or canals. Sometimes they came back; sometimes they did not. The result was a striking number of female-headed households among the Irish in the immigrant generation, again obviously enhancing maternal over paternal influence on the next generation.

Among the children of the immigrants in the late nineteenth and early twentieth centuries, family patterns and gender roles changed once again. Second-generation Irish men and women, for example, married far later than the immigrant Irish and were much more likely than the Irish-born to never marry. It was the second generation, then, not the immigrant one, that most resembled their cousins in Ireland. Indeed, in Worcester, Massachusetts, the average ages of marriage for second-generation men and women in 1900 was virtually the same as the average age for women and men in Ireland in 1901, but a significant two to three years on average *later* (two for men; three for women) than Irish immigrants in Worcester.

This is not entirely surprising. The American-born children of immigrants in almost all ethnic groups married later than their immigrant parents. Sons and daughters of immigrants living at home with their parents played a vital role in keeping immigrant family economies afloat. Multiple-income families that could rely on a father and adult or adolescent children's wages could even aspire to some prosperity and to buying a house of their own.

Parents were thus reluctant to let children marry early, but American-born children themselves, fearful of the costs of marriage, may have been reluctant to marry too. Second-generation Irish men and women who hoped to move beyond their parents' lowly economic level worried about hindering their careers by early marriage. For the many second-generation Irish women who were moving up into white-collar jobs as stenographers, bookkeepers, nurses, schoolteachers, or even doctors, marriage would not simply slow their careers but would end them, for they would not work after marriage. As Howard Chudacoff has pointed out, immigrant sons and daughters would also have to forego the new rich world of urban entertainment and popular culture emerging at the turn of the century if they took up the duties and obligations of marriage.

Though all children of immigrants married later than their parents in the early twentieth century, second-generation Irish married much later than the children of other immigrants. It appears that in addition to the needs of the family economy, the entertainment available in the city, or the interest in their own mobility, a stern Catholicism may have had a powerful effect on the first American-born generation of Irish. Catholicism did not by itself force the second-generation Irish to delay marriage or forego it altogether, but its stern moral codes seemed to work symbiotically with the economic pressures of their parents' family and their own yearning for self-improvement to convince them to postpone marriage or avoid it altogether. Hugh McLeod has noted that on the West Side of New York, Catholicism had become the arbiter of respectability: "it seems fair to interpret the militant respectability of these Catholics as a means of protecting their families from aspects of real life that were unpleasantly prominent. Their Catholicism looks less like the famous opium (Marx's notion of religion as an opiate for the masses) than a stimulant to the sanctification of values that offered a basis for pride in a situation of suffering and humiliation and some defense against its effects."[3] It is difficult to determine for certain, but it appears that both second-generation men and women had become strong adherents of Catholicism, if not more devoted than their parents, than, at least, certainly more integrated into the church's institutional practice and obedient to its dicta than the earlier immigrant generation. The huge numbers of American-born Irish priests that began to flow out of American seminaries at the turn of the century as well as second-generation Irish religious women out of novitiates testified to the central place Catholicism would play in their lives.

Of course, at the turn of the century the vast majority of second-generation men and women would eventually marry, if late in life. The proportion of female-headed households also seemed to decline in the second generation among Irish Americans, as Irish men moved into less dangerous jobs, and were more sensitive to church teachings about family responsibility. Once second-generation men and women married, however, it appears that they would have children at about the same rate as the immigrants, although, because of their later age of marriage, they ultimately had smaller families than the immigrants. Opposition to birth control, or as it was called in the early twentieth century, "race suicide," became a marker of Irish Catholic identity, distinguishing Irish Catholics from the sinful and inferior Protestants who practiced family limitation.

In marriage, important differences emerged between second-generation men and women. Irish Americans figured prominently in the urban culture of the turn of the century, from vaudeville skits and songs to early movies and comic strips, and a recurring theme was the chaotic transition from a working-class community to "lace curtain" middle-class respectability. As Ronald Ebst, William Williams, and others have pointed out, this process was depicted in a profoundly gendered way. In virtually everything from Harrigan and Hart's "Mulligan Guards" to Finley Peter Dunne's "Mister Dooley" to the comic strip Maggie and Jiggs, American-born women stood, like their immigrant mothers, for a future of ambition and respectability; men for a past of working-class communalism. Few historians have studied the gender dimensions of Irish social mobility, but broad statistics indicate that American-born Irish women often outperformed second-generation men in the economic realm, and hints in the literature of white-collar American-born women turning up their noses at their rough blue-collar, second-generation Irish male counterparts lend credence to the popular culture distinction. Studies like Paula Kane's also suggest that the church worried more about male than female mobility because they feared males who were too ambitious would be tempted to abandon their faith in search of status and riches. They did not expect many women to follow careers, so they worried less about these temptations for them.

There is evidence that many of these patterns emerging among Irish American Catholics in the nineteenth and early twentieth centuries continued to dominate the Irish Catholic community through the middle of twentieth century. Immigrant women outnumbered men in most years from the 1930s on, just as they had before. Among second and even third or later generations of Irish Americans there is scattered evidence of single women's occupational success, late ages of marriage for both men and women, significant proportions of men and women remaining unmarried as bachelor uncles or maiden aunts, high fertility rates for married women, and stout opposition to birth control and abortion. The cultural and social upheavals in American life that broke up older notions of Irish American identity and fractured the Irish American community in the 1960s also scrambled these patterns in Irish American gender roles and family life. In the new post-1960s world of the feminist revival, the sexual revolution, and the declining authority of the Catholic Church, Irish American notions of men and women's roles and sexual and family norms would be drastically altered.

NOTES

1. Janet Nolan, *Ourselves Alone: Women's Emigration from Ireland, 1885–1920* (Lexington: University of Kentucky Press, 1989), 91–92.

2. Kevin Kenny, *The American Irish: A History* (Harlow, U.K.: Longman, 2000), 154.

3. Hugh McLeod, "Catholicism and the New York Irish: 1880 to 1910," in *Disciplines of Faith: Studies in Religion, Politics, and Patriarchy*, eds. Jim Obelkevich et al. (New York: Routledge, Kegan, and Paul, 1987), 350.

CHAPTER TWO

Irish Americans in Politics

In 1954, when the famed British political scientist D. W. Brogan wrote his definitive study, *Politics in America*, he noted the peculiarly important role of Irish Americans in American politics: "Until well into the twentieth century, the 'governing classes' ... were the Irish."[1] By this he did not mean that Irish Americans were a "ruling class," something altogether different, but rather that "the Irish became in most regions outside the South, the providers of a professional political class."[2]

Irish prominence in American political life emerged only slowly in fits and starts during the colonial era, but flowered during the American Revolution and its aftermath. As David Doyle notes, the Revolution and perhaps as importantly the later triumph of Democratic-Republicans under Jefferson opened up opportunities for men like **Thomas McKean**. As noted earlier, the conjunction of the Jeffersonian revolution and the crushing of republicanism in Ireland in the 1798 rebellion brought a flood of highly politicized and largely Protestant Irish exiles to America, and they rose almost meteorically to prominence in American politics in the 1790s and early 1800s. In the first half of the nineteenth century, descendants of Ulster Presbyterians, from the second-generation Irish Andrew Jackson (who gave his name to an era) to Presidents James Knox Polk and James Buchanan and vice president and powerful Senator John C. Calhoun, were at the forefront of American politics. Irish Anglicans had enjoyed greater political prominence in the colonial era, but they, too, flourished in the early republic: George and Dewitt Clinton, governors of New York, were the best examples perhaps, but **Michael Walsh**, the rough and tumble Democratic leader of mid-nineteenth-century New York City, was another, if of a very different sort.

Protestant Irish prominence in American politics continued even long after such people stopped identifying themselves as Irish. The great nineteenth-century bosses like Richard Croker of New York and Christopher Magee of Pittsburgh were of Irish Protestant background, for example. More important, presidents Woodrow Wilson and Richard Nixon were also descendants of Irish Protestant immigrants. Yet few people in America thought of Wilson and Nixon as Irish. When Nixon, the descendant of Irish Quakers, confronted John F. Kennedy, the great-grandson of Irish Catholic immigrants, it was Kennedy, not Nixon, who was considered "Irish."

Thus, despite the political prominence of Irish Protestants throughout American history, when Brogan wrote of the Irish as a governing class, he meant Irish Catholics, and most of his readers understood him to be doing so. For no other ethnic or racial group in America has politics been more important than for Irish American Catholics. For example, in the last half century, three Irish American Catholics, John McCormack, **Thomas "Tip" O'Neill**, and Thomas Foley, have ruled the House of Representatives as Speaker of the House, the highest post for the politicians' politician. Over approximately the same time, Irish Americans including Terence McAuliffe, Paul Kirk, Lawrence O'Brien, John Bailey, J. Howard McGrath, and James Farley have acted as the chairmen of the Democratic Party. Today, Terence McAuliffe and Edward Gillespie, both Irish Americans and both graduates of Catholic University, serve as chairmen of the Democratic and Republican Parties respectively. In 1962, the President, Kennedy, the Speaker of the House, McCormack, and the Senate's majority leader, Michael Mansfield, were all Irish American Catholics.

And yet the peculiarly strong Irish American involvement in politics has not been only been at the leadership or elite level. There is evidence that at least by the end of the nineteenth and beginning of the twentieth centuries, Irish immigrants have been quicker to seek naturalization and entry into American politics than other ethnic groups. For example, in 1885 in Worcester, nearly two-thirds of Irish immigrant men had sought naturalization, compared to only 22 percent of French Canadians and 16 percent of Swedish newcomers.

The prominence of Irish Catholics in American politics has prompted many important questions for historians and political scientists, but two seem most important. The first and most obvious is: Why have Irish Americans been so much more involved in politics than other American ethnic groups? And the second is: What did the Irish do with this political power after they gained it—that is, what did Irish American Catholics believe the purposes of political power were?

Explanations for Irish prominence in politics usually begin with the culture and history of Ireland. This seems reasonable enough, for what would appear to more clearly distinguish the Irish from other ethnic groups than the distinctive culture and experience they brought with them to America? Indeed, it must be true at least in part that their culture or experience explains their political prominence because the Irish in the United States reacted to the new American environment very differently than any other group, such as the Germans, Italians, and Poles.

The Irish were one of the few peoples coming to America who had experience with Anglo-American forms of government, including everything from parliamentary elections to trials by jury. As Alexis De Tocqueville himself remarked on a trip to Ireland in the 1830s, most peasants participated little in these institutions, which often served more as instruments of their oppression than either as mechanisms for their representation or as safeguards of their rights. Nevertheless, they had a familiarity with the forms of Anglo-American government, and over the course of the nineteenth century gained more and more experience in manipulating them. A succession of mass movements, such as the Catholic Emancipation in the 1820s and for the Repeal of the Act of Union in the 1840s, and still later the Land League agitation for land reform and Home Rule in the 1880s, all helped mobilize the Irish peasantry and exposed them to the techniques of political organization. The Irish, Thomas Brown argues, became the most politicized peasantry in the world in the nineteenth century.

In addition to the experience they gained in organizing to influence the government in the nineteenth century, Irish immigrants had also learned in Ireland what the government could do for them. Even before the famine—but certainly during it—the government often addressed economic distress through government employment projects. As Cormac O'Grada points out, such projects did not help much during the famine—indeed, they may have made the suffering of poor peasants worse—but the precedent, that the government can and should provide employment to those who do not have it, may have stuck with Irish immigrants who came to America.

There were other inheritances from Irish experience that may not have been directly related to the political process but may have helped the Irish become more successful in it. Among them, perhaps the most important, was the strong emphasis in Irish peasant culture on communalism. From rural secret societies like the Whiteboys or Ribbonmen to O'Connell's mass protests to the Land League's boycotts, Irish peasants were schooled in the importance of group solidarity and its potency as a political weapon. Perhaps less important, but worth noting, Daniel Patrick Moynihan points to aspects of Irish self-discipline, reflected in late marriage patterns, as a useful trait for people working their way through political organizations. Moynihan ruefully notes: "The incredible capacity of the rural Irish to remain celibate awaiting their turn to inherit the family farm was matched by generations of assistant corporation counsels awaiting that opening on the City Court bench."[3] Others have suggested that Irish Americans inherited a concern for security from their old country's troubled history, which made them prize safe, if low-paying, jobs in civil service over the pursuit of entrepreneurial opportunities offering high rewards but also high risk. All these points to a greater or lesser extent help to explain the Irish preference for and success in politics, for something in their background must have made them more prominent and successful in politics than any other American ethnic group.

Yet Irish American interest might have also reflected not so much advantages the Irish Americans had over other groups as their disadvantages relative to others. They did not have the useful skills to move them quickly into higher-paid work in the private economy, for example; the capital to buy a farm, start a business, or move to new regions with strong economies; or the entrepreneurial values to maneuver in the private, capitalist economy. German and Scandinavian immigrants enjoyed the former advantages; Jews and some Asian groups the latter. The Irish may have become America's "governing class" less out of confident exploitation of inherited values and skills, therefore, than in a desperation to find in politics some kind of economic "niche" that they could call their own.

Nevertheless, citing any number of skills, experiences, or values inherited from Ireland does not fully explain why Irish Americans became so thoroughly involved as critical players in American politics. Here comparisons to the Irish in other parts of the diaspora are useful. In Canada and Australia, Irish Anglicans and even Ulster Irish Presbyterians often played important roles in politics, but neither there nor in Britain did Irish Catholics emerge as a "governing class." Why did the Irish carve out that role for themselves in the United States but not elsewhere?

One explanation may be that the Irish who migrated to these other parts of the world had less need for politics than the Irish in the United States, either because they came from backgrounds that better prepared them for the economies of their new homes or they found ample opportunities in the private sectors there. Some historians have argued that Irish immigrants were more economically successful in Australia, New Zealand, and Canada, especially in their ability to establish their own farms in the rural areas of those countries. Some Irish Americans in the eastern United States themselves wondered in the early twentieth century whether they had been forced into politics because of their region's limited opportunities, while Irishmen farther west thrived on the abundant job openings in private businesses produced by dynamic western economies. Still, the need for politics by itself probably did not account for Irish political prominence in the United States. The Irish in Britain were probably more needy but not nearly so successful, and the Irish in many places in the Midwest or West, like St. Paul or San Francisco, were very successful in politics, electing Irish American mayors and U.S. senators and establishing political machines even though they also enjoyed success in the private economy and achieved easy social acceptance.

A second explanation might be that nowhere else did Irish Catholics have sufficient numbers to establish themselves politically. Irish Catholics in Canada may never have had enough numbers to support their political ambitions, except in some isolated instances. Even in Toronto, where the Irish Catholic population was sizable by the late nineteenth century, the closest thing to a machine in local politics in that Ontario city was the local Orange order, which secured jobs in the city government for its Irish Protestant and other Protestant members. Irish migration into Britain was heavily Catholic, and though the Irish made up significant proportions of the populations of Liverpool, Glasgow, and other cities, they never constituted a very large proportion of Britain's entire population. Irish Catholic migration into Australia, however, was strong throughout much of the nineteenth century, and the Irish made up a larger proportion of Australia's white population than that of the United States until well into the twentieth century. Yet as Patrick Farrell astutely notes, "it is not the size of minority which counts politically but how it relates to the existing political system." He points out that the Irish in Australia were distributed "remarkably evenly across a vast continent. Irish concentrations were few and minor." Farrell argues, "had they been heavily concentrated in particular areas, as they were in some cities in the United States—bluntly, had they dominated a particular electorate, it is likely they would have compelled attention to their presence and grievances."[4]

J. Matthew Gallman, in his comparative history of Irish migration into Liverpool and Philadelphia during the years of the famine migration, makes something of the same point, but from a different perspective. Gallman points to the American tendency through most of the nineteenth century to concentrate decision making at the local level, in contrast to a British tendency to concentrate power higher up in national authority. This could mean that in America, an ethnic group like the Irish might wield real power in local arenas that they had a chance to dominate, while in Britain, and to a lesser extent Canada or Australia, they would be forced to compete in broader national or provincial arenas, where their numbers had much less potency.

Farrell's and Gallman's points are well taken and are undoubtedly important keys to the differences between Irish politics in the rest of the diaspora, but raw numbers and the importance of local arenas alone did not guarantee Irish political power in the United States. The Irish rarely constituted a majority of the population in any American big city, and their proportion of the populations of most cities fell steadily through the late nineteenth century, even as their political power appeared to rise. In some cities, St. Paul for example, the Irish dominated politics through the twentieth century even when they were a small minority, and in other cities like Philadelphia, the city with the second-largest Irish population in the nation in the nineteenth century, they did not elect a mayor until the 1960s.

Farrell and Gallman are right, however, in pointing to the political systems, or as we might say more broadly, political cultures or environments where the Irish settled as important keys to the extent of their political interest and success. There are some obvious differences in such systems. Perhaps most obvious was the American commitment to universal suffrage as early as the 1820s, compared to the persistence of restrictions on the vote in Britain, and limits, if less burdensome, in Canada and Australia as well. The key to Irish American political niche building in America was that even the poorest Irish immigrant man had a piece of political capital—a vote—that might be invested in earning material benefits for himself and his family.

There are any number of other possible important structural differences distinguishing the opportunities offered by Britain, Australia, or Canada on the one hand and the United States on the other. Perhaps more than anything else, however, the pivotal role that Irish American Catholics came to play in nineteenth- and twentieth-century America as political middlemen or brokers between outsiders and insiders may best explain how they rose to political power and prominence and made themselves America's governing class. Though some may dispute how well the Irish represented others, few can dispute that their ability to negotiate among many ethnic groups was a key to their success. As Brogan himself argued, these other European immigrant groups and their descendants were critical to the Irish emergence as a "governing class" in the nineteenth and twentieth centuries. In Britain and Australia, there were no large groups of immigrants besides the British and the Irish through most of the nineteenth and early twentieth centuries. In Australia, for example, immigrants or descendants of immigrants from Britain and Ireland made up over 90 percent of the population until the 1940s. Canada, like the United States, began receiving immigrants from Eastern Europe in the late nineteenth and early twentieth centuries, but not in nearly the same numbers as in the United States at that time. Moreover, in Canada, a relatively small number of Irish Catholics also faced a huge language minority, the French Canadians, who were hardly amenable to Irish Catholic manipulation or leadership. Irish politicians in American cities thus operated in ethnically plural environments. As the second-generation Irish, ambitious and eager for political prominence, grew to maturity in the late nineteenth century, they found cities where old Anglo-Saxon Protestant elites were on the run and a host of new immigrant groups offered the prospect for power.

Whether they could take advantage of these opportunities and for how long varied from city to city and state to state. They were successful in New York City until the 1930s, when a coalition of Italians and Jews rose to compete with them (though they continued to have success outside Manhattan). They were never successful in Philadelphia, where Republican party bosses fended off the Irish by joining an unusually large resident white Protestant population with blacks, new immigrant Jews, and Italians. In Chicago, Irish Americans took over a multiethnic machine crafted expertly by the Czech political genius, Anton Cermak, and after Cermak's death in 1933, ruled the city for decades after. The individual differences, however, were not as important as the overall truth: the Irish in America, at least in northern and Midwestern America, could take advantage of a broad ethnic pluralism to gain power. The Irish in other places, Britain and Australia, where there were few ethnic others, and in Canada, where the Irish could not easily manipulate them, could not.

Not everyone agrees with this argument. Steven Erie, in his excellent study of Irish American machine politics *Rainbow's End*, directly disputes the Irish brokering role elaborated here. He argues: "urban machines did not incorporate immigrants other than the Irish. The machine's arsenal of resources was far more modest than it sometimes appeared.... Limited as these prizes were, the Irish jealously guarded them, parsimoniously accommodating the later arriving Southern and Eastern Europeans and blacks." Erie summarizes: "Having already constructed a minimal winning coalition among old immigrants—that is, Western European—voters, the established machines had little need to naturalize, register, and vote later ethnic arrivals."[5]

Erie is right to be skeptical about how and why Irish Americans performed this brokering role. Irish Americans, negotiating their way through American ethnic groups, excluded as well as included groups in the coalitions they built. Most often, the Irish played delicate balancing acts among various ethnic groups to maintain their own power. They were often parsimonious, because jobs or nominations for office offered to members of new groups were taken from their own people, and, as Elmer Cornwell has pointed out, Irish Americans could and would not give up such positions easily because politics was so important to them economically. Yankees, Germans, and Jews could fall back easily on other professions or business, but, for the Irish, politics *was* their business, perhaps in some cities and towns the *only* business that they could call their own. They were thus trying to build coalitions that could ensure majorities without exposing themselves to serious challenge.

Still, Erie's characterization of Irish-led machines does not necessarily undermine the importance of the brokering role to Irish political prominence in America. Even among the machine bosses there are examples of Irish Americans managing to maintain political prominence in diverse cities through much of the twentieth century and, therefore, even as the "new immigrants" began fighting their way to political power. And if we broaden the discussion and consider Irish American politics generally, not just urban machines, the peak of Irish American Catholic political power, the 1930s through the 1960s, again, came precisely when other white ethnics were on the rise. What is important here is not whether they were always including new groups—they were not—or whether they incorporated new groups for anything but self-interested motives—they did not—but that, unlike the Irish in Canada, Australia, and Britain, they found in urban America from the late nineteenth through the middle of the twentieth century a diverse, ethnically plural environment, fluid enough for them to manipulate on their way to power. All sorts of changes, such as the emergence of media politics, not negotiated politics; the "assimilation" of white ethnics; the rising power of racial minorities in political arenas; and the opening up of opportunities for Irish Americans in other professions and businesses have all recently reduced though by no means eliminated the prominence of the Irish American politician.

Once the Irish achieved political power, how did they use it? That is the second critical question raised about Irish American politics. Here much of the focus has been on the Irish involvement with machines and a supposed Irish political preference for a politics of personal connections and favors to individuals, such as jobs, the turkey at Christmas, and the peddler's license, as opposed to a politics of ideas and issues and programs and legislation distributing benefits to everyone. Though the Irish in this light seem the consummate political technicians, bereft of any ideological leaning, many historians and social scientists have wondered whether the Irish preoccupation with personal politics really reflected a fundamental Irish American conservatism and resistance to change. Irish Americans, so this argument goes, were interested in exploiting the American political system, not in changing it.

Some have seen this distinction rooted in cultural differences. Richard Hofstadter gave explicit voice to this notion nearly fifty years ago in his *The Age of Reform*:

> Out of the clash between the needs of the immigrants and the sentiments of the natives there emerged two thoroughly different systems of political ethics.… One, founded upon the indigenous Yankee- Protestant political traditions, and upon middle class life, assumed and demanded the constant, disinterested activity of the citizen in public affairs, argued that political life ought to be run, to a greater or lesser degree than it was, in accordance with general principles and abstract laws apart from and superior to personal needs, and expressed a common feeling that government should be in good part an effort to moralize the lives of individuals while economic life should be intimately related to the development of individual character. The other system, founded upon the European backgrounds of the immigrants, upon their unfamiliarity with independent political action, their familiarity with hierarchy and authority, and upon the urgent needs that so often grew out of migration, took for granted that the political life of the individual would arise out of family needs, interpreted political and civic relations chiefly in terms of personal obligations, and placed strong personal loyalties above allegiance to abstract codes of law or morals.[6]

Hofstadter suggests the latter political system was rooted generically in nineteenth- and early twentieth-century immigrant culture and conditions, but observers from the mid-nineteenth century to the present have understood it as characteristically Irish. Journalist Jack Beatty has suggested the peculiarly Irish tinge to this privacy regarding politics by telling a story (a favorite of historian Thomas O'Connor as well):

> A Beacon Hill lady once went ringing doorbells in Irish South Boston on behalf of a high-minded candidate for the School Committee. At one house, an Irish housewife listened politely to the lady's pitch for her paladin, and then asked, "But doesn't he have a sister who works for the schools or who has something to do with the school system?" The Beacon Hill lady was shocked at what she took to be a suggestion of patronage. "I assure you madam," she replied, "he is not the kind of man who would ever use his position to advance the interests of his sister!"

To which the South Boston housewife responded "Well, if the son of a bitch won't help his own sister, why should I vote for him?"[7]

It would be hard or probably impossible to judge how many Irish American politicians practiced a "machine style" of politics, much less were part of the formal organization of a machine. There were legions of them who would not fit easily into either political category: For example, Thomas Walsh, the populist senator from Montana in the 1920s and attorney general under Roosevelt in the 1930s; Frank Murphy, the reform mayor of Detroit and governor of Michigan in the 1930s; Eugene McCarthy, the liberal senator and presidential candidate from Minnesota; and Father Drinan, the liberal Jesuit congressman in Massachusetts hardly seem like machine politicians.

Moreover, as Hofstadter suggests, urban immigrants of many cultures, not just the Irish, supported political machines in the nineteenth and twentieth centuries, and some, like the Italians or Jews, ran their own machines. Indeed, as George Washington Plunkitt, the famous second-generation Irish boss in New York's Tammany machine was quick to point out in 1905: "Philadelphia ruled almost entirely by Americans was more corrupt than New York where the Irish do almost all the governin.'"[8] Yankee-led machines did not just dominate many cities like Philadelphia in Plunkitt's era, but many states as well, such as the Platt machine in New York or the Brayton machine in Rhode Island.

Steven Erie points out that all of the above may be true but it also remains true that there is still good reason to identify the Irish with machine politics: "No other group made the same contributions to the building of the urban machines" in America, he says.[9] Not only did the Irish run more city machines in America than any other group, Erie points out, but Irish American–run Democratic machines were, on the whole, more successful and lasted longer than machines run by other ethnics or Republican Anglo-Protestant machines on the city or state level.

If Irish Americans seemed particularly if not uniquely identified with political machines and a machine style of politics, were they, then, merely hacks sunk in corruption, defending an old oppressive order, and resisting meaningful reform? Opinions of bosses and reformers and which ones better served the needs of the people have varied radically over time. Most contemporary, largely Anglo-Protestant observers in the nineteenth and twentieth centuries found little good in Irish-dominated machines. The muckraker Lincoln Steffens was an exception. Though certainly aware of Irish bosses' corruption, he also began to probe the reasons for their success, and in some cases came to grudgingly admire both the bosses as men and the roles that they played in their neighborhoods. Indeed, it was Steffens, trudging up the stairs of the Hendricks Political Club in Boston's West End in 1915, who elicited the most famous defense of boss politics in American history from the consummate Irish American ward boss, **Martin Lomasney**. Lomasney, a Steffens favorite, told Steffens: "There's got to be in every ward somebody that any bloke can come to—no matter what he's done—and get help. Help, you understand, none of your law and justice, but help."[10]

Less romantic but more significant was sociologist Robert Merton's analysis of the machine in his massive, magisterial *Social Theory and Social Structure*, published in 1949. Merton acknowledged that machines violated standard moral codes, but he argued that their persistence and durability, despite all the attacks on them, suggested that they performed certain essential "latent" functions in American cities that no other institutions or organizations did. Merton believed that several subgroups appreciated political machines; in fact, they needed them. Quoting Lomasney, he argued that machines served deprived classes not only in the benefits they provided but in the ways that they provided them. Merton contended that "the machine politician ... is better integrated with the groups which he serves than the impersonal professionalized, socially distinct and legally constrained welfare worker."[11] The machine also served the lower classes by providing a means of mobility for its ambitious male members, Merton suggested. Poor and working-class boys like James M. Curley or "Big Tim" Sullivan could aspire to be a boss some day and reap the benefits of the boss's power. Yet machines, Merton asserted, also met needs of other subgroups, most notably businesses, legal or illegal, by simplifying the chaos of government bureaucracies for legitimate business or protecting illegal but popular "businesses" like gambling, after-hours drinking clubs, and prostitution from government intrusion.

Not long after Merton rehabilitated the machine through his social science analysis, novelist Edwin O'Connor wrote a loving paean to the Irish boss in his Pulitzer Prize–winning and best-selling novel *The Last Hurrah*. Based loosely on the life of James Michael Curley (Curley, himself, called it "that book about me"), O'Connor described his fictional Irish boss with rich affection, contrasting him sharply with his so called "reform" Anglo-Protestant enemies and insipid, middle-class Irish American successors.

By the time a new generation of historians took up the history of political bosses and machines in the burgeoning of American urban history in the

1960s and 1970s, the tide had turned in evaluations of the contributions of bosses and machine politics to American politics. Few historians then were apologists for machines or bosses, but they had become skeptical of the bosses' enemies, the so-called reformers, who sought new forms of government, city manager or commission systems, or suffrage changes that served their elite interests and disenfranchised the poor. Historians in the 1960s and 1970s were thus sympathetic, if cautiously so, to bosses, Irish or otherwise. As Howard Chudacoff stated in his broad survey of American urban history:

> An assessment of Boss Politics must extend beyond issues of morality and fair play. Men like Croker and Tim Sullivan would not have lasted as long as they did, if they had not served real needs of large segments of the urban population. Bosses were both villains and heroes and something more.... Here was the ideology of boss politics: positive government, the belief that government existed to help people.[12]

In recent years, some historians have once again become critical of the Irish bosses. Writing in the late 1980s, as African Americans and other minorities seemed intent on following the Irish example by creating their own modern machines, Steven Erie disputed whether machines offered substantial opportunities for upward economic mobility and, as noted, questioned whether machines did much to integrate immigrants into the American political system. He condemned Irish bosses not so much for their corruption, which was offensive to middle-class sensibilities and pocketbooks, but for their sellout of the poor through the distribution of piddling favors when wholesale changes in the economy would have helped them much more. He concludes:

> The machine's organizational maintenance needs—building citywide electoral pluralities, securing necessary party financing, placating the business community—introduced a conservative strain into Irish American urban leadership, resulting in lost opportunities to represent working-class political interests more fully. As they learned to manipulate the levers of urban power, Irish bosses turned their backs on more radical forms of working-class politics.[13]

This critique of the Irish American politician's lack of vision is more recent than attacks on their corruption but has nonetheless been powerfully argued by many over the last few decades. None stated this point more succinctly than Daniel P. Moynihan: "In a sense, the Irish did not know what to do with power once they got it…. They never thought of politics as an instrument of social change—their kind of politics involved the processes of a society that was not changing."[14]

Erie and Moynihan suggest here that Irish American politics has been not so much pragmatic as conservative. As the cliché runs: not to have an ideology about the goals of politics is to, in fact, have one. That is, by failing to cash in their power for dramatic changes, Irish American politicians suggested their basic satisfaction with the American economic and political systems. That has convinced many historians that Irish Americans have always been basically ideologically conservative, but their conservatism has been hidden by their focus on the techniques and practices of gaining political power.

Such perceptions of Irish American Catholics as fundamentally conservative have been strengthened by the recent rise of explicitly conservative Irish Catholic intellectuals and the even the more recent shift of many Irish American Catholics into the Republican Party. As noted earlier, over the last half century, a group of Irish American conservatives have emerged that have been neither tacit nor shy in asserting an ideologically rigorous conservatism, and, by the 1980s, a substantial proportion of Irish Catholic voters had switched their allegiances to an increasingly conservative Republican Party.

The antagonism to radicalism and commitment to older familial and cultural values that lie at the heart of these recent Irish American conservatives' ideology have deep roots in Irish American history. Irish American Catholic leaders had worried about the excesses of republican fervor very early in the nation's history, and excoriated abolitionists and others who seemed intent on tinkering dangerously with the fragile existing order. Most Irish American Catholics eventually came to accept and embrace republicanism; it was after all the official ideology of the nation. Yet, as noted earlier, they did not hesitate to level their guns at socialism when it first began to gain a following at the end of the nineteenth century. After that period, Irish Americans became rigidly and vociferously antisocialist and anticommunist, climaxing in the McCarthy crusade of the 1950s.

Historians have often assumed that Irish Americans' Catholicism lay at the heart of this conservatism. It certainly played an important part. The church's crusade against socialism in the 1910s, led by Bishop McFaul of Trenton but endorsed by many others, and the powerful and unyielding anticommunism of the "American Pope," **Cardinal Spellman** of New York and Catholicism's best-known public voice, Bishop Fulton Sheen, in the 1950s, testified to Catholicism's influence. Antiradicalism became an article of faith for Irish

American Catholics and an emblem of identity that proved their Catholic and American identities were compatible and mutually reinforcing.

Nevertheless, there may have been other and more practical reasons inspiring Irish American antiradicalism. Socialists threatened Irish Americans' political and labor interests at a crucial moment at the turn of the century, when the Irish were beginning to secure control of many city governments or labor unions, for example. Irish politicians and voters thus turned against the Socialists to defend their new-found power and the spoils it afforded. As Erie suggests, "the machine ultimately tamed Irish voters as well as leaders ... Irish enthusiasm for labor politics dimmed as ever larger numbers were brought into the patronage system."[15]

Not all Irish Americans opposed radicalism, however. Indeed, some of the most prominent socialist or communist leaders or voices in late nineteenth- and early twentieth-century America were Irish Americans, **Peter J. McGuire**, **Mary Harris "Mother" Jones**, **Elizabeth Gurley Flynn**, and William Z. Foster.

Furthermore, if most Irish Americans were antiradical, did that automatically make them conservative? It may well be that Irish American political ideology may simply be too hard to fix in the categories of right and left that historians and other scholars have used to map out the American political spectrum. If Irish Americans have often seemed hysterically antiradical and rigidly antagonistic to cultural changes in family or sex roles, they have also often been consistently skeptical of unregulated free-market capitalism and thus longtime supporters of a government role in the economy. Such positions contradict essential tenets of almost all American conservatives. John McGreevy's *Catholicism and American Freedom* makes clear recently how sharply and persistently Catholic social teaching has diverged from mainstream American political ideologies over the last century and a half.

Even taking note of the paradoxes of Irish American ideology, however, it is important to point out that within the narrow ideological confines of Irish American politics in the twentieth century, many if not most Irish Americans perhaps even to the present day have stood on the left of American politics, though perhaps only slightly and even "curiously" left. Though the history of the Progressive movement has largely been written as the work of middle-class Protestants, old professionals, "new class" bureaucrats, new professionals, and reforming women, urban Irish American and other Catholic as well as Jewish working-class representatives in state legislatures across the Northeast and Midwest actually fought and won some of the Progressive era's most important social welfare, economic regulation, and even political reform victories. "Give the people what they want," said **Charles Francis Murphy,** boss of Tammany Hall in the 1910s, and his men in Albany, including Alfred E. "Al" Smith and "Big Tim" Sullivan, did so, through a whole host of social and economic reforms. John Buenker shows such urban ethnic reform efforts took place not only in New York, but also in Massachusetts under state representative **Martin Lomasney** and in Illinois, under Governor Edward Dunne. In the New Deal era, Irish Americans in New York and Boston may have been wary backers of Roosevelt, but most supported the Democrats nonetheless. Furthermore, **Edward "Ed" Kelly** in Chicago, who proclaimed "Roosevelt is my religion," and David Lawrence in Pittsburgh built their machines on Roosevelt's largesse, in return for strong votes for the New Deal. Even today, after the cultural revolutions of the 1960s and the Reagan political revolution of the 1980s, polling data and some survey data suggest that Irish Americans' own curious kind of liberalism is not yet extinct, though, as noted earlier, there have been important regional distinctions, particularly between Irish American voters in New England and those in the Mid-Atlantic states. In the end, then, Irish American Catholics' political ideology remains an open and in many respects confusing question that demands further scholarly exploration.

NOTES

1. D. W. Brogan, *Politics in America* (New York: Harper and Brothers, 1954), 96.

2. Ibid., 97.

3. Daniel Patrick Moynihan and Nathan Glazer, *Beyond the Melting Pot* (Cambridge, Mass.: MIT Press, 1963), 227.

4. Patrick Farrell, *The Irish in Australia: 1788 to the Present* (Cork: Cork University Press, 2001), 116.

5. Steven P. Erie, *Rainbow's End: Irish Americans and the Dilemmas of Urban Machine Politics, 1840–1985* (Berkeley: University of California Press, 1988), 6–7.

6. Richard Hofstadter, *The Age of Reform: From Bryan to FDR* (New York: Knopf, 1955), 9.

7. Jack Beatty, *The Rascal King: The Life and Times of James Michael Curley, 1874–1958* (Reading, Mass.: Addison-Wesley, 1992), 11.

8. Ronald H. Bayor and Timothy Meagher, eds., *The New York Irish* (Baltimore: Johns Hopkins University Press, 1996), 3.

9. Erie, *Rainbow's End,* 3.

10. Howard Chudacoff, *The Evolution of American Urban Society* (Englewood Cliffs, N.J.: Prentice Hall, 1981), 143.

11. Robert Merton, *Social Theory and Social Structure* (Glencoe, Ill.: The Free Press, 1957), 75.

12. Chudacoff, *The Evolution of American Urban Society*, 142.

13. Erie, *Rainbow's End*, 8.

14. Moynihan and Glazer, *Beyond the Melting Pot*, 229.

15. Erie, *Rainbow's End*, 8.

CHAPTER THREE

Irish American Nationalism

"If Ireland could be freed by a picnic, she'd be an empire by now." So said **Finley Peter Dunne**'s fabled character Mr. Dooley, commenting in his own trenchant way on the phenomenon of Irish American nationalism. Dunne's skepticism about the limited efficacy of this often frenzied nationalist activity should not obscure his wonder at the extent of the frenzy. Nationalism—the commitment to restore some political autonomy to the old country—was an essential part of Irish American life almost from the birth of the American republic. From the **United Irish Exiles** in the 1790s and early 1800s to the Repeal movement in the early 1840s to the **Fenians** of the 1860s, the **Land Leaguers** and Home Rulers of the 1880s to the **Friends of Irish Freedom** and members of the American Association for the Recognition of the Irish Republic in the late 1910s, and the **Clan na Gael** over much of the late nineteenth and twentieth centuries to the reborn nationalists of **NORAID** and the "**Four Horsemen**" of the 1970s and 1980s, Irish Americans have invested considerable resources of time and money into freeing the old country. The picnics, not to mention the speaking tours, fund drives, conventions, drilling and training, secret arms purchases, sympathy strikes, and protests, were, as Dunne suggests, too numerous to count and suggest how important nationalism was to Irish America.

Irish American nationalism was unique within the Irish diaspora. Nowhere else in the world outside of Ireland itself did nationalism gain the same breadth of support, inspire the same intensity of interest, or nourish such militant and radical strains of nationalist fervor as it did in the United States. Patrick O'Farrell suggests: "Irish nationalism, as such, was never strong in Australia [and] … such nationalism as did exist was strongly constitutional in main character."[1] In a famous incident, a **Fenian** partisan made an attempt on the life of Prince Alfred, Duke of Edinburgh, in Australia in 1868, but as Patrick O'Farrell notes, "Fenianism was too strong a meat for the average Irish Australian stomach."[2] The virtual universal condemnation by Australians of the would-be assassin pointed up both the weakness of the movement there and the reasons why. In simple terms, Australia was part of the British Empire: republican nationalism, particularly nationalism committed to violent revolution against the government of the United Kingdom, was tantamount to treason. What could be ignored or even honored in America would be cause for prosecution in Australia. Yet it may have run even deeper than the simple formality of the law. Some Australian historians have recently argued that a deep-seated identification with Britain, its culture, and its economic and political interests has been fundamental to Australian life over the last few centuries. Canada (at least in Ontario) was only slightly more fertile ground for Fenianism than Australia, for many of the same reasons. It was not only the imperial context but the small size and feeble strength of the Catholic Irish community there pitted against a powerful and militant Orange order that hindered revolutionary republican nationalism. Andy Bielenberg has summed up Irish nationalism in the British Empire: "The revolutionary and republican traditions of Irish nationalism were not strong in a colony where the British connection remained crucial to the economic and political well-being of the white population."[3]

Yet if nationalism was uniquely important to Irish America, there is much that is still in question about it. The most fundamental question has been: Who within the Irish American population has been most committed to nationalism, and why? Were they the upwardly mobile, seeking a place in American society through Irish liberation? Or were they workers, seeing class enemies on both sides of the Atlantic? Or the poor, alienated from the United States and longing for home? Or political exiles fixated on the old country's fate? Or transatlantic revolutionaries committed to the spread of republicanism?

Some historians have identified upwardly mobile ambitious Irish Americans as the critical players in the nationalist movement, and note their constant invocation of American ideals and experience in their nationalist rhetoric. Those invocations, such scholars suggest, testify to the hopes of these upwardly mobile nationalists to use the struggle for Irish freedom to help them find a place in American life. Thomas Brown argues that "the ambitious whose energies had earned them ... humiliations ... but also some degree of economic and social progress" were the ones most interested in freeing Ireland. Brown quotes a speech by the nationalist Michael Davitt to an

Irish American audience to explain why those "ambitious" men and women wanted to free Ireland: "You want to be regarded with the respect due you," Davitt stated, "that you may thus be looked on, aid us in Ireland to remove the stain of degradation from your birth ... and [you] will get the respect you deserve."[4]

Other historians disagree. Eric Foner and Kerby Miller believe that the rank and file of the nationalists came from much further down the social scale. Foner points to Irish American workers as the heart of the nationalist movement in America, as they become increasingly aware that the oppressors of their peasant relatives in Ireland were much like the industrial "aristocrats" who oppressed them here. Miller believes that such workers were embittered by the harshness of their experiences with American capitalism, felt alienated in the New World, and poured their emotion and energy into the homeland's cause. Miller also suggests that real leaders of this nationalism in America were not upwardly mobile American "wannabes" but Irish exiles. They were men like John Devoy, who lived out their American lives in spartan simplicity, focusing myopically, relentlessly, and fanatically on Ireland's cause. Nationalist leaders were, a sympathetic Englishman wrote in the mid-nineteenth century, "much more unreasonable animals" than Brown's anxious members of the middle class. The Irish nationalist leader in America, that observer continued, is more often "a dreamer, an enthusiast, a poet. Instead of making himself a career in the new country, he dreams of what he can be doing for the old."[5]

The differences in the understanding of who the American nationalists were and why they were committed to nationalism inevitably leads to further questions: What effect did the nationalist movement have on the Irish American community? Did it ease Irish integration into a broader American society as the ambitious middle class hoped? Or did it slow such integration, encouraging Irish Americans' ethnic consciousness and riveting their attention on the old country, not this one?

It would seem natural to assume that Irish American nationalism must have slowed Irish integration into the American mainstream. Could a people whose gaze seemed fixed on the old country's fate be very interested in assimilating into their new one? In the language of today's immigration scholarship such a people seem "transnational," moving back and forth between two identities and two cultures. Ironically, however, the predominant interpretation of Irish American nationalism for decades has contended that Irish American nationalism facilitated rather than hindered Irish assimilation into American life. William Shannon made this point nearly half a century ago: "The reality was that the Irish nationalist was one of the ways in which the Irish in this country learned what it was like to be an American."[6] They learned to be American through nationalism because they wanted Ireland to become just like America: modern, prosperous, respectable, and democratic. In trying to make Ireland over in America's image, these historians argue, such Irish American nationalists sought and sometimes received the approbation and support of Yankee or mainstream Americans, helping ease them into American society.

Some historians have raised a more specific question about the effect of nationalism on the Irish community's adjustment to the broader American world. Those scholars debate whether Irish Americans' participation in movements to liberate Ireland encouraged the Irish to seek changes in American politics or society as well; or, conversely, whether Irish Americans' fixation on Ireland's needs diverted their attention and sapped their interest in reform in America. Eric Foner has taken the former position. He has argued that nationalism helped ease Irish Americans into the American labor and reform movements in the nineteenth century by raising Irish Americans' consciousness of oppressive elites and institutions. Other scholars, such as David Emmons, are more skeptical. Emmons wonders whether Irish American workers' preoccupation with Ireland blinded them to their needs in America and hindered them from making common cause with other ethnics who shared their American economic interests.

There is little evidence of any concern for Ireland's fate among the Scotch-Irish or Irish Anglican immigrants who flooded North America in the colonial era. Undoubtedly some Catholic refugees like the Carrolls in Maryland or perhaps even the Sullivans, who were Anglican converts in New Hampshire, felt some lingering sympathy for the Stuart kings their families had served, but such sympathy, if widespread, never manifested itself in broader movements.

As noted earlier, it was not until after the revolution, with the coming of the **United Irish Exiles** in the 1790s, that Irish American nationalism began to emerge. For most United Irish Exiles, however, Ireland's rebellion was but part of a broader, worldwide revolution and the coming of a new republican age. As a republican catechism in Ireland ran:

What have you got in your hand? A green Bough.
Where did it first grow? In America.
Where did it bud? In France.
Where are you going to plant it? In the Crown of Great Britain.[7]

In the United States then, most of the United Irish Exiles were quick to point to America's revolution and subsequent republican government as a model for Ireland, or conversely, as Thomas Emmett and William MacNeven did, point to Ireland's long history of colonial oppression and sectarian division as a model for what Americans might avoid.

There is so little written on Irish American nationalism in this period that we know very little about who backed it. There was some suggestion of support of the new nationalism by Irish Americans at lower levels of the economic hierarchy: the **Society of the United Irishmen of America** counted members from among working-class artisans in Philadelphia and other cities. Still, all evidence suggests that Irish American nationalism at this stage seemed largely a top-down movement, initiated and kept alive by the remarkable group of United Irish political exiles. It would be hard, however, to see this elite's backing of nationalism, bathed in American republican rhetoric, as the quest of an insecure Irish middle class for American acceptance as Brown and other historians would depict later Irish American nationalists. These early United Irish Exiles were largely Protestant, often well educated, from middle-class or gentry families in Ireland. They did not suffer from the insecurities that aspiring Irish Catholics in a Protestant-dominated American world would endure later in the nineteenth century.

Whether interest in the old country's fate eased or retarded Irish American entry into a broader American life is hard to say. Certainly Federalist enemies feared that Irish immigration was contaminating America with foreign revolutionaries, but Irish Americans would help rout the Federalists by the early 1800s and themselves become part of the ruling Democratic-Republican establishment. It seems more likely that identification by America's United Irishmen with the still struggling Ireland may have made them especially fierce and urgent reformers in the United States. For almost all the exiles the cause of republicanism was the same in Ireland as it was in America, and so their nationalism did little to divert their attention from American reform. Indeed, for members of the United Irish Exiles like James MacNeven and Thomas Addis Emmett, acute awareness of their nation's sorry history of colonial oppression and sectarian division inspired their efforts to ensure that Catholics in America would achieve their full civil rights.

We know even less about the next important if brief episode in Irish American nationalism: the efforts of Irish Americans to mobilize in behalf of Daniel O'Connell's movement to repeal the Act of Union in the early 1840s. This movement appeared to have very different roots than the earlier one. It began, as David Doyle has pointed out, among the Catholic Irish petty shopkeepers and skilled manual workers of Boston—"the obscure inhabitants of Boston ... of no note or position"—as the British consul noted.[8] The Boston leaders, Doyle points out, included the editor of Boston's *Pilot* newspaper, but also a coal dealer and a hack driver. None of the old Protestant leaders were involved, a reflection of the sea change already at work in Irish America as Catholic migrants began to dominate Irish American communities in northern cities. There is some further evidence of this sea change in the statistics of donors to the Repeal movement, gathered by Oscar Handlin in his *Boston's Immigrants* years ago. Handlin found that over four-fifths of Boston's donors to the Repeal movement were from the southern three provinces or the four counties of south Ulster in Ireland, all predominantly Catholic regions. Though originating among humble Catholic Irish newcomers, the Repeal movement eventually achieved some cachet among both notable Catholics and non-Catholics. Prominent American politicians like former President John Tyler and his son attached themselves to the movement. Repeal won non-Irish support at local levels as well. Brian Mitchell has pointed out in his study of the Lowell Irish that "Lowell's Yankees perceived the political turmoil as a wrong to be redressed and characterized it [the Act of Union] as an undemocratic denial of political rights."[9]

Because we know so little about the Repeal movement, it is hard to know what moved its leaders, members, and donors to back it. Doyle quotes a contemporary account that suggests the early Boston Irish organizers of the movement were working-class immigrants "sensitively alive to the sufferings of their fellow countrymen."[10] If the original modest men who founded the movement in Boston had their eyes focused strictly on the homeland, it is impossible to say what moved later backers of the organization. Did their solicitation of prominent non–Irish American politicians reflect a deeper need by the Irish in the American Repeal movement for acceptance by American society? Or was it simply a strategy to gather the greatest possible clout to pressure the United Kingdom's leadership?

What is also unclear is the ultimate effect of the movement on the Irish community. The American Repeal movement's outreach to non-Irish supporters may have helped integrate Irish Americans into American society, but it more likely revealed the inability of the still-evolving Irish Catholic community to construct and sustain a new separate community and identity. On the whole, Kerby Miller argues, the American Repeal movement's short and "unimpressive" history "testified that Irish America was not yet sufficiently populous or mature to sustain a prolonged agitation without the support of native institutions."[11] Moreover, even if the American Repeal crusade may have helped Irish Americans gain a modicum of acceptance from some of their non-Irish neighbors, it did little to integrate them into American reform movements. Though Daniel O'Connell, the leader of Repeal in Ireland, was a staunch opponent of slavery, for example, the American Repeal Association refused to follow his lead. Indeed, the American repealers openly repudiated O'Connell's attacks on American slavery, to the bitter chagrin of American abolitionists.[12]

If Miller and other historians have found the American Repeal Association to be too small and weak to have much of an effect on Irish immigrant adjustments to American life, neither he nor anyone else would make the same judgment of the Fenians. Founded in 1858, only about fifteen years after Repeal dissolved, the Fenians would become, as Miller himself has pointed out, "the most popular and powerful ethnic organization in Irish American history."[13] As Miller has argued, "in the early nineteenth century Irish leaders such as O'Connell had paid little regard to Irish America; however, [after the Fenians,] from the 1860s onward nationalists at home were heavily dependent on Irish American approbation and funds."[14] Surprisingly, despite the Fenians' critical importance to the Irish American community, most studies of them have merely been narrow chronicles of their leaders' factional fights or studies of the Fenians' diplomatic consequences, not deep analyses of their supporters and their motives. It seems clear that the Fenians had broadly based support—the first really mass-based movement in Irish American history—but there is little or no probing of the social or economic backgrounds and social status of its members or donors at even a local, much less national, level. Were they the upwardly mobile Irish in their communities, local elites yearning for some form of American acceptance? Or were they poorer men, perhaps alienated by their American experience and still yearning for Ireland? There are no rigorous studies even of Fenian elites. In the absence of such studies the best single analysis of the Fenians remains Kerby Miller's discussion of them in his magisterial *Emigrants and Exiles*. Miller says of the Fenians that "impoverished Irish Americans were most homesick and most attracted to the nationalist dream: partly because such emigrants were most likely to share archaic outlooks rooted in peasant parochialism and Gaelic traditions; partly because American experiences of poverty and proscription corroborated and alienated affections from their adopted country."[15]

If there is no better analysis of who the Fenians were and what motivated them than what Miller has to offer, it is, however, perhaps possible to suggest something about what they meant to the Irish American community and its place in American life. Fenianism, with its aggressive republicanism, fit more closely with official American ideology than the Repeal movement, which had simply attempted to restore an Irish parliament under the king. Though the Civil War squeezed some of the edge, exuberance, or even brashness out of American republicanism, as George Frederickson argued long ago, Americans were still certainly familiar with the republican vocabulary that the Fenians used. Americans also had their own grudges against England in the 1860s, some long-term, but others recent legacies of Britain's pro-Confederate politics during the Civil War. There was, then, widespread sympathy for the Fenians among Americans, from national political leaders like Congressman Nathaniel Banks to local newspapers and community leaders in cities across the country.

America, then, offered a uniquely hospitable environment for the growth of republican nationalism. Some Fenians, such as the Civil War hero Patrick Guiney, capitalized on the harmony between American republican traditions and Fenian Irish ones to open up new avenues for Irish Americans into American labor and reform politics. Guiney, colonel of the famous Irish American Ninth Massachusetts Regiment and a strong backer of Lincoln and abolition, ran for Congress on the workingmen party's ticket after the war. It is not known, however, if Fenian nationalism had a similar effect on the commitment to reform or class consciousness of other Fenian leaders or members of the rank and file. That certainly seems plausible, but remains to be studied.

The broader effect of Fenianism, however, appears to have been not to integrate Irish Americans into American society but to strengthen the newly forming Irish American Catholic community's conscious sense of its separate identity. The Fenians may have welcomed the sympathy of their American neighbors for tactical reasons if nothing else, but they could stand on their own. Rather than reconcile most Irish Americans to the United States, Kerby Miller argues, it appears that Fenianism may have exacerbated their sense of grievance and alienation in America, as well as fixed their attention on Ireland. Miller concludes that the Fenians thus encouraged a sharpening ethnic consciousness among Irish Americans and nourished their sense of social and cultural separation from other Americans.

If Fenianism has inexplicably been understudied, then the next great episode in Irish American history, the **Land League** and Home Rule agitation of the 1880s, has attracted substantial attention from historians and the most sophisticated analyses of any episode in Irish American nationalism. Indeed, it is in their discussions of the Land League that the controversies over who backed nationalism and why first emerged. It was, for example, in his study of the American Land Leaguers and Home Rulers that Thomas Brown defined the typical Irish American nationalist to be a middle-class immigrant or second-generation Irish American, eager for upward mobility and American acceptance. Conversely, it was in *his* study of the Land League that Eric Foner argued that working-class men supplied the bulk of nationalist supporters. Foner noted the scores of Land League branches founded in New England factory towns and Pennsylvanian and Western mining towns. Workingmen, not shopkeepers, lawyers, or even clerks filled those branches and often led them, Foner contended, and these workers were not seeking upward mobility through a remaking of Ireland in America's image, but a revolutionary change in the old country's economic and political systems. They were moved, he believed, by a visceral kind of class antagonism, born out of their own struggles with American capitalism. **Patrick Ford** and his newspaper, the *Irish World*, were the leader and the voice of this radical wing.

Subsequent analyses of Land League members deepened and enriched but perhaps also complicated the depiction of who the nationalist support- ers were and why they enlisted in the Land League crusade. Victor Walsh added another dimension to Brown's and Foner's contrasting class analyses by pointing to the varied Irish regional origins of immigrant Land League supporters. Examining the backers of the Land League from the various Irish neighborhoods of Pittsburgh, he discovered middle-class Irish Land Leaguers hailing from the eastern province of Leinster, who seemed much like Brown's aspiring assimilationists, but he also found workingmen largely from Munster who fit Foner's characterization of emergent labor radicals. Walsh noted that Pittsburgh's impoverished immigrants from the western, traditional province of Connaught seemed left out of the nationalist agitation entirely. Other his- torians, like David Brundage and myself, noticed the signal importance of women for the movement, who were organized in the branches of the Ladies Land League. Indeed, in Worcester, I found the women of the Ladies Land League to be the most active and successful fund raisers of any of the Land League branches in the city. Irish American society permitted women few opportunities for a public role, but in Worcester, these women, largely second- generation white-collar workers, jumped at the chance for such a role when the nationalist movement offered them such an opening—even if it meant defiance of their communities' priests and political leaders.

The variety of such opinions on who backed the Land League and why does not mean we can find no clear patterns in the Land League's supporters. Brown and Foner, for example, are not irreconcilable. In Denver and Worces- ter, David Brundage and I both found Land League movements dominated by middle-class leaders eager to couch their agitation in American rhetoric and attract Yankee American support. Yet we also found working-class nationalists and women challenging this middle-class leadership. It seems likely that the strength of different classes, even of women versus men or of immigrants of various Irish regional origins in the local Land League branches, probably varied according to local circumstances across the country. Such circumstances might include, for example, the proportion of immigrants from each Irish region who settled in a particular city or town, the potential for working-class solidarity there, the size of the local Irish American middle class, or the nature of a relations between Irish Americans and their native-stock Yankee neighbors in that community.

Like their analyses of supporters and their motivations, historians' estimate of the consequences of the Land League and Home Rule movements also vary. Brown believed that any liberating potential Irish Americans might have found in the nationalist movement came to naught. In the end, he believed that the Land League crusade and its laudable "ethical concerns" and "generosity of spirit" were sacrificed to the grubby exigencies of American politics. Nevertheless, the political power that the Irish achieved, Brown contended, did them little good. It opened no doors to private status and acceptance, and the Irish sank into an obsession for "power for its own sake, apart from the community's needs." Irish Americans, Brown stated, became "an embittered people," drowning in self-pity, their very political successes intensifying their "sense of isolation and the narcissism that flowed from it."[16] Foner saw a more hopeful outcome for the Land League. He and Paul Buhle, who studied the Land League in Rhode Island, both found close links between Land League branches and assemblies of the Knights of Labor or other union organizations. Foner pointed, for example, to the founding of the New York Central Trades Union at a Land League meeting, and he and Buhle offered several other examples of Land League branches virtually transforming into Knights of Labor Assemblies in northeastern Pennsylvania mining towns or industrial cities like Providence. For Foner and Buhle, Land League nationalism was a mechanism of assimilation, but of a very special kind: a vehicle for the integration of Irish American workers into American reform and labor movements.

Little work has been done in Irish American nationalism between Parnell's fall in 1891 and the Easter rebellion in 1916, but what has been done underlines the movement's diversity. The **Clan na Gael** suffered severely from controversy over factional squabbles that led to the sensational murder of Dr. Philip Cronin, an opponent of the ruling leaders, but it continued to limp along through the 1890s. Constitutional nationalists founded their own organizations such as the United Irish League. David Brundage has noted important trends among physical force nationalists and constitutional nationalists in the two or more decades between the Land League of the 1880s and the Easter Rebellion of 1916. Physical force nationalists in the Clan na Gael seemed to become more socially conservative over that time, abandoning their interest in economic or social reforms after the 1880s, moving away from earlier anti-clericalism to embrace of the church, and growing skeptical of women's roles in the movement. Constitutional nationalists had little interest in economic reforms either, but reflecting a kind of cosmopolitan liberalism, they were more open to women's participation in the nationalist cause and took a more cautious approach to the church and its role in the envisioned Irish nation. It would seem that the physical force men probably came from the working and lower middle classes, and the constitutional nationalists from higher up the social scale, but without a study of memberships we do not know for sure.

In 1916, this quiet phase in both Irish and Irish American nationalism ended, and a new phase began. After 1916, but especially after 1918, Irish America would erupt in a new nationalist frenzy. The **Friends of Irish Freedom**, founded in 1916, would boast hundreds of thousands of members when nationalist momentum began to surge after the end of the war, and the FOIF's competitor, the American Association for the Recognition of the Irish Republic, also enlisted thousands of members. In addition, hundreds of thousands of Irish Americans bought the bonds of the new revolutionary Irish Republic.

Here again, however, aside from few local studies, it is impossible to determine exactly who joined and why. In Butte, Montana, David Emmons has found that the nationalist cause roused thousands of workers, who rallied to a vision of a radically reformed Ireland much like Foner and Buhle's workers had in the 1880s. In New York, women played a prominent role in agitating the cause. In Worcester, Massachusetts, second- and third-generation middle-class Irish Americans, who had been indifferent to the Irish cause for decades, suddenly caught the nationalist fever. If this suggests broad support cutting across class, gender, and generational lines, it is probably accurate, for the surge of interest beginning after World War I in 1918 and cresting in 1920 and 1921 appeared to dwarf any previous nationalist movement in Irish American history.

Clearly, there was a tangle of motives inspiring or provoking this diverse group of new nationalists. Despite the evidence from Butte and from some other parts of the country, class identification between Irish American industrial workers and Irish peasants was probably not as strong in this phase as it had been earlier. This was in part because of changes in Ireland. Many Irish peasants now owned their farms, purchasing them from their landlords through government-sponsored schemes. This was also in part due to changes among Irish Americans in the United States. There were fewer immigrants now, for example. As important, the bulk of American-born Irish were not mired in the lowest ranks of the economic hierarchy, but enjoyed respectable if modest prosperity as skilled blue-collar or lower white-collar workers. Irish Americans may also not have had the same ideological resources that their predecessors in the 1880s had had either. Working class republicanism, still flourishing in the early 1880s, had helped to inspire earlier Land League radicals. Yet it was long dead by the time the new nationalist phase began in 1918, and leaders of the Irish American community, priests, mainstream unionists, and politicians, had been waging an aggressive war on socialism and other forms of radicalism for a generation by then.

More powerful motives for interest in nationalism now came from the prospects for nationalist success in Ireland and the effects of World War I on the Irish American community. Simply put, Ireland seemed as close to winning some kind of real autonomy after World War I as at any time in its history, and Irish Americans seemed to recognize that fact. World War I had also created a new context for Irish American nationalism. For the American-born Irish, Woodrow Wilson had ironically provided a neat ideological bridge from their American patriotism to Irish nationalism by declaring that World War I had been fought to win self-determination for all nations. If it was in the best traditions of Americans to believe Poland or Yugoslavia should be independent, Irish Americans reasoned, then it was certainly acceptable for them—even incumbent upon them—to wish the same for Ireland. The other legacy of the war was less idealistic: the tension emerging among ethnic and religious groups, provoked by war hysteria and heightened by the postwar economic hard times. This tense atmosphere of ethnic competition and conflict heightened Irish Americans' ethnic consciousness, and as a corollary, intensified their interest in Ireland's fate.

If Irish American nationalism fed off those tensions, it in turn helped exacerbate them. Edward Cuddy has pointed out that the revival of Irish nationalism in America enraged some Anglophile and anti-Catholic American leaders, who understood it as a clumsy effort to twist the nation's foreign policy against its own interests and meddle in the internal affairs of Britain, a trusted ally. These attitudes, Cuddy argues, clearly fed into the anti-Catholic sentiment of such movements as the Ku Klux Klan. Indeed, in some cities, Ulster Protestant "Orange" immigrants mobilized in opposition to Irish American nationalism, and became early backers of the Klan when it returned in the early years of the "tribal twenties."

After the Treaty of 1921 established the Irish Free State and ended the Irish war for independence, Irish American nationalism virtually disappeared for more than forty years. There was some interest in the Irish republican side of the civil war, but that faded quickly, and only a dwindling Clan na Gael kept the cause of reuniting Ireland alive thereafter.

It was only with the revival of the "troubles" in Ulster in the 1960s that nationalism again caught fire. It appears—though there is no study to prove it—that in the initial civil rights phase of the movement there was broad support for Ulster's Catholics in the United States, both inside and outside the Irish American community. Some of the earliest organizations, such as the National Association for Irish Justice, grew out of the American "New Left" and invoked the same anticolonial principles in their support for Ulster's civil rights struggle as the anti–Vietnam War movement or the fight for racial minority rights in the United States did. Some of these people, like Brian Heron, the grandson of the Rebellion of 1916 hero James Connolly, had vital connections to Irish nationalism. Others may have been young people with few or no links to Ireland, who were drawn to this cause as part of a broader revolutionary struggle. Older nationalist hands organizing first in the American Committee for Irish Freedom also rallied to the cause, however, and they had very different ideological perspectives. Many were very conservative in their American politics but committed to violent overthrow of British rule in Ireland. In between probably lay an amorphous, largely unorganized population of Irish Americans of various generations, who initially understood the struggle as simply one more step in a broad, liberal, civil rights crusade, much like Martin Luther King's effort to win civil rights for African Americans.

By the early 1970s, the clutter of these early American responses to Ulster had largely been cleared. The Irish American nationalist left faded away, paralleling trends in Ireland, where the Official IRA, with its leftist goals and political, not military, strategies declined. The Provisional IRA, or "Provos," broke with the official IRA in 1969 and pledged itself to guerrilla war and the nationalist objective of reunification. The "Provos" flourished in the maelstrom of Ulster violence in the early 1970s. Hardcore nationalists in America organized the Irish Northern Aid Committee (**NORAID**), linked up with the Provisionals, and became the principal Irish American group involved in the Ulster crisis.

There has been no scholarly study of NORAID's membership. Observers as disparate as Andrew Greeley and Pete Hamill have suggested that NORAID drew significant numbers of young Irish Americans of the third generation or later, who latched on to the nationalist cause in their search for a meaningful ethnic identity. Such people were disillusioned with the artificiality of the "shamrocks and shillelaghs" Irishness of their parents, Hamill suggests. Like many of their young American contemporaries in the 1960s, he believes, the young Irish American nationalists sought to find a more authentic ethnic self, and they looked for it in the new nationalist struggle.

Andrew Wilson, in his *Irish America and the Ulster Conflict: 1968–1995*, acknowledges that some younger Irish Americans may have been drawn to NORAID, but asserts that "militant nationalist groups were still dominated by those born in Ireland."[17] Immigrants from the 1920s, particularly old IRA hands like Michael Flannery, Wilson notes, played a critical role in the founding of NORAID. Yet immigrants of the 1950s generation probably made up a larger proportion of NORAID's members, Wilson estimates. These people, he suggests, included Catholics who had fled Ulster in the 1940s and 1950s and still felt the stings of prejudice from their youth, and immigrants from the south, particularly the borderlands, who came from longtime republican families. Yet there were probably other immigrants from the southern republic, Wilson contends, who found in the nationalist movement simply another opportunity to get together with friends and socialize. All of these southern immigrants had left an Ireland still steeped in the republican nationalist and Catholic pieties of the new nation—De Valera's Ireland—and the legacy of these memories may have influenced them too.

Intriguingly, it appears that few of the most recent waves of immigrants, the illegals and others of the 1980s, for example, have had much interest in the Ulster conflict. For them the Ireland of De Valera is distant and to many, discredited, and they left a southern Ireland already wary and skeptical of IRA violence in the north. As noted earlier, many of these new immigrants also live in an uneasy if close relationship with the fifties' immigrants, dependent on the older hands for jobs but also resentful of that dependence.

In terms of class, there is again no rigorous analysis of today's nationalist supporters, particularly NORAID's membership. The few third-, fourth-, and later-generation Irish in the organization were most likely middle-class people for whom the angst of identity in a rootless modern world might seem most pressing. Yet most of NORAID's money was raised in small contributions, Wilson points out, and through a network of bars in major urban or inner suburban areas of settlement, suggesting support from low white-collar and blue-collar Irish Americans.

Whether nationalism helped or hindered Irish integration into the American mainstream by this time in Irish American history is not an issue. Almost all barriers to their integration had fallen already, and Irish Americans could be as integrated as they wanted to be. Indeed, if a search for identity moti-vated some American-born Irish nationalists now, it reflected the revolution in American society and culture in the 1960s that had discredited older no-tions of assimilation and now celebrated the nation's multiethnic roots. For blue-collar and lower white-collar immigrants and American-born Irish na-tionalists, support for Ulster's IRA provisionals may have reflected a differ-ent response to changing American contexts. Many observers have noted the paradoxical combination of conservatism on American issues and militancy on Irish ones among the ACIF and **NORAID** activists of the 1970s and 1980s. Some have speculated that racial and other changes since the 1960s, threaten-ing Irish American political power or challenging traditional Catholic values, may have frustrated some of these Irish Americans. Beleaguered at home, they identified with the beleaguered Catholics in Ireland and admired and supported the IRA Provos' willingness to fight back. This theory is, in the end, again, only speculation.

It is also important to make clear that the physical force nationalism em-bodied in NORAID enlisted but a sliver of Irish America in consistent support. Given the size and resources of Irish America, NORAID's membership and the amount of its contributions even in its best days were tiny. At its first peak of popularity in the early 1970s, NORAID could still only count about 10,000 members, and at its second peak, during the hunger strike crisis, it could raise but $250,000 in six months.

There was a group of political figures, Senators Edward Kennedy and Daniel Patrick Moynihan, Governor Hugh Carey, and Congressman **Thomas P. "Tip" O'Neill**, who defined a moderate, constitutional nationalist position on Ulster issues, much in the tradition of the Home Rulers of the 1880s. They op-posed violence and the IRA, but also criticized British government and Ulster unionist policies in Northern Ireland. It is impossible to know how many Irish Americans supported these constitutional nationalists, the "**Four Horsemen**," and since there has been no mass-based organization backing their position, it is just as impossible to know what kind of people they may have been. It is a guess and that is all it can be at this point, but it seems likely that beyond the tiny number of militant nationalist "true believers," there is a much larger proportion of Irish Americans for whom the Northern Ireland conflict is one of many issues that vaguely relates to the Irish American identity they have defined for themselves, and it fades in and fades out of their attention with changing circumstances.

As important as nationalism has been to Irish America, we still know very little about it. In particular, through most of the significant episodes of Irish

American nationalist history, we know little about who in the Irish American community supported nationalism and why they did so. While the Land League has received significant attention by excellent scholars, few studies of the Fenians, the FOIF, AARIR, or even recent history's NORAID have probed beneath the Irish American nationalism's elite leadership or diplomatic consequences.

NOTES

1. Patrick O'Farrell, *The Irish in Australia: 1788 to the Present* (Cork: Cork University Press, 2001), 197.

2. Ibid., 215.

3. Andy Bielenberg, ed., *The Irish Diaspora* (Harlow, U.K.: Longman, 2000), 221.

4. Thomas N. Brown, *Irish American Nationalism: 1870–1890* (Philadelphia: Lippincott, 1966), 22.

5. Kirby Miller, *Emigrants and Exiles: Ireland and the Irish Exodus to North America* (New York: Oxford University Press, 1985), 339.

6. William Shannon, *The American Irish: A Political and Social Portrait* (New York: Colliers, 1974), 133.

7. David Wilson, *United Irishmen, United States: Immigrant Radicals in the Early Republic* (Ithaca, N.Y.: Cornell University Press, 1998), 14.

8. David Doyle, "Irish in North America 1776 to 1845," in *A New History of Ireland*, vol. 5, *Ireland Under the Union*, ed. W. E. Vaughn (Oxford: Clarendon Press, 1989), 710.

9. Brian C. Mitchell, *The Paddy Camps: The Irish of Lowell, 1821–1861* (Urbana: University of Illinois Press, 1988), 73.

10. Doyle, "Irish in North America," 720.

11. Miller, *Emigrants and Exiles*, 278.

12. Several historians believe that this repudiation was conscious and deliberate, part of a broad attempt by Irish immigrants to distance themselves from blacks and win acceptance as whites. See the following chapter, "Irish Americans and Race."

13. Miller, *Emigrants and Exiles*, 336.

14. Ibid., 343.

15. Ibid., 342.

16. Thomas N. Brown, *Irish American Nationalism, 1870 –1890* (New York: Lippincott, 1966), 180–181.

17. Andrew Wilson, *Irish America and the Ulster Conflict: 1968–1995* (Washington D.C.: Catholic University Press, 1995), 73.

CHAPTER FOUR

Irish Americans and Race

For five days beginning on July 13, 1863, New York City was bedlam. Rioters, provoked to protest the imposition of a federal military draft law, began to run free to loot, maim, and kill. African Americans, their freedom now one of the war's principal goals, became the special target of the rioters' violence. By the middle of the week, the mobs seemed intent, as Iver Bernstein states, "not merely to destroy but wipe clean the tangible evidence of a black presence in New York City."[1] On the waterfront, rioters lynched African American William James and burned his body. On the Upper West Side, members of a white gang took turns stabbing the black William Williams and smashing him with a loose cobblestone. Later, another crowd pulled a crippled black coachman, Abraham Franklin, out of his home and lynched him, and one of the young gang members dragged his body through the streets by the dead man's genitals.

Not all, but many—and perhaps in certain of these incidents, even most—of the rioters were Irish Americans. It was, for example, a "young Irishman," sixteen-year-old Patrick Butler, who obscenely paraded Franklin's body through the streets. It became a commonplace in New York in the middle of the nineteenth century and many other parts of America that no one was more virulently antiblack and more insistently antiabolitionist than the Irish. Their racist anger was not confined to African Americans on the East Coast, however. In California in the 1870s, Cork-born Irish immigrant **Denis Kearney** thrilled the crowds on the San Francisco sandlots with his attacks on Chinese immigrants. There and on a tour across the nation, the pugnacious Kearney ended every speech with the booming refrain: "the Chinese must go."

In the middle of the nineteenth century then, Irish Americans earned a reputation as being among the most intensely racist people in America. In recent years, they have become the focus of arguments made by a school of American historians who have changed the writing of American history through their interpretations of a single word: "whiteness."

The first scholar to discuss whiteness was Alexander Saxton, in his *The Rise and Fall of the White Republic*, but it was an explosion of books by David Roediger, *Wages of Whiteness*; Theodore Allen, *The Invention of the White Race*; and Noel Ignatiev, *How the Irish Became White* in the late 1980s and early 1990s that both established whiteness as major interpretation in American history and identified the Irish as the premier examples of a people who learned how to "become white." Of these, Roediger's book was perhaps the most sophisticated and influential. David Brody has called Roediger's work an example of "charismatic" history—history that "is received as kind of historical revelation."[2]

Trends in popular culture and American politics seemed to combine to make this a "ripe moment," in Brody's phrase, for the "revelations" of the whiteness school. Some of Roediger's points, at least the focus on Irish racism, had already been long rehearsed in popular culture. Movies and television had been depicting Irish policemen, politicians, and others as racists since a revolution in ethnic representation in the media in the 1960s. An image of conservatism that began with the movie *Joe* evolved into the Irish as archetypes of racists in movies from *Serpico*, *Ragtime*, and *True Confessions*, to *L.A. Confidential* and television shows like *Homicide: Life on the Streets*.

Yet it was a "ripe" moment in other ways. Ronald Reagan had made significant inroads among Democratic working-class voters, deflating the hopes of a generation of labor historians who had celebrated working-class resistance to American capitalism. Many of the whiteness historians are labor historians themselves, but they took dead aim on their colleagues, particularly Herbert Gutman and Sean Wilentz. Gutman and others, the whiteness historians assert, had ignored the virulent racism of the white working class that had long prevented it from mounting a serious challenge to American free market capitalism.

Yet this was also a ripe moment because of a broad, multidisciplinary assault among scholars all over the world on "essentialist" notions of race—notions that somehow racial groups were rooted in unchangeable biological differences. Rejecting "essentialism," scholars began to emphasize the contingent nature of historically constructed racial identities. Societies and cultures—in short, people, not nature—made physical attributes such as eye shape or skin color into race. Barbara Fields' essay in 1982 on the construction of the black race in America was a key turning point in this intellectual trend to understand race as a constructed and not biological phenomenon.

Whiteness scholars have argued that if the black race is not a biological given, than the white race is not one either. They were committed to "interrogating" whiteness, probing the specific interests and culture that define people identified as white and answering questions such as: How did whiteness come to be? Who won the right to identify as white? Why did they want to become white? What bonds of solidarity have held white people together?

Irish Americans were a key to this exploration for many reasons. One reason, as noted above, is simply that the Irish seemed so violently racist. In addition, the Irish seemed to offer a good example of an immigrant people who "became white"—that is, they left their native land with no consciousness of a racial identity but learned to be "white" in America. Indeed, the Irish example has seemed especially interesting for whiteness scholars because the Irish had been oppressed in their own country by an invading colonial power. The Irish, oppressed at home and poor in America, should have made common cause with blacks in America, and their failure to do so seemed symptomatic of what was wrong with the working class in the United States. They therefore offered a good test case of the logic of class solidarity in America. Roediger and James Barrett have recently pushed this interest in the Irish further, noting that the Irish, themselves infected with white supremacy, seemed to play an important role in spreading its "disease" to other immigrants who followed them. The whiteness scholars are thus not just trying to explain racism or the special virulence of Irish racism, but rather they want to use the Irish to explain how white supremacy flourishes even among the immigrant poor in America. Since they began their focus on the Irish, as Eric Arnesen says, "the phrase 'how the Irish became white' has been repeated so often as to have become cliché. To numerous scholars the notion that the non-white Irish became white has become axiomatic."[3]

Whiteness scholars begin their argument about Irish whiteness in Ireland. Their purpose is to establish at the very least that the Irish were innocent of racism there; that Irish immigrants knew nothing about white supremacy in Ireland before they came to America. Theodore Allen moves beyond that point. He insists that because the Irish endured racial oppression in their own country, "no immigrants ever came to the United States better prepared by tradition and experience to empathize with the African Americans than the Irish, who were emerging directly from the historic struggle against racial oppression in their own country."[4] Allen, Roediger, and others all pay particularly close attention to Daniel O'Connell, the great Irish nationalist of the early nineteenth century, and his opposition to slavery, as well as an appeal issued by Ireland's Anti-Slavery Society to the Irish in America in 1842, calling on Irish Americans to fight for the abolition of American slavery. O'Connell's stubborn anti-slavery stand, the "Appeal," and the warm reception that African Americans Charles Lenox Remond and Frederick Douglass received in Ireland convince the whiteness historians that Irish immigrants came to America not even just ignorant of race, but predisposed to be sympathetic to nonwhites.

Ignatiev and Roediger argue that the mass of Irish immigrants then *chose* to become members of what was being touted as a superior race in America over solidarity with their fellow poor blacks and Chinese. Roediger speculates that there was a possibility up through the 1830s, perhaps, that the Irish might have chosen to cast their lot with fellow poor blacks or at least remained indifferent to America's racial division. Yet, he says the Irish later came to insist on their own whiteness and on white supremacy. He acknowledges that "within the constrained choices and high risks of antebellum American politics," this choice seemed "quite logical"—but it was a choice nonetheless.[5] In this sense, the whiteness literature sounds but another note on the persistent broad theme of Irish American history as tragedy: here the tragedy was a cruel "Sophie's Choice" imposed on a suffering people and their moral failure in yielding to the "pleasures" and "privileges" of whiteness.

Why, then, did they make this choice? Whiteness historians cite a number of reasons. Perhaps, in the broadest sense, all believe that Irish Americans were seeking acceptance. For Roediger, Ignatiev, and the historian Mathew Jacobson, "it was not clear" throughout much of the antebellum period "that the Irish were white." As Jacobson has argued: "Beginning in the 1840s American comment on the 'Irish character' became not only more pejorative but also more rigidly cast in racial typology."[6] American writers, cartoonists, and so-called scientific experts hammered away at Irish violence, emotional instability, and contentment in squalor. Therefore, Irish workers embraced white supremacy and deliberately chose it over an alliance with blacks and other racial outcasts in order to avoid descending or becoming mired in a racial "otherness" themselves. Roediger contends that the Irish were able to parlay their growing political clout into a "lasting marriage" with the Democratic Party that simultaneously bolstered that party in the north, gave birth to "new ideologies stressing the importance of whiteness," and erected a powerful political bulwark against nativist attacks on Irish rights to citizenship.[7]

But what did whiteness offer them? Roediger contends that the biggest gains were psychological. When the Irish became white they won the public deference and courtesies afforded whites but denied blacks or Asians. They basked in the privileges of white skin that set even the lowliest of Irish laborers or domestics above the richest and best-educated African or Asian Americans. And yet if white supremacy was seductive for the Irish and other white workers, Roediger believes that in the long run it paid no concrete benefits. Most whiteness historians have been quick to deny other historians' contentions that Irish American hostility to nonwhites grew out of a competition over real and material benefits. Roediger and Allen deny that the fears the Irish expressed over African American job competition were anything but a cover for other motives. Indeed, on the contrary, whiteness scholars argue, the false sense of white racial solidarity with white owners and managers that Irish workers gained through the embrace of white supremacy frequently diverted their frustrations with capitalist inequities into assaults on blacks and Asians. It thus robbed them of the chance to build a broadly based, powerful, multiracial class alliance that might have actually improved their lot.

Whiteness historians have found other reasons for the marked militancy of Irish American white supremacy. Allen asserts that despite increasing sympathy for the abolition of slavery in the Vatican and among Catholics worldwide, Archbishop Hughes and other American Catholic clerics steadfastly opposed abolition, lest they endanger the Catholic Church's tenuous position in the United States. Church leaders preached opposition to the abolition of slavery on two grounds, Allen contends. First, they argued that it was unpatriotic, because it challenged the existing legal and constitutional sanctions for slavery—indeed, it threatened a revolution in American social relations that might destroy the country altogether. Second, Allen points out, Catholic Church leaders harped upon the close relationship between abolition and evangelical Protestantism and the anti-Catholicism that seemed so pervasive among the abolitionists.

David Roediger looks to broader, deeper, and perhaps subtler conflicts in Irish Americans' "inner" or emotional life for the special virulence of their white racism. The shrillness and violent emotionalism of Irish immigrant whiteness, Roediger suggests, seemed to lie in the pain and guilt of an immigrant people uprooted from rural settings of longstanding traditions and suddenly thrust into the new and brutal conditions and harsh disciplines of urban, industrial life. They longed for the pleasures of the rural home, dance, easy conviviality, or laughter, for example—simple pleasures that not only seemed lost in the new urban industrial environment, but forbidden or at least severely limited by its demands for industrial discipline. The exigencies of the new world, Roediger contends, also often hastened the breakdowns of old moral standards. Men left cities often in search of work. Tramping about the country far from their own women, they sometimes succumbed illicit sexual pleasures. Irish women, for their part, were sometimes forced into prostitution. Roediger knows that Ireland's extraordinarily rigid sexual puritanism would only fully emerge in the late nineteenth century, but he suggests that Irish culture restricted and closely policed sexuality even before the Great Famine. The new sexual indulgence Irish immigrants practiced in antebellum America, he believes, must have therefore conjured up guilt and unease among Irish newcomers, who were used to a tradition of more rigorous sexual discipline.

Longing for an old world that was lost, and not only gone, but its pleasures forbidden in the new world, Irish Americans, Roediger suggests, projected the anxieties and desires of their inner turmoil on to African Americans. In doing so, they thus expressed those longings and desires and, by labeling and mocking them as the behavior of racial inferiors, condemned them at the same time. Irish Americans, Roediger argues, had an almost "monomaniacal" fixation on interracial sexuality. Roediger maintains that this almost pornographic fixation on black-Irish intermarriage revealed not just Irish fears but Irish projections of their own sexual longings on to blacks, already a powerful theme in American racial discourse. The ferocity of Irish attacks on blacks, especially in the draft riots of 1863—the mutilation of bodies in particular—and Patrick Butler's lurid parade of Abraham Franklin's body, he suggests, revealed how deeply the immigration experience had broken Irish Americans and how much the turmoil of their "inner life" was channeled into hostility toward African Americans. If Irish Americans chose whiteness for strategic reasons—however mistaken—to bolster a shaky status in a new world, they enforced it with an especially virulent hatred that reflected the pain of their transition to that new place.

As it has grown in popularity, naturally enough the "whiteness" school has provoked criticism. In the fall of 2001, the *Journal of International Labor and Working Class History* sponsored a symposium on whiteness in history, featuring a lead critique offered by the historian of labor and African Americans, Eric Arnesen, and responses by distinguished historians like Barbara Fields, Eric Foner, David Brody, and James Barrett. In 2002, Peter Kolchin, a historian of slavery, also addressed the writing on whiteness in American history in his article "Whiteness Studies: The New History of Race in America" in the *Journal of American History*. These critiques testify to the continuing importance of whiteness as an interpretive tool in the study of American history. Even most of the harshest critics of the whiteness historians recognize the value of exploring the history of white identity as an historical construction rather than as a biological fact. Still both the *ILWCH* symposium authors and

Kolchin raise critical and important points about the whiteness historians' interpretations. Though these criticisms are useful in examining the specific case of Irish American whiteness, neither Kolchin, the *ILWCH* authors, nor to my knowledge any other historian of Irish America has attempted a sustained critique of interpretations of Irish American whiteness. There are issues or points of argument, then, about that interpretation that need to be raised specifically in terms of Irish American history as well as those raised in the broader context of whiteness.

Few of the critics of whiteness, for example, have ventured to examine the whiteness' historians examination of Irish history. Yet the Irish background figures prominently in whiteness arguments, most notably in Allen's, and to a lesser extent in Roediger's, but in an implied sense in all of them. As they suggest, O'Connell did stalwartly back the abolitionist cause even against Irish American criticism, but it is less clear how deep or wide support for that cause ran in Ireland. It is very difficult to try to probe beyond the nationalist leadership or members of Ireland's antislavery societies to determine how future Irish immigrants to America among the Catholic peasantry in Ireland felt about blacks and slaves. Awareness of black Africans among common people in Ireland is hard to find, but there are scraps of evidence available. Notable, for example, was the occasional appearance of the word "nager" as a term of opprobrium in the speech of Irish peasants in the early nineteenth-century novels of William Carleton, once a peasant himself. In Carleton's story "The Poor Scholar," published in 1844, for example, a peasant who cared for the sick young scholar of the title tells a Catholic Bishop, "but sure my Lord, we couldn't be such nagers as to let him die."[8] Yet it is not clear from this whether blacks or Africans or even "nagers" were anything more than an empty category for Irish peasants, mere phrases, which they had picked up from an outside world but which had no emotional resonance in their own. Whether Irish Catholics came here as readymade abolitionists seems unlikely, but it still seems safe to say that they had no interest in and only the dimmest comprehension of the racial oppression of black Africans.

Whiteness historians would argue that it mattered less what Irish immigrants understood about Africans before they left than what they felt about their own condition when they arrived. Were the Irish ever in danger of being officially or legally treated as nonwhite; that is, were they in danger of being excluded from the country or denied their rights of citizenship? Foner, Arnesen, and others point out that the Irish were "white on arrival," defined so by naturalization laws since 1790 that made European immigrants, but not Asians or Africans, eligible for citizenship. Foner contends that "in terms of legal and political rights European immigrants never had to become white."⁹ Foner, Fields, and Arnesen argue that Jacobson, Roediger, and other white- ness historians mistake racialization of the Irish for a definition of them as nonwhite. Critics like Kevin Kenny and Barbara Fields contend that no amount of "racialization" of white immigrants like the Irish was applied with the same vigor, sweep, or thoroughness as the racial categorization of African Americans. Kenny contends that "there are degrees of racial discrimination and ... racism cannot be understood at the level of cultural stereotype alone; the perspectives of labor, politics, and citizenship laws must be added to the picture."¹⁰ Fields is even more insistent: "Whatever the various racializers of European immigrants do, there is one thing that they do not do, and that is to assign European immigrants to a biological category on the basis of the one drop of blood by any known ancestry rule that applies to African Americans." She goes on to contend "a chasm ... separates race as applied to European immigrants and as applied to person of African descent ... racialization is the rotten plank by which whiteness scholars try to bridge the chasm."¹¹

If the Irish were never in danger of being cast out as nonwhites, they were nonetheless subject to prejudice, discrimination, and bitter hostility by many Americans for their Irish background or Catholic faith or, more often, both. It is fair and indeed smart to ask, as whiteness historians do, whether Irish claims to white racial solidarity undermined those prejudices and eased their accep- tance into the white Protestant-dominated mainstream. Useful here are points made by both Kolchin and Arnesen about paying close attention to the variety of social relations and the structuring of power in different regions and locales of the United States. As David Gleeson has pointed out, white solidarity in the South appeared to soften religious tensions and conflicts and win Irish Ameri- cans ready acceptance there. It also appears that, as Moses Rischin suggested long ago, the Irish led anti-Chinese agitation in California reinforced white solidarity enough to smudge or largely erase internal ethnic divisions in San Francisco and ease Irish entry into the white mainstream there as well. There are other reasons for Irish Catholic acceptance in the South and West—their tiny numbers in the South meant that they posed no threat to ruling Protes- tants there, and in the West they arrived before dominating Protestant elites could take root—and yet white solidarity from shared racial antipathies seems to have played a role in both places. In the Northeast and parts of the Mid- west, however, antagonism between white Protestants and Catholics would persist for decades—in New England for a century—structuring political al- legiances, social affiliations, and job hiring practices. It would be ridiculous or even obscene to compare this religious tension and hostility to the brutal oppression endured by African or even Asian Americans. Yet a depiction of late nineteenth-century and early twentieth-century politics and social life in many eastern or even Midwestern American cities that does not take into account religious tensions would be unrecognizable to not only most historians who have studied those places but also to the people themselves who lived there then.

Not only did Irish assertions of white supremacy fail to soften hostility against the Irish in the Northeast and parts of the Midwest, but such assertions may have actually exacerbated it in those regions. It was not just Irish numbers nor was it the poverty and the crime and disorder that they seemed to bring with them that disturbed many northern native-stock Americans in the 1840s and 1850s. Many Protestant Americans in the North were also angry, as Tyler Anbinder points out, because they believed that the Irish had become allies of the slave conspiracy. Irish anti-abolitionism seemed to feed northern Know-Nothing and Republican Party antagonism against the Irish; just as the converse was true in the South, where it garnered the Irish some acceptance.

Even if we have questions about the whiteness' scholars contentions about the Irish becoming white and why, we still need to explain why Irish Americans turned their backs on African and Asian Americans, people who often shared their occupations, neighborhoods, taverns, and dance halls—indeed, people who sometimes shared their beds. All the evidence suggests that Irish men or more often women were vastly overrepresented among white spouses and lovers of African or Asian Americans, for example. White supremacy was an understandable but not necessarily inevitable option for Irish Americans. Conversely, if Irish immigrants' solidarity with fellow nonwhite workers was not "natural" either, whiteness historians are right to consider whether Irish solidarity with nonwhites could at least have been possible, and thus consider why it did not take place. In the Irish American case specifically, even if the reasons for the Irish American rejection of solidarity with nonwhites should appear self-evident, it is incumbent upon those of us who study Irish Americans to understand why the Irish seemed so much more insistent on their white identities, and, conversely, more bitterly hostile to blacks than most other groups in America for most of their history. Whether we accept the whiteness historians' arguments or not, why did the Irish in mid-nineteenth-century America think it not simply unnatural but unthinkable and even detestable to make common cause with nonwhites?

First, it may be useful to explore further what the Irish were fighting for. Whiteness historians, as noted, suggest that the Irish were fighting to be included as white, but few critics agree. It seems more likely that the Irish were fighting to preserve whiteness and its special privileges because they very quickly understood themselves to be white. Kevin Kenny suggests that "to have asked the immigrants themselves how they became white would surely have been to ask a nonsensical question ... that they were white was self-evident."[12] What the Irish said they feared over and over again was that blacks or Chinese immigrants might come to enjoy the freedom and rights of whites. Yet it was not a fear of black or Chinese freedom alone. It was also a fear that once those groups became free, they and their patrons, a powerful Republican Party and rich industrialists, would overpower the Irish and the Celts' own allies. In other words, the Irish were not trying to become white—they were fighting to prevent the elevation of nonwhites to a new status that would render whiteness and its resources and privileges irrelevant. Such an argument does not explain how the Irish became white—a key goal for whiteness historians intent on exploring how immigrants learn race and make it their own—but seeing Irish racial hostility as a defense of white boundaries rather than an attempt to become white seems a more straightforward interpretation of Irish antagonism towards blacks and their own explanation of it.

To say the Irish were defending whiteness rather than trying to become white presumes that there was something in whiteness worth defending. As we have seen, most whiteness historians have argued that whiteness offered the Irish no concrete benefits, but other historians disagree. Arnesen argues that such contentions fail to take into account "how racially segmented labor markets produced wage differentials favorable to whites or allowed whites to maintain occupational monopolies, how municipal employment was reserved for whites, and how legalized segregation ensured white workers access to public resources."[13] Whiteness historians retort that if Irish American racial enmity was really about concrete economic benefits, why did the Irish single out black and Asian competitors for exclusion from the job marketplace? If the Irish fought with blacks or the Chinese over jobs, why did not the Irish fight with Germans or native-stock Americans, or even people from other counties in Ireland over them?

The short answer is that they did. In 1880, the *New York Times*' editors wrote with exasperation that "the hospitable and generous Irishman has almost no friendship for any race but his own. As a laborer and politician he detests the Italian. Between him and the German American citizen there is great gulf fixed ... but the most naturalized thing for the Americanized Irishman is to drive out all other foreigners, whatever may be their religious tenets."[14] Open warfare with their next biggest rivals, the Germans, may have been less frequent than with blacks, but that may have been because the Germans were less likely to compete for the same jobs and were less vulnerable to Irish attacks. Irish battles with later immigrant Italians and Jews and attempts to exclude them from unions or workplaces were common enough, however, and Irish political conflicts with Poles, Italians, and Jews shaped northern urban politics for much of the twentieth century.

And the Irish fought each other, also. Roediger suggests that those battles were common in the 1830s but had died out later. That may have been true in New York City (though even there, leaders worried in the 1850s about county rivalries undermining Irish unity), but it certainly was not true in smaller cities like Lowell and Worcester, where intracounty rivalries over jobs and power ripped Irish communities apart in the late 1840s and continued to divide them into the 1850s, until Know-Nothing assaults forced the Irish factions together.

Allen and Roediger argue that even if the Irish were given to battle with other groups over jobs, they really should not have found nonwhites particularly challenging competition. The ease with which the Irish cleared blacks off New York's docks or out of its service quarters underlined the feebleness of northern blacks' competition, and Allen suggests that southern blacks never expected to come north to give substance to the deepest fears of the Irish.

One could point out that Irish immigrants could not be sure that blacks would not come north, but what is more important is why the Irish would expect or indeed dread it, and resist such an "invasion" before it happened. In the end, Irish immigrant poverty and economic vulnerability are not enough to explain the ferocity of the Irish defense of whiteness' benefits, concrete or psychological. The Irish did not act like the Germans or other white groups not just because they were poorer but because they were from Ireland and had learned "lessons" there that shaped their reactions to race relations in America. Theodore Allen entitled one of his chapters "Ulster Comes to America," and the phrase is very appropriate, but neither Allen nor any of the other historians of Irish whiteness fully appreciated how complex the Irish legacy of group relations was, or how important this complicated legacy would be to Irish American attitudes about whiteness in America. The whiteness historians essentially saw only people who had suffered, who knew nothing about white supremacy over blacks, and who appeared willing to follow their leader Daniel O'Connell as he linked arms with the crusade for the abolition of slavery. Yet they hardly probed beyond a superficial glance at what perspectives on social status, group relations, and mob violence Irish men and women might have brought to America that might have shaped Irish relations with blacks and Asians.

The first perspective was a historical one, but in Ireland more than most countries, history has never been distant; it has always a living dimension of the present. The English conquest of Ireland in the sixteenth and seventeenth centuries did not merely impose a new government over an old set of social relations. It revolutionized those social relations. A native Irish and Old English Catholic aristocracy was not so much eliminated as deliberately overthrown and then pushed into the underclass. Those that did not convert to Protestantism lost their lands. Some managed to hold on as what Kevin Whelan has called an "underground gentry," and acted as middlemen between the new lords and the tenants below. Others merely faded into the ranks of common farmers, or worse, sometimes fell into the ranks of the degraded cottiers. As the famous observer of Ireland Arthur Young reported in the 1770s: "The lineal descendants of the old families are now to be found all over the island working as cottiers on lands which were once in their own. In such great revolutions of property, the ruined proprietors have usually been extirpated or banished. In Ireland the case was otherwise." As Young elaborated, the old Catholic gentry, now impoverished, did not forget their past status: "it is a fact that in most parts of the kingdom the descendants of the old landowners regularly transmit by testamentary deed memories of their right to those estates which belonged to their families."[15] Such memories were also nourished by Gaelic poets, who sang about English upstarts and the crude nouveau riche displacing the legitimate old families and ruling their lands with overweening boorishness. Over time, old statuses and lineages may have grown confused, as old gentry middlemen suffered in the post-1815 economy and, conversely, some former peasants clawed their way out of poverty to become "strong" or moderately prosperous farmers. Yet even in the early nineteenth century, Irish Catholics retained a powerful sense of dispossession that was not merely national but personal. In the 1830s, travelers like Alexis de Tocqueville and his companion Gustave de Beaumont, for example, met a man on a coach in Ennis in County Clare who recounted in remarkable detail every dispossessed Irish noble family and their lands in the surrounding region.

This sense of Catholic dispossession animated Irish nationalism in the early nineteenth century. In the early and mid-nineteenth century, a sense of revenge and a desire to overthrow the existing order and return to Catholic supremacy still simmered and flashed below the more polite discourses of O'Connell's Emancipation or even the Repeal movements. In the 1810s and the 1820s, a commentary on the book of Revelation, "Pastorini's Prophecy," predicting that the Protestants would soon be cast down and Catholics returned to their land and power, circulated throughout Ireland, gaining special credence among the island's poorest Catholics. The notion, however, remained not merely general but personal for many Irish peasants as late as the 1840s. Patrick Connor in Ballykilcline, County Roscommon, for example, invoked his family's ancient claims to his land in a dispute with the crown over his failure to pay it rent in that decade.

Such lingering memories, perhaps, did more than fuel grand nationalist agitations or small village rebellions. Such memories must have made these Irish peasants, many of whom would soon flee to America, painfully aware of the vulnerability of status and power. As Arthur Young suggested, the nature of the English conquest was not to "extirpate" or "banish" the aristocracy or rule through or over it as conquerors would do in Poland, but rather to drag it down and degrade it, and this made Irish immigrants in America different than Germans, Poles, or Italian migrants who came to America. Those other immigrants did not have the same memories of such a loss, nor the same sense of how easily a people could be toppled from high status and humiliated.

And yet the lessons Irish peasants brought from Ireland were not merely history lessons of past glories so easily lost. There were also lessons drawn from present realities violently fought over. Irish peasants lived in an economy of scarcity where virtually the only means of economic success or even survival was through the land. Indeed, individual ambition, as Kerby Miller and Robert Scally have hammered home, seemed dangerous, for if someone was to win in this zero-sum economy fixed on the land, than someone else, inevitably, would have to lose. In the face of a ruinous depression and a tightening land market, Irish peasants often organized into secret societies, such as the Whiteboys, Captain Rock, and the like. Many and perhaps most societies organized to help peasants maintain a precarious hold on the status quo and to hold back changes that threatened to plunge them further into poverty and hopelessness. Most often, secret societies aimed their violence at fellow peasants who broke the rules of the "moral economy" and communal solidarity, such as a local tenant who broke ranks and took over the holding of a displaced fellow.

If secret society resistance was usually rooted in local struggles of economic give and take, that did not mean that secret society conflict did not reflect or reinforce broader ethnic or religious group divisions. This was most evident in the province of Ulster, particularly its southern counties, and the northern counties of Leinster and Connaught. In these Ulster borderlands, on either side of the province's border, both Catholic and Protestant populations were large enough to create an atmosphere of tense competition that could transform even everyday encounters or local economic competition into broad sectarian conflict. Even farther south, however, sectarianism often infused local conflicts. De Tocqueville's Catholic informants in the 1830s in Kilkenny, Cork, or Galway, for example, frequently remarked bitterly about local landlords who

allegedly cleared their land of Catholic tenants and replaced them with Protestants. Whether these reports were true or just rumors, they testified to the
sensitivity of sectarian competition in all parts of Ireland. James Donnelly also
documents, for example, the broad and deep influence of Pastorini's prophe-
cies and sectarianism on the Captain Rock secret society violence that erupted
in Munster in the 1820s. So great was the Rockite conviction in Pastorini that
thousands of them rose in an abortive insurrection in northwestern Cork in
January 1822, believing that they were helping to make the prophecy come to
pass. Moreover, at least six Protestant churches were burned by secret societies in Limerick, Kerry, and Cork during the Rockite troubles. Grievances over
tithes to be paid for the support of the established Church of Ireland in the
1830s, an upsurge in aggressive Protestant evangelization, and the spreading
popularity and power of the Orange Society in the early nineteenth century
also helped fuel this sectarian bitterness.

The surge of secret society resistance helped make early nineteenth-century
Ireland a rough and sometimes brutal society. Added to the chaos were faction
fights, massive brawls fought out at country fairs, sometimes invested with economic interests, sometimes extended family rivalries, and sometimes seemingly pointless battles among local leaders and their followings. Such violence
would subside by the 1840s with the substantial improvement of the police
in Ireland. Still traditions of violence, mob brawls, and secret society attacks
and threats were hardly unknown to the Irish men and women who came to
America during the famine years.

Such traditions of violence, a painful history of the vulnerability of status,
and lessons of mutuality and group solidarity, all played out in a society acutely
aware of sectarian boundaries, followed the Irish to America and must have
shaped how they understood group relations here. Secret societies emerged
here, such as the Molly Maguires in the Pennsylvania coal fields in the 1860s,
but also among workers on the Baltimore and Ohio canal in the 1830s and the
railroads in central Massachusetts in the 1840s. Yet it was not the transfer of the
forms of organization that is so important, but the transfer of the understanding among Irish immigrants of how groups related to one another. Indeed, it
may be important that the very areas along the Ulster borderlands, where sectarianism seemed especially virulent and laced conflicts over economic issues,
were also the areas overrepresented among Irish immigrants to America until
at least the famine and maybe later. Among them group solidarity, boundary
maintenance, and violence had become commonplace. It may also be useful
to remember that major Irish Catholic clashes with Irish Protestants may have
occurred about as frequently in America as conflicts between Irish men and

American blacks. Indeed, seven and eight years after the draft riots of 1863, Irish Catholics and Irish Protestants fought bitter battles on New York's West Side, the latter battle in 1871 a shootout that cost sixty-two lives.

As noted earlier, David Roediger argues that it was not just what the Irish brought with them from the Old World but the very transition of Irish Americans from Ireland to America that helped fuel the passion of their racism. Wrenched out of pastoral if impoverished Ireland, they landed in an urban industrial world that not only cut them off from nature but imposed harsh and numbing new disciplines on them. Roediger focuses more specifically on the emotional conflicts Irish Americans must have felt about the discrepancies between their sexual behavior in America and the moral codes of Ireland. This argument is powerful and sophisticated. Roediger is smart enough to know that Irish sexuality and marriage behavior were in transition in the mid-nineteenth century, but he still believes that Irish sexual morality was very strict then. He points out for example that Irish culture, even in the early nineteenth century, had little room for illegitimacy, and those rates were very low. Still, premarital sex may have been much more common in the pre-famine era than such rates suggest, for the Irish seemed fearful then not so much of sex than of unmarried mothers and fatherless children. If marriage was valued and illegitimacy discouraged at that time, some historians believe that rich and earthy attitudes about sexuality were also common. On the whole, Irish understandings of sexuality and sexual practice in the early nineteenth century were probably much more complicated than Roediger allows. The bulk of the Irish may have become sexual prudes in the late nineteenth century; it is not clear, however, that earlier in that century they were as well.

Yet Roediger's point remains: Why then were Irish Americans apparently so obsessed with a black sexual invasion across their racial borders? The fear might have also stemmed not so much from Irish emotions centered on sex than feelings focused on the defense of group boundaries and an understanding that sexual transgression of an ethnic boundary had a particularly powerful meaning. The Irish, as not only the poorest of whites, but also having the most single women among their immigrants, might have felt particularly vulnerable to African and Asian Americans crossing those boundaries. The very fact that Irish women were, indeed, more likely to wed nonwhite men than women of other white groups reveals how uniquely porous among all white ethnic groups Irish boundaries with nonwhites were. A fear of racial intermarriage may have been rooted in this fact. But was it a fear of black sexuality or of Irish helplessness? Roediger and Robert Lee both note that Irish men also worried about Chinese men preying on Irish women. Yet the Irish did not talk about Chinese men in the same way as they talked about black men. Like most Americans, Irish Americans understood Chinese men as dangerous, but not as sexually potent males. They rather were seen as sinister in an effete and devious way. Indeed, Denis Kearney himself derided the Chinese male as sexless.

While Roediger focuses on the importance of Irish American sexuality in nourishing their racism, Theodore Allen has been impressed with the powerful effect that Catholic leaders had on their Irish flocks' views of slavery. Allen suggested that these church leaders' positions grew out of American circumstances. In doing so he preserves the purity of the ideological innocence that Irish immigrants inherited from Ireland. John McGreevy, in his study of relations between American Catholics and American liberals, dismisses the notion that American bishops were out of tune with broader Catholic opinion, and argues that opposition to abolition was deeply rooted in Catholic thought. Almost no Catholics in the United States, he points out, not just Irish, but German and French Catholics as well, backed abolition. "Catholic opposition to abolition cannot be reduced to the particular American racial dynamic," he says.[16] Many Catholic intellectuals around the world accepted slavery as a legitimate if tragic institution. "Fearful of social disorder and unwilling to distinguish the suffering of slaves from other human miseries," McGreevy argues, "Catholics lumped immediate slave emancipation with a religious and political radicalism that threatened the foundations of society."[17]

In the end, there are many, many questions about Irish whiteness that remain unanswered. Indeed, it seems that there are too many. Ignatiev and Allen notwithstanding, Roediger's analysis of Irish whiteness remains the best, and it is simply a few short chapters in a book-length essay. For a phenomenon that has seemed so central to a major reinterpretation of American history, Irish American whiteness thus is woefully understudied. This seems true of the story on both sides of the Atlantic. No historian of Ireland has as yet seriously or comprehensively addressed the issues of the Irish background to Irish American racism. Yet even if, as suggested in this chapter, that background was crucial to teaching Irish immigrants lessons about group relations that they would later tragically apply in America, it is critical not to see such an outcome as an inevitable playing out of the Irish inheritance in an American environment. The "whiteness" historians are right: Carleton's stories notwithstanding, the Irish did not know white supremacy and white racial oppression of blacks before they came here. It is the intersection of Ireland's lessons in group relations with the very specific racial dynamics of American life that shaped Irish American racial attitudes. It was not just a place, however, but

also a specific place in a specific time. Irish American attitudes seemed to
be hammered into a tragically racist mode in the middle of the nineteenth
century, precisely when issues of slavery and race moved to the center of political discourse in America, blowing up into civil war. Whatever the full story
of how the Irish learned to translate their own understanding of group relations into white supremacy, the role of the Democratic Party at that time,
exploiting white racism in the antebellum era to shore up its support in the
North, must be considered important. Much also needs to be done in fixing
more precisely the timing of Irish racist hostility, assessing the variations from
community to community, analyzing the demographics and backgrounds of
Irishmen involved in antiblack or anti-Chinese violence, and trying to find
evidence — perhaps in sources like the thousands of letters Kerby Miller has
discovered — of what Irish immigrants themselves had to say about race. Like
everything else, but perhaps even more so in this case, it would be useful
as well to look at how these Irish "lessons" about group relations learned in
Ireland played out in other environments, such as Canada or Australia. What
were Irish Australian relations with aboriginal people like? Or Irish Canadians
with native peoples? Both Canada and Australia also had powerful and successful anti-Asian immigration movements. What role did the Irish in both
places play in those movements?

Whatever the reasons, most Irish Americans rejected standing with nonwhite minorities and embraced notions of white supremacy through the middle decades of the nineteenth century. They also often did so not with a quiet
acquiescence but a passionate, shrill enthusiasm. Would they continue to do
so in succeeding years? The record was mixed.

Interestingly, Irish and Irish American nationalists were often quick to side
with colonial peoples of any sort outside of Ireland and America who were
fighting the British or even the new American empire. In 1879, for example,
nationalists in Ireland celebrated the Zulu resistance in South Africa. At that
time, Michael Davitt and his fellows were launching the **Land League** agitation in Ireland, and they self-consciously evoked the similarities between Irish
peasants' fate and those of oppressed people like Africa's blacks throughout the
world. Though O'Connell's early cry for abolition did not find support in Irish
America, these later anticolonial sentiments did. As David Doyle and Mathew
Jacobson have pointed out, Irish American nationalists virulently opposed the
first steps toward American empire in the late nineteenth century, finding
American subjugation of the Filipino revolutionaries little better than Britain's conquest of Ireland. As the **Clan na Gael** camp of Worcester, Massachusetts put it in 1902: "It is eminently fitting and proper that we who are banded

together in the fight for Irish freedom should condemn any movement, which has for its object the subjugation of people whether in Ireland or the Philippines."[18] On the other hand, as David Doyle and Thomas McAvoy have pointed out, while Irish American nationalists rejected the notion of American empire, some prominent Irish American clerics, such as Father Denis O'Connell and **Archbishop John Ireland**, both Irish born, embraced American imperialism as a chance to spread an Americanized Catholic church's influence around the world. It is also important to note that nationalists both in Ireland and Irish America also backed the revolt of the Boers (the white Afrikaner oppressors of local blacks in South Africa) against the British Empire with more enthusiasm and more concrete help than they afforded the Zulus.

At home, Irish Americans appeared to remain stubbornly hostile to African or Asian Americans through the late nineteenth and early twentieth centuries. Though some like John Boyle O'Reilly, perhaps the most popular and influential Irish American writer of his day, championed African American interests, many Irish Americans continued to fight nonwhite efforts to claim equal rights. Irish Americans backed exclusion of Japanese as well as Chinese immigrants by the turn of the century, and played prominent roles in small antiblack riots in New York and a major one in Chicago in 1919. Irish American songs and comic farces were also often laced with racist language—in one of vaudevillian Pat Rooney's songs the refrain ran "to teach the Chinese how to die."

The old values of group and neighborhood solidarity, virtues that enriched Irish American life in many respects, seemed to continue to also nurture Irish American (and other Catholics') resistance to cooperation with nonwhite peoples until well into the twentieth century. Both John McGreevy and Gerald Gamm have detailed this Catholic, often Irish American, communal resistance. In 1974 and 1975, that resistance exploded across the nation's television screens when the heavily Irish American Boston neighborhoods of South Boston and Charlestown erupted in riots against court-ordered busing to racially integrate the city's schools.

The busing crisis, however, may have obscured a substantial degree of change among Irish Americans on race. By the time South Boston and Charlestown erupted, most Irish had moved up the economic ladder and out of old neighborhoods. Tightly bound working-class Irish communities like South Boston had increasingly become anachronisms. As John McGreevy has pointed out, even when the church opposed abolition in the nineteenth century, official church teaching had not countenanced the crude racism that defined blacks as inferior beings. Now Irish American Catholic clergymen in many cities stepped forward to advance the cause of integration. Irish American Cardinal Patrick O'Boyle, for example, integrated Catholic schools in Washington after World War II, before public school integration and in the face of stiff resistance. In the struggle for civil rights in the 1950s and 1960s, then, the institutional Church in America had cautiously but deliberately swung its weight against racism. Finally, by the middle of the twentieth century, the Democratic Party, once the bulwark of racism, had begun to change into a champion of civil rights. No study has been done, but quick looks at votes in the U.S. House of Representatives for the 1964 Civil Rights Act and even the much more contested 1966 open housing bill reveal that Irish American Democratic congressmen from the North backed those pieces of legislation almost unanimously. Many Irish Americans as well as other white ethnics abandoned the Democrats because of the party's stands on these issues. Yet for those who stayed, membership in the Democratic Party, like participation in the Catholic Church, may have helped educate them into racial tolerance.

By the 1960s and 1970s, Irish American relations with racial minorities were complicated, so much so that it might be impossible to say that there was one Irish American response to their nonwhite neighbors. Andrew Greeley's survey data suggests that Irish Americans had become among the most liberal of American ethnoreligious groups on civil rights issues by that time, but voting data from the same era reveal that Irish Americans were streaming out of the Democratic Party just as it was becoming a champion of those issues. Boston's busing crisis of the mid-1970s neatly reflected this complexity of Irish racial attitudes: if Irish Americans like school committee members Louise Day Hicks or John Kerrigan were prominent in protests against busing for racial integration, then Irish Americans like Senator Edward M. Kennedy and Judge Wendell Arthur Garritty, who issued the busing order, were also prominently in support of it.

NOTES

1. Iver Bernstein, *The New York City Draft Riots: Their Significance for American Politics and Society in the Civil War* (New York: Oxford University Press, 1990), 27.

2. David Brody, "Charismatic History: Pros and Cons," *International Labor and Working Class History* 60 (2001): 44

3. Eric Arnesen, "Whiteness and the Historian's Imagination," *International Labor and Working Class History* 60 (2001): 13.

4. Theodore Allen, *Invention of the White Race* (New York: Verso, 1994), 1:169.

5. David Roediger, *The Wages of Whiteness: Race and the Making of the American Working Class* (New York: Routledge, 1995), 144.

6. Mathew Jacobson, *Whiteness of a Different Color: European Immigrants and the Alchemy of Race* (Cambridge, Mass.: Harvard University Press, 1998), 48.

7. Roediger, *Wages of Whiteness*, 141.

8. William Carleton, *Traits and Stories of the Irish Peasantry* (Dublin: Mercier Press, 1973), 310–311, see also 264.

9. Eric Foner, "Response to Eric Arnesen," *International Labor and Working Class History* 60 (2001): 58.

10. Kevin Kenny, *The American Irish: A History* (Harlow, U.K.: Longman, 2000), 69.

11. Barbara Fields, "Whiteness, Racism and Identity," *International Labor and Working Class History* 60 (2001): 50.

12. Kenny, *American Irish*, 68.

13. Arnesen, "Whiteness and the Historian's Imagination," 12.

14. Tyler Anbinder, *Five Points: The Nineteenth-Century New York City Neighborhood that Invented Tap Dance, Stole Elections, and Became the World's Most Notorious Slum* (New York: The Free Press, 2001), 405.

15. Kevin Whelan, "An Underground Gentry? Catholic Middlemen in Eighteenth Century Ireland," in *Irish Popular Culture, 1650–1850*, eds. James Donnelly and Kerby Miller (Dublin: Irish Academic Press, 1998), 149.

16. John T. McGreevy, *Catholicism and American Freedom: A History* (New York: Norton, 2003), 52.

17. Ibid., 56.

18. Timothy J. Meagher, *Inventing Irish America: Generation, Class, and Ethnic Identity in a New England City, 1880–1928* (Notre Dame, Ind.: University of Notre Dame Press, 2001), 259.

PART III

Important People, Organizations, Events, and Terms

Ancient Order of Hibernians   Founded in St. James Church in New York, the Ancient Order of Hibernians grew to be the leading Irish ethnic fraternal organization in America by the end of the nineteenth century and remains an important one today. The AOH traces its origins to secret societies in Ulster such as the "Defenders," which protected Catholic interests and allied with the Society of United Irishmen there in the conflicts culminating in the rebellion of 1798. In fact, most of the charter members of the Hibernians gathering in St. James Church were from Ulster, and they drew their charter from an unnamed society in Ireland. The AOH's early history is hard to trace, but the order appears to have been closely associated with the defense of Catholic interests from nativist attacks in the 1850s. In the latter half of the nineteenth century, the order faced two serious problems: a factional split, which led to the creation of two orders in 1884, and condemnation by the Catholic clergy, who suspected the AOH of links to violent secret societies like the Molly Maguires in northeastern Pennsylvania. The factional fights divided the local divisions in New York City from those in the rest of the country over a range of issues: finances, interpretation of Irish descent qualifications for membership, and nationalist politics. The two orders eventually submitted to the arbitration of Bishop McFaul of Trenton and were reunited in 1898. Attacks on the order by some clerics and bishops following the Molly Maguire controversies troubled the Hibernians throughout the 1880s, but in 1895 a committee of the hierarchy cleared the organization of all suspicion. In the 1890s and early 1900s the AOH thrived, officially adding military companies and a Ladies Auxiliary in 1892 and 1894 respectively. By 1906, Hibernian men and women together totaled over 175,000 members. At the turn of the century, the order became a strong voice for preserving Irish culture in America, encouraging the Irish language movement by endowing a chair in Gaelic at Catholic University and lobbying for the teaching of Irish history in public and parochial schools. It also endorsed Irish nationalism and was especially militant under the presidency of Matthew Cummings, when the AOH aligned itself with physical force nationalists. Factional splits during the Irish Civil War in the 1920s and rapidly declining rates of immigration from Ireland sapped the strength of the Hibernians, and its membership fell to about 20,000 in 1940, remaining at that level though most of the late twentieth century. However, the Hibernians continued to be active in many of their old causes. In the 1960s and 1970s, the AOH became involved in the "Troubles" in Northern Ireland, helping form the Irish National Caucus in 1974 and the Ad Hoc Committee for Irish Affairs.

Boucicault, "Dion" Dionysius Larner   Boucicault was a key figure in the evolution of the Irish American stage and even more important in the evolution of images of the Irish in American popular culture. As William Williams has said, Boucicault worked hard in his many plays to transform the Irish peasant buffoon into a comic hero.

Boucicault was born in Dublin in about 1820, descended from old Huguenot settlers in Ireland (though there were rumors that he was the illegitimate son of a family friend). He began his acting career in London, gaining his first big break in 1841, in the play *London Assurance*. In 1853 he came to America with Agnes Roberts, his common-law wife. He lived and acted for several years before going back to Europe, and then returned to settle in the United States in 1870. Boucicault wrote over 200 plays, but his most famous were the series of *Colleen Bawn* (1860), *Arrah na Pogue* (1864), and *The Shaughran* (1874). In the latter he created a character, Conn, a clever rakish peasant who became Boucicault's featured role for the rest of his life and was the archetype of the new Irish comic hero. Boucicault's plays were immensely popular with Irish American audiences, but surprisingly, rarely overtly nationalist. For example, in *The Shaughran*, British army officers are portrayed less as brutal oppressors than as well-meaning, if bumbling, administrators of the law.

Carroll Family of Maryland   The Carroll family of Maryland was the leading Catholic family in British North America in the eighteenth century. Charles Carroll of Carrolton, for example, was the only Catholic to sign the Declaration of Independence. Though cultivating themselves as Anglo colonial landed gentry, they were of Irish ancestry, and their Irish experience was fundamental in shaping their understanding of themselves and their strategies of adjustment in America.

The Carrolls traced their lineage far back into the history of Ireland, when the family dominated the Ely O'Carroll, a region encompassing parts of Counties Laois, Offaly, and Tipperary. They tried hard to hold on to their land during the tumult of the sixteenth and seventeenth centuries through rapidly shifting alliances, crafty bargaining, and stubborn resistance, but the Carrolls, like most Irish families, steadily lost ground to English Protestant conquerors. Elizabeth's armies and then Cromwell's soldiers overwhelmed Irish resistance and confiscated the Irish elite's lands. Despite heavy losses during Cromwell's time, the family hung on until the late 1680s, when Charles Carroll emigrated to Maryland. Educated as a lawyer and with good connections to Maryland's proprietors, the Calvert family, upon arrival Carroll briefly became the colony's Attorney General.

The Glorious Revolution that same year deposed James II, broke the Catholic cause in Ireland, and forced Catholics like Carroll from the government in Maryland. Charles Carroll, however, continued to serve the Calvert family in Maryland as part of the family's hidden establishment in the colony. Through the help of his patron, smart marriages, and sharp negotiation as a banker and land speculator, he built up his holdings from over 1,000 acres to 47,000 acres in 1720. Charles Carroll was extraordinarily conscious of his Irish heritage, naming his properties after longtime Carroll castles and estates in Ireland: Litterluna and Climihara were two thus named. He also brought to Maryland an ancient genealogy of the Carroll family written in Irish. Most importantly, the family's experience in Ireland (where his cousins were already rapidly descending into the peasantry) drove him to fight and scheme to hold on and add to his lands in Maryland. Though brought up as an Anglo colonial gentleman, Charles's son (also named Charles) was well aware of his Irish ancestry—his "descent from princes of Ireland"—and maintained the family genealogy, translating it into English. Like his father, he went to great lengths to maintain the family holdings, even to the point of refusing to marry his son Charles's mother until the boy proved worthy of preserving the family fortune. That son, the third Charles, or as he is often called, Carroll of Carrolton, was far less conscious of his Irish ancestry than his grandfather and father. He was educated at the English college at the Catholic St. Omer's in French Flanders and studied law in Paris and London. Nevertheless, he too remained staunchly Catholic, and his Irish inheritance and Catholic faith would nourish his alienation from the English monarchy. In 1759, he wrote to his father from Europe: "I can't conceive how any Roman Catholick, especially Irish Roman Catholick, can consent to live in England or any of the British dominions if he is able to do otherwise." In 1770, Charles Carroll of Carrollton became a spokesman for the resistance to the British Empire's taxes on Marylanders, waging a newspaper war over both taxes and state support for the established church against advocates of the empire. In 1776, he participated in a mission to French Canada with Benjamin Franklin, Samuel Chase, and his cousin Father (later Bishop) John Carroll. He was a member of the Continental Congress until 1778, when he resigned to become president of the Maryland State Senate. He became a prominent figure in the Federalist Party after the Constitution was ratified, serving in the United States Senate briefly and the Maryland State Senate. After Thomas Jefferson was elected president in 1800, Carroll retired from public life, though he occasionally appeared at ceremonial occasions such as the opening of the Baltimore and Ohio railroad in 1828. He died in 1832.

Clan na Gael   The Clan na Gael was the most important revolutionary or physical force nationalist organization in Irish American history. For over fifty years straddling the turn of twentieth century, the Clan kept the cause of violent overthrow of British rule in Ireland and the establishment of an independent Irish Republic alive.

The Clan was founded in New York City in 1867 by men from various factions of the Fenians. They had come together to plan the kidnapping of Prince Arthur of Connaught, who was then visiting the United States. They hoped to hold the British prince as a hostage for the release of republican prisoners in Ireland. The men also hoped that they could reconcile quarreling Fenian factions and revive the Fenian Brotherhood as an effective nationalist force. Yet the Fenians seemed to be fading quickly, and so the conspirators created a new organization, the Clan na Gael, or, as it was sometimes called, United Brotherhood. The Clan was a secret society with elaborate rituals and coded communications. It was organized into local camps and regional districts, and was headed by a national executive. From the beginning it was strongest in the large Irish American communities of the Northeastern and Midwestern big cities, but camps were organized in small towns in rural states like Arkansas and Iowa. In the 1870s, the Clan engaged in a number of schemes to advance the cause of Irish revolution: contracting with John Holland to build a submarine to defeat the British navy (Holland did indeed develop a usable submarine, but for the United States—not the Clan); or hiring a whaling ship, the Catalpa, to successfully rescue Fenian prisoners in Australia. By 1877, the Clan's membership had risen to 11,000 members. In the late 1870s and early 1880s, it collaborated with other Irish Americans in the Land League, seeking to use that organization to foment revolutionary sentiment in Ireland. After the demise of the Land League, the Clan helped found and direct the Irish National League for the same purpose. Yet through the 1880s the Clan suffered severely from internal factional troubles. In 1881, Alexander Sullivan and two other members of the national board, Michael Boland and Denis Feeley, gained control of the Clan and ruled it dictatorially. Nicknamed the "Triangle" and relying on a powerful base in Sullivan's well-organized Chicago Clan camps, the Clan fostered a dynamite terrorist campaign in England in 1883 that enraged leaders of the Irish Republican Brotherhood, the Clan's sister organization in Ireland. American Clan members led by John Devoy were also upset at the Triangle, and in 1887, Devoy created his own Clan na Gael. Even the murder of an anti-Sullivan Clan member, Dr. Patrick Cronin, in Chicago in 1889, did not fully discredit the Triangle, and the two factions limped along, fighting each other, until they were finally unified in 1899.

Reunited, the Clan continued to seek opportunities to help the Irish revolutionary cause, backing the Boers against Britain in 1899, meeting with Russian and French diplomats to seek assistance against Britain (before the Triple Entente allied Britain, France, and Russia), and fighting to disrupt the increasingly close partnership between the United States and Britain. Moderate or constitutional nationalism had revived by the end of the nineteenth century, but the Clan refused to work with the representatives of moderate nationalism, the United Irish League of America or John Redmond's Irish Parliamentary party. Instead, the Clan sought a reconciliation with the Irish Republican Brotherhood in Ireland, which it achieved in 1911. Throughout World War I, Clan leaders worked closely with the IRB to link revolutionaries in Ireland with England's enemy, Germany. During the Irish revolution, the Clan split again: John Devoy opposed Eamon De Valera through the Clan's popular front organization, the Friends of Irish Freedom, while other Clan members like Joseph McGarritty backed De Valera and his American Association for the Recognition of the Irish Republic. These factions persisted through the Irish Civil War. When De Valera gave up the armed fight in 1926 and entered the politics of the Irish Free State, however, McGarritty and the remnants of the Clan in America broke with him and remained true to the concept of armed struggle. By this time, however, the Clan was tiny. The great decline in Irish immigration to America in the late 1920s and 1930s meant there was little infusion of new blood into the Clan. In 1934, the Clan split again—this time in a fight between traditionalist conservative nationalists and socialists. In 1938, the traditionalists under McGarritty helped the Irish Republican Army diehards in Ireland undertake a bombing campaign in England. In 1940, the death of McGarritty and World War II virtually extinguished the Clan. In the 1950s, a persistent small group sent funds to support a new IRA campaign, but after the demise of the new bombing effort in 1962, the Clan faded away. A few camps survived into the 1980s, but by the 1970s the Clan's role was largely taken over by new organizations like NORAID.

Coughlin, Reverend Charles Reverend Charles Coughlin, the famed "radio priest," played a vital role in the rise of populist movements in the midst of the economic turmoil of the 1930s. He both led and embodied a vicious Catholic anti-Semitism that reflected the sometimes nasty parochial underside to the Catholic militancy that characterized Irish American life in the twentieth century.

Charles Coughlin was born in Canada in 1891 of Irish ancestry (his great-grandfather emigrated there in the 1820s). He was ordained a priest of the Archdiocese of Detroit in the United States in 1923. He was assigned to a parish in the Detroit suburb of Royal Oak, Michigan, where his Catholic parishioners felt embattled and defensive after the Ku Klux Klan burned crosses there during the "tribal twenties." To build up the parish, Coughlin built a shrine to St. Theresa, "The Little Flower," a nun who had died young after extraordinary suffering and had only recently been canonized by the Catholic Church. To raise funds for the Shrine, Coughlin began to speak on local radio in 1926, on a program called the "Golden Hour of the Shrine of the Little Flower," which focused almost exclusively on religious and devotional subjects. A polished orator of the "old school," Coughlin's distinctive style turned out to be extraordinarily effective on radio. Though born in Canada, he spoke with a slight Irish brogue, trilling his R's to hide a slight speech impediment. By 1927, he could be heard on radio in twenty states.

In 1930, he began speaking on the economic problems caused by the Great Depression. Mixing elements of Catholic social thought such as points from Pius XII's *Quadregessimo Anno* condemning "despotic economic institutions" and long-time themes in American populism such as the commitment to an expanded money supply, Coughlin assailed the bankers, both American and European, for artificially restricting the money supply in America and causing the Depression. He also attacked President Herbert Hoover, the Federal Reserve, and other government officials and establishments. In his speeches he invoked powerful religious imagery, comparing, for example, the three years that it took veterans to get the bonuses due them for their service in World War I to Christ's three hours on the cross. Yet if Coughlin appeared to assail the status quo, he was also strongly anticommunist. He saw both the communists and the bankers as conspiratorial elites preying on average people. In the midst of the Depression, this message made Coughlin increasingly popular. By 1930, his audience had grown to almost thirty million listeners.

In 1932, Coughlin backed Franklin Delano Roosevelt for president, but after Roosevelt won, Coughlin quickly began to criticize him. In 1934, Coughlin created the National Union of Social Justice. By 1936, he had turned against Roosevelt entirely, blasting him on his radio show and in his paper, *Social Justice*, which he founded that year. That same year, he established his own political party and ran North Dakota congressman William Lemke against Roosevelt. To offset Coughlin's appeal to Irish and German Catholic voters, the Democratic Party recruited Monsignor John A. Ryan to speak for the president during the 1936 campaign. Though Lemke was defeated, Coughlin remained popular even as he became increasingly anti-Semitic. In his broadcast in response to the Nazis' attack on Jews in the infamous *Kristallnacht*, or "Night of the Broken Glass," Coughlin seemed to apologize for the attacks, arguing that the Nazis rightly saw that Jews were Communists and a threat to the German nation. In the United States, some of Coughlin's partisans began organizing as members of Christian Front clubs and began attacking Jewish neighbors in Manhattan's Washington Heights neighborhood, parts of Brooklyn, and Dorchester and other neighborhoods in Boston. Coughlin's anti-Semitic attacks cost him listeners, but he remained popular. Despite his vitriolic anti-Semitism, Catholic church officials were slow to condemn him. His first bishop, Archbishop Michael Gallagher, a former fiery Irish nationalist, was sympathetic to some of Coughlin's economic arguments and reluctant to curb him. His second bishop, Archbishop Edward Mooney, was more antagonistic. Mooney publicly condemned the *Kristallnacht*, for example, and frequently fought with Coughlin. Nevertheless, he remained cautious about forcing Coughlin off the radio, and the priest remained on the air until 1940. The church moved to prevent him from engaging in politics after World War II began, and the government threatened to accuse Coughlin of treason for his pro-Nazi opinions. Coughlin continued to serve as a priest in Michigan before retiring in 1966. He died in obscurity in 1979.

Daley, Richard J.   Richard J. Daley was the last of the great Irish American city bosses. He was mayor of Chicago from 1955 to 1976 and chairman of the Cook County Democratic Party for several years more than that. Over that period, he not only dominated Chicago politics but was a critical force in state and national politics.

Richard J. Daley was a third-generation Irish American born on May 15, 1902. He grew up in Bridgeport, a largely Irish and Polish Catholic neighborhood of modest bungalows on Chicago's South Side. The neighborhood would be his lifelong home. After graduating from De La Salle, a Catholic commercial high school, he took the first step in his political career by winning the presidency of the Hamburg Social and Athletic Club, a South Side organization that counted as members a number of young men who would later become powerful Chicago politicians. Daley was elected supposedly because he could type and, more importantly, he was quiet and knew how to keep his counsel. Many observers believe that the Hamburg's members were heavily involved in the Chicago race riot of 1919, though there is no direct evidence that Daley himself participated. Daley soon attached himself to Joseph "Joe" McDonough, the alderman and Democratic Party committeeman from his ward. When McDonough was elected county treasurer, Daley followed his patron and wound up doing much of the actual administration of the office. In 1936, Daley was elected to the Illinois State Assembly and in 1939, to the State Senate. He served in the latter until 1946. In the early 1950s, Daley emerged as an important figure amid the chaos of a factionalized and beleaguered Chicago Democratic Party. In 1955, he won the Democratic Party primary election for mayor over the incumbent Martin Kennelly, and the general mayoral election over Robert Merriam.

Initially, Daley ruled in traditional machine fashion. He doubled taxes between 1955 and 1963 to finance machine patronage and contracts. At this point, Daley depended heavily on African American Congressman William Dawson and Dawson's South Side black machine to win elections. In 1963, Dawson's black voters proved essential to Daley in helping him defeat Benjamin Adamowski, who played upon Polish ethnic pride and white small homeowner anger over taxes to mount a stiff challenge to Daley. After this election, Daley altered his strategy. He began to renew Chicago's downtown (the "Loop"), in the process building a constituency of developers, downtown businessmen, contractors, and construction unions. To pay for development and other capital expenses and to supply new sources of funds for the city's ambitions, he began to flex the machine's muscle in Springfield (the state capital) and in Washington. From 1955 to 1977, the federal proportion of the city's capital budget would grow from 9 percent to 32 percent. At the same time, Daley began to cultivate the small homeowners who had been deserting him over taxes. His city agencies and party committeeman paid close attention to the delivery of basic city services, garbage pickup, street and sidewalk repair, and street cleaning in these middle-class neighborhoods. Between the downtown renewal and the delivery of these city services, Chicago developed a reputation as "the city that works" — a powerful contrast to other cities like New York, Detroit, and Philadelphia, which were losing white middle-class residents, plagued by deteriorating downtowns, and locked in stalemates of racial conflict. There was another side to this success, however. As Daley cultivated these new constituencies he abandoned his old black allies. While the machine delivered public housing and welfare services to poor blacks, it also helped maintain Chicago's rigid segregation through its housing construction and school policies, and it also encouraged black political decline. By the 1970s, the machine's power was cracking, undermined by new city union demands, court-ordered limits on patronage, renewed minority unrest, and a series of scandals that took down some of Daley's most powerful allies and closest friends: Matthew Danaher, Thomas Keane, and Edward J. Barrett.

Daley was not just a local power, but through much of his career, a national one. In the 1950s, he emerged along with David Lawrence of Pennsylvania and others as a Democratic Party kingmaker. He is widely credited with helping John F. Kennedy squeak through in the 1960 presidential election by making sure that he produced enough votes for Kennedy to win the vital state of Illinois. In 1968, the oppressive tactics of his police and his own harsh rhetoric at the Democratic Convention in Chicago alienated a new force of Democratic liberals who took over the party after the election. By 1972, the party had virtually abandoned him.

Dooley, Dr. Thomas   "Tom" Dooley became an important symbolic figure for Americans generally, but Catholics and Irish American Catholics in particular, during the height of the Cold War through his work as a doctor in Vietnam and Laos. He came to embody a compassionate and young but vigorous Cold War warrior, a far more sympathetic anticommunist figure than the dark, glowering, oafish Senator Joseph McCarthy and helped create a bridge to John F. Kennedy's youthful, idealistic Cold War American nationalism. Though only half Irish in ancestry, his backers and handlers frequently depicted him as a typical Irish American "regular guy," which seemed to enhance his popularity.

Dooley was born in St. Louis on January 27, 1927 into a prominent Irish American family. He attended the University of Notre Dame and St. Louis University's medical school before joining the Navy and serving on a medical mission in Vietnam. There he quickly established a reputation for public charisma as well as a commitment to service, and attracted the attention of CIA officials seeking to shore up American support for Ngo Dinh Diem, the South Vietnamese president. The CIA thus moved to make Dooley a spokesman for Diem in America and capitalized on his personal appeal to make him a popular symbol of American anticommunism in Vietnam by early 1955. Dooley, however, was also gay and, for the times, relatively open about his sexuality, which led to a secret Navy investigation and his quiet resignation from the service in 1956. He continued to be a key anticommunist figure, however, moving to a mission in Laos where he served for the next four years. He was also still a popular figure in the United States, trumpeted by the Vietnam lobby as a secular saint and by Catholics as a folk hero. He died on January 18, 1961.

Draft Riots of 1863   On July 13, riots erupted in New York, beginning as a
protest against the implementation of a new conscription law and spreading to general mayhem over the course of the following week. Resistance to
the new draft law emerged in Boston and in the coal fields of northeastern
Pennsylvania as well, but never matched the intensity or scope of the New
York riots. Irish Americans played critical roles in all of these draft riots, particularly the New York City one, and the anti-black violence that marked
the New York riot has seemed emblematic to many historians of the pervasiveness and ferocity of Irish American racism in the nineteenth century.

In March 1863, the Union government passed a national conscription
act, which made all men aged twenty to thirty-five and all unmarried men
aged thirty-five to forty-five liable for conscription into military service.
Names were to be collected in house-to-house canvasses and submitted
to lotteries in each congressional district. Draftees could escape service
by presenting an acceptable substitute or paying $300. Many in the Irish
American community had already tired of the war. They were saddened by
heavy losses among Irish regiments at Antietam and Fredericksburg and
angry at the government for placing the abolition of slavery at the center
of the war effort, after the Emancipation Proclamation was formally issued
on January 1, 1863. Among Irish Americans in the Pennsylvania coal fields,
resistance to the war, mixed with protests over labor grievances, had already become common by 1862. Irish miners armed themselves and rioted
against a Pennsylvania state conscription law that year. The next year, Irish
miners and some German farmers protested again, but there was no open
insurrection when the draft law was instituted in the summer of 1863. This
was not the case in Boston and New York. In Boston the resistance was brief
and largely concentrated in the city's mostly Irish North End. On July 14,
1863, scuffling broke out between neighborhood crowds and provost guards
who had come into the North End to execute the draft. As the police and
militia arrived, the fighting became more general and a full-scale riot
erupted, lasting through the night. Six people died, but there was no loot-
ing and no attack on the city's blacks. The riots in New York were far more
devastating, a virtual insurrection that shut down the city for five days after
July 13. On the morning that the draft lottery was to begin, the protests
began with attacks on provost marshal offices. Many skilled artisans and
German immigrants also protested that day, but that evening they turned
against the riot when it degenerated into indiscriminate and savage violence. By the middle of the week, poor Irish Americans working in semi-
skilled industrial jobs or as laborers were heavily represented among the

rioters. The violence was general, aimed at prominent Republicans, city officials, Protestant organizations and, increasingly, African Americans. Attacks on African Americans had become more frequent in the months before the riots, but during the riots they became extraordinary in their breadth and ferocity, involving assaults, stonings, mobs, lynchings, mutilations of corpses, burning of African American homes and businesses, and destruction of charitable institutions. Rioters burned the Colored Orphan's Asylum, for example. Even white shopkeepers who served blacks were targeted. Though rioters focused on blacks and prominent Republicans, they did also occasionally attack Germans, Jews, Chinese peddlers suspected of relations with white women, and even fellow Irish Catholics who sought to quell the revolt. A mob assaulted Colonel Hugh O'Brien of the Eleventh New York Volunteers, for example, the day after he had ordered cannon fire to clear Second Avenue. Rioting spread over most parts of the city but was especially virulent in what was then the upper East Side (around Second Avenue and Twenty-second Street) and the West Side dock areas. Historians dispute the extent of unrest on the Lower East Side in the "Bloody Ould" Sixth Ward. Eventually the dispatch of regular army troops, which included Irish American soldiers fresh from Gettysburg, put the riot down. There were about one hundred dead in the official counts, but it is likely that there were many more deaths that went unrecorded.

Dunne, Finley Peter   In 1893, the musings of the fictional Mr. Martin Dooley began a commentary and narrative about the Bridgeport section of Chicago. Finley Peter Dunne composed these pieces within the limits of journalistic deadlines and newspaper limitations, yet their art is penetrating, imaginative, and enduring, and through his character and alter ego "Mr. Dooley" he became one of the most important observers of American life at the turn of the century.

Dunne was born in 1867, from parents who had both come to Chicago from Ireland. Peter, one of eight children, was the only one to attend high school, but graduated last in his class. In 1884, he began as a reporter at the *Telegram* in Chicago. With some thirty papers operating in Chicago at that time, the newspaper life was lively and varied, with an emphasis on immediacy and brief, realistic details. This urban journalism's penchant for realistic expression was a disciplining forge for any new reporter. Dunne apparently was successful enough to be recruited by the *Chicago Daily News* before he was eighteen, where he learned the craft of succinct editorial writing well enough to cover the Chicago White Stockings on the road during the years 1885 through 1887. During the course of his travels, he also wrote other stories in dialect, and his efforts led to a new job as a political reporter at the *Chicago Times*, where he wrote political pieces using Irish dialect.

After some experimentation and changing newspapers, Dunne began writing his Martin Dooley characterization in the *Chicago Evening Post* from a Bridgeport saloon on October 7, 1893. The columns, with their skillfully written realistic dialogue and narratives, continued until 1898, over time growing more pessimistic, trenchant, and satirical. Charles Fanning, in his *Exiles of Erin*, presents a representative collection, classifying some twenty-two pieces in a selected chronological thematic arrangement:

1. Memories of the Great Hunger, the crossing from Ireland, and the first years in the United States
2. Daily life in Bridgeport in the 1890s
3. Characterizations of Bridgeport residents
4. The comic and painful effects of assimilation
5. Work, politics, and choices for Irish in American cities
6. Views of Irish nationalism
7. Strong indignation at ethnic poverty in Chicago

Dunne would go on to write about larger journalistic issues, but his contribution to American literary realism is noted by both William Dean Howells and Theodore Dreiser, and James T. Farrell, writing after Dunne, attributed wisdom to Dooley at the beginning of *Young Lonigan*. (John Henry Meagher, hereafter JHM)

Farrell, James T.   James Farrell was one of the most prolific and important novelists in Irish American history. Unlike his contemporaries Fitzgerald or O'Hara, Farrell wrote about working- and lower-middle-class Irish Americans and probed the very heart of Irish American life in the first half of the twentieth century.

Born in 1904 on the South Side of Chicago, Farrell grew up in a working-class neighborhood that was to become the primary focus of his earlier and most notable works of fiction. Mary Daly Farrell, his mother, was one of the seven children of Julia and John Daly, who came from County Westmeath in Ireland. Mary married James Farrell, a son of a former slave overseer and Confederate soldier. James, who was able to read and write, became a teamster, a "scripper," and a dispatcher, and was a loyal union member. He was remembered with affection by Farrell as proud but kind, and an embodiment of the working class of Chicago.

Farrell's parents sent James, their second oldest son of three, to live with his maternal grandparents, the Dalys, nearby. This was a step up from his parents' apartment. He was able to go to Catholic schools from first to twelfth grade, enjoying baseball and his studies—especially after Sister Magdalen made a special impression on him in the eighth grade. He showed interest in becoming a priest but went to St. Cyril's high school, which he remembered as both propagandistic and authoritarian though also morally supportive. The Daly family moved into Washington Park, the neighborhood that was the setting for the Studs Lonigan novels and stories, while he was in high school.

Throughout high school he was a good student and not troublesome, wrote for the school monthly *Oriflamme*, played sports, wrote stories for "recognition and self-expression," and worked as a telephone clerk. After graduation, he worked full-time at the same company and shared his wages with his family. He began night classes in 1924 at DePaul but gave up in March of the following year, and began work at a gas station, saving money to begin studying at the University of Chicago in June. There he took writing courses and read widely and deeply in history, politics, sociology, psychology, and education from authors such as Dewey, George H. Mead, Thorstein Veblen, Nietzsche, Bertrand Russell, Mencken, Theodore Dreiser, Sherwood Anderson, Sinclair Lewis, and James Joyce. This period not only solidified his intention to be a writer, but convinced him to focus his writing on his Irish American past in Chicago. Lewis Fried notes: "Farrell believed his life was intimately and irrevocably bound to his urban past. His fiction almost obsessively deals with the poverty of his parents, the crippling parochialism of the South Side's Irish Catholicism, the suffocating middle-class pieties of the relatives who raised him. Yet these themes also serve as a prologue to his novels that deal with the liberation he saw promised by what he believed was the city's culture of democracy."

These times in his life would be the subject matter for much of his early and most famous works. His best known novels, *Young Lonigan* (1932), *The Young Manhood of Studs Lonigan* (1934), and *Judgment Day* (1935), narrate the dissolution of a second-generation Irish American young man in Chicago, restricted by the conformity of family, church, and neighborhood. Farrell saw the set of novels as a logical, psychological, and sociological sequence leading to the death of the hero, Studs. In contrast, he also wrote a second series of books that chart the liberation of another young man, Danny O'Neill, from the same section of Chicago. Narratively spanning the years 1909 through 1927, this set of novels includes *A World I Never Made* (1936), *No Star Is Lost* (1938), *Father and Son* (1940), *My Days of Anger* (1943), and *The Face of Time* (1953) and was called by Farrell the

O'Neill-O'Flaherty series (although the primary hero throughout remains Danny O'Neill). It is a set of novels that Farrell wanted to write first, but he doubted his ability to do it and so instead began the Studs series. Throughout this period, Farrell was also writing short stories that involved the same subjects and characters of the novels, such as "Studs" (1930), "Jim O'Neill" (1932), "All Things Are Nothing to Me" (1932), and "Boyhood" (1929). Farrell went on to write many more novels, stories, and critical pieces, but the first eight novels and early short stories established his place in American and Irish American literature. (JHM)

Fenians The Fenians were the first mass-based nationalist movement in Irish American history and they had a profound effect on nationalism in Ireland and America. Though their attempts to free Ireland by violent revolution or by invasions of Canada proved spectacularly inept, their recruitment efforts and fundraising educated an entire generation of immigrants in nationalism and republican ideology and set a precedent for the vital role Irish Americans would play in succeeding nationalist movements.

Several Irish nationalist organizations established in New York, such as John Mitchel's Irishmen's Civil and Republican Union and the Emmet Monument Association helped to cultivate the ground for the Fenians in the 1850s. The Fenians emerged after John O'Mahony, a veteran of the attempted Young Ireland rising of 1848, wrote to his former Young Ireland compatriot James Stephens in Ireland in 1857 about the establishment of a revolutionary nationalist organization. Stephens set up the Irish Republican Brotherhood as a republican revolutionary organization in Dublin on March 17, 1858, and O'Mahony established the Fenians in New York City the very same day, to mobilize Irish Americans in support of the Brotherhood. The initial notion, then, was that the IRB would raise an army in Ireland and the Fenians would supply it with the "sinews of war": guns (a hoped-for 50,000 rifles), money, and additional men. O'Mahony, a Gaelic language scholar, named the Fenians after the legendary ancient Irish warrior band. The Civil War was initially thought to be a hindrance to Fenian growth, but actually seemed to spur it, as Thomas Clarke Luby and Stephens recruited extensively among Irish American soldiers in the Union Army. The Fenians held their first convention in Chicago in 1863, when three hundred delegates representing sixty-three branches or circles formalized the organizational structure with a Head Center and Central Council of five, elected O'Mahony Head Center, and issued a Declaration of Independence for the Irish Republic. By the end of the war in 1865, the Fenians counted an estimated 50,000 members, and the time seemed ap-

propriate for the "final call"—a rising in Ireland. Irish American soldiers
had already landed in the old country, and a number of officers with extensive Civil War experience led by Colonel Thomas Kelly set up a military
council there. But the British government cracked down on the IRB in
Ireland in September 1865 and the rising was put off. This crackdown
revealed the Fenians' weakness: almost all of its strength in men, arms,
and money was in the United States, separated from Ireland by a British-
dominated ocean. Some American Fenians began to look for a another
way to help Ireland or at least strike a blow at Britain by attacking Britain's
colony Canada. A general anti-British sentiment in America and what the
Fenians believed were sympathetic meetings with President Johnson and
Secretary of State Seward encouraged this hope. Meanwhile, growing dis-
enchantment with O'Mahony erupted at a special Philadelphia Congress
in October 1865. The Philadelphia Congress ousted O'Mahony and set up
a Senate led by William Roberts, who urged a strategy of invading Canada. O'Mahony created his own rump faction, ostensibly committed to a
strategy of supplying the revolution in Ireland, as opposed to an invasion
of Canada. Yet in February 1866, the British parliament suspended habeas
corpus and carried out another series of raids in Ireland. In April of that
year the O'Mahony faction struck first at Canada to preempt the Roberts
faction. The O'Mahony faction's assault on Campobello Island turned
into a fiasco when General George Gordon Meade (of Gettysburg fame)
intercepted the Fenians and seized their ship. Undeterred, the Roberts
wing launched their own invasion of Canada from Buffalo and St. Albans,
Vermont in May 1866. Some Fenian Union army veterans made it across
the Niagara River and fought a successful skirmish with Upper Canada
militia, but President Johnson condemned the invasion, ordered the arrest of the Fenians, and the government dispatched troops and a revenue
cutter to block the Fenian retreat back to Buffalo. Almost all those arrested
were quickly released, but the Roberts wing suffered a severe blow. Back
in Ireland, the Irish American military council pressed Stephens to call
for an uprising there, finally deposing him and raising the rebellion in
1867. Some rebels prematurely attacked a Coast Guard station in Kerry
in February 1867, and there were further scattered skirmishes in Cork in
March, but none to any effect. Irish Americans from the O'Mahony wing
had tried to supply the rebellion with guns and men on the ship *Erin's
Hope*, but the men were arrested almost as soon as they landed. In 1868,
the Supreme Council of the IRB in Ireland declared the whole uprising
a debacle and broke off relations with their Irish American counterparts,

the Fenians. In America, Colonel John O'Neill, who had won the lone small victory in the 1866 Canadian invasion, rallied some diehards for another attempt on America's northern neighbor from the Lake Champlain area of Vermont. Yet his weak organization was riddled with spies, and the newly elected President Grant and his administration was firmly hostile. A small Fenian force barely made it across the border before they were driven back and O'Neill arrested. O'Neill tried again with about forty men in 1871, hoping to link up with the rebellious *metis* of western Canada, but was arrested again. The Fenians were a spent force by then, but limped on. O'Mahony returned as Head Center in 1872 and then James Stephens in 1879. By then, however, the Clan na Gael had surpassed the Fenians as the principal physical force Irish nationalist organization in America. Jeremiah O'Donovan Rossa held a final Fenian Convention in 1885 and the Fenians officially expired in 1886.

It is easy to make fun of the Fenians as revolutionary bunglers, but given the size of the project they attempted—challenging the most powerful empire in the world—it is hard to believe that they ever had any chance at success. What is more important is how broadly popular they were and how they rallied thousands to the cause of Irish republican nationalism. Despite clerical opposition, they not only recruited tens of thousands of members but mobilized 100,000 sympathizers for a rally in New York in 1866, and tens of thousands for picnics and protest meetings in cities from Worcester, Massachusetts to San Francisco.

Fitzgerald, F. Scott   F. Scott Fitzgerald was probably the most important novelist in Irish American history. His *The Great Gatsby* has become part of the American literary canon. Yet he also reflected trends in Irish American life at the turn of the century, particularly the social ambitions and disappointments of second- and third-generation Irish Americans at the beginning of the twentieth century.

F. Scott Fitzgerald was born in 1896 in St. Paul, Minnesota, and grew up in an age of turmoil and conflict. A descendant of the composer of "The Star Spangled Banner," his father Edward came from a southern family in Maryland while his mother Mary "Mollie" McQuillan was the beneficiary of her immigrant grocer father's success in St. Paul. Edward's business failure led to a move of the family to Buffalo and then back to St. Paul, where F. Scott went to St. Paul Academy and wrote for the school newspaper. In 1911, at the age of fifteen, he was sent to Newman School, a Catholic preparatory school in New Jersey where he met Monsignor Sigourney Fay and Shane Leslie, who were interested in Irish Nationalism and Irish American participation in Irish independence. From Newman he was conditionally accepted to Princeton, where in 1917 he stayed for a semester, thriving in the social scene, writing scripts, and neglecting his studies. In the same year, he joined the Army, and while stationed at Fort Leavenworth and then Montgomery, Alabama, he wrote *This Side of Paradise* (1920) and fell in love with Zelda Sayre, a daughter of an Alabama Supreme Court judge whom he later married in 1920. That year also saw the publication of *This Side of Paradise* and some of his stories in *The Smart Set* and *The Saturday Evening Post*, his most successful economic venue. Later living in New York, the couple enjoyed a celebrity lifestyle while he worked on novels, stories, and plays (*The Beautiful and Damned* and *The Vegetable*) that were at best a mixed success. The celebration of things Irish in 1917 and 1918 had long been abandoned, and like Blaine Amory, the Irish-born hero of *This Side of Paradise*, Fitzgerald appeared "tired" of it. In 1924, Scott and Zelda met Pound and Hemingway in France and then went to Rome, where he continued to work on *The Great Gatsby* (1925). On the Riviera he also met Gerald Murphy, an American whose son had contracted tuberculosis and who had given up his promising painting career to care for him.

Although the Fitzgerald marriage was disintegrating, his writing continued. It never returned enough satisfaction or money for him, however. Through two years in Paris, the Riviera, Rome, back in the United States in 1927, again in France in 1929, and in Switzerland, Zelda was first treated for mental and emotional illness while Scott wrote short stories to pay the bills instead of working on novels. Returning to America in the midst of an economic depression in 1931, Zelda and Scott settled near Baltimore where, hospitalized at Johns Hopkins Hospital in 1932, Zelda wrote an autobiographical novel, *Save Me the Waltz*, which appeared to some to anticipate or undercut Scott's *Tender Is the Night*. Later, living in Asheville, North Carolina hotels and not writing with much energy and creativity, Scott no longer felt he could care for his 14-year-old daughter Scottie, whom he left with Harold Ober, his agent. His return to Hollywood, his failing creative powers, alcoholism, and Zelda's deterioration led to his failing health, and he died in the apartment of Sheila Graham, his lover, on December 21, 1940, at the age of forty-four.

Irish matter was not a primary focus in his writings, although there are references to minor characters and stereotypes of Irish people in many of the stories and novels. However, his view of Catholicism echoes the critiques of other Irish American and Irish writers, including his contemporary James Joyce and the past realism of Finley Peter Dunne. Malcolm

Cowley suggested that Fitzgerald was split between participating in and observing the upper-class life: "Like Dunne he had been accepted into the ruling Protestant group, and unlike Dunne he wrote about that group, so that his Irishness was a little disguised, but it remained an undertone in all his stories; it gave him a sense of standing apart that sharpened his observation of social differences." To the extent that Fitzgerald seemed to grow increasingly critical of wealth, Robert Rhodes sees the author's view of the Irish as growing more important in the novels through *Tender Is the Night*, and speculates even beyond to the unfinished *The Last Tycoon*. Rhodes sees what was implied by Cowley's comment in Fitzgerald's vision of the class structure from the top down, in a time when the Irish were at lower levels of the social strata. (JHM)

Flynn, Elizabeth Gurley   Born in Concord, New Hampshire, on August 7, 1890, Elizabeth Gurley Flynn dedicated her life to labor and radical causes. Her father, Thomas Flynn, worked as a civil engineer and her mother, Annie Gurley, labored as a tailor. Elizabeth descended from a long line of Irish rebels, and the Bronx apartment she grew up in often served as a meeting place for Irish nationalists and socialists. Her parents encouraged her radicalism from a young age. By fifteen, Elizabeth had quit school and was speaking on soap boxes on street corners. She was arrested with her father while still a teenager for speaking without a permit.

Flynn gained national notoriety as a member of the Industrial Workers of the World. A revolutionary anarcho-syndicalist organization that formed in 1905, the IWW sought to help workers take over the means of production from capitalists and bosses. Flynn joined the IWW in 1906 and quickly became known as the "rebel girl" as she traveled the country agitating, organizing, and speaking in support of strikes, free speech movements, and the overthrow of the capitalist system. Flynn participated in support of some of the largest and most important strikes in the first two decades of the twentieth century. She rallied and raised money for the predominantly immigrant and poorly paid textile strikers in the Massachusetts towns of Lawrence, Lowell, and New Bedford in 1912, and in Paterson, New Jersey, in 1913 and 1914, for example. The unrelenting Flynn was involved in IWW-initiated, free-speech conflicts in Missoula, Montana (1908) and Spokane, Washington (1909–1910). Flynn came to the aid of numerous like-minded radicals in legal trouble, such as the Sacco and Vanzetti defense fund (1919–1926), and she raised money and support for the victims of the Palmer Raids, who were arrested in the antiradical hysteria after World War I. She also helped establish the American Civil Liberties Union in 1920.

Flynn paid a price for her demanding schedule. A brief marriage to Jack Archibald Jones in 1908 fell apart, with Flynn leaving their child to be raised by her mother and sister. She had a torrid affair with fellow IWW leader Carlo Tresca. In 1926, she collapsed from exhaustion and ceased her busy activist schedule for a decade. She returned to radical politics in 1936, and in 1938 joined the Communist Party. In 1940 the ACLU expelled her because of her Communist Party membership. She rose rapidly to the highest levels of the Communist Party, based primarily on her reputation as a rebel and IWW agitator. She was one of the Communist Party's more popular speakers and columnists, writing frequently for its newspaper, the *Daily Worker*. Flynn was arrested along with other Communist Party leaders in 1951 under the Smith Act, which made being a member of an organization that promoted the overthrow of the United States government against the law. It was the tenth time she was arrested for her activism. After her conviction, she spent three years at Alderson prison (1955 to 1957). Once released from prison, Flynn was determined to revive a Communist Party shattered by Cold War harassment. In 1961 she became the first female national chair of the Communist Party. She died in the Soviet Union on September 5, 1964, where she was given a state funeral. (Joseph Turrini, hereafter JT)

Ford, Patrick   One of the most important journalists in Irish American history, he was a lifelong powerful voice in America for Irish nationalism. His most influential years, however, were in the 1880s, when he became the American leader of the left wing of the great Land League agitation, and came to embody a new kind of Irish American radicalism.

Patrick Ford was born in Galway in 1837. Orphaned at an early age, he was brought to Boston by his guardians in 1844. He attended public schools in Boston and the Boston Latin School, and later took a job as a printer and journalist for William Lloyd Garrison's famous paper the *Liberator*. It was in Boston that Ford confronted anti-Irish and anti-Catholic prejudice during the rise of the Know Nothings in the 1850s. This made him increasingly conscious of his Irish identity and Ireland's plight as an oppressed nation. Ford believed that life in America lifted Irishmen out of "the littleness of countyism into the broad feeling of nationalism." Ford moved from Boston to New York and established his own newspaper, the *Irish World*, in 1870, which he edited until his death in 1913.

The *Irish World* became a strong advocate of Irish nationalism, printing a regular column in the 1870s on the Skirmishing Fund, an effort to encourage guerrilla war in Ireland, for example. Yet Ford moved beyond simple calls for freedom for Ireland. Jolted by the hardships of the Depression of 1873 and influenced by a host of radical thinkers like Henry George, Ford began to see the need for social and economic reform and the links between the cause of peasant tenants in Ireland and beleaguered American farmers and industrial workers. In 1878, he renamed his paper the *Irish World and Industrial Liberator*. During the Land War crisis of 1881 and 1882, he backed Henry George's land nationalization program for Ireland, allying with Michael Davitt and the Ladies Land League. He also raised funds for the League in America, soliciting money directly through his paper and sending it to his radical allies in Ireland. In 1881 and 1882 he was raising far more money for the League than the League's official treasurer. By 1882, the *World* counted a circulation of over 60,000 readers. In 1886, Ford would back Henry George for Mayor of New York City in an historic race that marked a high point of Irish American radicalism. Sobered by clerical condemnations of George, Ford abandoned his strident radicalism and became much more culturally and economically conservative. His paper remained a force in Irish American affairs, however, and still backed an independent Irish republic. In the early 1900s, the *World* boasted nearly 120,000 readers.

Four Horsemen   The "Four Horsemen" were the Irish American political leaders Senator Edward M. "Teddy" Kennedy of Massachusetts, majority leader and later Speaker of the House Thomas P. "Tip" O'Neill of Massachusetts, Senator Daniel P. Moynihan of New York, and Governor Hugh Carey of New York. They became the heart of the constitutional or moderate wing among Irish American nationalists after the eruption of the most recent phase of the "Troubles" in Northern Ireland in the 1960s. Their commitment was to a peaceful solution to the Ulster crisis, opposing IRA violence but with sympathy to Catholic Irish interests in Ulster.

The Four Horsemen emerged as spokesmen for constitutional or moderate nationalism in the late 1970s. Leaders of Northern Ireland's Social Democratic Labor Party like John Hume and the Foreign Office of the Republic of Ireland had become concerned about the popularity in America of the IRA and their supporters in NORAID. John Hume of the SDLP and Garret Fitzgerald, Sean Donlon, and Michael Gillis in the Irish Foreign Office worked hard to get prominent Irish American politicians to condemn the IRA's violence and establish an enduring Irish American counter to NORAID. Those efforts paid off when the Four Horsemen attacked support for the IRA on March 17, 1977. Yet all of the Horsemen were also committed to the defense of Catholic Irish interests in Ulster, both because of their own Irish Catholic roots and in the interest of their Irish American

Catholic constituencies. Thus in 1978, along with Senators Joseph Biden of Delaware and Gary Hart of Colorado, they assailed the British government for its seeming indifference to reports of human rights abuses by its police and military. On a trip to London, Congressman O'Neill made those points explicitly, provoking criticism in the English press but winning approval from the Irish government and the SDLP. During the hunger strikes of the early 1980s, the influence of the Four Horsemen and other moderate nationalists seemed to wane as that of militants like NORAID grew. By the mid 1980s however, the tide had turned again, as the Horsemen and a new Friends of Ireland group formed in the United States Congress seemed to help push the English government along toward the conclusion of an Anglo-Irish agreement. Carey's fall from power and O'Neill's death broke up the Four Horsemen, but constitutional or moderate nationalists continued to exert great pressure through the American government for a resolution to the Ulster crisis.

Friends of Irish Freedom   From the Easter Rebellion in 1916 until 1920, the Friends of Irish Freedom was the principal mass-based organization in the nationalist movement. It would eventually fade from prominence as its leaders incurred the wrath of Eamon De Valera, leader of the Irish Republic, then at war with Britain. The history of the FOIF reflects the sometimes differing and even competing goals of Irish American and Irish nationalists.

The FOIF was created by leaders of the Clan na Gael, who believed that they needed a mass-based "front" organization to more effectively carry on their effort to enlist American aid against England in World War I. The Clan organized the FOIF at an "Irish Race" meeting of over 2,000 carefully chosen delegates in New York in March 1916. The new organization's stated purpose was to "bring about the independence of Ireland." Its membership was open to all individuals who sympathized with its goal, including women, and the Friends encouraged existing Irish societies to join as affiliates. Soon after its formation, Ireland erupted in rebellion during Easter Week and the FOIF organized meetings in New York and Boston in support of the rebels. It was only when the British government moved to execute the Easter Week leaders, however, that Irish American support began to swell, and the FOIF organized a very successful nationwide protest on May 8, 1916, to condemn the executions. The FOIF worked to keep the United States from joining Britain and France in World War I up until almost the very moment that the nation entered the war in April 1917. World War I forced the FOIF to tread lightly in assertions of Irish independence and opposition to Britain, now an American ally, but a crisis over conscription in Ireland and the rising popularity of Sinn Fein encouraged the FOIF to call another race convention in May 1918 to once again assert Ireland's right to independence. When the war ended, the FOIF and its leaders swung into action. Just a month after the armistice, during the week between December 8 and December 15, 1918, the FOIF organized meetings all around the nation demanding self-determination for Ireland. In succeeding months the FOIF would call a Third Irish Race Convention, raise one million dollars for a "Victory" fund for Irish revolutionaries, and create an American Commission for Irish Independence to lobby for Ireland at the Paris Peace Conference. At its high point in 1919 and 1920, the FOIF claimed over 100,000 full members and 175,000 associates (members through affiliated organizations). Increasingly, FOIF leaders found themselves at odds with Woodrow Wilson and his proposed League of Nations and they therefore cultivated Republican support in Congress. When Eamon De Valera arrived in the United States, he believed that he should have greater control of the nationalist movement in America and quarreled with FOIF leaders Daniel Cohalan and John Devoy over fundraising and strategy. When De Valera created his own organization, the AARIR, the FOIF began to decline. After the signing of the treaty with Britain in December of 1921 and the FOIF's support of the new Free State as opposed to De Valera's republicans in the ensuing Irish Civil War, the FOIF's decline was precipitous. A few branches survived into the 1930s, but it was all but extinct thereafter. In 1989, a faction broke off from the principal American backer of the IRA, NORAID, and called itself FOIF, but the new organization had no connection to the old one.

Friends of Ireland for Catholic Emancipation   The Friends of Ireland for Catholic Emancipation was a loose collection of organizations formed in the late 1820s to lend support from the Irish American community to Daniel O'Connell's Catholic Association and its agitation in Ireland for Catholic emancipation. Though it had little influence on that agitation, the Friends of Ireland societies were perhaps the most important nationalist societies in the era between the Society for United Irishmen in the 1790s and the Repeal Association in the 1840s. It was also probably the first Irish nationalist organization dominated by Catholics and reflected the transition from Protestant to Catholic Irish immigration to America taking place in the 1820s and 1830s.

Efforts to win Catholics in Ireland full civil rights after the Penal Laws took effect dated back to the eighteenth century but were troubled by factionalism throughout the early nineteenth century. In 1823, Daniel O'Connell brought these factions together in the Catholic Association and transformed the agitation into a mass movement that raised money from thousands of peasants and mobilized them in mass protest meetings. The Association contested elections for Parliament in 1826 and 1828 and helped elect O'Connell himself to a parliamentary seat in County Clare. In 1825, Irish immigrants in New York formed the first American society in support of O'Connell's movement. Old '98 exile William Sampson spoke at a meeting backing O'Connell, where he claimed that Ireland's struggle was akin to the American fight for independence. His exiled colleague James McNeven wrote the new society's memorial to O'Connell, not only backing emancipation, but urging O'Connell to fight for a federal relation with Britain. The New York Friends fell apart as O'Connell concentrated more on the Emancipation movement and ignored the members' calls for a more aggressive nationalism. Still, in 1826 and 1827 meetings were held and Friends organized in cities from Boston and Washington to St. Louis. In 1828, Philadelphia formed a Friends Society and New York revived its Friends Association, and in 1829, several smaller cities, Troy (New York), Bardstown (Kentucky), Savannah, New Orleans, and Detroit established organizations. By the late 1820s there were about thirty such Friends associations in cities across the United States. Despite these numbers, these societies had little effect on the Emancipation movement. They never met in a national meeting and raised little money—only about $5,000—for Ireland. The Friends included Protestants in almost all their branches—George Washington Park Custis headed the Friends group in Washington—but the bulk of their members were probably Catholic.

Gaelic Sports in the United States   Gaelic sports, like the Gaelic language, became an important element in the Irish cultural revival in the United States in the early twentieth century. They have persisted as a critical social and cultural force in the lives of twentieth- and twenty-first-century immigrants from Ireland to America, as those immigrants have adapted clubs, associations, and cultural practices that they knew in Ireland to the American environment.

Irish homegrown sports such as hurling seemed in decline in Ireland and were little known and neglected in America when Irish leaders intent on preserving Irish culture founded the Gaelic Athletic Association in Thurles in 1884. In 1888, the GAA sent teams of footballers and hurlers to the United States on a mission later termed "the American invasion" to stage matches in New York, Boston, Providence, Philadelphia, and other cities. The "invasion" was not a commercial success, but it did help spark renewed interest in Irish sports. In New York City, Gaelic sports proved critical to creating enduring county societies (societies made up of people born or ancestors born in specific counties, like the Mayo or Cork societies), as each society sponsored its own team. These teams competed against one another in the Irish County Athletic Union, which later became a New York GAA affiliated with the GAA in Ireland. Gaelic sports clubs also sprang up in other cities. Chicago's first club appeared in 1890, and by 1893 the city boasted fifteen clubs. Clubs also formed in San Francisco, Boston, Philadelphia, and Detroit. Gaelic sports in America flagged with the declining numbers of immigrants after 1930, but repeated tours of teams from Ireland helped keep interest alive. In 1947, Cavan and Kerry played the all-Ireland football final at the Polo Grounds, the only Gaelic sports final ever played outside Ireland. By the 1950s, the world of Irish sports in America was divided between a New York association and a North American Board that represented the rest of the country. American Gaelic sports remained competitive at the end of the twentieth century, dominating biennial tournaments with "diaspora" competition from Canada, Australia, and Britain in the mid 1990s.

Gibbons, Cardinal James   Cardinal James Gibbons was one of the most important churchmen in the history of the Catholic Church in America. He was the leader of church liberals at the end of the nineteenth century as they tried to forge a new relationship between the Irish American–dominated church and American society.

James Gibbons was born in Baltimore in 1834 to Irish immigrant parents, but his father decided to return to Ballinrobe in Mayo after the panic of 1837, and so young James Gibbons grew up in Ireland. His father ran a small shop and tavern in Ballinrobe. The family suffered severely during the famine—Gibbons's father and sister both died. In 1853, Gibbons, his mother, and the rest of his family returned to the United States. Gibbons attended seminary in Baltimore and was ordained a priest in 1861. His first assignment was at St. Patrick's parish in the city and he then became pastor at St. Bridget's parish. He served as vicar of North Carolina and bishop of Richmond, Virginia, before returning to Baltimore to become archbishop in 1877.

He quickly established himself as a leader of the American church. Though small and seemingly frail, he was quick, polished, and politically adroit. In the 1880s and 1890s he led the liberal faction of the American Catholic hierarchy, which sought to accommodate the church to American culture. It included John Ireland, John Keane, and Denis O'Connell, all Irish immigrants, and several second-generation bishops and priests, while second-generation Irish Michael Corrigan and Bernard McQuaid and a number of German bishops led their conservative opponents. Among Gibbons's signal accomplishments was the winning of Vatican approval for Catholic workers to join non-Catholic labor unions, specifically the Knights of Labor. Gibbons and the liberals' broader efforts to open the church to American culture came to naught when in 1899 Pope Leo XIII condemned a heresy he vaguely defined as "Americanism." Cardinal Gibbons, however, continued to serve as the chief spokesman for American Catholicism and remained the ranking archbishop in the nation until he died in 1921. Though he had long avoided Irish nationalist issues, urging immigrants and their children to quickly Americanize, he endorsed the Irish nationalist movement in a major meeting at Madison Square Garden in New York in the fall of 1918.

Gordon, Mary   Gordon has been labeled a Catholic and woman writer. Her writing, while containing religious and feminist elements, more strongly reflects her own inward search for her identity as a daughter, scholar, wife, and mother. Her distinctly autobiographical fiction has focused on her Irish-Catholic childhood, such as her first novel *Final Payments* and *The Other Side*. These novels criticize harsh Irish culture and reflect Gordon's perception of her own family and childhood and early adulthood as told in her memoirs, *Seeing Through Places*. In *Final Payments*, Gordon also revisits her relationship with her father, a Jew who converted to Catholicism. Gordon's father was a staunchly conservative Catholic and Gordon weaves elements of his identity into the father's character in this first novel. While Gordon's later fictional work, such as *Rest of Life* and *Spending*, departs from this early concentration on ethnic and Catholic themes, feminist and religious elements remain an important part of her writing. Yet her work persists in reflecting issues that concern her life and experiences. Gordon maintains a personal style in her nonfiction essays and books, and candidly shares her personal views on contemporary political issues like abortion and the American Catholic church. In her two memoirs, *Shadow Man* and *Seeing Through Places*, Gordon describes her personal struggles with her family's controlling Irish Catholicism and her father's hidden identity as a Lithuanian Jew.

Born in Far Rockaway, Long Island, on December 8, 1949, Gordon grew up in the predominantly Irish American suburb of Valley Stream, New York, near the borough of Queens. Her parents were Anna Gagliano, a legal secretary, and David Gordon, a writer and publisher. After her father's death in 1956, Gordon and her mother lived with her grandmother in Valley Stream. Gordon earned a B.A. in English from Barnard College (1971), an M.A. in English from the University of Syracuse (1973), and entered the Ph.D. program there the same year. Gordon has taught at Dutchess Community College in Poughkeepsie, Amherst, and Barnard. Gordon has won several awards for writing, including the Janet Heidinger Kafka Prize (1979, 1981) and the Lila Wallace-Reader's Digest Writers' Award (1992), and has received honorary doctorates from several institutions. Her body of work includes five novels, three collections of short stories, and two books of memoirs. She has edited works by Virginia Woolf and has written a study on Joan of Arc. Her works include: *Final Payments* (1978), *Company of Women* (1981), *Men and Angels* (1985), *Temporary Shelter* (1987), *The Other Side* (1989), *Good Boys and Dead Girls and Other Essays* (1991), *Rest of Life: Three Novellas* (1993), *Shadow Man* (1996), *Spending: a Utopian Divertimento* (1998), and *Seeing Through Places: Reflections on Geography and Identity* (2000). Mary Gordon is currently the Millicent C. McIntosh Professor of Writing at Barnard College and is married to Arthur Cash. (Mary Elizabeth Fraser Connolly, hereafter MEFC)

Great Wagon Road   The Great Wagon Road, also known as the Irish Road, the Pennsylvania Road, the Valley Road, or the Lancaster Pike, runs for some 800 miles east of the Appalachians from Pennsylvania to Georgia, and was the primary land route for thousands of immigrants and settlers, mostly Scotch-Irish, German, and English, to the Southern back country during the eighteenth and early nineteenth centuries. The road had its origins as an Iroquois hunting trail known as the Great Warrior's Path. By 1744, the English had assumed control of it as pressure from traders and settlers had forced the Indians off the trail. The route evolved from narrow wooded paths to rugged roadways that would carry thousands of migrants and livestock, packhorses, and horse- and ox-drawn wagons—hence its being named the Great Wagon Road. It began in the city of Philadelphia, a primary point of arrival for European immigrants, and ran west through what was then or would later become Lancaster, York, and Gettysburg, Pennsylvania, then turned south through Hagerstown, Maryland, crossing the Potomac at Watkin's Ferry, and proceeded through the Great Valley of Virginia, through Winchester, Harrisonburg, Staunton, Lexington, Fincastle, and Big Lick (Roanoke), then into the Carolinas, running past Salem and Charlotte, then diverging, with routes past both Newberry and Camden, finally reuniting and terminating at Augusta, Georgia. Philadelphia was the principal market center of the road, but by the time of the American Revolution, way stations such as Lancaster, Winchester, Salisbury, and Camden had become major trading centers as well. Travel back and forth along the Great Wagon Road was greatly facilitated by ordinaries (houses that supplied food and rooms), taverns, and inns (which also served as the original courthouses), while barges and other watercraft served as ferries across streams and rivers. The religious emotionalism of the Great Awakening was also facilitated by the road, with the spread and mixture of missionaries and believers of Moravian, Baptist, Presbyterian, and Methodist predilection. For want of settled churches and schools, the latter sect was of particular attraction.

After 1768, another branch of the road known as the Wilderness Road deflected a large portion of migrants from the deep South to the west. Explored and pioneered by Daniel Boone, it left Big Lick in Virginia and proceeded west through the Blue Ridge Mountains into Tennessee and the Cumberland Gap into Kentucky. The Great Wagon and Wilderness roads declined with the rise of the railroad in the mid-nineteenth century, but the invention of the automobile gave them a new significance, as these routes became part of the nation's highway system. Roadways of log and plank were paved, and ferries and covered bridges were replaced with concrete bridges. Many portions of the road or stops along the way have been preserved as historic sites. Much of the original ethnic flavor of settlements along the routes remains: Scotch-Irish in the Great Valley of Virginia and the upper Carolinas, and German in such towns as Gettysburg and Hagerstown. (W. John Shepherd, hereafter WJS)

Harrigan and Hart   Ned Harrigan and Tony Hart were the most famous performers playing comic Irish roles in nineteenth-century America. More importantly, the comic farces that Harrigan wrote and that he and Hart played in were the most important and powerful efforts in American popular culture to define a new kind of Irish stage character, the urban working-class Irish American.

Edward "Ned" Harrigan was born on "Cork Row" in the Corlears Hook neighborhood of New York in 1844. He was a third-generation Irish American. Hart was born Anthony Cannon, a child of Irish immigrants, on St. Anne's Hill, an Irish neighborhood in Worcester, Massachusetts, in 1855. Harrigan began his working life as a sailor before launching his career as an entertainer in 1867 in San Francisco. He teamed up with Tony Hart for the first time in 1871. Their first major stage success occurred in 1872 and 1873, in a run at Tony Pastor's Vaudeville House in New York City. Over the next few years they would become the most famous comic team in America and would remain partners until 1885. Hart was only a performer; Harrigan was the creative genius. He wrote thirty-six plays and eighty sketches between 1870 and 1879. By the end of the 1870s, he had phased out the variety acts and vaudeville in his company's performances and focused strictly on full-length plays, which were enormously successful. Between the 1870s and 1890s, twenty-three of his plays ran for at least one hundred performances in New York theaters. The "Mulligan Guard" series, featuring Dan Mulligan, his wife Cordelia, and their Irish, German, Chinese, and African American neighbors and rivals in New York City's immigrant neighborhoods, became his most famous characterizations. They often invoked crude ethnic stereotypes, especially in their depictions of African and Chinese Americans, but for most theatergoers the sometimes elaborate recreations of immigrant New York seemed powerfully evocative of the city's streets. William Dean Howells once exclaimed, referring to Harrigan and Hart's work, "you lose the sense of being in the Theater." Harrigan's company toured almost every year, and each play had between four and seven songs that often became nationally popular. They included "Babies on the Block," "Maggy Murphy's Home," and "Going Home With Nelly after Five."

Harrison, George   George Harrison was probably the most important American figure in the running of guns from the United States to the IRA provisionals in Northern Ireland after the rebirth of the "troubles" in Northern Ireland in the 1960s.

Harrison was born in the small town of Shammer in Mayo in 1915. Even as a small child he became involved in IRA activities during the Irish Civil War. He joined the IRA officially at the age of sixteen. In 1938 he emigrated to the United States, served in the United States Army during World War II, and engaged in a variety of jobs before becoming a security officer for the Brinks Company. Unlike many Irish Americans who backed the IRA "Provos" in the 1970s and 1980s, Harrison was an avowed socialist, militant trade unionist, and a lifelong supporter of anti-imperialist causes around the world, once suggesting that he would rather visit Cuba than return to his native Ireland. Harrison began sending guns to the IRA as early as the 1950s, but became critically important to the IRA after the revival of conflict in the North in the late 1960s. By 1973, he was sending three hundred to four hundred guns, including machine guns, to Northern Ireland every year. In 1981, he was brought to trial with some of his associates by American authorities. Though not convicted, his gunrunning network was disrupted. By that time, however, he had shipped an estimated 2,000 to 2,500 guns to Ireland at a cost of over one million dollars.

Hughes, Archbishop John J.   Archbishop John Hughes was perhaps the best example of militant and authoritarian Catholicism in the mid-nineteenth century. His militancy has been thought by some to be representative of Catholic sentiment in his era and it was in many ways, but in others, like his opinions regarding relations with non-Catholics, other bishops and Catholics were far less fierce and unyielding than he. Still, he foreshadowed the Catholic militant style that would become universal in the twentieth century. Some have seen his aggressive, pugnacious rule as the American origin of the ghetto and clerical Catholicism brought from Ireland. This is not necessarily true, as the development of Irish American Catholicism was more complex than that, but Hughes was the most visible and perhaps most powerful Catholic bishop in mid-nineteenth-century America. He was a fierce sectarian, politically assertive, and a convinced believer in hierarchical authority.

John J. Hughes was born in Annaloghan, County Tyrone in 1797 into a moderately prosperous Irish farming family. (Today his family farm home is on display at the Ulster Folk Park in Omagh, Tyrone.) In the wake of the 1798 rebellion, Tyrone and Ulster were wracked with sectarian feeling and violence, and that apparently made an impression on Hughes. He emigrated to the United States in 1817 as the end of the Napoleonic Wars plunged the Irish economy into depression. He took a position as a gardener at Mt. St. Mary's College in Emmitsburg, Maryland, while studying for the priesthood. He was ordained in 1826, spent time as a priest in Philadelphia, and was named coadjutor bishop of the New York diocese in 1838. Bishop Dubois, then the reigning bishop of New York, suffered a stroke two weeks later and Hughes took over management of the diocese. He would not formally become bishop of the diocese, however, until Dubois died in 1842. In 1850, the New York diocese became an archdiocese and he became its first archbishop. Hughes was an aggressive defender of Catholicism and its interests. In 1830 he sent a false report of a Catholic invasion of Pennsylvania to an anti-Catholic newspaper there and then ridiculed the credulous, nativist editor when the man printed the story in his newspaper. Hughes was quick to debate on stage or in the press any nativist who assailed the church, and was also quick to mobilize Catholic power. New York City, with its huge and growing Catholic population and a strong Democratic Party, was a good place for a Catholic bishop to practice such brinksmanship. In 1841, Hughes backed his own candidates for state assembly, perhaps forming the only Catholic political slate in American history. In a tense environment in 1844, he warned nativist leaders that "if a single Catholic church is burned in New York, the city will become a second Moscow." He believed that the vast floods of newcomers from Ireland and Germany signified that Catholics had entered a new era, and that some day they would come to dominate the United States. He built twenty-three parishes in Manhattan alone over the twenty-six years of his reign. His jewel was the grand St. Patrick's Cathedral on Fifth Avenue, on what was then the far northern periphery of the city. He envisioned his new cathedral as a symbol of that new, ascendant Catholic power. Hughes's vision of the church was strictly hierarchical. He opposed the power of lay trustees in parishes, and managed to suppress most trustees and gain diocesan ownership of all New York's churches despite the state legislature's opposition. He asserted diocesan control whenever possible over religious orders as well.

Finally, Hughes was one of the most visible and outspoken bishops of his time on public issues. He opposed the Fenian republican revolutionaries but was ambiguous in his criticism. He was far more forthright on the great issue of the day: slavery. He condemned attempts to abolish slavery. He believed slavery was but one more condition in an hierarchical society. He argued that the relation between a master and a slave differed only in degree—not kind—from a parent's rule over his or her children. He argued that the paternalist slaveowner's care of the slave compared favorably with the living conditions that poor workers endured under the "mockery" of free labor in the capitalist North. Like most Catholic thinkers of the day, he also believed that the abolition of slavery would be too great a threat to the social order to risk eliminating in anything but the most gradual way.

Indentured Servitude   Indentured servitude, a system that legally restricted the freedom of laborers, originated from labor shortages in Great Britain and the American colonies as well as from the growing displacement of farmers by market changes and agricultural "improvements." Contract labor was historically based upon conditions of poverty, with deception and force sometimes used to obtain laborers who surrendered their freedom and agreed to work for specific periods of time, usually four to seven years, as repayment for transportation, housing, or training expenses. Some contracts were similar to apprenticeships, while others were imposed on criminals whose sentences were commuted if they agreed to servitude in the colonies. The importation of white indentured servants constituted nearly half of all white immigrants prior to 1776, including the vast majority of the Irish and a high proportion of the Scotch-Irish. It was more profitable as a short-term labor source than the use of free labor or the enslavement of Indians, though in the long-term, the most effective solution was to increase the supply of enslaved Africans. A labor-intensive cash crop such as tobacco required a large work force, and many of the first indentured servants were farm laborers. By 1620, the colony of Virginia offered a fifty-acre grant to owners per servant as an incentive for planters to import more laborers from England. In practice, the servant would sell him- or herself to an agent or ship's captain before leaving the British Isles. In turn, the contract would be bought by a buyer in the colonies to recover the cost of passage across the Atlantic—a passage usually in steerage and under poor conditions. Criminals convicted of capital offenses in England could be transported in lieu of a death sentence that was often imposed for even the most petty thefts. Many orphans were indentured to keep them off the poor rolls, debtors were sold for repayment of amounts owed, and some people simply indentured themselves just to survive. "Redemptionists" were immigrants permitted a certain period of time after arrival in America to raise unpaid portions of their transportation costs, perhaps from family members already present. Failure to do so resulted in them becoming ordinary indentured servants. In most cases, the work of indentured servants was unskilled household or agricultural labor—however, demands for skilled craftsmen such as weavers or carpenters provided better chances for negotiation of shorter contracts. There were regional differences in the situation of indentured servants, with conditions generally better in the mid-Atlantic and New England colonies. Treatment on the large plantations of the South could be far worse. Slave owners tended to view slaves as long-term investments whose value lessened if mistreated, whereas short-term indentured servants were often abused without concern, since they were only useful to a specific amount of time. Not surprisingly, runaways were frequent, so courts increasingly required identification and travel papers. If servants worked their full indenture, they received freedom dues based on Hebrew Law from the Old Testament. Practices varied, but indenture contracts often dictated that servants were to be freed with a certain amount of money, a piece of land, or perhaps a spouse, while manumitted slaves simply depended upon the generosity of the owner. Although its prevalence waned by the 1790s, indentured servitude existed in North America until at least the 1830s, and it remained legal in the West Indies and South America until the early twentieth century. (WJS)

Ireland, Archbishop John   John Ireland was one of the most important and powerful leaders in American Catholic church history. He was the most articulate and urgent voice in the liberal or Americanist Party of the American church hierarchy in the 1880s and 1890s, urging an Americanization of Catholic immigrants through the practical steps of acculturation, such as the temperance movement and accommodation to public schools.

Born in 1838 in Burnchurch, County Kilkenny in Ireland, John Ireland's family fled the ravages of the famine, taking ship to Canada, then moving south to Vermont before eventually settling in St. Paul, Minnesota. He had already begun to appreciate America's promise for future wealth and power when he was sent to seminary in Meximieux and Montabel in France, where the pretensions and jibes of his classmates confirmed his American loyalties. In 1861, he came back to St. Paul to be ordained a priest before going to serve as chaplain of the Fifth Minnesota Regiment in the Civil War in 1862 and 1863. In 1875, he was named coadjutor bishop in St. Paul and succeeded Bishop Grace there in 1884. He became the vital force in the liberal faction of the Catholic hierarchy, allying with James Gibbons, John Keane, and others on behalf of such causes as the establishment of a Catholic university and petitioning Rome to allow Catholics to remain members of the Knights of Labor. Ireland himself was a strong advocate of temperance and urged accommodations with public schools and open engagement with America's Protestant majority. He opposed ethnic clannishness and immigrant resistance to assimilation, leading to several clashes with German Americans as well as an ill-fated effort to establish poor Irish immigrants from Connemara on the Minnesota frontier rather than let them huddle together in big cities. He believed strongly in America's destiny in the world and in the opportunity for the Catholic Church in the United States to take advantage of America's rise to spread its influence. Locally in St. Paul he was enormously powerful, not only in ruling his diocese, but as a civic figure in St. Paul society and politics. He died on September 25, 1918.

Irish Language in America   Most Irish immigrants who came to the United States spoke English, but a substantial proportion between one-fifth and perhaps as many as one-third throughout much of the nineteenth century may have also spoken Irish as their first language. Irish immigrants rarely held on to their language and fewer still passed it on to their children. It appeared to endure best in isolated places where chain migration had created heavy concentrations of Irish language speakers such as the Donegal people on Beaver Island in Lake Michigan or the Dingle peninsula immigrants on Hungry Hill in Springfield, Massachusetts, but in most cities the pressure of American culture and the lack of a broad, well-funded institutional commitment meant that the language quickly eroded. Irish Catholic parochial schools, for example, unlike German, Polish, or French Canadian schools almost never taught the Irish language.

There were efforts to preserve the language. Organizations dedicated to Irish language preservation and education date back to at least 1858 and New York's Ossianic Society. Members of the Society included the Fenian revolutionary leaders John O'Mahony and Michael Doheny, who believed the Irish language was critical to Irish understanding of a separate Irish national identity. Philo-Celtic Societies devoted to the Irish language emerged in Boston and Brooklyn in the 1870s. Michael Logan of Brooklyn emerged as a key figure in the language movement in that decade and the next, promoting education in Irish and publishing (with a successor) *The Gael* from 1881 until 1904. In the 1890s, the language revival won the backing of the Ancient Order of Hibernians and other Irish American organizations, and the AOH raised money for a chair in the Irish language at the Catholic University of America. In 1898 the Gaelic League of America was founded, counting twelve affiliated organizations, several in New York City, and others in Boston, Philadelphia, Providence, and Springfield. In 1905 and 1906, Douglas Hyde, founder of the Gaelic League in Ireland, toured the United States on a very successful fundraising drive. In the 1910s and 1920s, American Gaelic League clubs suffered from the political infighting of nationalist groups engaged in backing the Irish revolution and republicans in the Irish Civil War, as well as from the decline of Irish immigration after the 1930s. There has been a revival of interest in the Irish language, however, since the 1960s. Several universities—Boston College, Notre Dame, Catholic University, and New York University—have offered it as part of their Irish Studies programs and Gaelic League branches still flourished in Washington, New York, Chicago, Ann Arbor, and New Orleans throughout the 1990s.

Irish Studies   The study of Irish culture—primarily its literature, language, and history—in American Universities extends back to the late nineteenth century, when universities like Harvard, imitating German universities, initiated the study of the Gaelic language. In 1896, the Ancient Order of Hibernians endowed a chair in the Irish language at the Catholic University of America in Washington, D.C. and began a tradition of the study of the Irish language at that university that has lasted until the present day. Throughout the twentieth century, other universities, most like Catholic University—that is, dominated by Irish American Catholics—offered courses in Irish literature and history. For example, Fordham University, a Catholic university in New York City, offered courses in Irish history and literature in the 1920s and 1930s. Nevertheless, Irish studies largely languished during most of the twentieth century. Despite Catholic University's language programs or Fordham's history and literature courses, most Irish American leaders of the Catholic Church were more interested in forging good American Catholics out of its many immigrant peoples and thus had little interest in perpetuating foreign cultures in America, even Irish ones. Indeed, such leaders had fought bitter battles with French Canadians, Poles, and Germans over the efforts to preserve homeland languages and customs and could hardly endorse Irish ethnic studies in their own schools. In the mainstream of American academics, Irish writers like Yeats and Joyce emerged as major figures in the literary canon, but there was little interest in Irish history in most American universities. Interest in Celtic languages also remained a narrow and rare specialization. It was in the rebirth and reinterpretation of Irish ethnic identity during the 1960s that Irish studies began to flourish in America. Just before that decade, Emmet Larkin, Arnold Schrier, Gilbert Cahill, and Lawrence McCaffrey met during an American Historical Association meeting to consider ways to promote historical scholarship on Ireland in the United States. Their discussions led to the founding of the American Committee for Irish Studies (later the American Conference) in 1960. This development of an overarching scholarly organization both reflected and encouraged the creation of Irish studies programs in universities around the United States. In 1982, the ACIS Guide identified 365 colleges and universities offering Irish studies courses or programs. By 1994, the number had grown to 454. Most colleges were sponsoring only small programs or single courses offered by an interested faculty member, but the numbers also included several comprehensive programs, such as those at Boston College, Catholic University, Notre Dame, and New York University, established in the 1970s, 1980s, or 1990s.

Jones, "Mother" Mary Harris   "Mother" Mary Harris Jones, a labor organizer, devoted her life to the improvement of working conditions for men, women, and children, particularly miners. Her devotion to the miners earned her the title "Miners' Angel." Born in County Cork in 1830, she immigrated with her family to North America in 1841, settling in Toronto, Ontario. Mother Jones did not begin her career as a labor organizer until the 1870s. Before that, she was a schoolteacher in Michigan, a seamstress in Chicago, and then a teacher in Memphis. There she met and married George Jones in 1860. They had four children, but in 1866 her husband

and children died in a yellow fever epidemic. Jones then returned to Chicago where she would begin work as a labor organizer.

Working as a seamstress in Chicago, Jones was confronted with the dramatic differences between the wealthy and impoverished and was drawn into the cause of organized labor, claiming to join the Knights of Labor in 1871. Through her connection with this organization, she observed and participated in the railroad strike in 1877 in Pittsburgh, Pennsylvania. This strike turned violent and the militia was called to break the strike. The Knights of Labor's equivocation over the usefulness of strikes in this instance compelled Jones to distance herself from this labor organization. She felt more needed to be done and that strikes were a necessary means to effect change.

In 1891, known as "Mother" to the miners whom she would call "her boys," Jones joined the United Mine Workers and began organizing workers throughout Virginia, West Virginia, Alabama, Pennsylvania, and Colorado. Her fame grew quickly, particularly after her work among miners in West Virginia during the 1897 strike. The president of the UMW, John Mitchell, called upon her to work there and in Pennsylvania in 1901 and 1902, specifically during the 1902 Anthracite Strike. During the strike of 1903, Mitchell sent her to Colorado to gain support for the UMW and to further the cause of a strike there. Ultimately, the strike failed when the miners were divided. During the strike, she had worked and lived among the miners and their families, was jailed several times, and repeatedly forcibly removed from Colorado. She proved her devotion again in 1912 when she returned to West Virginia's Kanawha Valley. She was arrested, tried, and sentenced to twenty years in prison. The sentence was overturned. Mother Jones returned to Colorado in 1913 to help organize the workers of Rockefeller's Colorado Fuel and Iron Company. The strike resulted in the Ludlow massacre, where the soldiers destroyed the striking miners' tent camp and killed eleven children and two women.

If Jones's principal work was on behalf of miners, she was nonetheless committed to labor's cause wherever she found it. In 1903, she led a children's march from Pennsylvania to Theodore Roosevelt's home in New York to call attention to the plight of children laboring in textile mills. She would later fight for women workers in the bottling industry.

By the 1920s, Mother Jones, while still actively pursuing the worker's cause, was engaged less frequently in individual cases. She continued to travel and give speeches in her nineties, making her base at the home of her friend Terence Powderly. Jones worked with various organizations throughout her career: the Socialists and Eugene Debs, the Industrial Workers of the World and Bill Hayward, and the Knights of Labor and Terence Powderly. Yet she was never an ideologue. Her heart and actions were with the workers and were focused on changing the immediate situation. She had no patience for politicians, theologians, and idealists who theorized about the future. She had even less patience for middle-class benevolent reformers and women's rights advocates whom she believed knew nothing of the worker's plight. Mother Jones's health began to fail and she retired to a farm in Maryland, where she died in 1933 at the age of one hundred. She was buried in Mount Olive, Illinois, in the Miners Cemetery. (MEFC)

Kearney, Denis   Denis Kearney was the most vocal and insistent advocate in America for the exclusion of Chinese immigrants and reflected the critical role of Irish Americans in that struggle.

Denis Kearney was born in Cork in 1847. At the age of eleven, he went away to sea, circumnavigating the globe while still a teenager. In 1870, he settled in San Francisco, where he ran a trucking business. In his early years in the city he was known to defend Chinese immigrants, attack organized religion, and scold workingmen for their political weakness and lethargy. He was not an uncritical labor advocate, occasionally attacking unions and denouncing strikes. In 1877, Kearney moved to the forefront of San Francisco's anti-Chinese movement. Anti-Chinese sentiment had deep roots in the city and state of California, but by 1877 a four-year depression and that year's great railroad strike seemed to make the city's workers especially receptive to the exclusion of Chinese immigrants. Workers gathered on the city's sandlots to protest their hardships and Kearney became their principal speaker. Self-educated, he was a powerfully emotional speaker, throwing off his jacket, gesturing forcefully, and shouting out his diatribes in a rich brogue. At the end of every speech he gave and every article he wrote, he concluded: "And whatever happens, the Chinese must go." He helped form and lead the Workingmen's Party in San Francisco, which won strong support in the elections of 1878. They were especially successful in winning delegate seats to the state constitutional convention. There they made an alliance with the farmer-backed Grangers to dominate the convention. Some believe that the constitution that the convention voted out did little to help workingmen, but it did include anti-Chinese provisions. In 1878 Kearney also began a tour of the country, harping on the same theme of Chinese exclusion. The response by workers was mixed, better at the beginning of the tour than the end, but his cross-country lectures seemed to convince many national politicians that Chinese exclusion had broad and fierce support among American workers. Back home in California, his popularity began to fade as early as 1879, attacked by trade union leaders who doubted his commitment to labor causes and resented his power. Kearney also undermined his own party by trying to lead it into an alliance with the Greenback Party, even as the Greenbackers were fading in importance. Kearney's influence subsequently declined, but he had been probably the key figure in making the exclusion of the Chinese a critical national political issue, which ultimately led to the passage of the Chinese Exclusion Act in 1882.

Kelly, Edward "Ed" Kelly became boss of the Chicago Democratic machine during Franklin D. Roosevelt's New Deal. His success suggested that Roosevelt's effect on Irish political machines was complex. Roosevelt "made" some machines—Kelly's in Chicago and David Lawrence's in Pittsburgh—even as he helped undercut others such as Tammany in New York City. Kelly was important also in securing Irish control of the Democratic machine in Chicago, which would one day produce Richard J. Daley, the last great Irish American boss.

Edward Kelly was born in the "back of the yards" (stockyards in the South Side of Chicago) in 1876. His father died young and Edward went to work to help support the family while attending night school to study engineering. In 1920, while he was the chief engineer of the Chicago Sanitary District, he met Patrick Nash, a sewer contractor. Kelly and Nash became political allies, cemented by $100 million in contracts that Nash secured from Kelly's Sanitary District. Chicago politics had been severely divided in the 1910s and 1920s as the colorful William "Big Bill" Thompson forged a competitive Republican Party to vie with the Democrats. Over the late 1920s, Mayor Anton Cermak, of Czech extraction, had put together a multiethnic Democratic Party coalition that finally vanquished Thompson's Republicans. Cermak was killed in 1933 when an assassin, trying to shoot Franklin Roosevelt, hit the Chicago mayor instead while he was visiting with the new president in Florida. Pat Nash, as chairman of the county Democratic Party, helped his friend Kelly become mayor and fill out Cermak's term. Kelly was then elected mayor for three terms over twelve years on his own. Kelly's success came largely through a cultivation of Roosevelt and the New Deal administration. Kelly had contact with Roosevelt even before Cermak's death, and after proving his strength with a smashing victory in the 1935 mayoral election, Kelly became Roosevelt's chief political liaison in Illinois. Hundreds of thousands of jobs in the WPA or other Roosevelt agencies went through the Kelly-Nash machine, as well as hundreds of millions of dollars in building contracts. For his part, Kelly delivered the vote for Roosevelt in Chicago, rolling up impressive victories and helping push legislation favorable to the New Deal through the Illinois legislature. As he himself wrote, "Roosevelt is my religion." He played a critical role in the effort to draft Roosevelt for a third term in 1940. His machine men packed the galleries at the Democratic convention in Chicago that year and set off an hour-long demonstration that stampeded the convention for Roosevelt (they would be famous for years after as the "Voice of the Sewer" because so many of the men in the galleries allegedly worked for the Sanitary District). By 1947, Roosevelt and Kelly's partner Nash were both dead and the Kelly regime was tarnished by charges of corruption and cronyism. Asked by Democratic boss Jacob Arvey to quit, Kelly stepped down and Martin Kennelly ran as the Democratic nominee for mayor. Kelly died in 1950.

Knights of Columbus   The Knights of Columbus became the embodiment of a militantly Catholic but patriotically American identity that dominated Irish America from the early twentieth century until the 1960s. Though multiethnic in membership, the Knights were founded and dominated by American-born Irishmen, who shaped it into an instrument and reflection of their aspirations and commitments as American patriots and faithful Catholics.

The Knights of Columbus was founded in New Haven in 1882 by Father Michael McGivney, a second-generation Irish American priest. McGivney hoped to establish a society that would provide insurance for the widows and surviving children of deceased Catholic men, saving these dependents from impoverishment and the poorhouse. He also wished to establish a society that would prove attractive enough to keep Catholic men from joining secret societies that had been condemned by the Catholic Church, like the Masons or Odd Fellows. The Knights spread slowly through Connecticut and Rhode Island, and by 1887 could count twenty-seven councils and about 2,700 members. In the 1890s, the order expanded into Massachusetts, where it was transformed in the ethnic and religious hothouse of the Bay State's social and political conflict. In its first decade in Connecticut, the Knights had been confident about easy Catholic assimilation into American life, but in Massachusetts in the 1890s, amid the revival of anti-Catholic nativism and grinding tensions between Protestants and Catholics, the Knights felt embattled, and led by American-born Irishmen like Thomas Cummings, became more militant in defense of Catholic interests. However, the Knights continued to be committed to American patriotism and understood their organization as broadly Catholic and multiethnic—not strictly Irish or Irish American. The Fourth Degree Ceremonial of the Order proclaimed: "Proud in the olden days was the boast, 'I am a Roman Catholic.' Prouder yet today is the boast, 'I am an American citizen.' But the proudest boast of all times is ours to make: 'I am an American Catholic citizen.'" Christopher Columbus became the symbol of this merger of American patriotism and Catholic devotion. The Knights praised Columbus not only as the first American, but the first American Catholic, and held him up as a powerful counter to white Anglo-Saxon Protestant Americans who invoked the Pilgrims as the first Americans. By 1897, the order had expanded to 16,000 members and by 1909 to over 230,000 Knights. The number of councils shot up from 300 to 1,300 in those twelve years. The 1910s and 1920s, however, were the critical growth years for the organization. From 1917 to 1923 alone, over 400,000 men joined the order. Most of them probably joined because of the Knights' work on behalf of American soldiers in France and at military posts in America during World War I. The Knights set up service centers at such camps, where they provided recreation and met other needs for soldiers. After the War, the Knights established employment offices to help veterans get jobs. By the 1910s, the Knights had also become the key community organization confronting anti-Catholic prejudice. In 1914, they established a Commission on Religious Prejudice led by Patrick Henry Callahan to sniff out the sources of prejudice and combat them. In the 1920s, the Knights created a Historical Commission to celebrate American ethnic diversity in the face of attacks by the KKK and other anti-Catholic, anti-immigrant movements. Among the books published by the Knights' Commission was W. E. B. Dubois' *The Souls of Black Folk*. While most fraternal societies declined precipitously in membership after the early twentieth century, the Knights of Columbus continued to thrive. In the 1950s, it boasted over one million members. It was a bastion of patriotism and anticommunism then, though some believed that it was slow to push for racial integration. By the Knights' hundredth anniversary in 1982, it had 1.6 million members and insurance assets of seventeen billion. Still, its importance as a touchstone of Irish American Catholic identity has declined since the upheavals of the 1960s remade Irish American life and undermined the old militant Catholic Americanism that the Knights had long embodied.

Land League   The Irish National Land League of America was organized to support the Land League in Ireland and the Irish League's efforts to reform the land system in Ireland and win some measure of political autonomy for the island. The Land League of America was the largest Irish American nationalist movement up to that point and second only to Irish American mobilization in behalf of the Irish revolution after World War I in the history of Irish America. The Land League of America's history also reflected the significant divisions that fragmented the Irish American community as that community entered a critical transitional period in the turn of the century era.

In the late 1870s, declining farm prices and bad weather created an agricultural crisis in Ireland that appeared to threaten famine in the western counties. Revolutionaries like Irishman Michael Davitt and Irish American John Devoy began to sense an opportunity in the agricultural hard times to build a mass-based nationalist movement energized by land reform issues. They hoped to combine it with the parliamentary obstruction of militant members of the Irish Home Rule party and create conditions that might spark a republican revolution in Ireland. This attempt to capitalize on all the various nationalist grievances and constituencies in Ireland and Irish America has often been called the "New Departure." The immediate vehicle for this hope would be the Land League, first founded by Davitt in Mayo in August 1879. It later became a national organization under the leadership of the Home Rule party leader, Charles Stuart Parnell, in October of that year. Some Irish Americans like Devoy were vitally involved from the beginning, and Irish American support was considered critical to the work in Ireland. In early 1880, Parnell toured the United States to raise money for the effort in Ireland. He visited sixty-two cities, raised $300,000, and helped plan an American Land League. In May 1880, delegates of that newly formed American Land League met in New York City. They were divided from the beginning. Clan na Gael revolutionaries like Devoy wanted a centralized nationalist organization in America with a central treasury, while moderate nationalists feared that the Clan would control a centralized organization and therefore pushed to give local branches the right to send the funds that they raised directly to Ireland. In the end a central treasury was established, but to appease the conservatives, a Catholic priest from Connecticut, Lawrence Walsh, was chosen as treasurer. Meanwhile, the economic radical Patrick Ford began to establish his own League, encouraging his branches to forward money to Ireland through his newspaper, the *Irish World*. Thus, from the beginning there were three factions in the movement: militant revolutionaries in the Clan na Gael committed to violent overthrow of British rule in Ireland, but largely uninterested in economic reform of Ireland; moderate or conservative nationalists, content with federal status or home rule in the Empire for Ireland, achieved by strictly constitutional methods; and Ford's radicals, backing the return of the land to Irish peasants through mass mobilization of the Irish peasantry. Over the next two years, these factions, along with their respective allies in Ireland, jockeyed for power within the Land League. On October 17, 1881, after Parnell and other leaders of the Land League were jailed, they issued a No Rent Manifesto, urging peasants to withhold their rents to push the United Kingdom government to further concessions on the land issue. Eight hundred and forty five delegates met at an American Land League convention in Chicago shortly thereafter and endorsed the No Rent Manifesto, but only as a political weapon for Home Rule and not as a first step in a radical remaking of the Irish land system. To underline their moderate position, they also unseated some Chicago Socialist delegates. Nevertheless, the Ford faction seemed particularly powerful at the convention. Ford raised more money for the League than the other two factions, and his economic radicalism was very popular among working-class Irish Americans in mill towns and mining villages across the United States. Ford's *Irish World* had proclaimed "the cause of the poor in Donegal is the cause of the factory slave in Fall River," and in January 1882, 12,000 labor union representatives met at Cooper Union in New York City to endorse the No Rent Manifesto. The women in the Ladies Land League also often backed Ford. Partly because the Ladies Land League branches backed the radicals, but mostly because their participation in the League violated gender roles, Bishop Gilmour of Cleveland condemned and excommunicated the Lady Land Leaguers in his diocese in May 1882. By that time, the tide had long since turned against the radicals in Ireland and thus also in America. Parnell had made a deal, the "Kilmainham Treaty," with Prime Minster Gladstone of England and disavowed the radicals, including his sisters, who were leaders of the Ladies League in Ireland. More importantly, strong farmers and other forces within the Land League in Ireland were wary of radical schemes for land redistribution. Membership in the American Land League had already began to decline by April 1882, when the Clan and conservatives dominated the American League's last convention and ganged up on the Ford radicals. The American League petered out by the fall of 1882 and eventually disappeared. In 1883, conservatives and Clan na Gael militants formed a new American National League, but that never caught on and foundered soon too. Though its history was short, the Land League was of great significance to Irish America. At its peak some estimate it may have had as many as fifteen hundred branches and half a million members, and Irish Americans in the League and out-side it may have sent as much as five million dollars to Ireland for famine relief, support of evicted farmers, backing for Home Rule, and funding for the Land League in Ireland.

Logan, James   James Logan was a prominent colonial Pennsylvanian states-man, merchant, and scholar. He was born on October 20, 1674, in Lurgan, County Armagh, Ireland, to Scottish-born Quakers Patrick Logan and Isa-bel Hume. Educated in the classics and serving briefly as a schoolmaster, he entered the shipping trade between Bristol and Dublin in 1697. Shortly thereafter, he met Pennsylvania founder William Penn and sailed with him in 1699 to the colony as his secretary. An apocryphal account of the voyage accurately reflects their respective attitudes. Logan helped fight off attack-ing pirates while the pacifistic Penn went below deck, and Logan replied to Penn's criticism by saying, "I being thy servant, why did thee not order me to come down?" Logan believed in a just defensive war and later suggested that Quakers who could not support defensive measures should not serve in the Pennsylvania legislature. In politics, he represented the aristocratic proprietary party supporting the Penn family, and served in numerous gov-ernment positions during his fifty-two-year career in Pennsylvania. These included Secretary of the Province and Clerk of the Provincial Council, 1701–1718; voting member and later President of the Council, 1702–1747; Acting Governor of the Province, 1736–1738; Mayor of Philadelphia, 1722–1723; and Chief Justice of the Supreme Court, 1731–1739. His dealings with fellow countrymen from Ireland is notable. With apprehensions about the Indians, in 1718 he granted extensive lands to the Scotch-Irish in Chester County, where they established Donegal Township, with the hope that these hardened Presbyterians could be a "frontier against any disturbance." He would regret this decision and later stated that "a settlement of five fam-ilies from the North of Ireland gives me more trouble than fifty of any other people." He further complained of their squatting on land without seeking legal title and was troubled by their numbers, stating that "it looks as if Ireland is to send all her inhabitants hither" and "that if they continue to come, they will make themselves proprietors of the province." Apart from his official duties, he became wealthy through land speculation and Indian trade. While engaging in the latter, he invented the "Conestoga Wagon," a heavy vehicle hooded with canvas against the weather that would transport generations of American westward. He was a voracious reader whose im-pressive library of over three thousand books was left to the city of Philadel-phia to start their public library. In 1714, he married Sarah Read, daughter of a prominent merchant, and they had five children. The Logans lived at "Stenton," the 500-acre family seat that he established near Germantown and where he hosted many visits by Indian ceremonial delegations. He was very successful in his relations with them—so much so that the chief of the Cayugas named his son Logan. After retirement from the Council in 1747, he spent much time at his estate devoted to study. Natural science was his great interest and his botanical investigations, especially his "Experiments Concerning the Impregnation of the Seeds of Plants," received scholarly recognition by the Royal Society in London. He also wrote on ethics and philology. He died at home on October 31, 1751. (WJS)

Lomasney, Martin   Martin Lomasney was the boss of Ward Eight in what was then called the West End of Boston in the late nineteenth and early twentieth centuries. He was the quintessential Irish American ward boss. In 1915, at the height of his political power, he told Lincoln Steffens, the famous muckraking journalist: "There's got to be in every ward somebody that any bloke can come to—no matter what he's done—and get help. Help, you understand, none of your law and justice, but help"—probably the most famous definition of the Irish American machine politics ethos ever uttered. Nicknamed the "Mahatma," he ruled his ward with almost total control and parlayed that control into becoming a power in city and state politics. He served in the Massachusetts state legislature, where his work reflected a newly emerging urban liberalism among Irish American politicians: support for a welfare state, government regulation of the economy, and favorable labor legislation.

Lomasney was born in Boston on December 3, 1859, the son of Irish immigrants from County Cork. Orphaned at an early age, he started to become a political force in his ward when he formed the Hendricks Club with his brother in 1885. By 1896, he had won election to the state senate. He would serve as an alderman in the Boston city government and as senator in the Massachusetts State Senate, but it was in the Massachusetts House of Representatives (or in its formal name, the General Court) that he would find his political home. He served in the House for several years and was a "potent force" during the Democratic renaissance of the 1910s. Yet it was his power behind the scenes, negotiating and dealing from his power base in Ward Eight to shape city politics, that made his reputation. Taciturn, modestly dressed, a regular churchgoer, and disdainful of parties and banquets, Lomasney has been overshadowed by his better known and more outgoing Irish American contemporaries: John F. Fitzgerald and James Michael Curley. Yet for almost forty years until his death in 1933, he ruled his ward almost absolutely and was a power in Boston politics that his more famous rivals fought or appeased but always respected.

McCarthy, Joseph P.   Joseph "Joe" McCarthy was a United States Senator from Wisconsin who became the symbol of rabid anticommunism in the 1950s. Of Irish Catholic ancestry, he seemed to also embody the virulent antiradicalism of Irish American Catholics, an essential component of their militantly Catholic, patriotically American identity in the first half of the twentieth century.

McCarthy was born on a farm in what was known locally as the "Irish settlement" in the small town of Grand Chute, Wisconsin. He was the son of Timothy and Bridget (Tierney) McCarthy and three of his four grandparents had been born in Ireland. McCarthy made little of his ethnic ancestry, but his mother and father were devoted Catholics and he himself was dutifully faithful to his religion, attending mass regularly and matriculating at the Jesuit Marquette University in nearby Milwaukee. McCarthy fancied himself a beer-drinking, steak-eating, poker-playing, earthy man's man. He read little and was largely unreflective.

In 1936, McCarthy lost his first race for public office, but three years later he won election as a judge. He served in World War II, though he would later grossly exaggerate his role in the war, telling false stories about wounds he allegedly sustained and combat missions he never flew. He actually served largely as a rear echelon officer. Yet in 1946 he ran for the Senate in Wisconsin as "Tail Gunner Joe" in the Republican primary against the scion of Wisconsin's famed LaFollette political dynasty, Robert LaFollette, and won a shocking upset. In the general election, he attacked the New Deal and Harry Truman, and raised the issue of softness on communism. The local Democrats brought the liberal bishop Bernard Shiel from Chicago to speak in the campaign, but McCarthy won an overwhelming victory. In the Senate, he was strongly conservative, opposing welfare, public housing, and foreign aid legislation. In fifteen major votes in 1947, for example, he voted conservative on all but one of them. In 1949, he leveled charges of communist sympathies against the city editors of the *Madison Capitol Times*. Three months later in a speech at the Catholic Wheeling College, he claimed to know of 205 known communists in the State Department. Over time he gave various other numbers: fifty-seven or eighty-one alleged communists. His allegations came in the wake of the fall of China to the Communists, and McCarthy had especially targeted the "China Hands," Far East experts in the State Department and other parts of the government in his attacks. It is not entirely clear why McCarthy launched his attack, except for it being an obvious attempt to find a winning issue to ensure his reelection. For years, many historians believed that Father Edmund Walsh, an Irish American Jesuit and the virulently anticommunist founder of Georgetown University's School of Foreign Service, had initially suggested the anticommunist crusade to McCarthy. That account is now disputed. Whatever his reasons for the anticommunist campaign, McCarthy's attacks were spectacularly successful from the beginning. Democrats who scoffed at him like Senator Joseph Tydings of Maryland went down to defeat in the 1950 elections, and the Republicans took back the White House in 1952. McCarthy himself won reelection in 1952 but with fewer votes than his 1946 margin of victory. In 1953 and 1954, McCarthy expanded his crusade to attacks on the United States Army for lax security. By late winter and early spring, his high-handed, clumsy attacks in that investigation had provoked rising opposition both within and outside his party, and his popularity began to erode. In June of 1954, Joseph Welch, a distinguished lawyer from an old established Boston law firm, attacked McCarthy in a televised encounter at the Army hearings that dramatically exposed the Wisconsin senator's clumsy oppressiveness. After McCarthy had made accusations against a young associate in Welch's law firm, Welch retorted, "Have you no sense of decency?" and the charge echoed throughout the country. Senator Ralph Flanders of Vermont had already suggested the censure of McCarthy, and on August 2, 1954, the Senate appointed a committee to investigate his abuse of power in the committee hearings. On December 2, 1954, McCarthy was censured by the Senate in a 67 to 22 vote. McCarthy faded quickly from political prominence thereafter, and died on March 2, 1957.

Throughout his rise, many observers believed that McCarthy drew especially strong support from Catholics and particularly Irish Catholics. There is certainly strong evidence of this. In March 1950, at the beginning of his anticommunist crusade, Catholic opinion on him ran 49 percent to 28 percent in his favor in one national survey, and at the height of his popularity, Catholic support ran as high as 53 percent to 23 percent. Irish Catholic senators like Patrick McCarran of Nevada were strong backers, as were local editors like Patrick Scanlan of the *Brooklyn Tablet*, a Catholic newspaper. Nevertheless, there were opponents in the Catholic and Irish American Catholic communities. In March 1954, Stephen Mitchell, chairman of the Democratic Party, refused to appear with McCarthy at a St. Patrick's Day dinner, urging Irish Americans to remember their heritage of oppression and stand against McCarthy's assault on civil liberties. When the censure vote finally took place, five Irish Catholic Democrats voted against him, two Irish Catholic Republicans voted for him, and John F. Kennedy did not vote.

McGuire, Peter J.   "P. J.," as he was often known, McGuire helped found the Carpenters and Joiners Union and was a powerful and often radical voice in the American labor movement for over thirty years at the end of the nineteenth century. McGuire was born in New York City on July 6, 1852. His parents, John J. McGuire and Catherine Hand, were Irish immigrants who raised their five children in a tenement house in New York City's Lower East Side. After John McGuire joined the Union army in 1863, Peter, just eleven years old but the eldest child, quit school and worked a number of odd jobs to support the family. In 1869, he became a woodworking apprentice at Haynes Piano Company and joined the Cabinetmakers Union. The seventeen-year-old also studied philosophy, history, and economics at Cooper Union, a continuing-education center that served as a haven for radicals and activists in New York City. At Cooper Union, McGuire met other kindred spirits, such as cigar maker and future American Federation of Labor president, Samuel Gompers. McGuire then embarked on a lifetime of labor and radical agitation. In 1872, he marched in support of the eight hour day. In 1874, he helped organize the Tompkins Square unemployment demonstration that was broken up by club-swinging police. He traveled widely, urging independent political action and support for the Workingmen's Party and the Greenback movement and mobilizing workers during the national rail strike in 1877. Throughout the 1870s, McGuire continued to work in the woodworking trade, primarily in piano shops, while increasing his political activities.

McGuire soon turned his political attention and energies to the formation of a national carpenters union. He was a prime mover in organizing the August 8, 1881, meeting that formed the Brotherhood of Carpenters and Joiners of America (renamed the United Brotherhood of Carpenters and Joiners of America in 1888). He was unanimously elected the first general secretary, the only full-time position in the union. McGuire worked tirelessly to make the Carpenters Union a progressive and growing organization that improved the everyday lives of carpenters while also working toward a transformed society. The union grew from just over 2,000 members in 1881 to more than 50,000 in 1890. During his two decades as secretary in the Carpenters Union, the average wage for carpenters more than doubled. McGuire and the Carpenters Union were on the forefront of all the important national labor movement activities of the period. McGuire drafted the convention call for the first meeting of the Federation of Organized Trades and Labor Union in 1881 and joined with Samuel Gompers in transforming it into the American Federation of Labor in 1886. McGuire stridently fought for the eight-hour workday while in office. By 1902, carpenters worked an eight-hour day in nearly 500 cities. McGuire is also considered by many to be the father of Labor Day, first celebrated in New York City in 1882.

The last years of McGuire's life ended tragically. After dedicating more than twenty years to the Carpenters Union, McGuire faced serious opposition as general secretary by political opponents amid rumors of embezzlement and incompetence. At the 1902 convention, McGuire, who was now wracked with a number of serious physical ailments and an increasing alcohol problem, resigned from the Carpenters Union. A forgotten, impoverished, and dejected McGuire died on February 6, 1906, leaving his second wife, Christina Wolff (whom he married in 1884) and four children. (JT)

McHenry, James The Irish-born McHenry was an influential member of the American Revolutionary generation. At one time or another in his life, he was a physician, soldier, prisoner of war, legislator, and cabinet officer. McHenry was essentially a conservative and upwardly mobile Ulsterman who was devoted to George Washington and to a lesser extent Alexander Hamilton.

After a classical education in Dublin, he left his native Ballymena, County Antrim, Ireland, for Philadelphia in 1771, and was followed by several family members the next year. His father, Daniel McHenry, and his brother John set up an importing company in Baltimore while James studied medicine under the celebrated Dr. Benjamin Rush in Philadelphia. An ardent patriot, no doubt influenced by Rush, James volunteered for military service in 1775, serving at a hospital in Cambridge, Massachusetts, and in 1776 was appointed Surgeon of the Fifth Pennsylvania Battalion. He and his unit were captured in the fall of Fort Washington, New York, in November 1776, though he was paroled the next year. Frustrated by his inability to assist wounded and dying prisoners of war, he turned his back on medicine and sought military advancement in other positions. He became a secretary to Washington in 1778 and was transferred to Lafayette's staff in 1780, where Washington intended McHenry's ability and caution to restrain Lafayette's exuberance. In 1781, he was commissioned a major in the Continental Army, though he resigned later that year to begin service in the State Senate of Maryland, from 1781 to 1786, and in Congress, from

1783 through 1786. A committed Federalist, he was a Maryland delegate to the Constitutional Convention of 1787, served as a member of Maryland's ratifying convention, and was a member of the Maryland commission that welcomed president-elect George Washington on his way to New York to assume the presidency in 1789. McHenry returned to the Maryland legislature where he served in the Assembly from 1790 to 1791 and served a second stint in the State Senate from 1791 to 1796. He succeeded Timothy Pickering as Secretary of War in Washington's second administration and was closely associated with the views and leadership of Alexander Hamilton. He retained his post after John Adams assumed the presidency in 1797, but fell increasingly out of favor over the quasi-war with France and his supposed machinations in favor of Hamilton. President Adams believed him disloyal and forced his resignation in 1800, with some alleging improprieties in his administration of the War Department. In 1802, a Congressional committee declined to investigate him, though he insisted on having an elaborate defense read on the floor of the House, which he published in 1803 as *A Letter to the Honourable Speaker of the House of Representatives of the United States*. After this he retired to his estate near Baltimore with his wife Margaret Caldwell, whom he had married in 1784. He published various minor works and opposed the War of 1812. Ironically, Fort McHenry, which was named for him, heroically resisted a British assault in 1814, thus saving Baltimore in the event immortalized in the national anthem, *The Star Spangled Banner*. (WJS)

Meany, William George Born in New York City on August 16, 1894, George Meany rose to become the most nationally recognized labor leader in the country for the more than two decades spanning the middle of the twentieth century. Meany's parents, Michael Meany and Anne Cullen, were American-born of Irish descent. Both of their families migrated from Ireland to the United States during the 1850s. Meany's family and the Bronx neighborhood that George grew up in were steeped in union politics, Irish nationalism, and Roman Catholicism. Michael Meany labored as a plumber and was active in the local plumbers' union. The younger Meany followed in his father's footsteps: he quit school at 14, served as a plumber's helper, and finished his apprenticeship, advancing to a journeyman plumber in Local 463 of the United Association of Plumbers and Steam Fitters of the United States and Canada in 1917. George also became the family provider after his father died in 1917. In 1919 he married Eugenia McMahon, a garment worker and member of the International Ladies Garment Workers Union. The couple had three daughters.

George moved steadily through the trade union bureaucracy, advancing from plumber to local union official, statewide leader, and eventually president of the AFL-CIO. He benefited from his father's activism in the plumbers' union when he was elected to the executive board of Local 463 in 1919, largely based on his standing as Michael Meany's son. Three years later, in 1922, he became a full-time union official when he was elected business agent.

Meany was a successful business agent, forcefully defending member rights and the United Association of Plumbers and Steam Fitters' jurisdiction against incursions from other craft unions. In the 1930s, his role expanded to include positions as a delegate to the New York City Central Trades and Labor Assembly and as a vice president and then president of the New York State Federation of Labor. He proved to be an able and energetic lobbyist for labor's legislative concerns in Albany while an official for the New York State Federation of Labor. He advanced to national office in 1939 when he was elected secretary-treasurer of the American Federation of Labor. Although the post was technically the second highest in the AFL, initially it was largely a functionary position, with AFL president William Green commanding virtually all of the authority in the national office. After World War II, however, Meany emerged as a forceful and active national leader in his own right. He lead the AFL's failed efforts against the antiunion Taft-Hartley bill in 1947, turned back the powerful and intimidating United Mine Workers Union of American president, John L. Lewis, in an angry exchange at the 1947 AFL Convention, and expanded the AFL's legislative activities and agenda when he helped create the Labor's League for Political Education prior to the 1948 presidential campaign. When William Green died in 1952, Meany was advanced to the presidency of the AFL without opposition.

George Meany served as president of the AFL and the AFL-CIO from 1952 until 1979. He scored his first important achievement when he guided the historic merger between the AFL and the CIO in 1955, reuniting a labor movement split since 1935. With Meany as president, the merged AFL-CIO gained substantial political clout and media attention during the 1950s and 1960s, but as the union percentage of the working population decreased, the labor movement also declined steadily over his twenty-seven years as president. The aging and socially conservative Meany had difficulty relating to the changing social dynamics created by the cultural revolution of the 1960s. An increasingly obstinate Meany at times recoiled from the civil rights movement, student activism, anti–Vietnam War mobilizations, and women's rights actions that transformed American society, culture, and politics. Under Meany, the AFL-CIO did not endorse George McGovern in 1972 because of his anti–Vietnam War politics—the first time since the New Deal that the AFL-CIO did not endorse the Democratic Party candidate in the presidential election. By the time Meany retired in November 1979, many felt that though he still garnered significant attention among national political leaders and in the media, he also embodied the AFL-CIO's resistance to change, which resulted in the labor movement's declining membership rates, decreasing political power, and isolation from other social movements. In March 1979, his wife of sixty years died. On January 10, 1980, just two months after he resigned as head of the AFL-CIO, the eighty-five-year-old William George Meany died. (JT)

Montgomery, Richard   Major General Richard Montgomery became an early hero of the new American republic when he was killed on December 31, 1775, while leading his troops in a forlorn attack on Quebec City, Canada. As the scion of a Church of Ireland gentry family, he also reflected the broad variety of origins of Irish immigration to America in the eighteenth century. He was born in Lifford, Donegal, Ireland in 1738, a son of Thomas and Mary (Franklyn) Montgomery. As members of a respectable Anglo-Irish family, Richard's father and elder brother were both members of the Irish Parliament. Richard was educated at Trinity College in Dublin and, as a third son, chose a military career and received a commission as an ensign in the Seventeenth Regiment of Foot (Irish) on September 21, 1756. He saw extensive action with his regiment during the Seven Years War (1756–1763), serving with distinction at the Siege of Louisbourg, Canada, in 1758, after which he was promoted to lieutenant; at Crown Point and Ticonderoga, New York, in 1759; and Montreal, Canada, in 1760. The Seventeenth Regiment then served in the Caribbean, taking part in the invasion of Martinique in 1761, after which Montgomery was promoted to captain, then to Havana, Cuba, which fell in 1762. In 1764, back in North America, Montgomery and the Seventeenth marched to the relief of Fort Detroit, which was besieged by the Indians as part of Pontiac's Rebellion. Returning to England in 1765, he became friends with Edmund Burke, Isaac Barre, and Charles James Fox, all critics of the British ministry. During this time, his military career stagnated, partly due to a lack of political patronage, and when his attempt to purchase a major's commission was blocked in 1771, the disappointed Montgomery sold his own commission and emigrated to New York. Although lacking title and patronage, Montgomery was not without means. He purchased a farm at King's Bridge, a few miles north of New York City, and renewed his acquaintance with Janet Livingston, a member of one of the colony's most influential families. Richard and Janet were married on July 24, 1773, and took up residence on her more substantial property at Rhinebeck. Although seeking the quiet life of a gentleman farmer, he became a patriot by both intellectual predilection and family connection. He was elected to the New York Provincial Congress in 1775 and selected as one of New York's two generals, along with Phillip Schuyler, to serve in the fledgling Continental Army. The two men led an invasion of Canada, with the more vigorous Montgomery assuming an ever greater role and command. He took the fortress of St. John's along with the city of Montreal in November 1775, for which he was promoted to Major-General, but was killed in action leading his troops in a desperate assault on the city of Quebec on New Year's Eve, 1775. Thereafter, the American campaign to add Canada as the fourteenth colony collapsed, resulting in an early British victory and America's first martyr of the general's rank. The fallen Montgomery was much lauded in prose and poetry and had several counties named in his honor. In later years he also became a symbol of Irish America at St. Patrick's Day celebrations and election campaigns. In 1818, with Janet still living, his remains, with great fanfare, were returned from Quebec and buried near a monument in his honor, at St. Paul's Churchyard in New York City. (WJS)

Murphy, Charles Francis "Charlie" Murphy was born in Manhattan in 1858, the son of Irish immigrants. He became the greatest leader in the history of Tammany Hall, the Democratic machine of New York and, perhaps, the greatest Irish American political boss in history. Physically tough and a natural leader, he developed a following at an early age. In 1880, he bought a saloon—though he himself never drank—and parlayed his popularity into leadership of the Gas House District on New York's East Side. In 1902, he ascended to the top of the Tammany hierarchy as Grand Sachem and Boss of the entire organization. The Hall was then suffering from scandal and attacks by reformers, but Murphy rebuilt the organization's fortunes over the next two decades. He won five out six mayoral elections from 1903 to 1917, turning back the challenge of William Randolph Hearst in 1905 and overcoming the boy reformer John Purroy Mitchel in 1917. (Mitchel, the grandson of the great Irish and Irish American nationalist, John Mitchel, had won in the mayoralty in 1913.) More importantly, Murphy extended Tammany's power into the state government in Albany. His protégés Alfred Emmanuel Smith and Robert Wagner led the state assembly and state senate respectively. Murphy later helped elect Smith governor and promoted his candidacy for the Democratic nomination for president of the United States in 1924. Murphy died that year and his last mayor, James Walker, is said to have lamented, "The brains of Tammany Hall lie in Calvary Cemetery." An ineptly led Tammany Hall declined soon after.

Murphy was important not just for his power but how he got it. He cleaned up the excesses of Tammany's vice rackets and shrewdly made peace with Brooklyn Democrats, feeding them patronage and offices. Yet he also committed the machine to backing reforms, if for no other reason than because it meant votes and warded off challenges by other ethnic groups or radical parties like the Socialists. "Give the people what they want," Murphy said. Tammany backed politicians helped pass a state civil rights law in 1912 that was hailed by the state's Jewish voters. Murphy also backed social and economic reforms initiated by Smith and Wagner in the legislature.

Murray, Philip   One of the most important union leaders in American labor history, Philip Murray was a key figure in the United Mine Workers, first head of the United Steel Workers of America, and the second president of the Congress of Industrial Organizations.

Murray was born on May 25, 1886, in Blantyre, Scotland, to Irish immigrants William Murray and Rose Ann Layden. His father was a coal miner and his mother a weaver in a cotton mill. Philip joined his father in the mines at age ten and went to union meetings with him. In 1902, the family emigrated to the mining town of Irwin, near Pittsburgh, Pennsylvania, where they had relatives. In 1904, Murray was elected president of a United Mine Workers of America local during an unsuccessful strike called after he was fired for fighting with a company official. He subsequently became a member of the UMWA's International Board in 1912, president of District 5 in 1916, and international vice president in 1920. An effective negotiator and knowledgeable about industry and economics, he worked closely with UMWA president John L. Lewis as his chief lieutenant for twenty-two years. He provided loyal support during the difficult decade of the 1920s, when competition from unorganized southern districts undermined UMWA control, defensive strikes failed, membership declined, and dissent racked the union. After the New Deal began in 1933, Murray was active in successfully reorganizing the UMWA and increasing membership under the impetus of federal legislation enabling employees to legally organize for collective bargaining. Murray's vision of labor and social justice was derived from his devout Catholic faith and family union tradition. In line with papal encyclicals on labor relations, he saw the rights and responsibilities of both employers and workers. He was Chairman of the Steel Workers' Organizing Committee from 1936 to 1942, and its successor, the United Steelworkers of America, from 1942 to 1952. Despite his debt to Lewis, who had appointed him to the Steel Workers' Organizing Committee, Murray could not avoid a break with his old patron. After repudiating Franklin Roosevelt in the 1940 election, Lewis retired as president of the CIO and was replaced by Murray, who served until his death in 1952. Because Murray remained committed to Roosevelt, Lewis charged him with disloyalty and removed him as UMWA vice president in 1942. Murray promoted labor cooperation during World War II and served as a member of the Combined War Labor Board, where he advocated price controls as well as taxes on excess profits. In 1943, he organized the CIO's Political Action Committee, to support Roosevelt's reelection the following year. He was also a member of the National Association for the Advancement of Colored People and worked to ensure that blacks received the full privileges of union membership. He condemned racial discrimination and directed the CIO to establish a Committee to Abolish Racial Discrimination. After the war, he strongly opposed the Taft-Hartley Act, which eliminated the closed shop and imposed a mandatory cooling-off period before striking. He also supported the campaign to purge communists from the CIO and led the 1949 convention delegates to expel eleven communist-dominated unions. Murray was married in 1910 to Elizabeth Lavery and they had a son, Joseph William Murray. Though Philip became a naturalized American citizen in 1911, he retained a Scottish brogue and often wore a kilt in public. He died on November 9, 1952, in San Francisco shortly before he was to attend the CIO convention in Los Angeles. (WJS)

NORAID   NORAID was the leading militant Irish American Republican organization in the United States after the renewal of the "troubles" in Northern Ireland in the 1960s.

NORAID was founded in 1969 when the Irish Republican Army split into factions: the "Officials," who wished to pursue development of a Socialist Republic, and the "Provisionals," who wished to wage a military campaign for narrowly nationalist goals. Michael Flannery, an old IRA veteran from the 1920s, traveled to Ireland to link up with the Provisionals, and Joseph Cahill and Dalthai O'Connel of the Provisionals cemented the link on a return trip to the United States. NORAID was headquartered in the Bronx and developed chapters across the country. By 1971, the organization counted sixty to seventy chapters and claimed 10,000 members. Its greatest strength was in large Irish American Catholic population centers such as New York, Boston, Philadelphia, Chicago, and San Francisco. In those cities, it appeared to draw most of its members and donations from working-class or lower-middle-class Irish immigrants who had left Ireland in the 1940s and 1950s. Indeed, it raised substantial amounts of its money from the small contributions it solicited at taverns and bars. NORAID grew swiftly in the first few years of the 1970s, capitalizing on American resentment of British internment and outrage at the "Bloody Sunday" killings in Derry in 1972. The organization languished in the mid-1970s, troubled by quarrels with other groups and with its identification as a backer of terrorism when the IRA commenced a broad bombing campaign. NORAID revived again in the early 1980s when Bobby Sands and other IRA members went on hunger strikes to gain status as political prisoners in United Kingdom jails. NORAID also sponsored several "Irish people" tours to Northern Ireland in the early 1980s, winning the organization favorable publicity. Yet as the IRA and Sinn Fein turned to a political strategy in the late 1980s, NORAID broke into factions. Older working-class members, committed to the armed struggle, abandoned the organization. Some created a new version of the Friends of Irish Freedom, which backed IRA diehards and opposed truces and new Sinn Fein political strategies.

NORAID claimed that its principal function was simply to raise funds for Catholic families in Ulster that had been injured or dispossessed by the struggle in Ireland, but British, Republic of Ireland, and U.S. authorities have all consistently argued that the bulk of NORAID money was spent on buying arms for the IRA in Northern Ireland.

O'Connell, Cardinal William Henry   William Henry Cardinal O'Connell personified the ultramontane (pro-Roman) conservative militant Catholicism as well as the authoritarian episcopal administrative style that dominated Irish American Catholicism from the early twentieth century through the 1960s.

O'Connell was born in Lowell, Massachusetts of Irish immigrant parents in 1859. He attended St. Mary's Seminary, Boston College, and the North American College in Rome, where he was ordained in 1884. He sedulously cultivated Roman contacts, rising to become rector of the North American College in 1895. In 1901, he succeeded James Healy as bishop of Portland, Maine, and in 1906, his Roman contacts helped him win appointment as coadjutor archbishop with right to succession in Boston. He became archbishop in 1907 and a cardinal in 1911. He would rule the Boston Archdiocese for over thirty years. Though personally friendly with members of Boston's Brahmins, he worked to build a separate Catholic community in Boston through the development of a vast and elaborate Catholic infrastructure. During just the seven years from 1922 to 1929, for example, forty-three Catholic parishes in the archdiocese opened new schools. In the 1910s, his regime suffered from a number of scandals, which, though never publicly exposed, weakened his power in national and international church politics. His attempts to concentrate all diocesan power in his own hands were also often thwarted by independent-minded priests or nuns in Boston. Still, he continued to rule in Boston until 1944 as the image of the authoritarian and grand prince of Irish American Catholic militancy.

O'Connor, Edwin   Edwin O'Connor is known as a chronicler of Irish American life in New England in the twentieth century. His *Last Hurrah* was not only a commercial success but has been hailed as one of the best evocations of Irish American politics ever written. Many found his *The Edge of Sadness* an even better piece, and it received the Pulitzer Prize in 1962.

O'Connor was born in Providence on July 29, 1918, but grew up in Woonsocket, a declining Rhode Island mill town of mostly French Canadians. His father was a doctor and his mother was a teacher who stayed home with her three children after teaching for three years. O'Connor attended public elementary schools and La Salle Academy in Providence, where he received a classical education in Greek and Latin, participated in the drama club, and ran cross-country. He chose to go to Notre Dame, and he so enjoyed it that after he had graduated, he returned each year to visit. As an English major, he thrived under the "Christian humanist" focus of his literature teachers, especially Frank O'Malley, whose Modern Catholic Writers course, which included works of Mauriac, Bernanos, and Maritain, was of great interest to him. It was to O'Malley and his classes that he would come back and speak in for years after, and to whom he dedicated *The Edge of Sadness*. When he had finished his undergraduate studies with *cum laude* distinction, he enrolled in the masters program at Notre Dame with a scholarship, but withdrew late in the first semester, deciding to follow an earlier decision to be a writer.

In 1940, having had some experience in radio at college, he became an announcer at WPRO in Providence, and then went on to work at Palm Beach, Buffalo, and Hartford radio stations. His primary goal, however, was to write, and at this time he wrote a number of short stories and radio scripts. When World War II began, he joined the Coast Guard, serving for three years on Cape Cod, patrolling the beaches and in Boston. There he befriended Louis Brems, a former vaudevillian and official greeter for Boston mayor Maurice Tobin, who told him many stories of politicians in dialect. He had already attempted a novel about his Coast Guard experience and he would begin another after he left the Coast Guard in 1945, while he continued in broadcast work in Boston. In 1946, he took up writing in earnest and began writing, teaching, editing, and interviewing to support himself. He found a room across the street from the *Atlantic Monthly*, and over the next several years it became his custom to visit the *Atlantic*'s writers and editors daily. Over a span of seven years, he wrote *The Oracle* and *The Last Hurrah* as well as numerous television reviews and short stories. Through the help of the *Atlantic*'s editor, Edward Weeks, he also participated in a series of weekly radio broadcasts on writing, edited scripts for Fred Allen, and helped write Allen's autobiography.

He visited Ireland in 1953 after a "near fatal" ulcer hemorrhage, and visited again in 1954, to compare American and Irish political customs, discovering more differences than similarities. When he returned, he intensified his work on *The Last Hurrah* in order to meet the deadline for a competitive new book literary award at the *Atlantic*, and submitted the manuscript in January 1955. The success of the novel was dramatic. He moved into a new home and bought a summer home and new car, but O'Connor's work habits and attitudes did not change. Former Boston mayor James Michael Curley claimed that he was the inspiration for the book and even went to the extent of claiming the deathbed scene as his, or at least that it would be his. O'Connor, however, said he became interested in politics not through observation of Curley but through visits when he was at Notre Dame to his Chicago classmates' homes and their parents regaled him with stories that he wrote down when he returned to school. O'Connor's *The Edge of Sadness* was published in 1961 and won the Pulitzer Prize in 1962. The novel is a first-person narration of a crossroads in the narrator's life after his return to priestly duties from rehabilitation. The novel's focus is on the narrator's coming to terms with his values as a Catholic and a priest. Arthur Schlesinger described it as a fusion "of the search for grace and the end of Irish America … into a single text. It is technically an impressive work, more complex in its construction than *The Last Hurrah*."

O'Connor went on to publish *All in the Family*, a novel that tells a story of political family continuing its legacy, which critics believed was modeled on the Kennedys. Arthur Schlesinger quotes the hero of *The Edge of Sadness* in describing Edwin O'Connor: "We all share in a shattering duality … every day in every man there is this warfare of the parts. And while all this results in meanness and bitterness and savagery enough … nevertheless the wonder of it all to me is the frequency with which kindness, the essential *goodness* of man does break through, and … in the long succession of these small redemptive instants … that the meaning and the glory of man is revealed." (JHM)

O'Connor, Flannery   In one of her letters, Flannery O'Connor recounts a conversation during which she was asked what an Irish Catholic was. She writes, "'You are in the presence of one,' says I, bowing." The reply is somewhat startling, since her novels and stories are so memorably Southern and in the number of characters, mostly Protestant. Her slight mockery of the stage Irish bow, however, confirms a full awareness of her response, and in other places she acknowledged that her Catholicism is Irish by way of Scotch-Irish Southerners, Jansenism, Mauriac, and de Chardin.

Her literary production by most standards was not large, but the fiction of both novels and short stories has attracted the interest of critics from the moment that the works were published in 1946 to her death in 1964 at the age of thirty-nine. Born in Savannah in 1925, she attended the Women's College of Georgia, graduated and then received an M.F.A. degree from the University of Iowa in 1947. Invited to join Yaddo in 1948, she resigned shortly afterwards in protest with Robert Lowell over a political issue. After remaining in the New York City area for a short period, she returned to her family home of Milledgeville, Georgia. In 1950, she suffered an attack of lupus, an incurable disease that had felled her father, and was hospitalized for nine months. The following year she settled in Milledgeville and remained there except for a visit to Lourdes in 1958 and occasional trips when she was invited to give talks at colleges and for other groups interested in her fiction.

In her life, she published two novels: *Wise Blood* (1952) and *The Violent Bear It Away* (1960) and a short story collection, *A Good Man Is Hard to Find, and Other Stories* (1955). Posthumously, *Everything That Rises Must Converge*, a short story collection (1965) and *The Complete Short Stories* (1971) were published, in addition to *Mystery and Manners: Occasional Prose* (1969) and her letters in *The Habit of Being* (1980). She had an interest in Pierre Teilhard de Chardin, a Jesuit priest who wrote *The Phenomenon of Man* and other philosophical and theological commentaries on the presence of divinity in human activity, and such interests deeply influenced her work. There is at once a practical and philosophical bent to her religious beliefs. Such a contrast or paradox is often the way critics see both the meaning and beauty of her fiction and the problems with it. (JHM)

O'Neill, Thomas P.   Thomas P. "Tip" O'Neill, third-generation Irish American, was majority leader and the Speaker of the House of Representatives in the 1970s and the 1980s. His years as Speaker were particularly important as he became the embattled symbol of an older Irish American politics with roots in the New Deal and the urban liberalism of the turn of the century, now threatened by the new conservatism of Irish American Ronald Reagan.

Thomas O' Neill was born in Cambridge, Massachusetts on December 9, 1912. His grandfather, Patrick O'Neill, was from Mallow in Cork and fled to America in the wake of the Great Famine in 1851. In Cambridge, Patrick found work with the city as a teamster. O'Neill's father, also named Thomas, worked as a bricklayer but was active in politics and became Superintendent of Sewers in the Cambridge municipal administration. O'Neill's father believed strongly in Americanization and the achievement of respectability, but Cambridge and Boston were suffused with religious and ethnic conflict, which left a lasting impression on his son "Tip." Indeed, later colleagues on Capitol Hill would be struck by how much resentments from the early days of this Yankee-Irish conflict persisted for O'Neill. On the other hand, "Tip" was an affable, natural politician. He began his own political career in 1934, while still attending Boston College, when he ran for the City Council. He lost that effort, but two years later after he graduated from college, he won a seat in the Massachusetts state legislature. In 1948, he became the first Democratic Speaker of the Massachusetts House in over one hundred years. In 1953, he took over John F. Kennedy's old seat in the United States Congress, when Kennedy ran and won a seat in the Senate. O'Neill made himself a power in the House, first under fellow Boston Irish Catholic majority leader and later Speaker John McCormack. In 1966, he broke with the Democratic administration over the Vietnam War, angering Lyndon Johnson but helping him make connections to new Democratic liberals. By 1973, O'Neill had become majority leader, leading the Democrats during the Watergate crisis, and by 1977, Speaker of the House. After Jimmy Carter's defeat by Reagan in 1980, O'Neill became the leading Democrat in the nation and his party's chief spokesman to counter Reagan. Initially badly bloodied in those battles, he fought back during Reagan's second term, though neither he nor the Democrats rolled back the Republican tide. O'Neill resigned from Congress in 1987 and died in 1994.

Orange Riots The Orange riots erupted on July 12, 1870, and on the same date in 1871, when members of the Loyal Orange Order and their supporters paraded through the West Side of New York City to commemorate William of Orange's victory over James II at the Battle of the Boyne in 1691, securing Protestant rule in Ireland. The riots reflected the persistence of religious tensions between Irish Catholic "green" and Irish Protestant "orange" in America. There had been riots and battles between Orange and Green before in New York City—for example, in 1824 in Greenwich Village—but the riots of 1870 and 1871 were by far the most lethal. Eight paraders or their opponents died in 1870 and sixty-two died in 1871. The riots in 1871 took place amidst breaking controversies over the corruption of William Marcy "Boss" Tweed's rule over the city and fed off those political tensions. In a broader sense, they helped sharpen the division among Irishmen between Protestants and Catholics. Most Protestants in America by this time had abandoned the definition of "Irishmen" in order to distance themselves from the Catholic Irish. As bloody as these battles were, conflicts over Orange Day parades and celebrations seemed less common in the United States than in Canada, where in the nineteenth century Protestant Irish immigration was proportionally heavier and the Orange order was an exceptionally powerful institution.

Paxton Boys   The Paxton Boys, largely Scotch-Irish frontiersmen in Pennsylvania, revolted against the colony's government and its Indian policy in 1763. For most of its history, colonial Pennsylvania was a proprietary colony in which members of the Penn family, who were originally Quakers but later became Anglicans, usually served as governors. Early settlers were primarily English, Irish, and Welsh Quakers, and later immigrants militant Scotch-Irish Presbyterians or Germans of various sects. Tensions abounded between the Quakers, who lived in and around Philadelphia, and the Scotch-Irish, who lived on the frontier along or near the Susquehanna River, with the Germans located both geographically and politically in the middle. By 1763, after nine years of Indian attacks during the French and Indian War and now assailed by the further depredations of Pontiac's Rebellion, beleaguered frontiersmen were increasingly angered by the failure of the Quaker-dominated Pennsylvania Assembly to provide adequate defense. On December 14, 1763, after word had circulated that some Indians were being sheltered at the Moravian Manor at Conestoga, about fifty men, certain that the Native Americans were providing aid and information to the enemy, brutally murdered six of them, including two women and a boy. Sympathetic Pennsylvanians moved fourteen other Conestoga Indians to Lancaster for protection while the frontiersmen, mostly from Paxton Township and calling themselves the "Paxton Boys," tracked them down. Two weeks later, these Indians, who were Christians, maintained a posture of prayer as each man, woman, and child was hacked to death. No one was ever arrested nor could witnesses be found for this crime. Colonial officials in Philadelphia were outraged, took steps to protect remaining Indians, and even tried unsuccessfully to export some of them to New York. However, the enmity of the Paxton Boys had not subsided, and hundreds of them marched on Philadelphia to eliminate any remaining Indians. They reached Germantown on February 5, 1764, where they were met by a delegation that included Benjamin Franklin. After some negotiation, they agreed to disperse, though they left two of their members to draw up a Declaration of Grievances which included requests for greater representation in the Assembly, protection against the Indians, and tax relief. The colonial government took no action, which only increased the divide between the two sides, even though fighting with the Indians subsided later in 1764 until the outbreak of the American Revolution in 1775. The western frontiersmen believed that the Quakers used pacifism as an excuse to leave the frontier undefended and gerrymandering to leave it underrepresented. The easterners were dismissive of these concerns, motivated both by self-interest and their moral revulsion at the violence of the settlers. This interregional impasse between differing interests and ideologies, a form of the typical split between the city and the countryside that affects most societies, would manifest itself during the events of the Whiskey Rebellion of 1794. (WJS)

The *Pilot* (the *Boston Pilot*)   A leading Irish American Catholic newspaper, the *Pilot* reached the zenith of its broad Irish American popularity under the editorship of the brilliant John Boyle O'Reilly in the late nineteenth century and his accomplished if less celebrated successors James Jeffrey Roche and Katherine Conway. For much of the nineteenth century, the *Pilot* was known as the "bible of the American Irish." By 1871, it had an estimated circulation of over 100,000 readers.

In 1829, Bishop Bernard Fenwick of Boston founded a paper called the *Jesuit*. Five years later, the bishop sold the paper to two laymen, Henry Devereaux and Patrick Donahoe. In 1836, Donahoe, who became the principal architect of its fortunes, renamed the paper the *Pilot* after a "popular and patriotic" journal of the same name in Dublin that strongly backed Daniel O'Connell and Catholic Emancipation. Donahoe strengthened the links with Ireland and Irish Americans by establishing a "missing persons" column for Irish immigrants seeking to reconnect with lost relatives in the United States, running regular reports of Irish news county by county, publishing Irish as well as Irish American poetry, fiction, and reviews of Irish drama, and, of course, faithfully following nationalist events. Oscar Wilde, Lady Gregory, William Butler Yeats, Dion Boucicault, and Fannie Parnell all wrote for the *Pilot*. Following Donahoe, the key figure in the *Pilot*'s rise was John Boyle O'Reilly, one of Catholic America's leading intellectuals and writers in the late nineteenth century, and well known in Irish and Irish American circles as a former Fenian and prisoner in Australia. Under O'Reilly, the paper was an eloquent advocate for black civil rights and the interests of workers and the poor, but skeptical about woman's suffrage. Roche continued the paper's commitment to social and economic reform. In 1908, the *Pilot* became the official voice of the Boston Archdiocese. Under clerical control, it became much more focused on the Church's activities in eastern Massachusetts and the paper lost its broad nationwide Irish American influence.

Powderly, Terence Vincent   Terence Vincent Powderly, labor leader and public servant, was born on January 22, 1849, in Carbondale, Pennsylvania, to Irish immigrants Terence and Madge (Walsh) Powderly. As a youth, he had little opportunity for education and was employed as a railroad switchman and later apprenticed as a machinist. He joined the International Union of Machinists and Blacksmiths in 1871, later becoming his local's president. His union activities and the Depression of 1873 left him jobless and blacklisted as a union agitator. Powderly joined the Scranton Local Assembly of the Knights of Labor in 1876 and rose steadily through the ranks until assuming the national leadership as Grand (later General) Master Workman, a position he held from 1879 to 1893. The Knights came into national prominence during his tenure, peaking in national membership and influence in 1886, but soon declined, riven by a divisive power struggle resulting in Powderly's removal and eventual succession by his protégé and betrayer, John William Hayes. Perhaps Powderly's greatest achievement, greatly aided by Cardinal James Gibbons, was to bring about reconciliation between the labor movement and the Roman Catholic Church, which had until that point distrusted and disapproved of labor organizations due to their secretive and ritualistic activities. In addition to his labor connections, Powderly served as a progressive mayor of Scranton from 1878 to 1884 and later practiced law in Pennsylvania. He was also a committed Irish nationalist, serving as a member of Clan na Gael and the Irish Land League. An avid campaigner for the Republicans in the 1896 presidential campaign, Powderly was rewarded by President William McKinley with the appointment as Commissioner General of Immigration in 1897. Unfortunately, Powderly's efforts to reform conditions at Ellis Island prompted President Theodore Roosevelt to dismiss him in 1902, though an investigation led to his reinstatement in 1906 as Special Immigration Inspector. Powderly then traveled to Europe to study immigration and issued a report advocating preselection of immigrants abroad and an even distribution of immigrants in the United States. Powderly next served as Chief of the Division of Information, U.S. Bureau of Immigration, from 1907 to 1921, and as the U.S. Department of Labor's Commissioner of Conciliation, from 1921 to 1924. He was also a world traveler, amateur photographer, and author of *Thirty Years of Labor* (1889) and his posthumous memoirs, *The Path I Trod* (1940). He died in Washington, D.C., on June 24, 1924. American labor historians have dismissed Powderly and the Knights as relics of the utopian traditions of the antebellum years and unsuited to the economic realities of the Gilded Age, especially in comparison with the rival American Federation of Labor, with its more apolitical craft unionism. Powderly was charged with being sensitive, vain, and naive. Recent studies of the Knights have transformed the view of them into that of an authentic working-class organization with a convincing critique of industrial capitalism. This has helped make the case that Powderly was not a pusillanimous utopian but a worthy if somewhat flawed hero who articulated the collective progressive vision of the working masses in the face of the inhumanity of the industrial capitalist system. In 1999, Powderly was honored as an inductee into the U.S. Department of Labor's Hall of Fame, joining figures such as rival Samuel Gompers and friend Mary Harris "Mother" Jones. (WJS)

Presentation Sisters   The Presentation Sisters were one of the most important Irish Catholic orders of religious women to send sisters to the United States.

The Presentation Sisters were founded in Cork, Ireland, in 1775 by Honoria (Nano) Nagle, a member of an Irish Catholic gentry family. Nagle, distressed that the Penal Laws had prevented Catholic education, was committed to the schooling of poor children. The first foundation of the Presentation Sisters in the United States was established in 1854, when five sisters came to San Francisco and took over a girls school. In 1857, they opened the first school for African American girls in California. In the 1870s, sisters from three convents in Ireland—Teranure, Clondelkin, and Tuam—settled in New York City to teach in parish schools, and a group went from Mooncuin to Dubuque, Iowa. Convents were later founded in Fitchburg, Massachusetts, metropolitan New York City, Iowa, and Fargo, North Dakota, and the Presentation Sisters staffed schools across the country. By 1960, they had over 1,400 sisters in the United States working in over 130 schools and other institutions.

Regulators   The Regulation or Regulator movement of North Carolina, from 1766 to 1771, is a notable case of militant political dissent in colonial

America. It was fundamentally a western movement, representing sections that resented the eastern-dominated colonial government that controlled the appointment of local officials. Westerners were unhappy with exorbitant fees, high taxes, corrupt officials, and multiple-office holders. Beginning in August 1766 with the erection of the Sandy Creek Association in Orange County, the Regulation spread quickly. The focus of discontent was in Orange, Rowan, and Anson counties, with some spillage into Granville, Mecklenburg, and Johnston counties. Settlers, many of them recently arrived from Pennsylvania and including both Scotch-Irish Presbyterians and English Baptists, sent various petitions to colonial authorities, refused to pay taxes, and used violence and intimidation against both officials and the courts. The first major incident occurred at Hillsborough, the Orange county seat, on May 3, 1768, when a hated county official, Edmund Fanning, had Regulator leaders Herman Husband and William Butler arrested after scores of armed men had shot up Fanning's home. In September 1768, an armed confrontation was only narrowly avoided between 1,400 militia, commanded by Governor William Tryon, and 4,000 settlers, primarily from Orange County. Amidst this ongoing turmoil, Regulators disrupted court proceedings in Anson and Johnston counties in 1768 and the superior court in Hillsborough in September 1770, where Husband, Butler, James Hunter, and 150 men assaulted several officers and attorneys. Those assaulted included the despised Fanning, who was whipped and his house destroyed. Retribution followed on May 16, 1771, when Tryon and nearly 1,200 militia, supported by artillery, routed over 2,000 Regulators after a two-hour battle at their main camp on Alamance Creek, near Hillsborough in Guilford County. This effectively ended the movement, as the defeated rebels suffered perhaps as many as thirty killed and 200 wounded. Seven ringleaders were executed and more than 6,000 men, nearly three-fourths of the back country's adult white male population, were forced to swear allegiance in return for pardons, though Husband, Hunter, and Butler were exempted. Many fled to other colonies—in fact, Husband would turn up in 1794 as a participant in Pennsylvania's Whiskey Rebellion. The bitter legacy induced many others who remained in North Carolina to become Loyalist supporters during the American Revolution. There was also a somewhat different Regulator movement in South Carolina, where members were primarily slave owners who acted between 1767 and 1769 as the enforcers of law and order in the back country. Facing a wave of depredations by wandering bandits and lacking local courts and jails as well as being frustrated by the leniency of the Charleston criminal justice system, they punished suspected robbers, prostitutes, and vagrants with whippings, house burn-ings, and banishment. They were also resentful of fugitive debtors, exces-sive legal fees, and underrepresentation in the colonial assembly. They also called for local capabilities to process land warrants and premiums on their crops. The South Carolinian Regulators only ceased operations with the South Carolina Circuit Court Act of 1769. (WJS)

St. Patrick's Day   Observance of the Feast of St. Patrick extends far back in to Irish history, but it was in America that mass public commemorations of the day in dinners, concerts, and especially parades became common-place. It was also in America that St. Patrick's Day became the traditional principal holiday of the Irish Catholic community. Invented in America from a variety of sources, St. Patrick's Day commemorations, particularly parades, were then exported back to Ireland.

Observances of St. Patrick's Day had deep roots in Irish culture. The feast was first listed in the Irish legal calendar in 1607 and the Vatican con-firmed its official importance in decrees in 1631 and 1687. Ordinary Irish peasants and farmers observed the day from early on at Catholic masses and in home rituals such as fathers drawing crosses on their children's heads with a charred stick, or children cutting out Celtic crosses. The wearing of shamrocks or bits of green ribbon was also common before the eigh-teenth century. Yet Catholics were not the only Irishmen to claim the day. Official celebrations of St. Patrick's Day by the government or the Prot-estant, established Church of Ireland elite ebbed and flowed throughout the seventeenth and eighteenth centuries. By the late eighteenth century, however, banquets and balls were common at Dublin Castle and in the early nineteenth century, so were elaborate military reviews. St. Patrick's Day commemorations in America would draw as much or more from other elements of Irish culture as from these Irish commemorations of the day. American commemorations, for example, would draw on the rituals of Pat-tern Day celebrations in Ireland. These rituals honored local saints and evolved by the eighteenth century into festivals of singing, dancing, and drinking. The proliferation of market fairs across Ireland in the modern era and the evolving traditions of entertainments and celebrations was another source from which Irish Americans would probably draw for celebrations of St. Patrick's Day. Sources in Ireland for the custom of parading on St. Patrick's Day are harder to identify. Few Irish peasants fleeing to America would have known much about Dublin Castle's military reviews. More may have witnessed or even participated in the grand processions orga-nized largely in Munster and Leinster by Daniel O'Connell's Catholic

Emancipation Association in the 1820s or by Repeal Associations in the early 1840s. Such "protest marches" were massive and included floats, bands, and people wearing or carrying boughs of green.

The first celebrations of St. Patrick's Day in America took place in the eighteenth century. They were sponsored by Protestant-dominated organizations such as the Charitable Irish Society of Boston, which organized a banquet on the day in 1737. Dinners and banquets became common in several cities after the American Revolution, and by the early nineteenth century often included both Catholic and Protestant Irishmen. The first parades are harder to date, but there appeared to be a procession of British army officers enrolled in the local Sons of St. Patrick to King's Chapel, the Anglican church in Boston in 1766, and a march of British soldiers and officers in New York in 1779.

It was in the nineteenth century, however, particularly in the 1840s and 1850s, that the commemoration of St. Patrick's Day began to take on its modern form. The day increasingly became an Irish Catholic and nationalist holiday: the essential sacred day of the emerging Irish American Catholic community, a marker of its identity, and a source of inspiration for its community solidarity. Parades began in small cities like Lowell, Massachusetts in 1830 or Worcester, Massachusetts in the late 1840s. In New York City, a convention of Irish societies took over organization of parades there in 1851, overriding the number of neighborhood processions that had grown up to create a single, massive, citywide procession. In 1853, the Ancient Order of Hibernians joined the New York City parade for the first time, and by 1860 there were 10,000 marchers in the New York parade. By the 1870s, parades in New York had become large marches, powerful symbols of Irish Catholic power, and even in small cities like Worcester they drew a thousand or more marchers. By that time, the AOH had emerged to play a critical role in the organization not only of the New York, but of also the Chicago and Boston parades. In the 1880s, however, enthusiasm for the parades slackened. Disputes between the AOH and the Convention of Irish Societies plagued the New York parades. More generally, the rise of Irish Catholic temperance societies in the Catholic Total Abstinence Union of America and the teetotalers' and Catholic cleric concerns over excessive drinking on the day sapped some support for the parade. Some nationalists also believed that the parade drained off money that should have gone to movements in Ireland like the Land League. Though parades would die out in some Irish American communities, they would revive in most places by the 1890s. By the middle of the twentieth century, the parade in New York City had grown to mammoth size: over 80,000 marchers and one million spectators by 1947, and in 1948, it drew President Harry Truman to the reviewing stand. Chicago revived its official parade in the 1950s and the city's South Side Irish neighborhoods began a parade in that decade as well. The St. Patrick's Day parade had become a powerful reflection of growing Irish power by the middle of the twentieth century.

Factions in Irish American communities have always fought over the proper celebration of the day. In the nineteenth century, fights between Irish Temperance men and Hibernians were especially common, and nationalist factions sometimes argued over control of banquets or parades. Because the parade came to represent the Irish American community on the march, different parts of the Irish American communities were always eager to assert their own definition of Irish American identity through the parade. In 1983, Michael Flannery, a founder and leader of the pro-IRA provisional group NORAID, was named Grand Marshall of the parade in New York City, prompting criticism from Catholic church and other Irish American leaders who decried IRA violence. More recently, Irish American gay men and lesbians sought inclusion in the New York and Boston parades, sparking battles with conservative Irish Catholic organizers of the parade, who believed that openly gay identities were not appropriately Irish. In Ireland, gay men and women have since marched in St. Patrick's Day parades without controversy.

By the twentieth century, if not much earlier, St. Patrick's Day celebrations had become commercialized by several industries seeking to exploit the day's marketing potential. In the early twentieth century, local makers of confections or souvenirs had roused the ire of the Ancient Order of Hibernians by selling candies in the shape of pigs or clothing or cards inspired by stage Irish stereotypes. Yet over the course of the twentieth century, greeting card companies, souvenir sellers, and whiskey distillers and beer brewers in particular, have made St. Patrick's Day a virtual national holiday. So important have St. Patrick's Day parades become as markers of Irish identity that the government and other promoters of tourism in Ireland began organizing parades in Dublin to encourage American tourists to come "home" to celebrate the day. By the 1970s, such parades had become standard features of mid-March festivals in Dublin and had spread to other Irish cities. In 1990, the Dublin parade boasted 6,000 marchers—1,000 of them from the United States—and was telecast back to thirty American cities.

Scotch-Irish Society of the United States of America   Until the early nineteenth century, Irish immigration to America consisted largely of people variously called Irish Protestants, Presbyterian Irish, Ulster-Scots, Scotch-Irish, or sometimes just Irish. Whatever term used, they had a strong sense of identity and a proud heritage, which they believed was threatened by the numerous Irish Catholics arriving in America after the Great Famine of the 1840s. As a result, in May 1889 businessman Thomas T. Wright, newspaper publisher Robert E. Bonner, newspaper editor A. C. Floyd, and Presbyterian pastors John D. Hall and John S. MacIntosh founded the Scotch-Irish Society of America to preserve Scotch-Irish history and promote fraternity among their descendants. Primarily an upper-middle-class organization with membership open to citizens and legal permanent residents of Scotch-Irish descent, it consisted of clergy, businessmen, politicians, and lawyers. Having no intention of being identified with the "mere Irish," the term "Scotch-Irish" was applied to persons descended from those who emigrated to America from Ulster and whose families had arrived in Ulster after 1600 from Scotland, England, France, and elsewhere in Europe. For about a dozen years before it faded into oblivion, the society held annual meetings in Scotch-Irish centers such as Columbia, Tennessee, and Pittsburgh, Pennsylvania, and published volumes titled *Proceedings and Addresses of the Scotch-Irish Society of America* (1889–1901). There were several state affiliates but only the Pennsylvania Scotch-Irish Society, founded in October 1889 by A. K. McClure and John S. MacIntosh, survived the demise of the national society. Besides holding annual dinners, featuring distinguished speakers such as Woodrow Wilson in 1901 and Herbert Hoover in 1917, the Pennsylvania Society supported projects and the publication of books promoting the Scotch-Irish role in American history. Among these were Henry J. Ford's *The Scotch-Irish in North America* (1915) and Wayland F. Dunaway's *The Scotch-Irish in Colonial Pennsylvania* (1944). Emphasis was on the importance of the Scotch-Irish in winning the American Revolution, securing the Constitution, taming the West, and providing leadership in higher education. Scotch-Irish individuals of particular note were celebrated, including presidents Andrew Jackson, James Polk, James Buchanan, William McKinley, and Woodrow Wilson; politicians James G. Blaine and Marc A. Hanna; banker Thomas Mellon; inventor Cyrus McCormick; architect Charles F. McKim; and musician Stephen Foster. The society also maintained close ties with Ulster and donated monetary assistance there during both world wars. In 1949, the society organized the Scotch-Irish Foundation, a Pennsylvania nonprofit corporation, to receive gifts and bequests as well as to collect and preserve books, documents, letters, journals, and other historical material about the Scotch-Irish for public, educational, and research use. It was first located at the Presbyterian Historical Society of Philadelphia and later moved to the Historical Society of Pennsylvania in Philadelphia. In 1961, the society broadened its base and transformed itself into a national organization named the Scotch-Irish Society of the United States of America. In 2000, it organized the Center for Scotch-Irish Studies to sponsor biennial symposia and publish the annual *Journal of Scotch-Irish Studies*, devoted to the scholarly study of Scotch-Irish people and their contributions to American history, language, music, material culture, and political and legal philosophy. (WJS)

Sisters of Mercy   The Sisters of Mercy have been one of the most important Catholic orders of religious women to come from Ireland to the United States. Their original work in Ireland and America largely involved charitable projects, orphanages, hospitals, and work with young women. They continued these charitable efforts in America but, like most orders of religious women, were increasingly drawn into teaching in the expanding Catholic parochial school system.

The Sisters of Mercy were founded in Dublin, Ireland in 1831 by Catherine Elizabeth McAuley. McAuley had been born into a Catholic middle-class family, but raised largely among members of the Anglo-Irish Protestant aristocracy. Loyal to her faith, she wished to promote an active role for women in the church. The Sisters of Mercy reflected a trend toward the establishment of an active apostolic women's religious congregation as opposed to a contemplative and cloistered one. They also reflected the gathering momentum of reform in the Catholic Church that would explode by the middle of the century in the Devotional Revolution. During that revival, the number of sisters as well as priests in Ireland would increase enormously, and they would become a vital and rich resource for the church in America. The Sisters of Mercy began sending nuns from Ireland to the United States in 1843, when eight sisters left the order's convent in Carlow for Pittsburgh. Three years later, more left Dublin for New York and in the next decade, groups left Naas and Kinsale in Ireland for Little Rock, Arkansas and San Francisco, respectively. Through the emigration of sisters from Ireland and recruitment of American-born Irishwomen, the Sisters of Mercy grew substantially in number. By 1929, there were over 9,000 Sisters of Mercy in sixty independent mother houses in the United States. Numbers dwindled after the 1960s—as they did for all Catholic religious orders—but the Sisters of Mercy have remained a powerful force in American Catholicism, counting over 6,000 members in the mid-1990s.

Smith, Alfred E   Speaker of the New York State Assembly, Governor of New York, and the first Irish Catholic candidate for president nominated by a major party, Smith embodied many critical facets of Irish American political life in the first half of the twentieth century. In New York he was a stalwart social and economic reformer, and as a presidential candidate his campaign crystallized urban ethnic Catholic support for the Democratic Party, but his defeat in that election was a powerful reminder to Irish Catholics of the continuing deeply held anti-Catholic sentiment that pervaded America.

Alfred Emmanuel Smith was born in New York City on December 30, 1873. His father was of mixed Italian and German ancestry and his mother Irish and English, but Smith himself always identified as an Irish Catholic. In 1885, his father died and Smith was forced to go to work to support his family. He became involved in politics through the local machine of the Lower East Side boss Tom Foley. Foley selected him to be a candidate for the state assembly. There he became friends with Robert Wagner (they roomed together) and the two would become critical players in a Democratic Party revival in Albany in the 1910s. In 1911, Smith became Democratic majority leader and in 1913, Speaker of the State Assembly. Along with Wagner, Smith became one of the New York state legislature's leaders in a great era of reform. After a fire in the Triangle Shirtwaist Company's rooms killed 146 women in 1911, Smith was chosen to be vice chairman of the Triangle Shirtwaist Commission (Wagner was chairman) set up to investigate factory working conditions. Smith and Wagner helped push through a whole host of factory safety and other regulatory laws recommended by the Commission. In 1918, Smith was elected governor and over four terms in Albany he continued his fight for progressive legislation. In his first term, he courageously resisted sentiment whipped up by Red Scare hysteria to expel Socialist members of the New York State Assembly. Charles Murphy, boss of Tammany Hall, was his critical backer throughout his career. In 1924, Murphy promoted him for the Democratic nomination for president, but the convention deadlocked for 109 ballots before turning to a weak compromise candidate, John Davis. In 1928, he won the nomination, but lost the election by an overwhelming 444 electoral votes to eighty-one. Religion clearly played a role in the contest, costing Smith Protestant votes throughout the country. His nomination, however, also electrified Catholic ethnics across the nation, who turned out for him in huge numbers. Some observers have called the election the "Al Smith" revolution in Democratic Party politics. In 1932, he sought the nomination again, attracting strong Irish American Catholic support in states like Massachusetts, but he lost to Franklin D. Roosevelt. Once a friend and ally of Roosevelt, Smith became increasingly alienated from the new president, excoriating New Deal policies, hobnobbing with rich corporate executives, and campaigning for the Republican presidential candidate, Wendell Wilkie, in 1940. Smith died in 1944.

Society of United Irishmen of America   The Society of United Irishmen of America was one of the chief organizational embodiments of the radical republican exiles who fled Ireland for the Untied States in the 1790s. It reflected their commitment to creating an independent Irish republic (it could be seen as the first important Irish nationalist organization in America) and the triumph of republicanism in the United States and throughout the world.

The Society of United Irishmen was created in Ireland in 1791 by nationalist radicals. They would eventually dedicate themselves to the overthrow of British rule and the establishment of a republic in Ireland. In 1794, it was proscribed by the British government. Hunted down and oppressed in Ireland, hundreds of radicals fled to the United States over the course of the mid- and late 1790s. Some sources suggest that an American branch of the Society may have been formed as early as 1795, but the first constitution of the Society dates to 1797. The constitution stated that the purpose of the Society was to "promote the emancipation of Ireland from the tyranny of the British government." Among its activities was the raising of funds to purchase the contracts of Irish radicals who had emigrated to the United States as indentured servants. However, the Society was also a nursery of hope for the spread of republicanism throughout the world, and it accepted non-Irish members. Beginning in Philadelphia, the heartland of the Irish republican radicals, the Society soon claimed branches all along the East Coast, from South Carolina to New York. It is difficult to determine how many members the organization had, but, at one point in the late 1790s, reports suggested that there were as many 1,500 members in the Philadelphia area alone. Members included Irish radical newspapermen, teachers, shopkeepers, and some skilled artisans. Its opponents, particularly members of the American Federalist Party, accused it of treasonous designs to overthrow the American government, then led by the Federalist president John Adams. When relations between the United States and France deteriorated during the XYZ affair in 1798, some Federalists suggested the American Society of United Irishmen was organizing to assist a French invasion, and passed the Alien, Naturalization, and Sedition Acts to suppress them and other Irish radicals. It is not clear when the Society disappeared, but new organizations like the Hibernian Provident Society, established in New York City in 1802, carried on its work.

Spellman, Cardinal Francis   Called by some the "American Pope," Francis Spellman dominated the Catholic Church in America during the middle years of the twentieth century and seemed the single best embodiment of the new Irish American identity: the militantly Catholic but fiercely patriotically American Irish American.

Spellman was born in Whitman, Massachusetts, in 1889 to middle-class parents of Irish ancestry. He attended Fordham College in New York and studied for the priesthood at the North American College in Rome. There he began the assiduous cultivation of Roman connections that had become critical for any ambitious American Catholic cleric in the twentieth century. Spellman made many friends then and in a later stint in Rome among members of the Roman Curia, the Vatican bureaucracy. None was more important to him, however, than Eugenio Pacelli, who became Vatican Secretary of State in 1930 and Pope Pius XII in 1939. Exploiting his Vatican connections, Spellman also made useful contacts among American politicians, most notably Franklin Roosevelt. In 1939, Pius XII named Spellman the archbishop of New York and, shortly thereafter, made him a cardinal. As archbishop of New York, Spellman became one of the great builders in American Catholic history, spending over five hundred million dollars on the construction or repair of 370 schools and ninety-two million dollars on the expansion of hospitals and social service agencies. He ran a very tight organization, centralizing purchasing and other functions in the diocesan administration and asserting strong control over his clergy.

Spellman played a prominent role far beyond New York in American Catholic and Irish life, both as an intermediary between the Church and American politicians and as a spokesman and symbol for an uncompromising and militantly anticommunist American Catholicism. He spoke out frequently against the evils of communism, gave careful support to Joseph McCarthy, blamed communist sympathizers for a gravediggers' strike in his diocese, and engaged in public spats with liberal Democrats like Eleanor Roosevelt. He also served as Military Vicar to the Armed Forces from 1939 until his death, established a strong connection with the military, and was an outspoken and unbending backer of the Vietnam War until his death in 1967.

United Irish Exiles   In the 1790s and early 1800s, several leaders of the Society of United Irishmen and the rebellion of 1798 fled Ireland or were sent into exile and settled in the United States. They became a powerful force in American politics, publishing nearly a score of newspapers between 1792 and 1812 and becoming critical voices for Thomas Jefferson's emerging Democratic-Republican majority party. Their vision of a nonsectarian republican Ireland and thus a republican nonsectarian Irish America had a powerful effect on Irish American life in their day. Though they were influential throughout the country, they were strongest in the nation's two leading cities, New York and Philadelphia.

The Society of United Irishmen was founded in Ireland in 1791, but by 1794 the British government had begun to crack down on the republican Irish nationalists, driving many of their leaders underground or into exile. Among those fleeing to America were Wolfe Tone, James Napper Tandy, and Archibald Hamilton Rowan. Tone would return to Europe after making contacts with the French in Philadelphia and would eventually enlist French support for an uprising in Ireland. Others like Napper Tandy would also return to Ireland, but many who fled that first crackdown or were forced into exile after the failure of the rebellion of 1798 settled in the United States. John Daly Burk, for example, fled Ireland to escape arrest as a leader of the United Irishmen in 1797, settling first in Boston, then New York, and eventually Virginia. Burk was a playwright (his works include "Bunker Hill," the first play written about the American Revolution), newspaperman, and historian. John Binns was an Irishman living in England and working for republican causes there before he was forced into exile. Binns settled in Philadelphia where he became an influential editor and politician. New York City attracted a remarkable trio of exiles after the failure of the Rebellion of 1798: Thomas Addis Emmett, William Sampson, and James MacNeven. Sampson and Emmett were lawyers and though both were Protestants they became stout defenders of New York's Irish Catholics. In 1813, Sampson defended the priest Anthony Kohlman, for example, in a famous case when Kohlman refused to break the seal of confession, a sacred obligation of secrecy for Catholic priests hearing the sins of their parishioners, to testify against a thief who had stolen from the priest's St. Peter's parish. Emmet and Sampson also defended Catholics arrested in an Orange-Green riot in 1824. They persistently argued for a republican vision of America that would brook no sectarianism, invoking Ireland's sorry history of religious conflict as an example of sectarianism's dangers. MacNeven was Catholic and a doctor trained on the European continent who collaborated with Emmet on a history of Ireland and with Emmet and Sampson participated in all of the important local Irish organizations of early nineteenth century New York. Singly or collectively, the three led such organizations as the Shamrock Friendly Association, which was linked to DeWitt Clinton's Democrats; the Emigration Society, which encouraged Irish colonization in the western United States; and the Friends of Ireland, in behalf Catholic Emancipation. Like most of the middle-class or aristocratic United Irish exiles, Emmett and Sampson were largely indifferent to workingmen's efforts to organize, but unlike some United Irishmen, Emmett opposed slavery. By the 1830s, the tide had begun to turn in New York and elsewhere against the United Irish exiles. Emmet was dead and MacNeven would retire to Washington. Sampson's fate symbolized the decline of the old exiles and the changes in the Irish American community. Sampson alienated newer Irish immigrants by opposing their hero Andrew Jackson on the issue of a national bank. In 1834, Sampson lost a bid to become state senator in a bitter and violent election, as new and largely Catholic Irish immigrants turned against him.

Walsh, Michael   Michael "Mike" Walsh was perhaps the most prominent Irish Democratic working-class politician in the antebellum period. He embodied a new kind of Irish politician and a new style of politics: the working-class populist rabble-rouser, violent in methods and speech, fierce in opposition to aristocrats, and stout in defense of republican equality. Yet he also embodied the rancid racism of those Irish Democrats.

Mike Walsh was born into a Protestant Church of Ireland family in the seaport town of Youghal in County Cork, Ireland, in 1810. His father was a cabinetmaker and a veteran of the 1798 rebellion. When Mike was still a small boy, the family emigrated to the United States and his father set up a furniture shop in New York. Mike Walsh became apprenticed to an engraver and traveled across the south in the 1830s before resurfacing in New York as a newspaper reporter in 1839. He eventually started his own paper, the *Subterranean*, and combined that voice with the "muscle" of his own political club, the Spartan Associates, founded in 1840. In 1841, he ran for Congress, endorsed by Bishop Hughes, but managed only to split the Democratic vote, which allowed the Whig candidate to win. In 1842, he traveled to Providence, Rhode Island, to join the Dorr radicals in their war on the Rhode Island state government and in 1844, he visited Brook Farm. Yet it was in New York that he made himself a force as the leader of the "Shirtless Democrats." Dressed in the rough clothes of a workingman but carrying a diamond-headed cane, he excoriated aristocrats, Yankee entrepreneurs, and the British Empire, and lashed at capitalism's reduction of workingmen to servile dependence in speeches laced with New York slang. Meanwhile, his Spartan Association backed his acrid rhetoric with the roughhouse tactics then becoming common in New York City politics. The combination helped elect him to the state assembly in 1846 and to Congress in 1852. However, by that time Walsh had become as much a Democratic Party apologist for Southern slavery as a fighter for working-men's rights. He had linked up with supporters of John C. Calhoun as early as 1843 in their mutual enmity against high-tariff Yankees and blacks, and by the 1850s the defense of slavery became his obsession. Defeated for reelection in 1854, he went to Europe to conduct some business but came back a broken man. Always a prodigious drinker, he drank himself to death on St. Patrick's Day in 1859.

The Whiskey Rebellion   The Whiskey Rebellion of 1794 was a back coun-try revolt of mostly farmers, many of them of Irish background, located in the Laurel Highlands of southwestern Pennsylvania. The rebellion focused on federal authority, especially the excise tax on whiskey. Following the American Revolution, there were many contributory issues to the increase of political partisanship that ultimately resulted in violent confrontation. Among these factors were debates about the rights and obligations of citizen-ship, the relationship between the federal and state governments, political representation and legitimate taxation, regional disputes between eastern commercial interests and western settlers, the future of westward expan-sion and the fate of the Indians, land rivalries with European powers such as Britain and Spain, and trade and navigation on the Mississippi River. Above all these issues was the hated and controversial excise on domesti-cally distilled spirits, primarily whiskey, enacted by Congress in 1791 at the instigation of the Secretary of the Treasury Alexander Hamilton, with the intention of both reducing the national debt and demonstrating the power of the new federal government. Back country farmers who distilled and drank whiskey in large amounts resisted federal tax collectors. In July 1794, despite the presence of a detachment of soldiers from Fort Pitt, hundreds of armed men attacked and burned the house of regional tax inspector John Neville after he refused to resign his position and surrender records associated with tax collection. From there, opposition spread until about 7,000 men marched to Pittsburgh, where they faked an attack on Fort Pitt and the federal arsenal there, destroyed private property, and rounded up and banished several residents they found disagreeable. Violence spread to western Maryland, where a Hagerstown crowd raised "liberty poles" and threatened the arsenal at Frederick. At about the same time, sympathetic "friends of liberty" mobilized in Carlisle, Pennsylvania, and back country regions of Virginia and Kentucky. Reports reached the federal government in Philadelphia that the western country was in chaos, with frontier separatists negotiating with representatives of Great Britain and Spain, two of the United States' most formidable European rivals. In response, the following month President George Washington issued a congressionally authorized proclamation ordering the rebels to return home and calling for militia from the states of Maryland, New Jersey, Pennsylvania, and Virginia. After inconclusive negotiations, Washington nationalized about 13,000 militiamen from the aforementioned states—roughly the size of the Continental Army he had commanded during the Revolution—and personally led the "Watermelon Army," as it was derisively called, west to attack and eliminate the insurgency. However, there were no battles and opposition swiftly collapsed as government troops occupied the region. A few rebels were tried, but the two convicted of treason were later pardoned by the president. Many Americans, particularly members of the opposition Jeffersonian Republican Party, were uncomfortable with the use of overwhelming governmental force. They feared such action could be a first step to absolute power. Federalists, however, believed that the most important result was that national authority triumphed over its first rebellious adversary and won the support of the state governments in enforcing federal laws within the states. It is of some note that Herman Husband, a Carolina Regulator twenty years before, was jailed in 1794 and 1795 for his minor role as an itinerant preacher who argued for political reform and moderate resistance to the tax. (WJS)

PART IV

Chronology of Irish America

1169	Normans invade Ireland from Wales
1315	Scots under Edward Bruce invade Ireland
1366	Statutes of Kilkenny prohibit intermarriage between English and Irish and English adoption of Irish language and customs
1495	Poyning's Law restricts power of Irish parliaments
1534	Henry VIII becomes head of the English Church
1541	Ireland raised from a Lordship to a Kingdom under Henry VIII
1595	Hugh O'Neill, Earl of Tyrone, and Hugh O'Donnell, Earl of Tyrconnell, begin war against England
1598	O'Neill's great victory at Yellow Ford in Ulster
1601	Defeat of O'Neill, O'Donnell, and the Spaniards by Mountjoy at Battle of Kinsale
1607	September 4, "The Flight of the Earls": Ulster lords Hugh O'Neill, Earl of Tyrone, and Rory O'Donnell, Earl of Tyrconnell, flee to Europe
1609	Chief Justice Sir James Ley's and Sir John Davies's "Orders and Conditions" issued, laying the framework for the plantation of Ulster lands by English and Scottish landowners and their tenants over the next several years
1625	Sixmilewater revival among Protestant dissenters in Ulster
1638	Signing of the National Covenant and Episcopacy abolished by the General Assembly in Scotland.
1636	The ship *Eagle Wing*, sailing from Belfast, aborts an attempt to reach New England due to storms
1641	Catholics own about 59 percent of the land in Ireland
	Irish uprising touches off fifteen years of war among a variety of parties, the King of England, the English parliament, the Gaelic Irish, and the Scots
1642	June 10: First formal presbytery established among Presbyterians in Ulster
1649	August 15: Oliver Cromwell begins his conquest of Ireland
1653	September: English parliament passes land settlement legislation and that eventually leads to the displacement of many Catholic landowners
1660	Restoration of Charles II
1672	About 100,000 Scots live in Ireland, largely in Ulster, and about 200,000 English live throughout the provinces, out of a total of about 1.3 million people in Ireland

1680	Evidence of Ulster Presbyterian settlement in Maryland
1682	Evidence of Ulster Presbyterian settlement in South Carolina
1683	Thomas Dongan appointed governor of New York
	Presbyterian minister Francis Makemie sails to America, where he begins preaching in Virginia, Maryland, and the Carolinas
1688	Catholics own about 22 percent of the land in Ireland
	Glorious Revolution deposes James in England and Scotland. Gates of Derry shut in face of James's troops in Ireland.
1689	Siege and relief of Derry
1690	Presbyterianism reestablished in Scotland
	First Synod of Ulster Presbyterians established
	William of Orange (William III) defeats King James II at Battle of the Boyne
1691	William's army defeats James's army at Aughrim, and Catholics surrender at Limerick and sign Treaty of Limerick
1695	Anti-Catholic Penal Laws introduced, restricting Catholic rights to education and bear arms
	First known American use of the term "Scotch-Irish" in Maryland
1696	April: Irish linen exports to England freed of duties
1697	September: Penal laws banish Catholic bishops and religious order priests
1699	The Wool Act passed by the British parliament prevents Irish woolens from being exported anywhere but to England
1700	Ulster produces 12,000 yards of linen
1702–1713	Queen Anne's War (War of the Spanish Succession)
1704	March: Test Act passed, requiring all officeholders in Ireland to take the sacrament according to the prescriptions of the established church, which excludes Protestant dissenters, such as Presbyterians, from holding office. Restrictions are also imposed on Catholic landholding.
1706	Francis Makemie creates first American presbytery of Presbyterian Church in Accomack, Virginia
1707	United Kingdom of Great Britain formed from the union of England and Scotland
1710	Ulster sends 1.5 million yards of linen to England
1711	The Irish parliament establishes the Linen Board to encourage investment in the linen industry

1715	Ulster's population estimated at about 600,000 people, out of a total population in Ireland of about 2.1 million. An estimated 200,000 of Ulster's people are Presbyterians.
1717–1718	First major wave of Scotch-Irish immigration to America, with over a dozen ships arriving in Philadelphia
1718	The "Five Ships" migration of Ulster Scottish Presbyterians go to Boston
1719	November: Toleration Act provides educational and religious liberties to dissenters in Ireland
	Rev. John Abernethy of Belfast Presbyterian Society declares all doctrine nonessential on which "human reason and Christian sincerity permitted men to differ," setting off a battle between New and Old Light ministers
1720	Declaratory Act passed by the British parliament, permitting that parliament to pass laws of sufficient force to bind the Kingdom of Ireland to Britain
1725–1729	Second wave of Scotch-Irish immigration to America, primarily to Pennsylvania
1727	First year of three years of poor harvests in Ireland
1734	Irish-born Gilbert Tennent insists on examinations of ministers in the Presbyterian church to show evidence of their conversion to bolster the church against the "declining power of godliness"
1735	William Tennent moves to Warminster township in Pennsylvania and begins his famous Log College, an informal seminary for preachers in the Great Awakening
1736	James Logan becomes the acting Governor of Pennsylvania
1737	The Charitable Society of Boston celebrates St. Patrick's Day with a banquet
1740	Ulster sends 6.4 million yards of linen to England
	March 8: Gilbert Tennent delivers his sermon *Dangers of an Unconverted Ministry*
1740–1741	Famine in Ireland kills up to one-fifth of the Irish population in what becomes known as "The Year of the Great Slaughter"
	Third wave of Scotch-Irish immigration, with the first movements beyond the confines of Pennsylvania to the southwest, through the Shenandoah Valley of Virginia, whose southern extremity opens out toward North and South Carolina
1744	The English take control of the Great Wagon Road

1754–1755	Fourth wave of Scotch-Irish immigration, settling mostly in North and South Carolina
1754–1763	French and Indian War
1756–1763	Seven Years War
1764	Paxton Boys uprising by largely Scotch-Irish frontiersman. They assault friendly native Americans and march on Philadelphia.
1766	The first St. Patrick's Day parade in North America undertaken by Irish-born soldiers in the British army quartered in New York City
1768	The Regulators first erupt in the North Carolina back country
1770	Charles Carroll of Carrolton emerges as a spokesman for the patriots opposing the British in the lead-up to the American Revolution
1771	May 16: Colonial militia rout the Regulator rebels at the Battle of the Alamance
1772–1773	Linen market collapses in Ireland, encouraging migration to North America
1771–1775	Fifth wave of Scotch-Irish immigration, spread out widely from New York to Georgia
1775	Catholics own about 5 percent of land in Ireland
	April: American Revolution begins
	November: Irish parliament agrees to the removal of some English troops to fight in America
1776	July 4: Declaration of Independence signed by Irish American Charles Carroll
	Nearly 600 Presbyterian congregations exist in the United States
1779	March 17: Parade by Irish-born, largely Catholic, soldiers serving in the British Army led by Protestant Colonel Lord Rawdon in New York City
1782	Henry Grattan and Ireland's parliament, inspired in part by the American Revolution, assert the Irish Parliament's independence of English interference
1783	January 20: Treaty of Paris ending the American Revolution and granting American independence goes into effect, after Britain reaches an agreement with France. Immigration from Ireland to America resumes, as an estimated 5,000 leave from Ulster ports and Dublin for the New World.

1783	St. Peters, the first Catholic church in New York, founded
1788	Holy Cross, Boston's first Catholic church, founded
	January: First fleet of convicts, including some Irish, lands in Australia
1789	John Carroll elected and confirmed by the Vatican as bishop of the new see of Baltimore, encompassing the entire United States
1791	October 18: Society of United Irishmen founded in Belfast
	September 26: First ship of convicts sent directly from Ireland lands in Australia
1794	July–November: Whiskey Rebellion erupts in western Pennsylvania against federal excise tax among backwoods farmers, largely Ulster Irish in background
1795	The Orange Order is founded in Ireland
	June 24: John Jay's treaty with Britain ratified by the Senate. Irish immigrant Republicans had opposed it over its concessions to Britain when the terms were announced in March.
	Wolfe Tone arrives in Philadelphia
1798	May 23: Rebellion in Ireland breaks out around Dublin. It spreads to the north in Ulster and south into Leinster, and ends September 8 with the defeat of a French invasion force at Ballinamuck.
	June 18 to July 14: Alien, Sedition, and Naturalization Acts passed by the Federalist government in Washington, changing the waiting period required for citizenship from five to fourteen years, authorizing the president to deport or imprison dangerous aliens and imprison or fine writers defaming the government. Matthew Lyon is prosecuted, imprisoned, and fined under the Sedition Act.
1799	February 9: Riot at St. Mary's Church in Philadelphia, between Irish Catholic Federalists and Irish Catholic and Protestant Republicans over the new Alien, Sedition, and Naturalization acts passed by the Federalists
	Thomas McKean elected governor of Pennsylvania
1800	December 3: Thomas Jefferson elected president, supported by most United Irish exiles and probably most Ulster Irish immigrants and their descendants
1801	January 1: Identical legislation passed by the parliaments in Britain and Ireland unite Britain and Ireland through an Act of

	Union. The Irish parliament is eliminated and Ireland gains seats in the United Kingdom's parliament in London.
1803	United Kingdom's Passenger Act sets requirements for provisions and passengers per ton for emigrant vessels. The rules discriminate against American vessels.
1803–1805	Irish trade had shifted from Philadelphia to New York City. 58 percent of ships leaving Ireland head for New York in these years.
1805	Robert Patterson, United Irish Exile, appointed Director of the Mint by President Jefferson
1815	The end of the Napoleonic Wars opens up the sea lanes to emigration traffic. 20,000 leave Ireland for North America.
1818	3,000 Irish-born are laboring on the Erie Canal
1819	Economic depression, the "Panic of 1819," in the United States temporarily discourages immigration from Ireland
1820	St. Louis Irish celebrate St. Patrick's Day with a dinner
1822	Irish-born Catholic Bishop John England, inspired by American republicanism, issues a constitution for his Charleston diocese
1823	Catholic Association established in Ireland to campaign for Catholic Emancipation and full civil rights for Catholics
1824	Catholic "rent" introduced by Daniel O'Connell transforms the campaign for Catholic emancipation by enlisting the peasantry and making it a mass movement
	July 12: Orange-Green riot in Greenwich Village, New York, between Protestant and Catholic Irish immigrants
1825	The New York City Irish form societies to back Daniel O'Connell's Catholic Emancipation movement
1826	Irish-born Catholic Bishop John England is invited to address Congress
	Catholic voters in Ireland, acting to achieve Catholic Emancipation, inflict defeats on opponents of Emancipation
1828	O'Connell wins a by-election in County Clare in Ireland for a seat in the United Kingdom's parliament. Though as a Catholic he is not allowed to take his seat, his victory convinces the government to grant Catholic emancipation.
	12,488 Irish immigrate to the United States, exceeding 10,000 for the first time since official counts began in 1820
	December 3: Second-generation Irish Andrew Jackson elected president

1829	April 13: Catholic Relief Act passed, granting Catholic Emancipation
1830	First St. Patrick's Day parade in Lowell, Massachusetts
1831	July 12, Orange-Green riot in Philadelphia between Protestant and Catholic Irish
1834	1,800 Irish laboring on the Chesapeake and Ohio Canal
	January 24: County Longford immigrants fight County Cork immigrant laborers working on the Chesapeake and Ohio Canal at Williamsport, Maryland, killing five of them
	August 12 to 15: Whites, including many Irish, attack African Americans in the "Flying Horse Riot" in Philadelphia
	William Sampson, United Irish Exile defeated in race for Congress by new Irish immigrant voters, signaling the passing of the exile's influence and the emergence of a new kind of Irish politics and leadership in America
	Convent of the Ursuline Sisters in Charlestown, Massachusetts is attacked by a nativist mob
	24,474 Irish immigrate to the United States, exceeding 20,000 for the first time since official counts began in 1820
	By this year 80 percent of Irish immigrants leave for North America from Liverpool
1835	Philadelphia Irish immigrant coal heavers on Schuylkill River go on strike, prompting a general strike in Philadelphia
1836	The Boston newspaper the *Jesuit*, founded in 1829, is renamed the *Pilot*
	30,758 Irish immigrate to the United States, exceeding 30,000 for the first time since official counts began in 1820
1838	January 7: John Hughes becomes coadjutor bishop of New York and after Bishop Dubois suffers a stroke two weeks later, Hughes takes control of the diocese
1840	Bishop Hughes of New York proposes that Catholics receive a share of the New York State education appropriation
1841	First broadly popular St. Patrick's Day parade in Boston
1842	University of Notre Dame founded in South Bend, Indiana
	Bishop Hughes creates his own slate of candidates for state elections. A nativist mob erupts in violent protest, stoning the bishop's house.
	51,342 Irish immigrate to the United States, exceeding 50,000 for the first time since official counts began in 1820

	August: A riot erupts in Philadelphia's southern suburb of Moyamensing, as largely Irish white workers attack African Americans
1843	Sisters of Mercy from Carlow in Ireland arrive in Pittsburgh. This is the first establishment of the Sisters of Mercy in the United States.
	Holy Cross College founded in Worcester, Massachusetts
1843–1844	The potato blight appears in North America, severely damaging crops in the northeastern United States. It may have been brought from there to Europe on vessels from New York, Philadelphia, or Baltimore.
1844	May 3: A riot erupts in Philadelphia's Kensington neighborhood, pitting Irish Catholics against Protestants, many of them Irish. Rioting erupts again on July 4. In all, thirteen people die and two Catholic churches are burned.
	James Harper elected nativist mayor of New York City. John Hughes promises to make New York "another Moscow" if nativists threaten any Catholic churches in the city.
1845	September: A potato blight, *Phytopthora Infestans*, appears for the first time in Ireland. Most of the potato crop, two-thirds to three-quarters, survives because the blight appears so late. The government under Peel also introduces public works schemes for relief and the purchase of corn meal for cheap sale to avoid famine.
1846	The potato harvest fails almost entirely due to the blight, and the government repeals the Corn Laws, permitting easier import of foreign grain
1846–1847	Winter: The effects of the potato crop's destruction hit home, causing severe cases of malnutrition. An unusually cold and rainy winter complicates the government's efforts to address the famine through public works, as many ill-clad poor suffer in the harsh weather.
1846–1851	763,125 Irish immigrants enter the United States during the years of the Great Famine
1847	February: The government of Lord John Russell introduces a new famine policy. The government temporarily sets up soup stations to feed the starving, offering an estimated three millions meals by the summer.

June: The government shifts responsibility for relief to poor law unions in Ireland. The "Gregory Clause" forbids relief to an occupier of more than a quarter acre of land, facilitating eviction.

105,536 Irish immigrate to the United States, exceeding 100,000 for the first time since official counts began in 1820

Suffering follows the Irish peasants on to ships to America. An estimated 30 percent die on ships to Canada; 9 percent on ships to the United States.

1848   February 29: Young Ireland "rebellion" erupts and peters out in Ballingarry, County Tipperary, Ireland

1849   The Order of the Star Spangled Banner (the Know- Nothing secret society) is founded in New York City

1851   The Great Famine ends in almost all parts of Ireland

Irish immigration to the United States peaks at 221,253. It will never be this large again.

1853   The Ancient Order of Hibernians march in the New York St. Patrick's Day parade for the first time

1854   The Know-Nothings rise to power in the wake of frustration over the Kansas-Nebraska Act, elect a mayor of Philadelphia and the governor and almost the entire legislature in Massachusetts, and show great political power in other states like Delaware and Indiana

1857   July 4: "Dead Rabbits" riot erupts on the Lower East Side of New York

July 25, The *Irish American*, a New York newspaper, begins publishing a regular weekly column, "Our Gaelic Department." It will continue to do so until 1915.

1858   March 17, Irish Republican Brotherhood and Fenians are founded simultaneously in Dublin and New York respectively

1860   Dion Boucicault's play, *Colleen Bawn*, opens

The St. Patrick's Day parade in New York City includes as many as 10,000 marchers for the first time

1861   April 12: Rebel troops fire on Fort Sumter in Charleston Harbor and the Civil War begins in America

Irish Immigration to the United States falls to 23,797 with the outbreak of the Civil War in America

1862   September 17: Irish American troops distinguish themselves at the Battle of Antietam in Maryland, but also suffer heavy casualties

September 22: Abraham Lincoln makes public his intention to issue the Emancipation Proclamation, freeing slaves in the Confederate states, effective January 1, 1863

December 13: Irish American troops distinguish themselves at the battle of Fredericksburg in Virginia, but also suffer heavy casualties

1863   January 1: Emancipation formally proclaimed. Many Irish Americans resent this act as establishing abolition as the principal purpose of the war.

Boston College founded

July 2–3: Irish Americans distinguish themselves at the Battle of Gettysburg, Pennsylvania

July 13–16: Draft riots erupt in New York City, paralyzing the city and causing one hundred deaths

Irish immigration to the United States rises to 55,916

1865   October: The Fenian convention in Philadelphia creates a government in exile: a Senate, House of Delegates, and Executive

1866   May 1: Riots erupt in Memphis, Tennessee between the largely Irish police force and Black union army veterans. Forty-eight people are killed. Four black churches and twelve freedman's schools destroyed.

Fenians attack Canada across the Niagara River from Buffalo, encounter Toronto militia, and are intercepted by American authorities on their retreat back to the United States

1867   March: Fenian uprising in Ireland is quickly put down

The New York City St. Patrick's Day parade includes 20,000 men, 44 bands, and 17 carriages

June 20: The Clan na Gael founded by representatives of Fenian factions

1870   After this year, most immigrants will leave for America directly from Irish ports, not from Liverpool. Most leave from Queenstown (now called Cobh) in the south of Ireland or Moville in the north.

Patrick Ford founds the Irish World in New York

The first Vatican Council decrees papal infallibility. Irish-born

	Bishop Edward Fitzgerald of Little Rock is one of two dissenters among the world's bishops.

1871   Tweed ring and Boss William M. Tweed fall

July 12: Riot over parade by Irish Protestants celebrating William's victory at the Boyne erupts in riot. Sixty-two people are killed.

1875   December: Jeremiah O'Donovan Rossa establishes "Skirmishing Fund" to raise money for guerrilla war in Ireland

1876   April 18: Six Fenian prisoners in western Australia are rescued by the Clan na Gael's hired whaling ship, the *Catalpa*, the "Emerald Whaler"

1876–1877   Fifty men and women indicted for crimes as members of the Molly Maguires in Pennsylvania coal fields. Twenty of the men are convicted and hanged.

1877   July: Great Strike on the B&O and other American railroads begins in Baltimore and extends across the country, as close as the United States ever comes to a general strike. A substantial proportion of the workers striking are Irish.

October 3: James Gibbons becomes archbishop of Baltimore

1878   July 21: Denis Kearney, Irish-born anti-Chinese agitator, begins a tour of the East and Midwest, proclaiming the need for the exclusion of Chinese immigrants

Michael Davitt tours the United States, foreshadowing the "New Departure" in his lectures

1879   August: The Land League founded in Mayo

October: The National Land League founded in Dublin

June: New Departure launched, linking physical force nationalists, land reformers, and parliamentary home rulers

1880   William Grace is elected mayor of New York City, the first Irish American Catholic to hold this position

January to March: Parnell tours the United States, visiting sixty-two cities, raising $300,000, and addressing both houses of Congress

May 18–19: American National Land League meets for first time in convention in New York City

1880–1883   Irish immigration to the United States exceeds 70,000 for every one of these years. The total for these years, 301,863, is the largest four-year total since the Great Famine.

1880	Only 980 men march in the St. Patrick's Day parade in New York City
1881	Philadelphia gives up its St. Patrick's Day parade
1881–1885	Boston does not stage a St. Patrick's Day parade
1881	The "Triangle" of Alexander Sullivan, Michael Boland, and Dennis Feely take control of the Clan na Gael
	Michael Logan publishes *An Godhal*, a Gaelic language monthly
1882	The *Irish World* boasts 60,000 readers
	The Knights of Columbus are founded in Connecticut by Father Michael McGivney
1884	John Ireland becomes bishop of the diocese of St. Paul, Minnesota
	Hugh O'Brien elected mayor of Boston, the first Irish American Catholic to hold this position
	Third Plenary Council of American Catholic bishops at Baltimore decrees that every parish should build a school and also authorizes a common catechism for all of the United States
	The Ancient Order of Hibernians splits into factions, pitting divisions located largely around New York City against divisions from the rest of the nation
	In the presidential election, some Irish nationalists urge Irish Americans to vote for the Republican, James G. Blaine, over the Democrat, Grover Cleveland. Few Irish American voters do so.
	The Gaelic Athletic Association is founded in Ireland
1886	St. Patrick's Day parade revives in New York City with 10,000 marchers
	April 8: Irish Home Rule party and British Liberals present First Home Rule Bill to United Kingdom parliament. The Bill is defeated in June by a split in the Liberal ranks and the defection of Liberal Unionists.
	Henry George runs for mayor of New York against the Tammany candidate, splitting the city's Irish American community
1888	The Gaelic Athletic Association sends teams of Irish Footballers to the United States in the "American Invasion"
1889	May 4: Dr. Cronin, opponent of the Triangle in the Clan na Gael disappears. His body is found on May 22.

	December: Captain O'Shea cites Charles Stuart Parnell as his wife's illicit lover in divorce petition
	The Scotch-Irish Society of America is founded
1890	The Irish-born population in the United States reaches its peak. There are 1,871,509 Irish immigrants in the United States.
	Archbishop John Ireland praises public schools in address to the National Education Association
	December 6: Irish nationalist party splits into pro-Parnell and anti-Parnell factions
1891	October: Charles Stuart Parnell dies
	May: Anti-Parnellites among Irish Americans form Irish National Federation of America
1893	February 13: Liberals and Irish Home Rule party present Second Home Rule Bill. It passes the Commons on September 1, but is defeated in the House of Lords on September 8.
	John Hopkins elected mayor of Chicago, the first Irish American Catholic to hold this position
	October: Finley Peter Dunne begins his Martin Dooley columns
1896	The Ancient Order of Hibernians endows a chair in Gaelic language at Catholic University
1897	Irish immigration to the United States falls below 30,000 to 24,421 for the first time since the Civil War
1898	Gaelic League founded in America
	Factions of the Ancient Order of Hibernians are reunited
1899	January 22, Pope Leo XIII condemns a heresy called "Americanism" in an encyclical called *Testem Benevolentiae*
1900	Second-generation Irish numbers reach their peak. There are 3,375,546 children of Irish immigrants living in the United States.
1901	The United Irish League of America is founded
1902	Charles Francis Murphy becomes boss of Tammany Hall in New York City
1904	Irish County Athletic Union created among Irish county societies in New York City
1905–1906	Douglas Hyde of the Gaelic League in Ireland tours the Unites States

1905   Sinn Fein radical nationalist party founded by Arthur Griffith and Bulmer Hobson

1906   Matthew Cummings ascends to leadership of the Ancient Order of Hibernians in America and pushes them to increasing militancy in their nationalism

1907   August: William Henry O'Connell becomes Archbishop of Boston

1908   Ancient Order of Hibernians, Ancient Order of Hibernians Ladies Auxiliary, and Ancient Order of Hibernians Juvenile Divisions together count over 195,000 members

The *Pilot* becomes the Archdiocesan paper for the Archdiocese of Boston

1912   April 1: The government introduces a Home Rule bill for Ireland

1913   January 16: Home Rule Bill passes the Commons but is rejected by the House of Lords on January 30

July 7: Home Rule bill passes the Commons again, but is again rejected by the House of Lords on July 15

July 12: Resolution adopted by a unionist mass meeting at Craigovan in Ulster to resist Home Rule by force

1914   May 26: Home Rule Bill passed by Commons and under the Parliament Act of 1911 does not have to pass the House of Lords

August 4: England declares war on Germany

September 18: The Home Rule Bill receives the royal assent and becomes law

1915   Ku Klux Klan revived at Stone Mountain, Georgia. The new Klan is now anti-Catholic and anti-immigrant as well as anti-black.

1916   March: Friends of Irish Freedom founded in mass meeting at Madison Square Garden in New York City

May 8: Friends of Irish Freedom organize a meeting to protest the United Kingdom government's executions of the leaders of the Easter Week rebellion

1917   April 6: The United States declares war on Germany and enters World War I on the side of the Allies

1917–1923   Over 400,000 Catholic men join the Knights of Columbus

1918   May: The Friends of Irish Freedom call another "Race Convention" to assert Ireland's right to independence

November 11: World War I ends

December: Sinn Fein wins seventy-three out of 105 Irish seats for the United Kingdom Parliament in Westminster

December 8: Mass meetings organized by the Friends of Irish Freedom endorse the Irish revolution

December 15: Mass meetings organized by Friends of Irish Freedom to endorse the Irish revolution

1919   January: Dail Eireann founded from the Sinn Fein party members who had been elected to the United Kingdom parliament but refused to take their seats there

January 21: Irish War for Independence begins

1920   F. Scott Fitzgerald's novel *This Side of Paradise* is published

1921   July 21: Truce in the War for Irish Independence starts and negotiations begin to end the war

December 6: Negotiators agree to treaty ending the Irish War for Independence and establishing the Irish Free State

1922   January 7: The Dail votes 64 to 57 to accept the treaty creating the Irish Free State

June 28: Civil war erupts in Ireland over the treaty's terms, particularly the oath of loyalty to the King and the partition of Ulster that leaves six counties out of the new republic

December: The civil war in Ireland comes to a virtual halt

1923   April 30: Official cease-fire declared in the Irish Civil War

May 24: The Irish Republican Army factions engaged in the Irish Civil War dump their arms

1925   F. Scott Fitzgerald's novel *The Great Gatsby* is published

1926   Reverend Charles Coughlin appears for the first time on the radio

1930   Reverend Charles Coughlin begins speaking on economic and political topics and his audience grows to thirty million

1932   Irish immigration to the United States falls to 539, the lowest non-wartime total since official statistics available

1932–1939   The number of Irish immigrants to the United States remains less than 1,000 per year in each of these years

1932   James Farley becomes chairman of the national Democratic Party

James Farrell's novel *Young Lonigan* is published

1934   Fred Allen, born John Florence Sullivan, inaugurates radio show, "Town Hall Tonight"

1936	The first of James Farrell's series of Danny O'Neill novels, *World I Never Made*, is published
	Frank Murphy is elected governor of Michigan
	Reverend Charles Coughlin helps forms a third political party, the Union Party, nominating Congressman William Lemke from North Dakota as their presidential candidate and Thomas O'Brien, District Attorney of Boston, as their nominee for vice president. Monsignor John A. Ryan, a New Deal supporter, appears on a national radio broadcast to back Franklin Roosevelt and counter Coughlin.
1938	Reverend Charles Coughlin justifies the Nazi horrors of the *Kristallnacht* attacks on Jews
	The tiny remnants of the Clan na Gael led by Joseph McGarritty back the IRA diehards engaged in a bombing campaign in England
1939	September 8: Francis Spellman installed as archbishop of New York
1940	Frank Murphy is appointed to the Supreme Court by Franklin Roosevelt
1941	Eugene O'Neill completes his play *Long Day's Journey into the Night*
1943	Eugene O'Neill completes his play *A Touch of the Poet*
1945	David Lawrence elected mayor of Pittsburgh. He will serve four consecutive terms.
1946	Irish-born William O'Dwyer elected mayor of New York City. He resigns in 1949 under fire to become ambassador to Mexico.
1947	Cavan plays Kerry on the All-Ireland Irish Football final played in the Polo Grounds in New York City
	The St. Patrick's Day parade in New York City boasts 80,000 marchers and is watched by an estimated one million spectators
1948	Paul Dever elected governor of Massachusetts, the Democrats take over the state's House of Representatives for the first time in about a century, and elect Thomas P. "Tip" O'Neill as Speaker
	President Harry Truman attends the St. Patrick's Day parade in New York City
	Irish immigration to the United States rises above 3,000 for the

first time since 1931, and remains above that number until 1966

1950   February 9: Joseph McCarthy speaks at Wheeling College in West Virginia, claiming that there are 205 communists in the United States State Department

1952   Dwight Eisenhower elected president with considerable Catholic, including Irish Catholic, support

The movie *Quiet Man*, directed by John Ford, opens

1954   July 30: Senator Ralph Flanders of Vermont introduces motion to censure Joseph McCarthy

April 4: Cardinal Spellman attends a communion breakfast in New York City, where Senator Joseph McCarthy is the principal speaker. This is widely interpreted as Spellman's endorsement of McCarthy.

November: Senate censures Joseph McCarthy

1955   Richard Daley elected mayor of Chicago for the first time

William F. Buckley founds the *National Review*

Flannery O'Connor's collection of stories *A Good Man is Hard to Find* is published

1956   December 11: The IRA launches a border campaign known as Operation Harvest. This campaign lasts until 1962 with few results and no support in the United States.

William Brennan appointed to the Supreme Court

1958   David Lawrence elected governor of Pennsylvania

1959   January 25: Pope John XXIII announces his intention to convene an Ecumenical Council

1960   January 30: John F. Kennedy announces that he is running for president

American Committee (later Conference) for Irish Studies begins

July: John F. Kennedy nominated for president by the Democratic Party convention in Los Angeles

November 8: John F. Kennedy becomes the first Catholic president of the United States

1961   Irish American Michael Mansfield becomes majority leader in the Senate

January 20: John F. Kennedy inaugurated president of the United States

1962	January 10: John McCormack of Boston becomes Speaker of the House
	October 11: Second Vatican Council opens
1963	Richard J. Daley beats back the challenge of Benjamin Adamowski in race for mayor of Chicago
	June: John F. Kennedy visits Ireland and speaks to the Dail
	November 22: John F. Kennedy is assassinated in Dallas
1964	Catholic school enrollment peaks this year. It will never again be as high in absolute numbers or proportion of Catholic school children again.
	Campaign for Social Justice established in Belfast to document discrimination against Catholics
1967	Irish immigration to the United States falls below 3,000 to 2,765
	May 17: Daniel Berrigan and eight others destroy files at a Selective Service office in Catonsville, Maryland
	October 27: Philip Berrigan and three others pour blood on draft records at the selective service office in Baltimore
	November 30: Senator Eugene McCarthy declares for the presidency, running as an antiwar candidate against the incumbent, Lyndon B. Johnson, of his own party
	The Northern Ireland Civil Rights Association, founded as a civil rights movement, emerges in Ulster to fight discrimination by the Northern Irish authorities and radically transform the Northern Irish government
	American Committee for Irish Freedom founded to support Catholics and nationalists in Northern Ireland
1968	March 18: Robert Kennedy announces his candidacy for president of the United States
	June 5: Robert Kennedy, senator from New York and candidate for the Democratic nomination for president, is assassinated
	July 29: Pope Paul VI issues encyclical, *Humanitae Vitae*, reasserting the Catholic Church's traditional opposition to "artificial means" of contraception
	October 5: Major street demonstration undertaken by civil rights protestors in Derry
1969	January: NICRA organizes a march from Belfast to Derry. They are attacked by loyalists at Burntoillet Bridge in County Derry.

August 12: Battle of the Bogside breaks out in Derry between loyalists and civil rights supporters

August 14–15: Six people killed and one hundred houses wrecked as violence erupts between Catholics and Protestants and the largely Protestant police

August 24: NICRA marches from Coalisland to Dungannon in Ulster to protest housing discrimination against Catholics

August: Bernadette Devlin of NICRA visits the United States

December: The IRA splits into Official and Provisional (often called "Provos") wings

1970   John McCormack resigns from the Congress

1971   August: Security forces in Northern Ireland intern over three hundred republican suspects

1972   January 30: Thirteen demonstrators killed in confrontation with British paratroopers in Derry on "Bloody Sunday"

July 21: The Irish Republican Army sets off twenty-two bombs in the Belfast city center, killing nine people

October: Desmond O'Malley, Minster of Justice in the Republic of Ireland, tours the United States condemning the IRA

1974   September 28: Three Irish American organizations endorse the Irish National Caucus as umbrella organization for their nationalist interests

Fall: Violent protests in the Irish American neighborhood of South Boston against busing for desegregation

1975   Fall: Violent protests in Irish American neighborhoods of South Boston and Charlestown in Boston against busing for desegregation

1976   The armory in Danvers, Massachusetts is robbed. Some of the arms are sent to the Irish Republican Army by George Harrison.

1976   Ireland Fund established to raise money from Irish Americans for cultural and charitable projects in Ireland

1977   January 4: Thomas P. "Tip" O'Neill becomes Speaker of the House

March 17: The "Four Horsemen"—Teddy Kennedy, Hugh Carey, Daniel P. Moynihan, and "Tip" O'Neill—issue statements condemning organizations committed to violence

1978   Four Horsemen and other congressmen assail British government for human rights abuses in Northern Ireland

1979	George Meany retires as president of the AFL-CIO
1980	Edward "Ted" Kennedy challenges James E. "Jimmy" Carter for the Democratic Party's nomination for president
1981	March 1 to October: Hunger strikes undertaken by Irish Republican Army men imprisoned in Northern Ireland seeking recognition as political prisoners. Bobby Sands begins the strike when he refuses food.
	March 17: Friends of Ireland, a moderate nationalist group, created in Congress
	May 5: Bobby Sands dies after hunger strike in an Ulster prison. Protests organized in the United States on behalf of the hunger strikers peak in the week after Sands's death.
	Prompted by sympathy for the hunger strike, NORAID fund-raising monthly contributions rise from $5,088 in February to $84,894 in June
1982	November 2: IRA gun runner George Harrison declared not guilty by jury at his trial in an American court because the jury accepts his contention that he was working with the Central Intelligence Agency
1983	Controversy erupts over the election of NORAID's Michael Flannery as Grand Marshal of the St. Patrick's Day parade in New York City
	May 13: Gabriel Megahey and four others from New York found guilty of running guns to the IRA in Ulster
1984	November: Fair employment guidelines for Ulster launched, named after Sean MacBride principles
	Ronald Reagan elected president, rolling up large majorities among Irish American Catholics in New York and other states, but not in Massachusetts
	John J. O'Connor becomes archbishop of New York
1984–1986	Peggy Noonan serves as special assistant to Ronald Reagan, writing many of his significant speeches
1985	November 15: An Anglo-Irish agreement signed as Margaret Thatcher and Garrett Fitzgerald, Taoiseach of the Irish Republic, agree to consult regularly and formally on Northern Ireland issues
1986	Sinn Fein and NORAID leaders meet for two days to discuss Sinn Fein's politicization strategy

1987	Three men plead guilty in American court for running guns into Ireland on the fishing vessel *Valhalla*
1988	Anthony Kennedy appointed to the Supreme Court by Ronald Reagan
1989	George Mitchell becomes Senate majority leader
	June 6: Thomas S. Foley becomes Speaker of the House
	July: NORAID breaks up over Sinn Fein's new political strategy. Some militants who wish to continue the armed struggle form a new version of Friends of Irish Freedom.
	October: Fair Employment Act passed to counter job discrimination in Ulster
1993	December 15: Downing Street Declaration by John Major of Britain and Albert Reynolds of Ireland assuring Sinn Fein a place in future political discussions, if the IRA abandons campaign of violence
1994	January: The United States permits Sinn Fein leader Gerry Adams to visit
	August 31: The IRA agrees to a cease-fire
	The American Conference for Irish Studies lists 454 colleges and universities offering one or more courses in Irish Studies
1995	Sinn Fein opens an office in Washington D.C.
	November: President Bill Clinton visits Northern Ireland
1996	February 9: The IRA ends its cease-fire with a bombing of Canary Wharf on the London docks
	The Irish dance and musical production "Riverdance" comes to New York
1997	Tony Blair and the Labor Party come to power in the United Kingdom
1998	April: The "Good Friday Agreement" is completed, calling for a new local government in Northern Ireland, a reform of the police, and decommissioning of arms by the IRA and other paramilitary groups
	May 22: The Good Friday agreement is submitted to a referendum in the north and south of Ireland, winning over 70 percent approval in Northern Ireland and over 90 percent in the Republic

PART V

Annotated Bibliography

IRELAND

Bourke, Joanna. *Husbandry to Housewifery: Women, Economic Change, and Home-work in Ireland, 1890–1914*. New York: Clarendon Press, 1993.

During this era, Irish women left work in the fields and other men's homes to perform housework for husbands, brothers, or other relatives. Bourke notes that at this time, the Irish rural economy was booming, as prices for Irish agricultural products and the island's agricultural production both rose. Thus, ironically, as Irish agricultural families grew richer, women's opportunities for work outside the home narrowed.

Boyce, D. George and Alan O'Day, eds. *The Making of Modern Irish History: Revisionism and Recent Controversy*. London: Routledge, 1996.

Over the last thirty or forty years, a controversy over revisionism has dominated the study of Ireland's history. The revisionists attacked old nationalist histories that the revisionists believed placed undue emphasis on British colonial repression in Irish history and overlooked the weaknesses of the new twentieth-century nationalist state. This collection includes essays discussing revisionists and their critics on topics such as the Great Famine, nationalism, the Home Rule movement, the 1916 uprising, and the Irish diaspora.

Clear, Catriona. *Women of the House: Women's Household Work in Ireland, 1926–1963*. Dublin: Irish Academic Press, 2000.

Housewives comprised the largest percentage of women working in this period. Clear questions the notion that women were cowed, and argues that women had more power than previously thought. She also believes that the new Republic of Ireland was not as misogynistic as previously thought, and doubts that a tightly coherent domestic ideology existed in Ireland during the early twentieth century.

Connell, K. H. *Irish Peasant: Four Historical Essays*. Oxford: Clarendon Press, 1961.

This is one of the most important studies of Irish family and marital behavior in the early nineteenth century. Connell argues that changing landholding patterns, the shift to pasturage, the growing size of farms, and the spread of the custom of impartible inheritance forced a change in marriage behavior, from early marriage in the older system before the Great Famine to distinctively late average ages of marriage in the late nineteenth and twentieth centuries.

Connolly, Sean J. *Priests and People in Pre-Famine Ireland, 1780 –1845*. Dublin: Gill and MacMillan, 1982.

An excellent survey of religious practice among the Irish peasants in the century or so before the Great Famine, it provides enormous insight into a broad array of topics, from sexual morality among Irish peasants to their ritual practices. Despite efforts to improve education and evidence of spreading devotionalism in the late eighteenth and early nineteenth centuries, Connolly finds most Irish laity woefully uninformed and practicing a faith that was a complicated amalgam of official orthodoxy, magical beliefs, and agricultural customs.

Connolly, Sean J., ed. *The Oxford Companion to Irish History*. Oxford: Oxford University Press, 1998.

This is a terrifically useful resource, with thousands of entries on every aspect of Irish history from ancient times to the present. The contributors include excellent historians of Ireland: Mary Daly, Vincent Comerford, Peter Gray, and Alvin Jackson, among others. It concentrates overwhelmingly on Irish history, but some topics in Irish American or the history of the Irish diaspora are covered too. The entries are generally short, ranging from about a hundred words for a definition of the Gregory Clause to over a thousand words in the entry on the Great Famine. The volume is also extensively cross-referenced.

Donnelly, James. *The Great Irish Potato Famine*. Phoenix Mill, England: Sutton Publishing, 2001.

This is a superb analytical narrative of the Great Famine's history, exploring in detail the famine's origins, its effects, and especially local and United Kingdom relief policies and administration. Donnelly does not accept the traditional John Mitchel notion that Ireland would have produced enough food to feed itself had its ports been closed and had no food been exported, but he makes a very strong, meticulously detailed argument against United Kingdom policy, particularly the United Kingdom's abdication of its role in relief and passage of legislation easing evictions after 1847.

Donnelly, James and Samuel Clark, eds. *Irish Peasants: Violence and Political Unrest, 1780–1914*. Madison: University of Wisconsin Press, 1983.

This is an excellent collection of essays on Irish peasant life. An essay by Donnelly on secret societies in Ireland is particularly interesting and helpful.

Donnelly, James and Kerby Miller. *Irish Popular Culture, 1650–1850*. Dublin: Irish Academic Press, 1998.

This is a rich collection of essays on Irish social and cultural history that addresses a wide array of topics. Particularly good are the essays by Miller on the declining Protestant presence in pre-famine southern Ireland, Ó Crualaoich on wakes, Malcolm on pubs, Ó Giolláin on patterns, Whelan on the Underground Gentry, and especially Owens on parades and processions during the Repeal movement.

Guinnane, Timothy. *The Vanishing Irish: Households, Migration, and the Rural Economy in Ireland*. Princeton, N.J.: Princeton University Press, 1997.

This is the newest and most sophisticated scholarly examination of Ireland's demographic history. It revises previous interpretations of the history of Irish marriage, sexuality, and marital fertility. On Irish fertility or childbearing, for example, Guinnane argues that while Irish fertility rates remained higher than in some other European urban societies, it began to drop at the end of the nineteenth and beginning of the

twentieth centuries, suggesting that the Irish were practicing some type of family limitation or birth control by that point. Moreover, since differences between Protestant
and Catholic fertility rates were not significant, high Irish Catholic birth rates cannot
be attributed to religious beliefs. In overall terms, Guinnane believes that Irish demographic patterns have not been unique or peculiar when compared to demographic
trends throughout rural parts of Europe.

Hachey, Thomas and Lawrence McCaffrey. *Perspectives on Irish Nationalism.* Lexington: University Press of Kentucky, 1989.

This is a collection of essays edited by leading historians of Ireland and Irish America. Several of the essays are excellent, but particularly interesting are the pieces on
folklore and nationalism by Thuente, and on literature and nationalism by Flanagan.

Hechter, Michael. *Internal Colonialism: The Celtic Fringe in British National Development, 1536–1966.* Berkeley: University of California Press, 1975.

A powerful and sophisticated argument by a leading theoretician of ethnic and national conflict, it sheds interesting light on the roots of Irish nationalism. Hechter argues
that while northeastern Ulster was largely integrated into Britain's industrial economy,
southern Ireland remained an "internal colony" in the United Kingdom, the conflict of
economic interests with the British metropolis thus nurturing Irish nationalism.

Jordan, Donald. *Land and Popular Politics in Ireland: County Mayo from the Plantation to the Land War.* New York: Cambridge University Press, 1994.

Jordan's book analyzes the changing fortunes of peasants in the western county of
Mayo over several centuries, but focuses in particular on the years just before, during,
and after the Land League agitation of the early 1880s. Jordan found that poorer tenants working smaller, economically untenable plots joined the Land League during
the agricultural crisis of the late 1870s, hoping for the redistribution of land from richer
tenants to poorer ones. Once it became clear that the league would not do that, many
of those small farmers left for America.

Kennedy, Liam, Paul S. Ell, E. M. Crawford, and L. A. Clarkson. *Mapping the Great
Irish Famine: A Survey of the Famine Decades.* Dublin: Four Courts, 1999.

These maps are based largely on returns from the Irish censuses of 1841, 1851,
1861, and 1871, but also includes maps drawn on other government statistical information, such as the Poor Law Inquiry of 1836. Focusing on topics ranging from manufacturing to average age of marriage to the percentage of Irish speakers, the maps graphically demonstrate both the critical regional distinctions in Irish economic and social
life and the dramatic effect of the Great Famine on both.

Larkin, Emmett. "The Devotional Revolution in Ireland." *American Historical Review*
77, no. 3 (June 1972): 625–652.

One of the most influential articles written in recent years on Catholicism in Ireland, Larkin contends that Catholic religious practice was remade in the nineteenth
century. A people steeped in a folk religion who were only loosely anchored to insti-

tutional Catholicism before the Great Famine became a rigorously disciplined and
devoted Catholic faithful after it, boasting one of the highest mass attendance rates
in the world and a surfeit of priests and nuns. Larkin attributed the change to the
famine's virtual destruction of an older traditional Gaelic culture and language and
the need of the Irish people to find a new cultural identity to replace the one that
they had lost.

Miller, David W. "Irish Catholicism and the Great Famine." *Journal of Social History*
9, no. 1 (1975): 81–98.

This is a very important article on Irish Catholicism in the pre-famine era. Using
a census of chapels and churches from the early 1830s, Miller provides estimates of
regular church attendance for a sample of Catholic chapels from different parts of the
island. Miller finds that mass attendance varied widely from the impoverished districts
of the west to the richer more modern areas of the east.

O'Grada, Cormac. *Black '47 and Beyond: The Great Irish Famine in History, Economy,
and Memory*. Princeton, N.J.: Princeton University Press, 1999.

This is a thorough and insightful study of the Great Famine in Ireland that addresses all of the critical questions: how does the Great Famine compare in mortality
and havoc to other famines past and present? Who died, and of what causes? Who left
for America and Britain? Who profited from the famine? What role did the landlords
play? Was the famine inevitable? Was the United Kingdom government's policy appropriate? Could that government have done more?

O'Grada, Cormac. *Ireland: A New Economic History, 1780–1939*. New York: Oxford
University Press, 1994.

A broad history of Ireland's economy by Ireland's premier economic historian, it
has an especially interesting and provocative analysis of the potato's role in Ireland's
population growth and a reevaluation of the significance of the end of the Napoleonic
Wars in 1815 on the Irish economy.

Poirtier, Cathal. *Famine Echoes*. Dublin: Gill and MacMillan, 1995.

This is a collection of folk memories drawn from the Folklore Commission Archives in Ireland. It is an interesting selection, including recollections by the children
and grandchildren of the Great Famine generation about stories their forefathers and
mothers told about the pre-famine period, starvation, relief, "gombeen men," landlords, emigration, and the legacies of the famine.

Scally, Robert James. *The End of Hidden Ireland: Rebellion, Famine, and Emigration*.
New York: Oxford University Press, 1995.

This is a beautifully written and finely argued study of the people of the townland of Ballykilcline, County Roscommon, in pre-famine and famine-era Ireland. Ballykilcline was part of a Crown estate. By an oversight by Crown officials, the peasants
there managed to avoid paying rent for several years. The Crown eventually evicted
them during the famine. The case produced sufficient evidence to permit Scally to

probe deeply into the inner life of this townland's people. The result is probably the richest analysis of a local Irish community from top to bottom in recent Irish historiography. Like Kerby Miller, Scally strongly argues for the importance of communal loyalties in structuring life among Irish peasants in this era.

OVERVIEWS OF THE IRISH IN AMERICA

Blessing, Patrick. *The Irish in America: A Guide to the Literature and the Manuscript Collections*. Washington, D.C.: Catholic University of America Press, 1992.

Though now over a decade old, this is still a helpful resource for the study of Irish American history. The bibliography is comprehensive and covers such sources as statistical resources and reference works as well as subject headings including politics, religion, labor, and nationalism. The guide to the archives and manuscript collections is unique. The volume also contains some useful statistics on Irish immigration to America.

Clark, Dennis. *Hibernia America: The Irish and Regional Cultures*. Westport, Conn.: Greenwood Press, 1976.

This is a wide-ranging survey of the regional differences in Irish American experiences. Clark takes to heart the critique of Donald Akenson and others that the Irish diaspora experience has been interpreted too much through the lens of the history of Irish Americans in large East Coast cities. The book thus has chapters not only on New England, New York, Pennsylvania and the Midwest, but also the South, Southwest, Far West and Northwest.

Cronin, Mike and Daryl Adair. *The Wearing of the Green: A History of St. Patrick's Day*. London: Routledge, 2002.

The book is a very useful and comprehensive survey of the celebration of St. Patrick's Day throughout the Irish diaspora. It begins with how Ireland commemorated the day largely as a religious holy day, but with some balls, banquets, and military reviews by the Anglo-Irish establishment in the late eighteenth and early nineteenth centuries. Cronin and Adair recount the emergence of the holiday as a major celebration in the colonies and later, the United States, Canada, Australia and Britain, and its eventual return to Ireland.

Dezell, Maureen. *Irish America Coming into Clover: The Evolution of a People and a Culture*. New York: Doubleday, 2000.

A broad, often insightful, and very readable survey of Irish America's history and particularly its current state, by a distinguished journalist. The chapters on women, the images of Irish Americans, and Irish American attitudes toward upward mobility are particularly interesting.

Doyle, David. "The Regional Bibliography of Irish America, 1880 to 1930: An Addendum." *Irish Historical Studies* 13, no. 1 (May 1983): 254–283.

Though ostensibly merely an addendum to Saemus Metress's bibliography of Irish America, Doyle also briefly but insightfully discusses the importance of regional distinctions in Irish American experiences.

Doyle, David and Owen Dudley Edwards. *America and Ireland, 1776–1976: The American Identity and the Irish Connection*. Westport, Conn.: Greenwood Press, 1976.

Among its many essays on Irish America and America's relationship with Ireland, this collection includes excellent essays on Irish music in America by Williams and the Irish in American labor by Montgomery.

Funchion, Michael. *Irish American Voluntary Organizations*. Westport, Conn.: Greenwood Press, 1983.

This is a very helpful, rich resource for the history of a wide range of Irish American organizations. The entries are long, detailed, well researched, and well argued. Entries on the Land League, the Fenians, Clan na Gael, and the Ancient Order of Hibernians, for example, are probably the best introductions to the histories of those major organizations, but the book also includes substantive histories of scores of less well-known Irish American associations and clubs.

Glazer, Michael. *The Encyclopedia of the Irish in America*. Notre Dame, Ind.: University of Notre Dame Press, 1999.

This is a mammoth, nearly one-thousand-page reference book, containing nearly nine hundred separate entries. Subjects include every important figure, event, organization, topic, or trend in Irish American history. For example, the biographies range from St. Brendan the Navigator to the contemporary actor Pierce Brosnan, with every important, novelist, architect, mother superior, politician, Fenian, and army general in Irish American history in between. This breadth makes it is exceptionally useful, but there are also very helpful special features, such as articles on the Irish American experience in different states or in important cities.

Kenny, Kevin. *The American Irish: A History*. Harlow, U.K.: Longman, 2000.

The best short history of the Irish in the United States and probably the best book to begin study of the subject. It is lucidly written, well informed, and comprehensive, running from the eighteenth-century Ulster Scot migration through recent Irish illegal immigrants in the 1980s. It provides useful short biographies of leading Irish Americans and addresses several important topics in the historiography of the American Irish, such as the roles of women, the whiteness controversy, and machine politics. It is arranged chronologically, with separate sections on such topics as labor, gender, nativism, politics, nationalism, and religion within each period.

McCaffrey, Lawrence. *The Irish Catholic Diaspora in America*. Washington D.C.: Catholic University of America Press, 1997.

Originally published in 1976, the book was revised, updated, and republished in 1997. McCaffrey's book is a broad short essay exploring both the Irish background in the old country and Irish American experiences in the New World. McCaffrey believes that the Irish were urban pioneers in America, blazing a trail in American cities for later ethnic and racial migrants. While not underestimating the harsh conditions Irish immigrants suffered in the United States, he points to the eventual broad and impressive success of later generations. He is critical, however, of the limited vision of Irish American politicians and the intellectual sterility of the Irish American dominated Catholic Church in America.

McLaughlin, Virginia Yans. *Immigration Reconsidered*. New York: Oxford University Press, 1990.

This is a collection of essays that covers a wide range of topics including African and Asian migration and comparisons of old and new American immigrant groups. Some of these essays are very helpful for a theoretical understanding of ethnicity, such as Charles Tilly's article on the importance of networks in immigration or Ewa Morawska's review of the historical and sociological literature on ethnicity and assimilation. The collection also includes a sharp, sophisticated, and provocative analysis by Kerby Miller of the emergence of the middle-class hegemony among Irish Americans at the turn of the century.

Miller, Kerby. *Emigrants and Exiles: Ireland and the Irish Exodus to North America*. New York: Oxford University Press, 1985.

This is by far the best overview of Irish immigration to North America. It is huge, dense, and comprehensive, covering all phases of emigration from the seventeenth century until the birth of the Irish Free State in 1921. It is encyclopedic in its wealth of detail, rich with statistics, and includes studies of thousands of immigrant letters. It is also sharply argued and is controversial in its assertions that, for example, Irish Catholic culture hindered Irish Catholic adjustment to the American economy; that many if not most Irish Catholic immigrants hated America and longed for home; and that middle classes in Ireland manipulated Irish nationalism to obscure their own responsibilities for Irish emigration. Miller also argues that because of their cultural inheritance from a Gaelic past, manipulation by Irish nationalists, and alienation in the harsh environment of a Protestant, urban industrial America, Irish Catholic immigrants understood their move to America more as an "exile" forced upon them by British oppressors than as a voluntary search for economic mobility.

O'Drudy, P. J. *The Irish in America: Emigration, Assimilation, and Impact*. New York: Cambridge University Press, 1985.

This is a very useful collection that boasts a number of important essays on Irish American life from the colonial era to the present. It includes excellent articles by Maurice Bric on the effect of Scotch-Irish and '98 rebels on early American politics, Deirdre Mageean on early nineteenth-century Irish emigrants, and David N. Doyle on

Irish American newspaper editors and their commitment to progressive reform at the turn of the century.

Shannon, William. *The American Irish*. New York: Colliers, 1974.

First published in 1963 with a second edition following in 1974, it follows the Irish Catholic experience in the United States from the early nineteenth century to the 1960s. Aimed at a broad public audience, it is not comprehensive but rather contains a series of vignettes on interesting figures and topics including James Michael Curley, John L. Sullivan, John F. Kennedy, and Tammany Hall. Shannon, who later became ambassador to Ireland, was trained as an historian, however, and the book offers intriguing historical insights into the differences between the San Francisco and Boston Irish and the transformation of Irish Catholic America at the turn of the century.

Literature

Fanning, Charles. *The Irish Voice in America : 250 Years of Irish-American Fiction*. Lexington: University Press of Kentucky, 2000.

This is a marvelous, comprehensive, and insightful survey of Irish American fiction from the early nineteenth to the late twentieth century. It is not a mere compendium but rather a sophisticated interpretation of Irish American literature and its relation to Irish American society as the two evolved over nearly two centuries. It pays due attention to leading lights like James Farrell, but also explores a wide range of authors including Maurice Egan, Mary Sadlier, and Edward McSorley, who were not well known but reflect important themes in Irish American life and thought.

Local

Bayor, Ronald and Timothy J. Meagher. *New York Irish*. Baltimore: Johns Hopkins University Press, 1996.

This is a collection of essays on the history of the Irish in New York City from the founding of New Amsterdam in the seventeenth century to the 1990s. There are twenty focused essays on topics such as Irish relations with African Americans and Chinese, Irish American nationalism in the 1890s and early 1900s, Irish immigrants in the city's clothing trade in the mid-nineteenth century, and Irish traditional music in the twentieth century. There are also overview essays for each of five major periods in the history of the city's Irish.

McCaffrey, Lawrence, ed. *The Irish in Chicago*. Urbana: University of Illinois Press, 1987.

This book contains an overview by McCaffrey and long, well-researched essays on politics, by Michael Funchion; Catholicism, by Ellen Skerret; and literature, by Charles Fanning. These essays are broadly comprehensive, rich in detail, and insightful. Skerret's essay, for example, traces the establishment of Irish parishes from the inner city in the nineteenth century to the suburbs in the mid-twentieth century, and explores the meaning of the religious life in those churches.

O'Connor, Thomas H. *The Boston Irish: A Political History*. Boston: Northeastern University Press, 1996.

This is a readable, comprehensive survey of Boston's Irish American political history. It traces that history from the nativist quarrels of the 1840s through the rise of Patrick Collins, James Michael Curley, John F. Fitzgerald, and Martin Lomasney in the heroic age of the turn of the century, to the new generation in the age of renewal and revival, such as John Hynes and John Collins.

Thernstrom, Stephan. *The Other Bostonians: Poverty and Progress in the American Metropolis, 1860–1970*. Cambridge: Harvard University Press, 1973.

This is considered the principal social mobility study of the era. Irish Americans figure prominently in this book, with Thernstrom arguing that Catholic groups like the Irish were hindered by Catholic culture from competing successfully with Protestants and Jews in the American economy.

Nativism

Higham, John. "Another Look at Nativism." *Catholic Historical Review* 44, no. 2 (1958): 147–158.

This is a coda to Higham's exceptional book on nativist movements in America, *Strangers in the Land*. In that book, Higham studied the rise and fall of nativist movements; here he points to the enduring patterns of social and economic discrimination and inequality that reflected and sustained ethnic tensions and conflicts.

Politics

Erie, Steven P. *Rainbow's End: Irish Americans and the Dilemmas of Urban Machine Politics, 1840–1985*. Berkeley: University of California Press, 1988.

This is the only real scholarly examination of the broad phenomenon of Irish American political machines. Sophisticated, comprehensively documented, and sharply argued, Erie divides the history of Irish machine politics into three phases: rise, consolidation, and decline. Erie argues that political machines did not serve the Irish well as a means of occupational mobility since jobs were few and most of them were only blue- or low white-collar positions with no futures. He also contends that Irish American machines were not useful in incorporating new immigrants into American politics and may have helped choke off a class politics that would have better served both American immigrants in the past and minorities today.

Popular Culture

Stivers, Richard. *A Hair of the Dog: Irish Drinking and American Stereotype*. University Park: Pennsylvania State University Press, 1971.

This is a study of the persistence of distinctively high rates of alcoholism among Irish Americans. Stivers suggests that Irish Americans indulged in excessive drinking in order to live up to conceptions of Irish identity forged in the stereotypes of popular culture.

Williams, William H.A. *T'Was Only an Irishman's Dream: The Image of Ireland and the Irish in American Popular Song Lyrics, 1800–1920*. Urbana: University of Illinois Press, 1996.

This is an extraordinary study of the image of Ireland, the Irish, and Irish Americans in American music. It is richly and imaginatively researched, theoretically sophisticated, smartly argued, and gracefully written, and ranges far beyond the music itself to discuss the rise of vaudeville, popular theater, Tin Pan Alley, and host of other topics. Williams argues that Irish Americans took over the construction of their own image as they rose to prominence in the entertainment industry in the mid-nineteenth century. Yet instead of eradicating old stereotypes of feckless, drunken "Paddy," they merely Americanized and inverted them, making an urban American Paddy, whose lack of ambition became communalism and whose drinking became conviviality.

Religion

Chinnici, Joseph. *Living Stones: The History and Structure of Catholic Spiritual Life in the United States*. New York: Macmillan Co., 1989.

Chinnici's work is part of a recent effort by American Catholic historians to look beyond the institutional history of the church and try to plumb what the faith meant to its laypersons, religious women, and clerics—what they thought they were doing when they prayed. Chinnici includes examinations of the spirituality of immigrants, Americanists, and social reformers, and features Irish Americans like Monsignor John A. Ryan and Archbishop John Hughes.

McDannell, Colleen. *Material Christianity*. New Haven, Conn.: Yale University Press, 1995.

This is a unique and insightful book that examines material culture—clothing, cemetery monuments, statues, and other objects used in the practice of Christianity in America. McDannell's analysis helps open broad new areas of lay Catholic, including Irish American lay Catholic, spiritual life in America. Two of the chapters focus on issues of special importance to Catholic devotional life: the origins of the marketing of holy water from Lourdes by priests at the University of Notre Dame and the dramatic changing of the decoration of Catholic churches in the mid-twentieth century.

Morris, Charles. *American Catholic: The Saints and Sinners Who Built America's Most Powerful Church*. New York: Random House, 1997.

This is a popular but very insightful and provocative history of the Catholic Church that argues flatly that the roots of the modern American Catholic Church are found not in Rome or in the early Spanish missions but in nineteenth-century Ireland.

Nineteenth-century Ireland, Morris asserts, bequeathed a "militant and bureaucratic style" to the American church.

Societies

O'Dea, John. *History of the Ancient Order of Hibernians and Its Auxiliary*. New York: National Board of the AOH, 1923.

This is an old-fashioned three-volume chronicle of the AOH's history that is narrowly institutional and largely a record of the order's national conventions. It is nevertheless a very useful source for tracing the Hibernian's national policies and tracking the official statistics of its membership up through the 1920s.

THE IRISH "DIASPORA" CONTEXT

Archer, Robin. "Why Is There No Labor Party?: Class and Race in the United States and Australia." In *American Exceptionalism: United States Working Class Formation in an International Context*, edited by Richard Halpern and Jonathan Morris, 56–72. New York: St. Marks, 1997.

Archer's essay is a fascinating exploration of why a labor party emerged in Australia but not the United States at the turn of the century. It is relevant to the history of the Irish in America for two reasons: first, because a heavily Irish working class mobilized into a labor party in Australia, but a similarly heavily Irish and Irish-led working class in America did not. Second, Archer also points out that labor in Australia combined the exclusion of Asian immigrants with class solidarity, which the Irish-led workers in San Francisco attempted to do as well.

Bielenberg, Andy, ed. *The Irish Diaspora*. Harlow, U.K.: Longman, 2000.

This is a collection of essays based on the papers of a conference that took place at the National University of Ireland at Cork. The essays are wide-ranging, addressing Irish experiences in India, South Africa, New Zealand, Australia, and Canada. There are several essays on the Irish in Britain, strong essays by Kerby Miller and Ruth Ann Harris on the Irish in the United States, and an excellent overview of the Irish in the British Empire by Bielenberg.

Campbell, Malcolm. *The Kingdom of the Ryans: The Irish in Southwest New South Wales, 1816–1890*. Sydney: University of New South Wales Press, 1997.

Campbell, influenced by Donald Akenson, points to the success of Irish immigrants in New South Wales to question "the American Orthodoxy" that the Irish "labored under some form of cultural disability" overseas. The book traces the remarkable career of Edward Ryan, a "Whiteboy" from Tipperary transported to Australia in 1816 for participation in an attack on a British barracks, who rose to become King of Galong

Castle and ruler over 300 square miles of grazing land by the 1840s. This is a sophisticated study that puts Ryan in the broad context of Irish Australian ethnicity.

Clarke, Brian. *Piety and Nationalism: Lay Voluntary Associations and the Creation of an Irish Catholic Community in Toronto, 1850–1895.* Toronto: McGill Queen's University Press, 1993.

A very important study of Irish Americans in Toronto that addresses the critical issue of how the devotional revolution or Catholic revival played out among Irish immigrants in mid-nineteenth-century North America. Irish Catholic women were more likely to take up the devotional and institutional zeal of the Catholic revival than men, who were absorbed in nationalist issues for much of the period.

Fanning, Charles. *New Perspectives on the Irish Diaspora.* Carbondale: Southern Illinois University Press, 2000.

This is a collection of eighteen essays examining the history and literature of the Irish diaspora. It includes insightful essays by Kerby Miller on the Scotch-Irish, Edward O'Day on the Irish regional origins of nineteenth-century Irish immigrants to New England, and George O'Brien on Frank McCourt's *Angela's Ashes.* It also contains poems by Eamon Wall and Terence Winch.

Fitzpatrick, David. "'A Peculiar Tramping People': The Irish in Britain, 1801–1870." In *A New History of Ireland.* Vol. 5, *Ireland Under the Union,* edited by W. E. Vaughn, 623–660. Oxford: Clarendon Press, 1989.

This is a sophisticated overview of Irish migration to Britain when the movement of Irish refugees across the Irish Sea began to reach flood stage. Fitzpatrick, a distinguished historian of Ireland and Irish migration to Australia, disputes notions that the Irish were ghettoized in British cities or created a self-conscious, well-organized ethnic minority.

Houston, Cecil and W. J. Smyth. *Irish Emigration and Canadian Settlement : Patterns, Links, and Letters.* Toronto: University of Toronto Press, 1990.

This excellent survey provides an important overview of Irish emigration into Canada, elaborating on the eighteenth-century Waterford-to-Newfoundland connection, the rising immigration of the early nineteenth century, the remigration of Canadian arrivals to the United States in the 1830s and 1840s, and the rapid decline of Irish immigration to Canada after the middle of the nineteenth century.

Katz, Michael. *The People of Hamilton, Canada West: Family and Class in the Mid-Nineteenth-Century City.* Cambridge: Harvard University Press, 1975.

One of the early quantitative community studies that analyzes the family and work lives of Irish immigrants in Hamilton. Katz finds that the Irish-born in Hamilton tended to marry earlier than the Irish in Ireland.

McDonagh, Oliver and W. F. Mandle. *Ireland and Irish Australia: Studies in Cultural and Political History.* London: Croom Helm, 1986.

This book includes essays by some of the most distinguished historians of the Irish in Australia: McDonagh on an overview of the Irish in nineteenth-century Australia and Patrick O'Farrell on the writing of Irish Australian history.

McGowan, Mark G. *Waning of the Green: Catholicism, the Irish and Identity in Toronto, 1887–1922.* Montreal: McGill University Press, 1999.

McGowan, like many others writing about the Canadian and Australian Irish, believes that the experience of the Irish in Canada differs from the "American model" of "typical American Irish ghettoes." He believes Irish Catholics in Toronto made a transition from Irish ethnic to Canadian imperial loyalties and merged successfully into the social and economic life of Toronto.

Murphy, Terrence and Gerald Stortz. *Creed and Culture: The Place of English-Speaking Catholics in Canadian Society, 1750–1930.* Montreal: McGill Queen's University Press, 1993.

This is an excellent and important collection of essays that explores the position of English-speaking Catholics (largely but by no means exclusively Irish in origins) ranged between a Protestant, imperial, English-speaking majority and a sizable and deeply rooted French-speaking minority. The essays are attentive to regional differences in this experience.

O'Farrell, Patrick. "The Irish in Australia and New Zealand, 1791–1870." In *A New History of Ireland.* Vol. 5, *Ireland Under the Union,* edited by W. E. Vaughn, 661–681. Oxford: Clarendon Press, 1989.

O'Farrell's chapter is an excellent overview of the early years of the Irish in Australia, tracing the Irish from the early convict days to the beginnings of mass free migration to the continent. O'Farrell believes Irish assimilation was relatively easy in Australia because they were initially such a large and important segment of the population, enjoyed competent leadership, and took advantage of the growing economy's opportunities.

O'Farrell, Patrick. *The Irish in Australia: 1788 to the Present.* Notre Dame, Ind.: University of Notre Dame Press, 2000.

This is the definitive work on the Irish experience in Australia. O'Farrell believes that the Irish were a large minority in Australia but were spread so evenly that they never achieved significant political power. He believes, however, that their huge presence as a distinct people in a society dominated by Anglo-Protestants also encouraged the development of a special kind of Australian tolerance.

SEVENTEENTH- AND EIGHTEENTH-CENTURY MIGRATION

Blethen, H. Tyler and Curtis W. Wood, Jr., eds. *Ulster and North America: Transatlantic Perspectives on the Scotch-Irish.* Tuscaloosa: University of Alabama Press, 1997.

This is a seminal collection of eleven academic essays selected from eighteen years of the Ulster-American Symposium that examine developments in Scotland and Ireland as well as in North America. Many of the essays are local studies that include demographic research, folklore, geography, and linguistics, greatly adding to existing Scotch-Irish historiography while debunking or clarifying many cherished myths. A major theme is the rapid Scotch-Irish assimilation into American society in contradiction to the theories of those who argue for the persistence of Scotch-Irish, British Borderland, and Celtic traits.

Cullen, Louis. "The Irish Diaspora of the Seventeenth and Eighteenth Centuries." In *Europeans on the Move: Studies on European Migration, 1500 to 1800*, edited by Nicholas Canny, 113–149. New York: Oxford University Press, 1994.

Cullen examines migration not just to the Americas but also to Europe in these centuries. He notes, for example, the substantial migration by Irish soldiers or recruits to European continental armies from the defeats of the sixteenth and seventeenth centuries until the middle of the eighteenth century. In his analysis of migrant numbers to the Americas—largely the Caribbean in the seventeenth century and North America in the eighteenth—he points out that it is very difficult to estimate the numbers of emigrants. His own calculations are very conservative. His estimates for the eighteenth century—perhaps little more than fifty thousand migrants in the entire period between 1729 and 1774—run far below what many American historians have suggested.

Dickson, R. J. *Ulster Emigration To Colonial America, 1718–1775*. Belfast: Ulster Historical Foundation, 1966.

This is acknowledged to be the best scholarly work on the pre–American Revolution eighteenth-century immigration from Ulster to North America of thousands of people of mostly Scottish background and Protestant religion. It offers a detailed examination of the economic, social, and political background of immigration, as well as information on the origins and motivations of the immigrants. A primary focus of the book is the effect of rents, prices, and wages as inducements to emigration.

Doyle, David N. *Ireland, Irishmen, and Revolutionary America, 1760–1820*. Dublin: Mercier Press, 1981.

This is probably still the best overall study of the eighteenth-century Irish migration, but it also has several additional features: a sober but full and original investigation into Irish Catholics among the pre-Revolutionary immigrants, an intelligent analysis of the complexity of Scotch-Irish politics in America, and a rich examination of the American Revolution's effect on politics in Ireland.

Dunaway, Wayland F. *The Scotch-Irish in Colonial Pennsylvania*. Chapel Hill: University of North Carolina Press, 1944.

This is a somewhat dated though still useful work gleaned from many Pennsylvania family, church, and county histories, as well as from the publications of Scotch-Irish societies. Dunaway traces and defends the use of the term "Scotch-Irish," discusses reasons for emigration from Ulster, and details the significant Scotch-Irish contributions to Pennsylvania politics and education. However, more could have been written in regard to religion, and he is soft on the murderous Paxton Boys.

Fogleman, Aaron S. "From Slaves, Convicts, and Servants to Free Passengers: The Transformation of Immigration in the Era of the American Revolutions." *The Journal of American History* 85, no. 1 (June 1998): 43–76.

This is an excellent summary of free, slave, and indentured migration to the Americas in the seventeenth and eighteenth centuries. It provides the best current statistics on Irish immigration in those centuries, as well as the best current estimates of servants and free immigrants among them. It also describes Irish perceptions of America and explores the reasons for the end of indentured servitude, such as changes in American ideas about slavery and freedom.

Ford, Henry Jones. *The Scotch-Irish in America*. Princeton, N.J.: Princeton University Press, 1915.

This is a pioneering scholarly study of the Scotch-Irish effect on American institutions and culture. He examines Scottish migration to Ulster in the seventeenth century, the causes of Ulster-Scot emigration to North America in the following century, and Scotch-Irish settlements in New England, New York, New Jersey, Pennsylvania, and along the frontier.

Green, E. R. R., ed. *Essays in Scotch-Irish History*. London: Routledge and Kegan Paul, 1969.

These five essays from a 1965 Ulster Historical Foundation symposium at Belfast's Queens' University address aspects of Scotch-Irish immigration to America. Though the essays are relatively brief, contributors E. R. R. Green, Maldwyn Jones, E. E. Evans, E. Wright, and Arthur Link raise important questions and suggest further avenues of inquiry. Jones's essay is perhaps the most important, his emphasis being the continuing Protestant migration after the American Revolution.

Griffin, Patrick. *The People with No Name: Ireland's Ulster Scots, America's Scotch-Irish, and the Creation of a British Atlantic World*. Princeton, N.J.: Princeton University Press, 2001.

This is the most recent and best examination of the Ulster Presbyterian migration to America in the first half of the eighteenth century. Griffin points out that these are an "elusive people to pin down." They did not call themselves Scotch-Irish, but others did, and they rejected definitions of themselves as either Scotch or Irish as well. Griffin points to their constant invention and reinvention of identity and culture in America. One of the strengths of the book is Griffin's emphasis and elucidation of the importance of the rise of the linen industry to Presbyterian life in Ulster and its effect on the migration.

Hoffman, Ronald. *Princes of Ireland, Planters of Maryland : A Carroll Saga, 1500–1782*. Chapel Hill: University of North Carolina Press for the Omohundro Institute of Early American History and Culture, Williamsburg, Virginia, 2000.

The Carroll family, descendants of the ancient Ely Carroll family of Offaly and northern Tipperary in Ireland, was the most important Catholic family in early American history. Charles Carroll of Carrollton signed the Declaration of Independence. This study traces the immigrant and first two American-born generations of the family, smartly placing them in the broad context of American history. Yet it also demonstrates how the Carroll's Irish inheritance critically shaped their family strategies for survival and success in America.

Jackson, Carlton. *A Social History of the Scotch-Irish*. Lanham, N.Y.: Madison Books, 1993.

This book is essentially an update of Leyburn, reflecting the more recent work of scholars such as David Doyle and Bernard Bailyn. Unlike Leyburn, who divided his study into equal parts, tracing the Scotch-Irish as they moved from Scotland to Ireland to America, Jackson's emphasis is primarily on the settlement of the Scotch-Irish in America. A good selected and annotated bibliography is included.

Jones, Maldwyn. "The Scotch-Irish in British America." In *Strangers Within the Realm: Cultural Margins of the First British Empire*, edited by Bernard Bailyn and Philip D. Morgan, 284–313. Chapel Hill: University of North Carolina Press, 1991.

This is an excellent overview of the Scotch-Irish migration to North America. It intelligently addresses the entire issue of who the Scotch-Irish were, including such questions as when that term was first used in North America, how Ulster Presbyterian immigrants defined themselves, and what cultural customs and values distinguished Scottish-descended Presbyterians in Ulster and Scottish Presbyterians in America. It also crisply and smartly reviews the best scholarship to its date on such topics as the regional distribution of Ulster Presbyterians in America, the fortunes of indentured servants, and Scotch-Irish agriculture.

Lehman, William C. *Scottish and Scotch-Irish Contributions to Early American Life and Culture*. Port Washington, N.Y.: Kennikat Press, 1978.

From a venerable sociologist rather than an historian, this account presents the Scotch-Irish as one of three component parts of Scottish immigration to North America: Lowland Scots, Highland Scots, and Ulster Scots (Scotch-Irish), rather than many other approaches, which present them singularly or as a component part along with the Anglo-Irish and the Native or Catholic Irish of Irish immigration.

Leyburn, James G. *The Scotch-Irish: A Social History*. Chapel Hill: University of North Carolina Press, 1962.

This now classic work combines both sociological and historical perspectives. Lucid prose describes the character and culture of this unique people, first in Lowland Scotland, then in Ireland, and finally in North America. Leyburn acknowledges their very real accomplishments in many fields, especially in government, but is also judicious in debunking many of the myths about them. In particular, though he found some earlier uses of the term "Scotch-Irish" in Britain, he supports the view that it only came into general use in America after the heavy Irish Catholic immigration of the mid-nineteenth century.

Miller, Kerby, Arnold Schrier, Bruce Bolling, and David Doyle. *Irish Immigrants in the Land of Canaan: Letters and Memoirs from Colonial an Revolutionary America, 1675–1815.* New York: Oxford University Press, 2003.

This is a mammoth collection of letters and memoirs from sixty-eight Irish immigrants to colonial and revolutionary America. The letters and memoirs are painstakingly edited with substantial notes and rich, interpretive introductions and interpolations. There are seven chapters and an epilogue. The documents in the first chapter are written from Ireland and address the causes of immigration. The second chapter describes the processes of migration, the networks, purchasing of tickets, and journey. Documents in the third through sixth chapters illustrate Irish immigrants in different occupations: farmers and planters; craftsmen, laborers, and servants; merchants, shopkeepers, and peddlers; and clergymen and schoolmasters. The letters and memoirs in the last chapter reflect Irish immigrants' diverse relationships to American political institutions and ideals, particularly the controversies surrounding the American Revolution.

Truxes, Thomas. *Irish American Trade, 1660–1783.* Cambridge: Cambridge University Press, 1988.

Truxes is concerned with the broad topic of trade between Ireland and America in the colonial era, and contends that it must be seen in a broader imperial framework as intercolonial trade within the context of the same imperial laws, financial mechanisms, and service institutions. He treats emigration as just one part of this trade, but makes a strong case that the volume of emigration from Ireland to what became the United States was larger than what other authors such as Dickson have suggested.

FROM REVOLUTION TO FAMINE

Doyle, David N. "The Irish in North America, 1776–1845." In *A New History of Ireland.* Vol. 5, *Ireland Under the Union,* edited by W. E. Vaughn, 682–724. Oxford: Clarendon Press, 1989.

This is probably the best single short overall discussion of Irish life in Canada as well as the United States in this period. It convincingly identifies the era as a critical turning point. It delineates, for example, the shift from a Protestant-dominated to a Catholic-dominated migration and the decline of Protestant-Catholic cooperation, both within the Irish group and between Irish Catholics and all other Protestants outside it.

Jones, Maldwyn A. "Ulster Emigration, 1783–1815." In *Essays in Scotch Irish History,* edited by E. R. R. Green, 46–68. London: Routledge, Kegan and Paul, 1969.

This is a superb and neatly comprehensive overview of Ulster Irish migration in this often neglected period. Jones provides important information on who the migrants were, how many came, why they came, where they came from, where they landed, and legislation governing the migration.

Light, Dale. *Rome and the New Republic: Conflict and Community in Philadelphia Catholicism Between the Revolution and the Civil War.* Notre Dame, Ind.: University of Notre Dame Press, 1996.

This is a thoughtful and well-researched analysis of how the immigrant Catholic church adapted to the American environment. Light points out the difficulties experienced by Irish-born bishops Henry Conwell and Francis Kenrick as they confronted republican dissenters, rebellious priests, and immigrants steeped in their own folk versions of Catholicism. He contends that the religion Irish immigrants came to practice in Philadelphia was not the one they brought with them from Ireland but instead the new devotionalism inspired by the worldwide Catholic revival, fostered by the papacy and imposed by the ultramontane on local Catholics.

McWhiney, Grady. *Cracker Culture: Celtic Ways in the Old South.* Tuscaloosa: University of Alabama, 1988.

This is a deliberately provocative if entertaining book. It is the boldest summary of the "Celtic South Thesis" argued by McWhiney and his colleague Forest McDonald. McWhiney spends less time here on the statistical evidence proving the South was Celtic than on what the ramifications of that Celtic domination were for Southern society. His argument is that the South's cattle and swineherding economy and its violent, hospitable, indolent, and honor-obsessed culture are but the latest manifestation of a Celtic culture that can be traced far back into time and contrast sharply with the ancient Anglo-Saxon culture transplanted to "Yankee" New England.

Way, Peter. *Common Labour: Workers and the Digging of the North American Canals, 1780–1860.* New York: Cambridge University Press, 1993.

This is an important study in American labor history, focusing on the dire straits and brutal working conditions of unskilled canal workers in the antebellum era. Many of those workers were, of course, Irish immigrants. Hired by contractors or gangs, they were routinely cheated by their bosses and constantly engaged in violence with Germans or men from other construction gangs or other counties of Ireland.

Wilson, David. *United Irishmen, United States: Immigrant Radicals in the Early Republic.* Ithaca, N.Y.: Cornell University Press, 1998.

This is the first study of the United Irish exiles and their effect on Irish Americans and the United States. It expertly details the reasons for the United Irishmen's migration and their role in influencing and shaping Irish American culture and politics. Wilson points to the exiles' belief in the revolutionary potential of their times and the possibility that Ireland, America, and indeed, the world could be remade in a new republican mold. Yet he also points to some of their failures: their indifference to or evasion of the plight of enslaved African Americans and oppressed workers.

THE FAMINE ERA

Overviews of the Era

Ferrie, Joseph. *Yankey's Now: Immigrants in the Antebellum United States, 1840–1860.* New York: Oxford University Press, 1999.

This is one of the most important and original studies of antebellum immigrants to appear in years and is a critically important book for understanding Irish immigration in the famine era. It is based on a massive sample of immigrants arriving in the Port of New York in the 1840s who Ferrie then traces into the United States census manuscript schedules for 1850 and 1860. Ferrie documents and explains better than anyone to date the Irish concentration on the East Coast and the failure of Irish immigrants to compete successfully against their fellow immigrant Germans and English in the American economy.

The Civil War

Miller, Randall. "Catholic Religion, Irish Ethnicity, and the Civil War." In *Religion and the American Civil War*, edited by Randall Miller, Harry S. Stout, and Charles Reagan Wilson, 261–296. New York: Oxford University Press, 1998.

This is a very important and intelligent discussion of the commitment of northern Irish Catholics to the Union cause in the Civil War, and the role of the Church in serving its faithful amid the war's chaos. Miller argues that Irish Americans in the North became increasingly frustrated and ambivalent about the war as casualties mounted at Antietam and Fredericksburg and as Abraham Lincoln enlarged the war's purposes to include the abolition of slavery. Such disaffection climaxed in the Draft Riots of 1863. Miller suggests that the later image of unqualified Irish commitment to the war was a public memory manufactured by Irish veterans after the war.

Local

Anbinder, Tyler. *Five Points: The Nineteenth-Century New York City Neighborhood that Invented Tap Dance, Stole Elections, and Became the World's Most Notorious Slum.* New York: The Free Press, 2001.

This is a rich and very readable history of the Five Points neighborhood in New York, which was dominated by the Irish for most of the nineteenth century. It powerfully conveys living and working experiences for Irish immigrants. One of the most important features of the book for students of Irish American history is Anbinder's trace of the Irish immigrants who settled in Five Points to the villages and indeed the estates that they left in Sligo and Kerry in Ireland, which graphically shows how immigrants used networks of kin and friends to survive in New York's most brutal slum.

Blessing, Patrick. " 'West Among Strangers': Irish Migration to California, 1850 to 1880." Ph.D. dissertation: University of California at Los Angeles, 1977.

A study of Irish immigrants in California, particularly the understudied southern part of the state, underscoring the opportunities that the western states offered Irish immigrants.

Burchell, R.A. *The San Francisco Irish, 1848–1880*. Berkeley: University of California Press, 1980.

Burchell's book richly documents the fact that Irish Americans enjoyed far more success in San Francisco than in eastern cities. The book makes expert use of statistical and other research to demonstrate the ease of Irish movement into white-collar occupations and their widely dispersed neighborhood settlement, as well as the processes and routes that took them to San Francisco. The book also discusses the Irish-dominated Catholic Church, nationalism, and politics in San Francisco during these years.

Clark, Dennis. *The Irish in Philadelphia: Ten Generations of Urban Experience*. Philadelphia: Temple University Press, 1974.

This is a study of the Philadelphia Irish from the founding of Penn's colony until the twentieth century, but, nonetheless, focuses largely on the Great Famine Irish migration and its aftermath in the nineteenth century. Clark makes a good case that the Irish adjustment in Philadelphia was easier than in other cities because Philadelphia's economy was dynamic, its housing cheap, and its neighborhoods rough but healthy. The book powerfully emphasizes the difference between Philadelphia and cities further north like Boston, where economies were sluggish, housing expensive, and slums crowded and squalid.

Ernst, Robert. *Immigrant Life in New York City, 1825–1863*. New York: Columbia University Press, 1949.

This is one of the earliest important works on immigration. It is a broad survey of immigrant life in New York, and is rich with details, ranging from the number of Irish-born policemen per ward to descriptions of the city's Irish American newspapers. It is thus still a very significant resource for the history of the Irish in New York City.

Gallman, Matthew. *Receiving Erin's Children: Philadelphia, Liverpool, and the Irish Famine, 1845–1855*. Chapel Hill: University of North Carolina Press, 2000.

This is an important and original study of the response of two cities to the flood of Irish immigrants in the 1840s and 1850s. As Gallman points out, he is not interested in the immigrants so much as the different environments of Liverpool and Philadelphia that they entered and how those different environments reacted to the problem of poverty that those immigrants exacerbated. Liverpool and Philadelphia were about the same size, but Gallman points to important differences in their political cultures that shaped their responses to the Irish newcomers: universal manhood suffrage in Philadelphia versus a narrowly restricted electorate in Liverpool, American localism versus British centralized national power, and an established church in Liverpool versus a fractious American religious pluralism.

Gerber, David. *The Making of an American Pluralism: Buffalo, 1825–1860*. Urbana: University of Illinois Press, 1989.

This is a broad study of ethnicity in Buffalo in the mid-nineteenth century that aims to explain how American ethnic groups are constructed, and thus how the pluralistic structure of American politics and society is constructed. The book discusses German as well as Irish immigrants, but the chapters on the Irish are exceptionally well researched, thoughtful, and well argued.

Gleeson, David. *The Irish in the South, 1815–1877*. Chapel Hill: University of North Carolina Press, 2001.

This is the first comprehensive scholarly survey of the Irish in this frequently neglected region. It covers all aspects of Irish life in the states of the old Confederacy: economic mobility, associations, politics, and race relations, and has a particularly useful statistical analysis of Irish occupational studies in cities. Gleeson argues convincingly that the Irish experience in the South was much more positive than in most parts of the northeastern United States.

Gordon, Michael. *The Orange Riots: Irish Political Violence in New York City, 1870 and 1871*. Ithaca, N.Y.: Cornell University Press, 1993.

This is a study of the two riots that occurred on the July 12 anniversary of the Battle of the Boyne in 1870 and 1871. The first riot cost eight lives and the second sixty-two. This study not only examines the riots but also the broader political context, including the city's struggle over Boss Tweed, which heightened tensions between Irish Protestants and Catholics in those years.

Handlin, Oscar. *Boston Immigrants, 1790–1865: A Study in Acculturation*. Cambridge: Harvard University Press, 1941.

This is probably the first modern historical study of any immigrant community to employ a sophisticated blend of quantitative techniques and cultural analysis. Though discussing all immigrants to Boston in this period, the book is really about the Irish since they so thoroughly dominated immigration to the city in that era. Handlin's depiction of Irish immigration to Boston is bleak—a tragedy for both Boston and the Irish. Boston's weak economy offered the unskilled peasant Irish who settled there little hope for improvement, and the conservative, ignorant, and impoverished Irish only divided what had been a liberal, civil, homogeneous Yankee town.

Kenny, Kevin. *Making Sense of the Molly Maguires*. New York: Oxford University Press, 1998.

This is a rich, subtle, recent analysis of the famous Molly Maguires, a secret society of miners in northeastern Pennsylvania who gained national attention when their members were executed for murders of mining company managers and officials in the 1860s. Kenny explores the roots of the Mollies in Ireland's (specifically West Donegal's) rural secret societies, discusses nativist attacks on the Irish in the mining districts, the relation between Pennsylvania's Mollies and the real labor unions among the miners, and the validity of the evidence lodged against the executed miners.

Mitchell, Brian C. *The Paddy Camps: The Irish of Lowell, 1821–1861*. Urbana: University of Illinois Press, 1988.

A thoughtful, thorough history of the Irish in early and mid-nineteenth-century Lowell. Mitchell's book traces the Lowell Irish community's evolution from a fragile accommodation with local Yankees to, with the coming of the Great Famine migration, the bitter and inflexible division between the two. Mitchell artfully explores class and regional tensions within Lowell's Irish community.

Religion

Dolan, Jay. *The Immigrant Church: New York's Irish and German Catholics, 1815–1865*. Baltimore: Johns Hopkins University Press, 1975.

This a superb study of New York's Irish and German Catholics from the grassroots or "people in the parish" level. The book examines the history of the Irish in Lower East Side parishes and examines in depth both the Irish populations and church instructional and social services. Between problems of poverty, constant mobility in search of work, and the weakness of the institutional religious tradition they inherited from Ireland, perhaps fewer than half the Irish attended mass regularly, and the poorest of the poor may have had only tangential links to the Church.

O'Connor, Thomas H. *Fitzpatrick's Boston, 1846–1866: John Bernard Fitzpatrick, Third Bishop of Boston*. Boston: Northeastern University Press, 1984.

This is a thorough study of the Boston Catholic bishop and his diocese during the Great Famine and Civil War era. Born American and educated in the Boston schools, Fitzpatrick was a very different leader than John Hughes of New York. Though devoted to the church's interests and resentful of Protestant prejudice, he was far more cautious in asserting the church's rights and far more committed to the assimilation of his flock into his beloved Boston society.

Nativism

Anbinder, Tyler Gregory. *Nativism and Slavery: The Northern Know-Nothings and the Politics of the 1850s*. New York: Oxford University Press, 1992.

This is the best recent examination of the Know-Nothings, the nativist secret society and political party that emerged in the mid-1850s as a major national force. The book reveals how frustrations over the Whig and Democratic politicians' refusal to grapple with the slavery issue fueled the rise of the Know-Nothings.

Knobel, Dale. *Paddy and the Republic: Ethnicity and Nationality in Antebellum America*. Middletown, Conn.: Wesleyan University Press, 1986.

This is a study of American attitudes about Irish Americans, employing a content analysis of magazines and other public texts. Knobel has found that until the early 1840s, Americans perceived the Irish as poor, feckless, and ignorant, but redeemable by the American republican environment. In 1844, following the bloody riots in Philadelphia and then the flood of hapless Great Famine immigrants, Americans became more pessimistic about the Irish, considering them racially—that is, genetically inferior and probably incapable of improvement.

Nationalism

D'Arcy, William. *The Fenian Movement in the United States, 1858–1886.* Washington: Catholic University Press, 1947.

This is still the only broad survey of the Fenian movement in the United States. Though largely a chronicle that sheds little light on the backgrounds of Fenian supporters or the broader meanings of the movement for Irish America and the United States as a whole, D'Arcy does thoroughly document the actions of the Fenian leaders O'Mahony, Stephens, Mitchel, and O'Neill among others, and, in particular, the personal and factional conflicts that divided them.

TURN OF THE CENTURY

Overview

Doyle, David N. *Irish America: Native Rights and National Empires, 1890–1901.* New York: Arno Press, 1976.

This is an important book that analyzes the responses of Irish Americans to American imperialism at the turn of the century. Doyle finds that many Irish American nationalists opposed such expansion, invoking Ireland's own fate at the hands of imperial Britain, while some Irish American Catholic church leaders, who identified strongly with America's mission in the world, endorsed America's imperial ventures. Doyle also has an important chapter analyzing the emergence of a "lace curtain" middle class among the Irish at the turn of the century.

Jacobson, Mathew. *Special Sorrows: The Diasporic Imagination of Irish, Polish, and Jewish Immigrants in the United States.* Cambridge: Harvard University Press, 1995.

This is a sophisticated comparative study of three American ethnic groups—the Irish, Jews, and Polish Americans—to America's war with Cuba and the conquest of the Philippines. It explores not only Irish opposition to the Philippines adventure but the "diasporic" popular culture of Irish American (as well as Polish and Jewish American) nationalism.

Meagher, Timothy, ed. *From Paddy to Studs: Irish American Communities at the Turn of the Century, 1880 to 1920*. Westport, Conn.: Greenwood Press, 1986.

This is a collection of essays on Irish American communities in Philadelphia, Chicago, St. Louis, San Francisco, and Lowell and Worcester, Massachusetts, at the turn of the century. The essays probe what happened in these communities as new generations matured and a middle class emerged. Those experiences varied, as might be expected, but in most of the communities, Catholicism seemed to become more important over time.

Local

Brundage, David. *The Making of Western Labor Radicalism: Denver's Organized Workers, 1878–1908*. Urbana: University of Illinois Press, 1994.

This study of labor in Denver is particularly sensitive to the Irish American workers who made up such a critical part of Denver's working class. Brundage delves into subjects like the Land League in Denver and the role of saloons in community culture, as well as Irish American participation in labor organizations and politics.

Connolly, James. *The Triumph of Ethnic Progressivism: Urban Political Culture in Boston, 1900–1925*. Cambridge: Harvard University Press, 1998.

The best recent history of the critical turn-of-the-century era in Boston politics, this book discusses the emergence of Irish dominance in the city. Original and provocative, Connolly reveals how Boston Irish politicians like James Michael Curley adapted progressive antiestablishment rhetoric to serve their own ends and forged a Boston Irish political tradition of ethnic grievances against Boston's ruling Yankee elite.

Emmons, David. *The Butte Irish: Class and Ethnicity in an American Mining Town, 1875–1925*. Urbana: University of Illinois Press, 1989.

This is a superb study of the Irish in the mining community of Butte, the most Irish city in America in 1900. Emmons examines Irish family life, residential patterns, institutions, and associations in Butte. He is particularly interested, however, in the way that the first wave of Irish-born miners created a tight ethnic community that monopolized work in the mines and nourished an intensely militant Irish nationalist movement but avoided strikes and protests against the Irish-born mine owner, Marcus Daly. Emmons believes that Irish communalism, not the embrace of middle-class values, inhibited working-class consciousness and activism.

Hirsch, Eric. *Urban Revolt : Ethnic Politics in the Nineteenth-Century Chicago Labor Movement*. Berkeley: University of California Press, 1990.

A study of labor's role in the city politics of Chicago, Hirsch characterizes the Irish role in labor politics as "militant reformism"—aggressive or even violent in tactics, but reformist, not radical, in goals.

Kazin, Michael. *Barons of Labor : The San Francisco Building Trades and Union Power in the Progressive Era*. Urbana: University of Illinois Press, 1987.

This is a study of the building trades' union's rise to power and dominance in San Francisco politics. The trades were led by Irish Americans, most notably Patrick H. McCarthy. Kazin's excellent book challenges the notion that AFL unions were apolitical and myopically conservative and thus, by extension, simple generalizations about the conservatism of Irish Catholic union leaders as well.

Perlmann, Joel. *Ethnic Differences : Schooling and Social Structure Among the Irish, Italians, Jews, and Blacks in an American City, 1880–1935.* New York: Cambridge University Press, 1988.

Perlmann's book is based on a massive research study of the relationship between schooling and occupational mobility among ethnic groups in Providence in the late nineteenth and early twentieth centuries. It is one of the most ambitious and carefully argued mobility studies. Perlmann found that Irish Americans began to match native-stock or "Yankee" school and occupational achievement after the turn of the century, pulling even by the 1930s. Perlmann also found no difference between the effects of Catholic schools and public schools on Irish Catholic economic achievement.

Wingerd, Mary L. *Claiming the City: Politics, Faith and the Power of Place in St. Paul.* Ithaca, N.Y.: Cornell University Press, 2001.

This is an exceptional local study that offers the best analysis yet of how Irish Americans expertly played a brokering role in turn-of-the-century America. Though they were a relatively small part of St. Paul's population, Irish Americans managed to build coalitions with some groups and marginalize others to put themselves at the very center of St. Paul's community life. Wingerd's study is comprehensive, with abundant attention to the religious, labor, and political dimensions of Irish power brokering.

Nationalism

Brown, Thomas N. *Irish American Nationalism, 1870 –1890.* New York: Lippincott, 1966.

This gracefully written and well-argued book was the most important study of Irish American nationalism in its time, and it remains an important work. Focusing largely on the American Land League and support here for the Home Rule movement, Brown argues that Irish Americans backed the liberation of Ireland in order to raise their own status in the eyes of their American neighbors. The heavily middle-class Irish nationalist leaders, Brown argues, needed independence to erase the stain of Ireland's hapless poverty. Many have since qualified this interpretation, but it remains a powerful insight into the motives of at least some of the nationalists. Brown also explores the relationship between American politics and Irish American nationalism.

Buhle, Paul. "The Knights of Labor in Rhode Island." *Radical History Review* 17 (1978): 39–73.

Buhle's article amplifies Eric Foner's insights in his article "Class, Ethnicity, and Radicalism" (see below) into the relationship between the Land League and the

Knights of Labor in Irish American communities. Buhle, like Foner, finds that Land
League nationalism helped ease Irish Americans into labor reform and recruitment
into the Knights of Labor in the early 1880s.

Carroll, Francis. *American Opinion and the Irish Question, 1910–1923: A Study in
Opinion and Policy.* New York: Gill and MacMillan, 1978.

This is still the best survey of American responses to the Irish question in the crucial years of the last efforts at Home Rule, the Easter Rebellion, and the Irish war for
independence. Drawing on newspapers and other sources, it provides comprehensive
documentation of American interest and reaction to these events.

Foner, Eric. "Class, Ethnicity, and Radicalism in the Gilded Age: The Land League
and Irish America." *Marxist Perspectives* 1, no. 2 (Summer 1978): 6–55.

This a groundbreaking article on Irish American nationalism by one of the best
American historians. Foner argues that Irish nationalism, particularly the Land
League, helped rouse the reform consciousness of Irish workers and ease them into
the Knights of Labor and the mainstream of the American labor movement. Foner
points to the close links between the Land League branches and the Knights of Labor
assemblies in New England mill cities and Pennsylvania and western mining towns. In
some cases, the Land League branches turned into Knights of Labor assemblies. Foner
disputes Thomas Brown's suggestion that Irish American nationalism was primarily a
movement of Celtic middle-class men seeking respectability, pointing instead to broad
working-class support for nationalism, motivated by class antagonism toward the Irish
aristocracy and British colonialism.

Funchion, Michael. *Chicago's Irish Nationalists: 1881–1890.* New York: Arno Press,
1976.

Chicago's branches of the Clan na Gael dominated that secret nationalist organization and the Clan wielded tremendous power in Chicago's Irish community through
the 1880s. Funchion's well-researched and smartly written book is a thorough study of
the Clan's rise in Chicago and its power in the city and outside it until the murder of
Dr. Cronin discredited the Chicago Clan at the end of the decade.

Walsh, Victor. "A Fanatic Heart: The Cause of Irish American Nationalism in Pittsburgh During the Gilded Age." *Journal of Social History* 15, no. 2 (Winter 1981):
187–204.

This is an interesting article that explores the sources of support for nationalism
within the Irish American community. Walsh has found that the regional origins of
the Pittsburgh Irish had a significant effect on who backed nationalism and what kind
of nationalism that they backed. Immigrants from Leinster were more successfully
economically and often supported constitutional nationalism, while Munster working-
class immigrants backed Patrick Ford's radical nationalists. Connaught immigrants living in Pittsburgh's "Point" neighborhood seemed sunk in poverty and never mobilized
in behalf of nationalism.

Nativism

Baltzell, Digby. *Protestant Establishment, Aristocracy, and Caste in America*. New York: Random House, 1964.

Baltzell's book traces the development of a Protestant elite subcommunity organized around men's eating clubs, preparatory schools, university social clubs, cotillions, and country clubs from the late nineteenth century to the middle of the twentieth century.

Higham, John. *Strangers in the Land: Patterns of American Nativism, 1860–1925*. New Brunswick, N.J.: Rutgers University Press, 1955.

This is still the best single book on nativist movements in late nineteenth- and early twentieth-century America. Higham, one of the most distinguished historians of American diversity, argues that there were major themes in American nativism: anti-Catholicism, antiradicalism, and Anglo-Saxon racism. Higham traces these themes through the rise and fall of such movements as the anti-Catholic American Protective Association, the Anglo-Saxon racist Immigration Restriction League, and the racist and anti-Catholic Ku Klux Klan.

Politics

Allswang, John. *A House For All Peoples*. Lexington: University of Kentucky Press, 1971.

Allswang analyzes the creation of the multiethnic Democratic coalition in Chicago in the 1920s. Anton Cermak, of Czech ancestry, was the architect of this coalition, but after Cermak's death it was taken over by two Irish Americans, Edward Kelly and Patrick Nash.

Buenker John D. *Urban Liberalism and Progressive Reform*. New York: Scribners, 1973.

This important but neglected book documents in exceptional detail the work of Irish American and other ethnic politicians for social, economic, and political reform in state legislatures across the Northeast and Midwest—states including Massachusetts, Rhode Island, Connecticut, New York, New Jersey, Ohio, and Illinois—in the 1910s. Buenker argues persuasively that conventional accounts of progressivism do not take into account this urban liberalism.

Karson, Marc. *American Labor Unrest and Politics*. Carbondale: University of Southern Illinois Press, 1958.

An older study of labor politics, it contains a full and detailed discussion of the Catholic Church's anti-Socialist campaign in the 1910s and 1920s and its effect on labor politics.

Kleppner, Paul. *The Cross of Culture; A Social Analysis of Midwestern Politics, 1850–1900*. New York: Free Press, 1970.

One of the earliest and most influential studies of American voting patterns by an historian of the "ethnocultural" school, Kleppner argued that the Midwestern electorate was divided not so much by class as by ethnicity and religion over the last half of the nineteenth century. Specifically, Kleppner distinguishes between "ritualists" (Catholics, including Irish Catholics and some Protestants, such as Lutherans and Episcopalians) and "pietists" (largely evangelical Protestants).

Leinenweber, Charles. "The Class and Ethnic Bases of New York City Socialism, 1904–1915." *Labor History* 22, no. 1 (1981): 31–56.

Leinenweber's article documents what most historians have suspected: that there were few Irish Catholics in the Socialist Party. He attributed their small numbers to the influence of the Catholic Church and Irish investment in New York's Tammany Hall political machine.

Religion

Cross, Robert. *The Emergence of Liberal Catholicism in America*. Cambridge: Harvard University Press, 1958.

This is one of the first and still one of the best argued and well-written discussions of the growth of a liberal faction in the American hierarchy and their conflict with conservatives over the Catholic church's adjustment to American culture and society. Though condemned by the Vatican, Cross believes that the liberals of the late nineteenth century set precedents for the Church's twentieth-century response to American life.

Curran, Robert Emmett. *Michael Augustine Corrigan and the Shaping of Conservative Catholicism in America, 1878–1902*. New York: Arno Press, 1978.

This impressively researched and well-argued biography is the first important work to explore the conservative side of the Americanist controversy in the late nineteenth century. Through a study of the conservative leader of that controversy, Archbishop Michael Corrigan of New York City, and his battles within his diocese with liberal priests like Edward McGlynn and outside it with James Gibbons and John Ireland, Curran provides a new perspective on the Americanist battles and the triumph of the conservatives within the Church.

Curran, Robert Emmet. "Prelude to 'Americanism': The New York Academia and Clerical Radicalism in the Late Nineteenth Century." *Church History* 47, no. 1 (1978): 48–65.

This important article traces the history of a special band of Catholic clerics, many of them, like Edward McGlynn, second-generation Irish Americans in the New York Archdiocese. These men were Catholic liberals who envisioned an Americanized church. They questioned parochial schools, endorsed a vernacular liturgy (in America, the English language), and backed social reforms. Their ideas never bore fruit, but

they were an early precedent for liberalism among Irish Americans in the Catholic
Church.

Dolan, Jay. *Catholic Revivalism: the American Experience, 1830–1900*. Notre Dame,
   Ind.: University of Notre Dame Press, 1978.

   Dolan examines a very important Catholic Church practice, the parish mission,
which took root in the mid-nineteenth century and flourished through the turn of the
century. The mission, akin to a Catholic version of a revival meeting, was a critical tool
in Catholic attempts to foster Catholic devotion among the laity. Dolan sees the missions and their message as harmonizing strongly with American values. Dolan moves
beyond the mission itself to examine the participants in missions in the New York City
parish St. Paul's, and finds that they attracted a broad range of people, particularly
skilled blue-collar and low white-collar workers.

Ellis, John Tracy. *The Life of James Cardinal Gibbons: Archbishop of Baltimore, 1834–
   1921*. 2 vols. Milwaukee: Bruce Publishing, 1952.

   This is an extensive biography of Gibbons, the leading Catholic prelate of his day.
Born in America of Irish parents, Gibbons was raised in Ireland when his family returned there. This book covers the principal controversies within the church in the late
nineteenth century: conflicts between Irish and Germans over ethnic representation
in the Church, questions about Catholic membership in the Knights of Labor, and
debates over Catholic relations with Protestants.

Ellis, John Tracy, ed. *The Catholic Priest in the United States: Historical Investigations*.
   Collegeville, Minn.: St. John's University Press, 1971.

   This is a collection of essays, with particularly useful ones by Gannon on the effects
of the Vatican's condemnation of modernism in clerical intellectual life and by Trisco
on canon law and the priesthood.

McLeod, Hugh. "Catholicism and the New York Irish: 1880 to 1910." In *Disciplines
   of Faith: Studies in Religion, Politics, and Patriarchy*, edited by Jim Obelkevich,
   337–350. New York: Routledge and Kegan Paul, 1987.

   This is a very interesting article about Irish American Catholicism in New York
City at the turn of the twentieth century. Based on sources from an Irish-dominated
Manhattan parish of that era, McLeod argues that Catholicism worked not so much
as a salve or narcotic for the discouraged impoverished, but more as an inspiration
and guide to working-class Irish attempting to achieve respectability and stability amid
harsh circumstances.

O'Connell, Marvin. *John Ireland and the American Catholic Church*. St. Paul: Minnesota Historical Society, 1988.

   This is a comprehensive biography of a critically important Irish-born churchman
by a seasoned historian of American Catholicism. O'Connell refrains from defining
Ireland as a liberal or his opponents as conservatives in the church's battles at the turn

of the century, and attempts to underplay the degree of divisions that split the church then. Nevertheless, this is a fully documented, gracefully written, and thorough rendition of Ireland's life.

Shannabruch, Charles. *Chicago's Catholics: The Evolution of an American Identity.* Notre Dame, Ind.: University of Notre Dame Press, 1981.

This useful book traces the evolution of an American Catholic group from the diverse ethnic groups of Chicago. Previous works had emphasized conflicts between Irish Americans and newer immigrants such as Italians or Poles, but Shannabruch points to the increasing institutional collaboration, rituals, and shared values and interests that tied these groups together under Irish leadership.

THE TWENTIETH CENTURY

Overviews

Greeley, Andrew. "The Success and Assimilation of Irish Protestants and Catholics in the United States." *Social Science Research* 72, no. 4 (1985): 229–235.

Greeley's survey data reported in this article reveals that Irish American Catholics had actually moved ahead of Irish American Protestants in occupational status by at least the 1920s.

Moloney, Michael. "Irish Ethnic Recording and the Irish American Imagination." In *Ethnic Recording in America: A Neglected Heritage,* 85–100. Washington, D.C.: Folklife Center, 1982.

A fascinating survey of Irish folk music recordings from the earliest home cylinder recordings of Galway-born piper Patsy Touhy in the early 1900s through the Clancy Brothers in the 1960s. Moloney analyzes important trends, such as the rise of a "hybrid" style mixing traditional and big band music in the 1940s and 1950s to the folk music revival of the 1960s.

White, Richard. *Remembering Ahanagran: Storytelling in a Family's Past.* New York: Hill and Wang, 1998.

White is a distinguished American Western and Native American historian. The focus of this book is the story of the author's mother, an emigrant from North Kerry, and her family, but the book is both a rich, insightful history of immigrants to America and a sophisticated probing of the different and often conflicting sources and uses of memory and history.

Politics

Crosby, Donald. *God, Church, and Flag: Senator Joseph R. McCarthy and the Catholic Church, 1950–1957.* Chapel Hill: University of North Carolina Press, 1978.

This is a very thoughtfully researched and closely argued analysis of Catholic support for McCarthy's anticommunist crusade. Crosby does not whitewash Catholic backing for McCarthyism but carefully delineates its dimensions and also fully explores anti-McCarthy support in the Catholic community as well. Although Crosby is concerned with support for McCarthy generally, he also investigates supporters and critics of the senator among Irish Catholics specifically.

Fisher, James T. *Dr. America : The Lives of Thomas A. Dooley, 1927–1961*. Amherst: University of Massachusetts Press, 1997.

Dr. Thomas Dooley served as a navy doctor in Vietnam at the end of the 1950s. The CIA and Catholic anticommunists in America backed and capitalized on Dooley's work in the war zone there to make him an heroic symbol of American Catholic anticommunism and proof of the need to resist communism in Vietnam. While serving as a public hero, Dooley led a complex private life as a gay man. Fisher's excellent study contends that Dooley served as a useful symbolic bridge for Irish American Catholics from the dark, heavy-handed "Red" hunting of Joseph McCarthy to the seemingly more idealistic cold warrior John F. Kennedy.

Local

Almeida, Linda Dowling. *Irish Immigrants in New York City, 1945–1995*. Bloomington: Indiana University Press, 2001.

This splendid book admirably fills a critical gap in the history of the Irish in America: mid- and late twentieth-century immigrants. Over the course of the century, a steadily rising proportion of these immigrants settled in New York, so Almeida's book focuses on the heart of this Irish immigrant experience. She expertly explores their reasons for leaving Ireland and their economic, social, and cultural adaptation to America. For example, she probes questions such as how the bleak Irish economy provoked this migration and how cultural and social organizations changed over time.

Bayor, Ronald. *Neighbors in Conflict: The Irish, Germans, Jews, and Italians of New York City, 1929–1941*. Urbana: University of Illinois Press, 1988.

This is an excellent study of the ethnic conflict that erupted in New York in the 1930s, provoked by the Great Depression and nurtured by the rise of fascism in Europe. It is particularly good for its analysis of the political and social conditions that exacerbated tensions between Irish and Jewish Americans in the city during that decade.

Beatty, Jack. *The Rascal King: The Life and Times of James Michael Curley, 1874–1958*. Reading, Mass.: Addison Wesley, 1992.

This is a very personal and comprehensive biography of James Michael Curley, written by a distinguished Boston journalist. Beatty is passionate about Curley, but critical of him as well.

Freeman, Joshua. *In Transit: The Transport Workers Union in New York City, 1933–1966.* New York: Oxford University Press, 1989.

This is a very important study of the Transit Workers Union in New York City by a distinguished labor historian. It is important for Irish American history because radical Irish immigrants, many of them veterans of Ireland's civil war in the early 1920s, played a crucial role in organizing and building the union.

Gamm, Gerald H. *The Making of New Deal Democrats: Voting Behavior and Realignment in Boston, 1920–1940.* Chicago: University of Chicago Press, 1990.

This is a sophisticated quantitative study of the "Al Smith Revolution" and the subsequent construction of the New Deal Democratic majority. Gamm found less of a "revolution"—a uniform conversion of Republicans to the Democrats or a surge of new voters to Smith and FDR—than a complicated process that mixed consistent Democratic support with some conversions and the emergence of new voters. Irish voters had been the most consistent Democrats before the New Deal, but their vote for Roosevelt declined from 1932 to 1940 even as their commitment to state and local Democrats rose.

McNickle, Chris. *To Be Mayor of New York: Ethnic Politics in the City.* New York: Columbia University Press, 1994.

This study of urban politics in New York City richly analyzes the rise and fall of Irish power in the city's Democratic party and city administration. The book focuses heavily on the postwar era, the decline of Tammany, and the rise of Robert Wagner Jr., but also offers interesting insights into the earlier years as well, such as Boss Charlie Murphy's efforts to deal with rising Jewish power in the city.

Moynihan, Daniel Patrick. "The Irish." In *Beyond the Melting Pot*, by Nathan Glazer and Daniel Patrick Moynihan, 217–287. Cambridge, Mass.: MIT Press, 1963.

This is a rich, lively, and provocative essay that offers extraordinary insights into Irish American politics, economic achievement, and Catholic culture, which can be extended far beyond New York to apply to the Irish in twentieth-century America. That does not mean it is always correct. Moynihan overstates the slowness of Irish occupational progress and underestimates Irish American commitment to reform. Nevertheless, it is one of the best short essays on Irish Americans ever written.

Religion

Broderick, Francis L. *Right Reverend New Dealer: John A. Ryan.* New York: Macmillan, 1963.

This is still the most comprehensive biography of the most important social thinker in American Catholic history. Broderick traces the influences of the Irish American populist Ignatius Donnelly and the nationalist Patrick Ford on the young Ryan, the son of Irish immigrants growing up in rural Minnesota. Broderick rightly contends that Ryan was the critical figure in shifting the church's official position from sullen hostility towards radicalism to its support of positive government intervention on behalf of working people.

Herberg, Will. *Protestant, Catholic, and Jew: An Essay in American Religious Sociology.* Garden City, N.Y.: Doubleday & Co., 1955.

Herberg's influential book describes the evolution of American ethnic diversity into the melting pots of Protestant, Catholic, and Jew. His tracing and explanation of this evolution, particularly of the transformation of Irish Catholics into American Catholics, is problematic, but the book captures the growing importance of religious identities in postwar America.

O'Toole, James M. *Militant and Triumphant: William Henry O'Connell and Catholicism in Boston, 1859–1944.* Notre Dame, Ind.: University of Notre Dame Press, 1992.

This richly contextualized and smartly argued biography focuses on one of the most important figures in twentieth-century American Catholicism: William Henry Cardinal O'Connell. O'Connell had often been depicted as the great exemplar of the trends that transformed American Catholic dioceses from loosely run collections of priestly fiefdoms to centralized, authoritarian bureaucracies and their bishops from products of complicated negotiations between Roman and American interests to creatures of Roman influence. O'Toole finds O'Connell less successful than contemporaries as an autocratic administrator, but clearly a reflection of the increasingly critical importance of Roman connections in the American Catholic Church.

IRISH AMERICANS: THE 1960S TO THE PRESENT

Byron, Reginald. *Irish America.* Oxford: Clarendon Press, 1999.

This is an anthropological study of Irish Americans in contemporary Albany and the meaning of their Irish American ethnic identity for them. Byron finds that most of the Irish Americans that he interviewed were of the fourth or fifth generation, and most (over 90 percent) of those born after 1945 were of mixed ancestry who chose to identify as Irish Americans. The book makes some useful points about regional diversity in the Irish American experience but is marred by unfamiliarity with Irish American historiography or even some of the better sources on the history of the Albany Irish.

Farrell, James A. *Tip O'Neill and the Democratic Century.* Boston: Little Brown, 2001.

This is an interesting comprehensive biography of O'Neill, the third-generation Irish American congressman from Massachusetts who rose to become majority leader and Speaker of the House. It rightfully follows O'Neill's career in Washington in some detail, but it also underlines the importance of his Massachusetts Irish roots in shaping his political outlook, skills, and tactics.

Freedman, Samuel. *The Inheritance: How Three Families and America Moved from Roosevelt to Reagan and Beyond*. New York: Simon and Schuster, 1996.

This book follows three families in New York, tracing their movement over the generations from loyal devotion to the Democratic party to an embrace of Reagan Republicanism, in an effort to probe deeply into the reasons for the breakup of the old New Deal coalition. One of the families that Friedman traces is Irish American.

Levy, Mark and Michael Kramer. *The Ethnic Factor: How America's Minorities Decide Elections*. New York: Simon and Schuster, 1972.

This is a useful discussion of ethnic political behavior in the 1960s, 1970s, and 1980s, which draws on some very interesting exit polling and survey data to trace Irish American and other ethnic partisan loyalties.

Waters, Mary C. *Ethnic Options: Choosing Identities in America*. Berkeley: University of California Press, 1990.

This is a critical book in the examination of the current meaning of ethnic identity for white ethnics in America. Waters argues that for these white Americans—Italians, Irish, Poles, and others—ethnic identity has become optional, not constrained or required. These ethnics can thus "choose" to be Irish, an identity that will serve certain emotional or psychological needs but is not forced upon them by discrimination or prejudice.

Wilson, Andrew. *Irish-America and the Ulster Conflict, 1968–1995*. Washington, D.C.: Catholic University of America Press, 1995.

This is a well-researched and meticulously thorough tracing of Irish American responses to the Ulster Crisis from the first surge of civil rights protests in the 1960s through the parallel rise of the IRA Provisionals and NORAID in the 1970s to the militant high point during the hunger strikes in the early 1980s and finally to the rise of constitutional nationalism and the movement toward the "Good Friday Agreement."

IRISH AMERICAN GENDER AND FAMILY

Diner, Hasia. *Erin's Daughters in America: Irish Immigrant Women in the Nineteenth Century*. Baltimore: Johns Hopkins University Press, 1983.

Still the best overall study of Irish women in nineteenth-century America, it discusses the causes of Irish women's migration, their successful economic adaptations, their sometimes troubled family lives, their suspicions of suffrage and feminism, and their active roles in religious life and secular social service. Diner argues that Irish women were economic migrants seeking better economic opportunities and they and their daughters found them, but the rigid sexual segregation in Ireland's Catholic culture and their poverty shadowed relations between Irish husbands and wives and complicated Irish family lives.

Diner, Hasia. *Hungering for America: Italian, Irish, and Jewish Foodways in the Age of Migration*. Cambridge: Harvard University Press, 2001.

This is an excellent book. Diner examines the importance of food in three ethnic cultures, Italian, Jewish, and Irish Americans, and finds that food played the least important role in Irish American culture, either in the substance of everyday life or as a marker of ethnic identity. Diner finds a number of reasons for this: the overreliance on the potato in the old country, the severe alienation of Irish Catholics from the Irish gentry (Italian immigrants, Diner, argues drew on the old country's aristocratic cuisine to create an Italian American cuisine in America; Irish Americans did not), and the prominence of drinking instead of food in Irish and Irish American cultures. Diner smartly points out that the relative absence of food in Irish American culture has important consequences for Irish American women's domestic roles.

Kane, Paula. *Separatism and Subculture: Boston Catholicism, 1900–1920*. Chapel Hill: University of North Carolina Press, 1994.

This is a pathbreaking study of lay Catholics in the Boston Archdiocese in the early twentieth century that is particularly important for its attention to the gendering of lay catholic roles at that time. It discusses in detail diocesan efforts to define domestic roles for Catholic women and offers some particularly interesting insights into Irish American men and social mobility.

Nolan, Janet. *Ourselves Alone: Women's Emigration from Ireland, 1885–1920*. Lexington: University of Kentucky Press, 1989.

This is a short but well-written and analytical study of the causes of Irish female emigration at the turn of the century. Nolan argues that constricting economic roles and social freedom combined with rising education encouraged women in Ireland to emigrate abroad in order to regain some status in new roles.

Tentler, Leslie. "Present at the Creation: Working-Class Catholics in the United States." In *American Exceptionalism: U.S. Working-Class Formation in an International Context*, edited by Rick Halpern and Jonathan Morris. New York: St. Martin's Press, 1997.

This is an excellent, insightful piece that makes a very important but often overlooked point. Though Protestant working-class men appeared to leave the major denominations and religion in the nineteenth and early twentieth centuries, Catholic working-class men from many ethnic groups were committed to their churches.

IRISH AMERICANS AND RACE

Allen, Theodore. *Invention of the White Race*. 2 vols. New York: Verso, 1994.

This is among the most important of the whiteness studies and by far the most ambitious. It pays a great deal more attention to Irish history than any of the others, but that attention seems marred by an outmoded understanding of the effects of the penal laws and some confusion over racial versus religious oppression in Ireland.

Arnesen, Eric. "Whiteness and the Historian's Imagination." *International Labor and Working Class History* 60 (2001): 3–32. See also the responses in the same volume of the journal: James R. Barrett, "Whiteness Studies: Anything Here for Historians of the Working Class?" (33–42); David Brody, "Charismatic History: Pros and Cons" (43–47); Barbara Fields, "Whiteness, Racism and Identity" (48–56); Eric Foner, "Response to Eric Arnesen" (57–60); Victoria Hattam, "Whiteness: Theorizing Race, Eliding Ethnicity" (61–68); and Adolph Reed, "Response to Eric Arnesen" (69–80).

This forum—an essay by Arnesen and responses by six scholars—is the most comprehensive, widely ranging, and insightful critique of the whiteness school to date. The contributors, five historians and two political scientists, are extraordinarily distinguished scholars in the field and are well equipped to comment on the issues raised by whiteness historians. They raise points from doubts about whether Irish immigrants were ever in danger of becoming white to questions about the "logic of solidarity," which suggests that Irish American workers should have naturally found allies among the nonwhite poor.

Bernstein, Iver. *New York City Draft Riots: Their Significance for American Politics and Society in the Civil War.* New York: Oxford University Press, 1990.

The best book on the Civil War draft riots of 1863, which included thousands of Irish immigrants and their children. Bernstein sets the riots in a broad context of economic, social, and political changes in New York during the Civil War, as a new Republican manufacturing elite rose to power and with the backing of the national government displaced an older Democratic merchant elite, threatening and frustrating the poor Irish allies of the Democratic merchants.

Gyory, Andrew. *Closing the Gates: Race, Politics, and the Chinese Exclusion Act.* Chapel Hill: University of North Carolina Press, 1998.

This is a new, well-researched, and powerful interpretation of how the exclusion of Chinese immigrants from the United States became law in 1882. Previous interpretations had emphasized labor's role in pushing such restriction from below. Gyory acknowledges the popularity of Chinese exclusion among Irish-led workers in California but he disputes the notion that workers outside California were seriously interested in barring Chinese immigration. Even Irish Americans in the East seemed indifferent to exclusion. It was the political parties, Gyory argues, trying to break a political stalemate with a dramatic stroke, that led eventually to the Exclusion Act.

Ignatiev, Noel. *How the Irish Became White.* New York: Routledge, 1995.

One of the most notable works in the whiteness controversy, it is the only book in the whiteness school to focus strictly on Irish American supremacy. It, nonetheless, suffers from a lack of focus, as it consists of a series of vignettes and biographies, does not seem to distinguish Irish Catholics from Irish Protestants, and overestimates Irish acceptance in late nineteenth-century America. Roediger's *The Wages of Whiteness* (see below) is a much more sophisticated and thoughtful treatment of Irish whiteness.

Jacobson, Mathew. *Whiteness of a Different Color: European Immigrants and the Alchemy of Race*. Cambridge: Harvard University Press, 1998.

One of the most important books in the recent discussion of whiteness, Jacobson thoroughly documents the racialization of several white immigrant groups, including the Irish, in nineteenth-century American popular and academic culture, but points out that the division of whites into separate, distinct races faded by the 1920s and 1930s, when all whites, including ethnics, began to be treated more often as simply a single "Caucasian" race.

Kolchin, Peter. "Whiteness Studies: The New History of Race in America." *Journal of American History* 89, no. 1 (2002): 154–173.

This is a significant critique of the whiteness school by a distinguished scholar of American slavery and race. Like other critics, Kolchin criticizes whiteness historians for failing to address more directly specific and concrete social and political group relations and for focusing too much on cultural representations of race in their exploration of Irish and other whites' racial identification.

McGreevy, John T. *Parish Boundaries: The Catholic Encounter with Race in the Twentieth Century Urban North*. Chicago: University of Chicago Press, 1996.

A sophisticated, smart, and rigorously fair study of Catholics (many of them Irish) and the question of race in northern American cities. It argues that Catholic traditional values of communalism and the church's centralized institutional structure (differing from Protestants and Jews, for example, in the extent of a congregation's control of their church) shaped a distinctive Catholic response to the great African American migrations north in the twentieth century.

McMahon, Eileen. *What Parish Are You From?: A Chicago Irish Community and Race Relations*. Lexington: University Press of Kentucky, 1995.

This study of St. Sabena's parish in the South Side of Chicago is one of the few studies of Irish American Catholic life at the neighborhood level. The parish, founded in the 1910s, flourished through the 1950s but became a racial battleground in the 1960s. MacMahon richly documents the parish's prosperous years, makes a good case for the parishioners as emblematic of the twentieth century's militant American Catholicism, and explores their painful and diverse approaches to the movement of African Americans into the neighborhood.

Roediger, David. *The Wages of Whiteness: Race and the Making of the American Working Class*. New York: Routledge, 1995.

The most important book in the "whiteness" historical school, it is sophisticated, smart, and readable. It argues persuasively how America's white workers forged a white identity at the birth of American industrialization in the antebellum era. The book is particularly good in its discussions of how a republican ideology shaped workers' identities. Roediger suggests that workers chose an illusory white egalitarianism and the psychological pleasures of racial superiority over a possible productive alliance with their fellow black workers. Irish workers figure prominently in this book, as Roediger tries to illustrate the cultural and political reasons why Irish workers chose whiteness.

Saxton, Alexander. *The Indispensable Enemy: Labor and the Anti-Chinese Movement in California*. Berkeley: University of California Press, 1971.

This book, by one of the nation's leading historians of American race relations, argues that the anti-Chinese movement was not a simple response to Chinese economic competition, but was shaped by ideological and psychological motives. He sees the movement as an effort by Democrats to revive their party after the Civil War by using racial appeals and without becoming tainted by the disloyalty that the party had suffered during the war. Labor unions in California also tried to use anti-Chinese appeals to rally workers outside the skilled trades and strengthen the position of craft workers. Anti-Chinese and later anti-Japanese movements inhibited real reform. Dennis Kearney and Frank Roney, both Irish immigrants, were important figures in the anti-Chinese movement.

INDEX

Indians, 278–79, 286; Paxton Boys and, 40, 295–96
individual ambition, 226
industrial revolution, second, 109
Industrial Workers of the World (IWW), 254–55
inheritance, 97, 100–101, 124, 176
intellectuals, 136, 139, 194
Invention of the White Race, The (Allen), 215, 216, 218, 220, 224
Inwood (Manhattan), 128
Ireland: 1950s, 151; cabbage patch rebellion (1848), 90; Celtic Tiger economy, 154, 168; contemporary views of famine, 60–61; cultural revival of 1990s, 168–69; Easter Rebellion, 1916, 119, 207, 208, 210, 257; economy, 1780s, 44–45; economy, 1800s, 54, 96–97; economy, 1930s, 123; economy, 1950s, 151; economy, 1990, 154; famine of 1740s, 65; Fenians and, 250–51; history, 28–29; in-migration, 151, 154; Irish Free State established, 210; land system, 63, 64; lineages, 225–26; local cultures, 14–15; marriage age, 176; opposition to slavery in, 216–17, 220, 224, 230; peasants purchase farms, 208–9; population growth, 45, 54, 63–65; precedents for racism, 216, 224–27, 229–30; rebellions, 119–20, 207–8, 210, 212, 227, 257, 308; romanticization of, 49–50; school system, 101, 126; tillage economy, 96, 100, 174, 176; Troubles (1960s and 1970s), 8, 237, 241, 256, 264–65. *See also* nationalism; republicanism
Ireland, John (Archbishop), 111, 116, 231, 261, 267–68
Irish America and the Ulster Conflict: 1968–1995 (Wilson), 211
Irish American Cultural Institute, 168
Irish American Protestants, 21–22, 56–57,

92, 155, 203. *See also* Ulster Presbyterians; Ulster Protestants
Irish Ancestral Research Association of Boston, 167
Irish bars, 168
Irish Brigade, 84, 149
Irish Catholic Americans, viii; 1980 data, 155; in American Revolution, 39; differences from Irish Presbyterians, 30–31; failure attributed to, 131–32; as governing class, 185, 187; history as tragedy, 5–6; migration to northern cities, 56, 57; militant American Catholicism, 115–20, 123, 160–62, 265–66, 274–75, 290–91; in poverty, 1970s, 156–57; racialization of, 83–84; sense of dispossession, 225–26; successes of, 155–57. *See also* American Catholic identity; Catholic Church; Democratic Party; Great Famine immigration; nationalism; nineteenth-century immigration; second-generation Irish Americans; third- and fourth-generation Irish Americans
Irish Civil War, 237, 241, 258, 264, 269
Irish County Athletic Union, 260
Irish diaspora, 15–16, 198; politics in, 185–87
Irish Folklore Commission, 62
Irish Free State, 99, 120, 241, 258
Irish immigrants: migration to southern and Western frontiers, 36–37; Ulster Catholics, 55–56; Ulster Presbyterians, vii, 20–23, 35, 42, 45, 302–4; Ulster Protestants (Church of Ireland), 26–27, 36. *See also* seventeenth-century immigration; eighteenth-century immigration; nineteenth-century immigration; turn of the century immigration; twentieth-century immigration